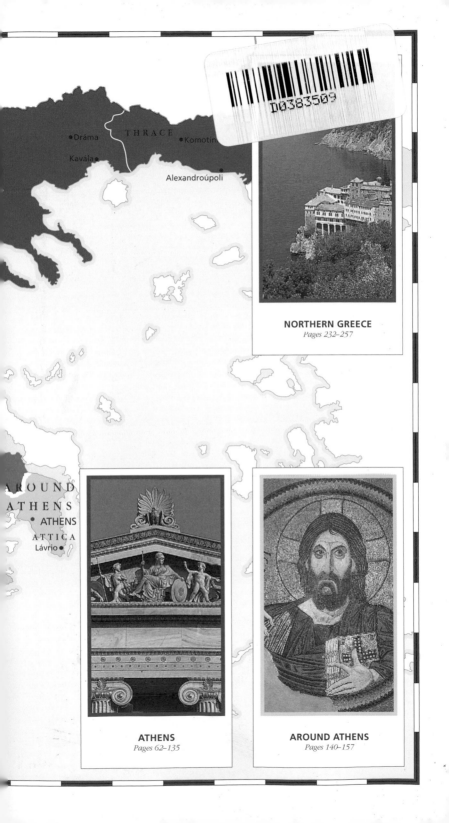

●Dráma

THRACE

Kavála●

●Komotiní

Alexandroúpoli

NORTHERN GREECE
Pages 232–257

AROUND
ATHENS
● ATHENS
ATTICA
Lávrio ●

ATHENS
Pages 62–135

AROUND ATHENS
Pages 140–157

D0383509

EYEWITNESS TRAVEL

GREECE
ATHENS & THE MAINLAND

EYEWITNESS TRAVEL

GREECE
ATHENS & THE MAINLAND

MAIN CONSULTANT: MARC DUBIN

DK

LONDON, NEW YORK,
MELBOURNE, MUNICH AND DELHI
www.dk.com

PROJECT EDITOR Jane Simmonds
ART EDITOR Stephen Bere
EDITORS Isabel Carlisle, Michael Ellis, Simon Farbrother,
Claire Folkard, Marianne Petrou, Andrew Szudek
US EDITORS Michael Wise, Mary Sutherland
DESIGNERS Jo Doran, Paul Jackson, Elly King, Marisa Renzullo
MAP CO-ORDINATORS Emily Green, David Pugh
VISUALIZER Joy Fitzsimmons
LANGUAGE CONSULTANT Georgia Gotsi

CONTRIBUTORS AND CONSULTANTS
Rosemary Barron, Marc Dubin, Mike Gerrard, Andy Harris,
Lynette Mitchell, Colin Nicholson, Robin Osborne, Barnaby
Rogerson, Paul Sterry, Tanya Tsikas

MAPS
Gary Bowes, Fiona Casey, Christine Purcell (ERA-Maptec Ltd)

PHOTOGRAPHERS
Joe Cornish, John Heseltine, Rob Reichenfeld, Peter Wilson,
Francesca Yorke

ILLUSTRATORS
Stephen Conlin, Paul Guest, Steve Gyapay, Maltings Partnership, Chris
Orr & Associates, Paul Weston, John Woodcock

Printed and bound by L. Rex Printing Company Limited, China

First American Edition, 1997

13 14 15 16 10 9 8 7 6 5 4 3 2 1

Published in the United States by
DK Publishing, 375 Hudson Street,
New York, New York 10014

**Reprinted with revisions 1998, 1999, 2000, 2001,
2002, 2003, 2004, 2006, 2007, 2009, 2011, 2013**

Copyright © 1997, 2013 Dorling Kindersley Limited, London

A CATALOG RECORD FOR THIS BOOK IS AVAILABLE FROM THE LIBRARY OF CONGRESS.

ISSN: 1542-1554

ISBN: 978-0-75669-503-3

THROUGHOUT THIS BOOK, FLOORS ARE REFERRED TO IN ACCORDANCE WITH
EUROPEAN USAGE; IE THE "FIRST FLOOR" IS THE FLOOR ABOVE GROUND LEVEL.

Front cover main image: Parthenon, Acropolis, Athens

MIX
Paper from
responsible sources
FSC
www.fsc.org   FSC™ C018179

**The information in this
DK Eyewitness Guide is checked regularly.**
Every effort has been made to ensure that this book is as up-to-date
as possible at the time of going to press. Some details, however, such
as telephone numbers, opening hours, prices, gallery hanging
arrangements and travel information are liable to change. The
publishers cannot accept responsibility for any consequences arising
from the use of this book, nor for any material on third party
websites, and cannot guarantee that any website address in this book
will be a suitable source of travel information. We value the views
and suggestions of our readers very highly. Please write to: Publisher,
DK Eyewitness Travel Guides, Dorling Kindersley, 80 Strand, London
WC2R 0RL, UK, or email: travelguides@dk.com.

◁ **Morning at Gýtheio harbour in the Peloponnese**

CONTENTS

**Black-figure bowl depicting
the god Dionysos**

INTRODUCING
ATHENS AND
MAINLAND GREECE

ANCIENT GREECE

Tower houses at Vátheia, Inner
Máni, in the Peloponnese

Fresco at Varlaám monastery at
Metéora, Central Greece

Greek salad

View of the
Acropolis in
Athens

Reconstruction of Ancient Olympia

HOW TO USE THIS GUIDE

This guide helps you to get the most from your visit to Mainland Greece. It provides expert recommendations and practical information. *Introducing Athens and Mainland Greece* maps the country and sets it in its historical and cultural context. *Ancient Greece* gives a background to the many remains and artifacts to be seen. The four regional chapters, plus *Athens*, describe important sights, with maps and illustrations. Restaurant and hotel recommendations can be found in *Travellers' Needs*. The *Survival Guide* has tips on everything from using a Greek telephone to transport.

ATHENS

Athens has been divided into two sightseeing areas. Each has its own chapter, opening with a list of the sights described. All sights are numbered on an area map, and are described in detail on the following pages.

Sights at a Glance
gives a categorized list of the chapter's sights: Museums and Galleries; Squares, Parks and Gardens; Churches and Historic Buildings.

All pages relating to Athens have red thumb tabs.

A locator map shows you where you are in relation to the rest of Athens.

1 Area Map
The sights are numbered and located on a map. Sights in the city centre are also shown on the Athens Street Finder *on pages 122–35.*

2 Street-by-Street Map
This gives an overhead view of the key areas in central Athens. The numbering on the map ties in with the area map and the fuller descriptions that follow.

Story boxes highlight special aspects of a particular sight.

Stars indicate the sights that no visitor should miss.

A suggested route for a walk is shown in red.

3 Detailed Information
The sights within Athens are described individually. Addresses, telephone numbers, opening hours and information concerning admission charges and wheelchair access are given for each entry. Map references to the Athens Street Finder *are also provided for orientation.*

MAINLAND GREECE AREA BY AREA

Mainland Greece has been divided into four regions, each of which has a separate chapter. A map of these areas can be found inside the front cover of the book.

1 Introduction
An introduction covers the history, character and geography of each region, showing how the area has developed over the centuries and what it has to offer the visitor today.

Each region can be identified by its colour coding, shown on the inside front cover.

A locator map shows you where you are in relation to the other regions in the book.

2 Regional Map
This shows the region covered in the chapter. The main sights are numbered on the map. The major roads are marked and there are useful tips about the best ways of getting around the area.

3 Detailed Information
All the important towns and areas to visit are described individually. They are listed in order, following the numbering on the Regional Map. Within each entry there is detailed information on all the major sights.

A Visitors' Checklist provides the practical information you will need to plan your visit.

4 Greece's Top Sights
These are given one or more full pages. Historic buildings are dissected to reveal their interiors. Many of the ancient sites are reconstructed to supplement information about the site as it is seen today.

INTRODUCING ATHENS AND MAINLAND GREECE

DISCOVERING MAINLAND GREECE

Ancient treasure of Greece

Four thousand years of civilization and waves of invaders have made Greece a patchwork of history and geography, from the northern snows of Epirus and Macedonia to the fertile plains of Thessaly and Attica and the sun-baked slopes of the Peloponnese. More than half of the Greek population live in the three largest cities, leaving much of the hinterland under-populated and untouched by 21st-century urbanization, with ruins of ancient temples and medieval castles still brooding over the deserted countryside. These pages offer an at-a-glance guide to the highlights of each region.

The ancient Parthenon on the Acropolis, Athens

ATHENS

- **The temples of the Acropolis**
- **Authentic café culture**
- **Treasures of the National Archaeological Museum**

The urban sprawl of Greece's capital surrounds an inner historic core overlooked by the imposing temples of the **Acropolis** *(see pp94–101)* and the hills of Attica. Despite its size, Athens retains a village charm, with little squares shaded by palm trees, cafés and tavernas at every corner and pots of geraniums growing on apartment balconies.

Atop the Acropolis, the Parthenon is a majestic sight. Below it, surrounding the remarkable **Tower of the Winds** *(see pp86–7)* and **Ancient Agora's** toppled columns *(see pp90–91)* lie the bustling street markets of the vibrant **Monastiráki** district *(see p117)*.

Dotted around the city are tiny churches dating back to its Byzantine heyday, like the delightful **Panagía**

Gorgoepíkoös *(see p105)* located in picturesque **Pláka** *(see pp102–3)*, where tourists and Athenians alike flock to soak up the thriving outdoor café culture.

The **National Archaeólogical Museum** *(see pp68–71)* with its impressive exhibits is unmissable, but the city also has many smaller museums, such as the **Benáki Museum** *(see pp78–9)* and the **Museum of Cycladic Art** *(see pp74–5)* with its enigmatic relics of Europe's oldest civilization.

AROUND ATHENS

- **Glorious Soúnio**
- **Opulent beach resorts of the Attica Coast**
- **Traditional tavernas**

The Athens suburbs have spread almost all the way across the upper Attica peninsula, but below the city is the appealing **Attica Coast** *(see p149)*, where a string of luxury resorts stretch south towards **Soúnio** *(see pp148–9)* and the soaring columns of

the Temple of Poseidon. The hinterland is much less attractive and largely industrial, however **Ancient Eleusis** *(see pp156–7)* and the spectacular **Monastery of Dafní** *(see pp152–3)* both merit a visit.

Sacred sites, including **Ancient Brauron** *(see p146)*, **Ancient Oropós** *(see p144)*, the ruined Temple of Nemesis at **Ramnoús** *(see p144)* and the evocative battlefield of **Marathónas** *(see p145)* are scattered across the peninsula, and on the east coast is **Rafína** *(see p145)*, a lively harbour with some great fish tavernas.

THE PELOPONNESE

- **Magnificent ancient sites at Olympia and Corinth**
- **Byzantine architecture**
- **Empty beaches and wilderness landscapes**

South of the Gulf of Corinth, the Peloponnese waits to be discovered. A region of

The beautiful Attica Coast at Cape Sounion

Spectacular clifftop monasteries, Metéora, Central Greece

immense beauty, with a mountainous interior, lush valleys and fine beaches, it is also home to some of Greece's most important ancient cities and temples, including **Ancient Corinth** *(see pp162–5)*, **Spárti** *(see p189)* and **Ancient Messene** *(see p201)*.

Byzantine ruins at Mystrás, Peloponnese

Its greatest strength is its wealth of hidden histories, from the ruins of the last out-post of Byzantium at **Mystrás** *(see pp192–3)* to the spooky Venetian fortress at **Monemva-sía** *(see pp186–8)*. However, no visit would be complete without seeing the region's key attractions – **Ancient Corinth** *(see pp162–5)*, the remains of Agamemnon's capital at **Mycenae** *(see pp178–9)*, the amphitheatre at **Epidaurus** *(see p184)* with its amazing acoustics, and **Olympia** *(see pp170–72)*, birth-place of the Olympic Games.

The Peloponnese has more to offer than just ancient ruins. Walkers are drawn to the **Loúsios Gorge** *(see pp174–5)*, a striking canyon where

monasteries nestle in wooded flanks and, dozing in the sun, elegant **Náfplio** *(see pp182–3)* and pretty **Gýtheio** *(see p198)* are simply delightful.

CENTRAL AND WESTERN GREECE

- **Ruins of Ancient Delphi**
- **Breathtaking Píndos Mountains**
- **Traditional Zagórian villages**

This vast region spells remote mountain wildernesses and fertile plains. **Ancient Delphi** *(see pp228–31)* attracts droves of visitors but the coastal towns of **Galaxídi** *(see p224)* and **Náfpaktos** *(see pp224–5)* also demand to be visited. The Parnassus massif cuts the province off from the plains of Thessaly and merges with the **Píndos Mountains** *(see p206)*, enclosing breathtaking scenery – much of it within nature reserves that provide refuge for bears and wolves, and a paradise for walkers.

In **Metéora** *(see pp216–17)*, monasteries perch dramatically on clifftops and in **Zagória** *(see p207)*, enchanting hamlets cling to the stark slopes of the Epirus range. **Pílio** *(see pp218–20)*, on the Aegean coast, is a forested penin-sula dotted with fishing villages and olive groves. To cap it all, the region has some fine beaches at **Párga** *(see p212)* and **Agios Ioánnis** *(see p220)*.

NORTHERN GREECE

- **Thriving city nightlife**
- **Unspoilt Préspa Lakes**
- **Splendid monasteries of Mouth Athos**

Macedonia and Thrace are Greece's least-explored regions, despite glorious beaches on the **Chalkidikí** peninsula and an array of rewarding archaeological sites. The old Macedonian capital at **Ancient Pélla** *(see p243)* and the temple site of Dion, slumbering beneath Greece's tallest mountain, **Mount Olympos** *(see p241)*, both warrant a visit. **Thessaloníki** *(see pp244–5)*, Greece's second largest city, has two world-class museums, the **Thessaloníki Archaeological Museum** *(see pp246–7)* and the **Museum of Byzantine Culture** *(see p244)*, and its lively nightlife attracts a young crowd.

Inland, ruined Byzantine castles crown hilltops along the line of the Via Egnatia that once connected Rome with Constantinople. The **Préspa Lakes** *(see pp236–7)*, a unique, multi-national nature reserve, has a dazzling array of flora and fauna and attracts an abundance of wildlife. The spectacular monasteries of **Mount Athos** *(see pp252–4)* are off-limits to female visitors but can be viewed by boat from the coast. The gorges of the **Néstos Valley** *(see p255)*, where the river flows through the Rodopi mountains, make for some of the loveliest scenery in Greece.

The gorgeous turquoise sea on the Chalkidikí peninsula, Northern Greece

Putting Greece on the Map

Occupying the southernmost tip of the Balkan peninsula, Greece divides into over 2,000 islands stretching from the Ionian Sea in the west to the Aegean Sea in the east. The mainland has borders with Albania, Bulgaria, Turkey and the former Yugoslav Republic of Macedonia and is home to most of Greece's 10.9 million people, with a third of these in Athens.

KEY

- Main international ferry service
- International airport
- Railway line
- Dual-carriageway
- Major road
- National boundary

A PORTRAIT OF MAINLAND GREECE

reece is one of the most visited European countries, yet one of the least known. The modern Greek state dates only from 1830 and bears little relation to the popular image of ancient Greece. At a geographical crossroads, Greece combines elements of the Balkans, Middle East and Mediterranean.

For a relatively small country, less than 132,000 sq km (51,000 sq miles) in area, Greece possesses marked regional differences in topography. Nearly three-quarters of the land is mountainous, uninhabited or uncultivated. Fertile agricultural land supports tobacco farming in the northeast, with orchard fruits and vegetables grown further south. A third of the population lives in the capital, Athens, the cultural, financial and political centre, in which ancient and modern stand side by side.

Fresco from Moní Frankavílla, Amaliáda

Rural and urban life in contemporary Greece have been transformed despite years of occupation and conflict, including a bitter civil war *(see p42)* that would surely have finished off a less resilient people. The society that emerged was supported with US aid, yet Greece remained relatively under-developed until the 1960s.

Rural areas lacked paved roads and even basic utilities, prompting extensive, unplanned urban growth and emigration. It has been said, with some justice, that there are no architects in Greece, only civil engineers.

For centuries a large number of Greeks have lived abroad; currently there are over half as many Greeks outside the country as in. This

Backgammon players at the flea market around Plateía Monastiráki̱ou in Athens

◁ Leading a mule on the streets of Monemvasía

The Píndos mountain range, from above the village of Vrysochóri

diaspora occurred in several stages, prompted by changes in the Ottoman Empire late in the 17th century. Most post war emigration was to Africa, the Americas and Australia.

RELIGION, LANGUAGE AND CULTURE

During the centuries of domination by Venetians and Ottomans *(see pp38–9)* the Greek Orthodox Church preserved the Greek language, and with it Greek identity, through its liturgy and schools. Today, the Orthodox Church is still a powerful force despite the secularizing reforms of the PASOK government in the 1980s. The query *Eísai Orthódoxos*

(Are you Orthodox?) is virtually synonymous with *Éllinas eísai* (Are you Greek?). While no self-respecting couple would dispense with a church wedding and baptisms for their children, civil marriages are now equally valid in law as the traditional religious service. Sunday Mass is very popular with women, who often use the services as meeting places for socializing much in the same way as men do the *kafeneía* (cafés).

Votive offerings in the Pantánassas convent

Parish priests, often recognizable by their tall stovepipe hats and long beards, are not expected to embody the divine, but to transmit it at liturgy. Many marry and have a second trade (a custom that helps keep up the numbers of entrants to the church). There has also been a renaissance in monastic life, perhaps in reaction to the growth of

Greek priests leading a religious procession in Athens

materialism since World War II.

The subtle and beautiful Greek language, another great hallmark of national identity, was for a long time a field of conflict between *katharévousa*, an artificial, written

Tavernas in the town of Náfplio

form hastily devised around the time of Independence, and the slowly evolved *dimotikí*, or everyday speech, with its streamlined grammar and words borrowed from several other languages. The dispute acquired political overtones, with the Right tending to champion *katharévousa*, the Left, *dimotikí*, with blood even being shed at times.

Today the supple and accessible *dimotikí* is the language of the nation. The art of storytelling is still as prized in Greece as in Homer's time, with conversation pursued for its own sake in *kafeneía* and at dinner parties. The bardic tradition has remained alive with the poet-lyricists such as Mános Eleftheríou, Apóstolos Kaldarás and Níkos Gátsos. The continuous efforts

made to produce popular and accessible art have played a key role in helping to keep *dimotikí* alive from the 19th century until the present day.

Both writers and singers, the natural advocates of *dimotikí*, have historically been important to the Greek public. During recent periods of censorship under the dictatorship or in times of foreign occupation, they carried out an essential role as one of the chief sources of coded information and morale-boosting.

DEVELOPMENT AND DIPLOMACY

Compared to most of its Balkan neighbours, Greece is a relatively wealthy country. However, by Western economic indicators Greece is poor and languished

An archaeologist helping to restore the Parthenon

at the bottom of the EU league table until the addition of ten new East European countries in 2004. The persistent negative trade deficit is aggravated by imports of luxury goods, an expression of *xenomanía* or belief in the inherent superiority of all things foreign. Cars are most conspicuous among these, since Greece is one of the very few European countries not to manufacture its own.

Greece still bears the hallmarks of a developing economy, with agriculture and the service sector accounting for two-thirds of the GNP. Blurred lines between work and living space are

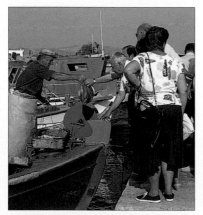

Selling fish at Vólos harbour, the Pílio

Barrels in the Achaïa Klauss winery at Pátra

the norm, with professional brass plates alternating with personal bell-buzzer tags in any apartment block. There is a tenacious adherence, despite repeated campaigns against it, to the long afternoon siesta. As a result, some workers have to endure commuting twice a day.

With EU membership since 1981 and a nominally capitalist orientation, Greece overcame its resemblance to pre-1989 Eastern Europe. The state no longer invests heavily in antiquated industries nor is the civil service of today overstaffed as part of a full-employment policy. After the turn of the millennium Greece saw an initial growth in its economy above the EU average, but due to uncontrolled government spending and the world financial crisis that started in the lates 2000s, the Greek economy faces a severe crisis. Industry has shrunk and unemployment has risen sharply. Tourism ranks as

the largest hard-currency earner, offsetting the depression in world shipping and the fact that Mediterranean agricultural products are duplicated within the EU. Greece's historically lenient entry requirements for refugees, and its pre-eminent status in the Balkans, have made it a magnet for Arabs, Africans, Kurds, Poles and Albanians for a number of years. Now protectionist procedures, such as stringent frontier clamp-downs and the deportation of all undocumented individuals, have been introduced.

The fact that the Greek state is less than 200 years old, and that it has had much political instability, means that there is little faith in government institutions. Life operates on networks of personal friendships and official contacts. The classic designations of Right and Left have only acquired their conventional meanings since the 1930s. The dominant political figure of the first half of the 20th century was Elefthérios Venizélos, an anti-royalist Liberal. The years following World War II have been largely shaped by the influence of

Statue of Athena standing beside the Athens Academy

Rooftops of Náfplio and Boúrtzi islet from the Palamídi fortress

House in the village of Psarádes, beside the Préspa lakes

three men: the late Andréas Papandréou, three times premier as head of the Panhellenic Socialist Movement (PASOK), the late conservative premier Konstantínos Karamanlís and the late premier Geórgios Papandréou (PASOK).

Since the end of the Cold War, Greece has been asserting its underlying Balkan identity. Relations with Albania have improved since the collapse of the Communist regime in 1990. Greece is the biggest investor in Bulgaria, and after a rapprochement with Skopje, it seems poised to be a regional power, with Thessaloníki's port (second largest in the Mediterranean) seen as the future gateway to the southern Balkans.

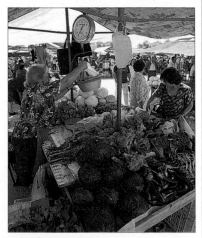

Man with a shepherd's crook in the village of Métsovo

HOME LIFE

The family is still the basic Greek social unit. Traditionally, one family could sow, plough and reap its own fields, without need of cooperative work parties. Today, family-run businesses are still the norm in urban settings. Family life and social life are usually one and the same, and tend to revolve around eating out, which is done more often than in most of Europe. Arranged marriages and granting of dowries,

though officially banned, persist; most single young people live with their parents or another relative until married, and outside the largest cities, few couples dare to cohabit. Despite the renowned Greek love of children, Greece has the lowest birth rate in Europe after Italy: less than half its pre-World War II levels. Owing in part to reforms in family and inheritance law, urban Greek women have been raised in status. Better represented in medicine and the law, many women run their own businesses. In the country, however, macho attitudes persist and women often forgo the chance of a career for the sake of the house and children. New imported notions and attitudes have begun to creep in, especially in the larger cities, but generally tradition remains strong and no amount of innovation or outside influence is likely to jeopardize the Greek way of life.

Wednesday market in Argos

Byzantine Architecture

Medieval churches are virtually all that have survived from a millennium of Byzantine civilization in Greece. Byzantine church architecture was concerned almost exclusively with a decorated interior. The intention was to sculpt out a holy space where the congregation would be confronted with the true nature of the cosmos, cleared of all worldly distractions. The mosaics and frescoes portraying the whole body of the Church, from Christ downwards, have a dual purpose: they give inspiration to the worshipper and are windows to the spiritual world. From a mountain chapel to an urban church there is great conformity of design, with structure and decoration united to a single purpose.

THE BEST OF BYZANTINE ARCHITECTURE

1. Thessaloníki *p248*
2. Mount Athos *pp252–4*
3. Arta *p213*
4. Monastery of Osios Loúkas *pp222–3*
5. Pátra *p169*
6. Moní Kaïsarianís *pp150–51*
7. Monastery of Dafní *pp152–3*
8. Athens *p80, p105, p108*
9. Mystrás *pp192–3*
10. Geráki *p189*

Small dome above narthex

The drum is pierced with as many as 40 windows.

The Pantokrátor, a mosaic of Christ in Judgment, is in the dome.

The iconostasis screen divides the altar from the main body of the church.

Side aisle

Four squinches support the dome.

Central apse

The west-facing porch may bear scenes from the life of the Virgin.

Ornamental brickwork was a 10th-century Greek invention.

Icon of Christ above the main door

Coloured marble flooring

Brickwork may alternate with layers of stone.

The three apses of the east wall often have ornamental brickwork on their curved exterior.

TYPICAL BYZANTINE CHURCH

Each church has a covered porch (narthex) to the west and an altar behind the iconostasis in the eastern apse. The nave typically has three aisles with the dome above the central square space. In a monastery the main church is known as the *katholikón*.

UNDERSTANDING FRESCOES IN A BYZANTINE CHURCH

The frescoes and mosaics in churches' interiors were organized according to a standard scheme. Symbolically, images descended from heaven (Christ Pantokrátor in the dome) to earth (the saints on the lowest level). The Virgin was shown in the semi-dome of the apse, with the fathers of the church below her.

THE VIRGIN MARY

Icons of the Virgin Mary abound in every Orthodox church, where she is referred to as Panagía, the All Holy. Her exceptional status was confirmed in 431 when she was awarded the title Theotókos "Mother of God", in preference to just "Mother of Christ".

Choirs of angels

Windows in drum

Christ Pantokrátor

The dome *is symbolically filled by the figure of Christ in Judgment, the Pantokrátor. Choirs of angels swirl around Him, and outside them stand the Old Testament prophets. This dome comes from Moní Perivléptou in Mystrás (see p192).*

Prophets

The Virgin and Child are in the curve of the apse, symbolically between heaven (the dome) and earth (the nave).

Archangels Michael and Gabriel, dressed like courtiers of a Byzantine emperor, honour the Virgin.

The Fathers of Orthodoxy, here in their episcopal robes, defined Orthodoxy in the early centuries.

Upper register of saints

The apse *is often hidden from public view by an elaborate iconostasis screen, through whose doors only the clergy are admitted. This apse is from Agios Stratigós in the Máni (see p199).*

Lower register of saints

Sand-filled tray for votive candles

The side walls *are decorated in registers. On the lowest level stand life-size portrayals of the saints, their heads illuminated with haloes. More complex scenes portraying incidents from the Gospels or the Day of Judgment fill the upper walls and vaults. This church is at Miliés in the Pílio (see pp218–20).*

Eleoúsa, *meaning "Our Lady of Tenderness", shows the Virgin Mary brushing cheeks with the Christ Child.*

The Virgin seated on a throne, *flanked by two arch-angels, is a depiction usually found in the eastern apse.*

Odigítria, *meaning the "Conductress", shows the Virgin indicating the Christ Child with her right arm.*

The Landscape of Mainland Greece

Greece is a land of rugged beauty. The narrow coastal belt is backed by cliffs in places while inland there are massive mountain ranges, gorges and cliffs, the haunt of eagles and vultures. The fantastic array of vegetation, including many species of spring wild flowers, is strongly influenced by the Mediterranean climate of long, hot and dry summers and mild, wet winters. Clearance of forests for agriculture and timber has produced a mosaic of flower-rich fields and areas of shrubs. This shrubland habitat is of two kinds: the dense aromatic bushes of *maquis* and the sparser *phrygana* with lower and more compact plants. Although the country's millions of goats destroy the vegetation with their constant grazing, one of the most romantic sights in Greece is that of flocks being herded through olive groves full of archaeological remains, as at Sparta in the Peloponnese.

Common poppy

Abandoned areas of cultivation soon revert to the wild. Larks and pipits feed and nest here and, in spring, wild flowers and butterflies are abundant.

Phrygana often covers bare slopes and rocky outcrops.

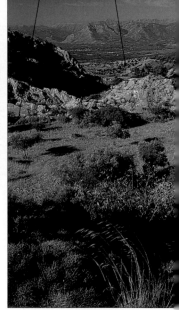

Hilly landscapes *with stately cypress trees standing tall and dark against the steep slopes are closely associated with Greece's archaeological sites. These, including the Byzantine town of Mystrás above, are worth visiting for their wildlife alone and in particular the spring wild flowers that mix rare orchids with daisies, poppies and marigolds.*

Olive trees harbour numerous birds and insects among their silvery-green foliage.

Spring flowers such as poppies and irises have a brief but prolific season.

MAQUIS AND PHRYGANA

Maquis shrubland dominates the landscape in this view of Mycenae. It is a mixture of rockroses and aromatic herbs. The more barren *phrygana*, in the far distance, has clumps of spiny vetches.

Olive groves *are found all over Greece at low altitudes; this one is at Argalastí in the Pílio. In spring, flowers grow in profusion in the shade of trees and attract a wealth of butterflies and beetles. Lizards hunt for insects in the twisted trunks that also provide nesting places for birds such as masked shrikes.*

Wetland areas, *such as the margins of Lake Stymfalía in the Peloponnese, are often used for farming. Usually fairly dry underfoot, they are rich in birds, amphibians and plants.*

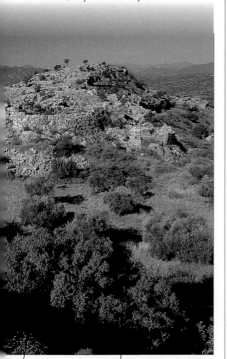

Areas of *maquis* provide ideal habitats for nesting birds such as warblers, serins and hoopoes.

Between the shrubs in open areas of *maquis*, orchids, tulips and other native flowers appear in the spring.

WILD FLOWERS OF GREECE

Greece is blessed with an extraordinary wealth of flowering plants. At least 6,000 species grow in the country, quite a few of them found nowhere else in the world. The floral richness is due in part to the country's diversity of habitats, ranging from wetlands, coastal plains and lowland *maquis* to snow-capped mountain tops. The growing period for many plants is winter, the dampest, coolest season, and the flowering periods run from March to early June, and again in September. Coastal areas of the Peloponnese are perhaps the richest in wild flowers.

The wild gladiolus has several varieties that are among the most showy spring flowers.

The tassel hyacinth is aptly named for its appearance. It grows on open ground and flowers in May.

Cytinus hypocistus is a parasite plant found growing close to the base of colourful cistus bushes *(see below)*.

Sage-leaved cistus is widespread in *maquis* habitats. Its colourful flowers attract pollinating insects.

White asphodel is often seen growing on roadside verges in many parts of Greece. Tall spikes of white flowers appear from April to June.

ORCHIDS

One of the botanical highlights of a visit to Greece is the range of wild orchid species that can be found in bloom between late February and May. All have strangely shaped, and sometimes colourful, flowers whose purpose is to attract pollinating insects.

The four-spotted orchid has spots on the flower lip. A plant of open hillsides, it flowers in April.

The naked man orchid has a dense head of pale pinkish flowers and favours open woodland.

The Greek spider orchid looks more like a bumblebee than a spider. It is found in *maquis* in early spring.

THE HISTORY OF GREECE

The history of Greece is that of a nation, not of a land: the Greek idea of nationality is governed by language, religion, descent and customs, not so much by geography. Early Greek history is the story of internal struggles, from the Mycenaean and Minoan cultures of the Bronze Age to the competing city-states that emerged in the 1st millennium BC.

Alexander the Great, by the folk artist Theófilos

After the defeat of the Greek army by Philip II of Macedon at Chaironeia in 338 BC, Greece was absorbed into Alexander the Great's Asian empire. With the defeat of the Macedonians by the Romans in 168 BC, Greece became a province of the Roman Empire. As part of the Eastern Empire, she was ruled from Constantinople and in the 11th century became a powerful element within the new, Orthodox Christian, Byzantine world.

After 1453, when Constantinople fell to the Ottomans, Greece as a political entity disappeared altogether. Eventually the realization that it was the democracy of Classical Athens which had inspired so many revolutions abroad gave the Greeks themselves the courage to rebel and, in 1821, to fight the Greek War of Independence. In 1832 the Great Powers that dominated Europe established a protectorate over Greece which marked the end of Ottoman rule. Greece re-established itself as a sizeable state, but the "Great Idea" – the ambition to re-create Byzantium – ended after Greece's disastrous defeat in the Greco-Turkish War (1919–22).

The instability of the ensuing years was followed by the Metaxás dictatorship and then by the war years (1940–48), during which half a million people were killed. The present boundaries of the Greek state have only existed since 1948, when Italy returned the Dodecanese. Now, as an established democracy and member of the European Union, Greece's fortunes seem to have come full circle after 2,000 years of foreign rule.

A map of Greece from the 1595 Atlas of Abraham Ortelius called *Theatrum Orbis Terrarum*

◁ The beginning of the 1821 Greek Revolution as shown in 1825 by L Dupré

Prehistoric Greece

Mycenaean gold brooch

During the Bronze Age three separate civilizations flourished in Greece: the Cycladic, during the 3rd millennium; the Minoan, based on Crete but with an influence that spread throughout the Aegean islands; and the Mycenaean, which was based on the mainland but spread to Crete in about 1450 BC when the Minoans went into decline. Both the Minoan and Mycenaean cultures found their peak in the Palace periods of the 2nd millennium when they were dominated by a centralized religion and bureaucracy.

PREHISTORIC GREECE

▨ Areas settled in the Bronze Age

Neolithic Head *(3000 BC)*
This figure was found on Alónnisos in the Sporades. It probably represents a fertility goddess who was worshipped by farmers to ensure a good harvest. These figures ind- icate a certain stability in early communities.

The town is unwalled, showing that inhabitants did not fear attack.

Cycladic Figurine
Marble statues such as this, produced in the Bronze Age from about 2800 to 2300 BC, have been found in a number of tombs in the Cyclades.

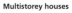

Multistorey houses

Minoan "Bathtub" Sarcophagus
This type of coffin, dating to 1400 BC, is found only in Minoan art. It was probably used for a high-status burial.

TIMELINE

	7000 Neolithic farmers in northern Greece		3200 Beginnings of Bronze Age cultures in Cyclades and Crete		2000 Arrival of first Greek-speakers on mainland Greece
200,000 BC	**5000 BC**		**4000 BC**	**3000 BC**	**20◆**
200,000 Evidence of Palaeolithic civilization in northern Greece and Thessaly		*"Frying Pan" vessel from Sýros (2500– 2000 BC)*		2800–2300 Kéros-Sýros culture flourishes in Cyclades	
				2000 Building of palaces begins in Crete, initiating First Palace period	

Mycenaean Death Mask
Large amounts of worked gold were discovered at wealthy Mycenae, the city of Agamemnon. Masks like this were laid over the faces of the dead.

Forested hills

The **inhabitants** are on friendly terms with the visitors.

WHERE TO SEE PREHISTORIC GREECE

The Museum of Cycladic Art in Athens *(see pp74–5)* has Greece's leading collection of Cycladic figurines. The remains at Mycenae are extensive *(pp178–80)* and the museum at Náfplio *(p182)* displays finds from this and other Mycenaean sites, as does the National Archaeological Museum, Athens *(pp68–71)*. Excavations at Nestor's Palace *(p201)* uncovered tablets written in Linear B script. These earliest examples of Greek language can be seen in the museum at nearby Chóra, together with frescoes and pottery from the palace.

Cyclopean Walls
Mycenaean citadels, such as this one at Tiryns, were encircled by walls of stone so large that later civilizations believed they had been built by giants. It is unclear whether the walls were used for defence or just to impress.

Oared sailing ships

MINOAN SEA SCENE
The wall paintings on the island of Santoríni were preserved by the volcanic eruption at the end of the 16th century BC. This section shows ships departing from a coastal town. In contrast to the warlike Mycenaeans, Minoan art reflects a more stable community which dominated the Aegean through trade, not conquest.

Mycenaean Octopus Jar
This 14th-century BC vase's decoration follows the shape of the pot. Restrained and symmetrical, it contrasts with relaxed Minoan prototypes.

1750–1700 Start of Second Palace period and golden age of Minoan culture in Crete

1525 Volcanic eruption on Santoríni devastates the region

1250–1200 Probable destruction of Troy, after abduction of Helen *(see p54)*

1450 Mycenaeans take over Knosós; use of Linear B script

Helen of Troy

1800 BC	1600 BC	1400 BC	1200 BC

1730 Destruction of Minoan palaces; end of First Palace period

Minoan figurine of a snake goddess, 1500 BC

1200 Collapse of Mycenaean culture

1600 Beginning of high period of Mycenaean prosperity and dominance

1370–50 Palace of Knosós on Crete destroyed for second time

The Dark Ages and Archaic Period

Silver coin from Athens

After 1200 BC, Greece entered a period of darkness. There was widespread poverty, the population decreased and many skills were lost. A cultural revival in about 800 BC accompanied the emergence of the city-states across Greece and inspired new styles of warfare, art and politics. Greek colonies were established as far away as the Black Sea, present-day Syria, North Africa and the western Mediterranean. Greece was defined by where Greeks lived.

Koúros *(530 BC)*
Koúroi *were early monumental male nude statues (see p70). Idealized representations rather than portraits, they were inspired by Egyptian statues, from which they take their frontal, forward-stepping pose.*

Bronze breastplate

MEDITERRANEAN AREA, 479 BC

◼ *Areas of Greek influence*

The double flute player kept the men marching in time.

Bronze greaves protected the legs.

Solon *(640–558 BC)*
Solon was appointed to the highest magisterial position in Athens. His legal, economic and political reforms heralded democracy.

HOPLITE WARRIORS

The "Chigi" vase from Corinth, dating to about 750 BC, is one of the earliest clear depictions of the new style of warfare that evolved at that period. This required rigorously trained and heavily armed infantrymen called hoplites to fight in a massed formation or phalanx. The rise of the city-state may be linked to the spirit of equality felt by citizen hoplites fighting for their own community.

TIMELINE

Vase fragment showing bands of distinctive geometric line patterns

900 Appearance of first Geometric pottery

1100 BC	1000 BC	900 BC
1100 Migrations of different peoples throughout the Greek world	**1000–850** Formation of the Homeric kingdoms	

6th-Century Vase
This bowl (krater) *for mixing wine and water at elegant feasts is an early example of the art of vase painting. It depicts mythological and heroic scenes.*

Bronze helmets
for protection

Spears were used for
thrusting.

WHERE TO SEE ARCHAIC GREECE

Examples of *koûroi* can be found in the National Archaeological Museum *(pp68–71)* and in the Acropolis Museum *(p97)*, both in Athens. The National Archaeological Museum also houses the national collection of Greek Geometric, red-figure and black-figure vases. The first victory over the Persians in 490 BC was commemorated by the mound of Athenian dead which still dominates the plain at Marathon *(p145)*. The museum at Sparta *(p189)* contains a bust of Leonidas, the Spartan king, who with his 300 hoplite soldiers was massacred by the Persians at Thermopylae in 480 BC.

The phalanxes
shoved and
pushed, aiming to
maintain an
unbroken shield
wall, a successful
new technique.

Gorgon's head
decoration

Characteristic
round shields

Hunter Returning Home *(500 BC)*
Hunting for hares, deer, or wild boar was an aristocratic sport pursued by Greek nobles on foot with dogs, as depicted on this cup.

Darius I *(ruled 521–486 BC)*
This relief from Persepolis shows the Persian king who tried to conquer the Greek mainland, but was defeated at the battle of Marathon in 490.

776 Traditional date for the first Olympic Games

675 Lykourgos initiates austere reforms in Sparta

600 First Doric columns built at Temple of Hera, Olympia

Doric capital

490 Athenians defeat Persians at Marathon

0 BC   700 BC   600 BC   500 BC

750–700 Homer records epic tales of the *Iliad* and *Odyssey*

770 Greeks start founding colonies in Italy, Egypt and elsewhere

Spartan votive figurine

546 Persians gain control over Ionian Greeks; Athens flourishes under the tyrant Peisistratos and his sons

630 Poetess Sappho writing in Lésvos

480 Athens destroyed by Persians who defeat Spartans at Thermopylae; Greek victory at Salamis

479 Persians annihilated at Plataiaí by Athenians, Spartans and allies

Classical Greece

The Classical period has always been considered the high point of Greek civilization. Around 150 years of exceptional creativity in thinking, writing, theatre and the arts produced the great tragedians Aeschylus, Sophocles and Euripides as well as the great philosophical thinkers Socrates, Plato and Aristotle. This was also a time of warfare and bloodshed, however. The Peloponnesian War, which pitted the city-state of Athens and her allies against the city-state of Sparta and her allies, dominated the 5th century BC. In the 4th century Sparta, Athens and Thebes struggled for power, only to be ultimately defeated by Philip II of Macedon in 338 BC.

Trading amphora

CLASSICAL GREECE, 440 BC

▮ *Athens and her allies*

▮ *Sparta and her allies*

Theatre used in Pythian Games

Temple of Apollo

Siphnian Treasury

Fish Shop
This detail is from a 4th-century BC Greek painted vase from Cefalù in Sicily. Large parts of the island were inhabited by Greeks who were bound by a common culture, religion and language.

Perikles
This great democratic leader built up the Greek navy and masterminded the extensive building programme in Athens between the 440s and 420s, including the Acropolis temples.

THE SANCTUARY OF DELPHI

The sanctuary *(see pp228–9)*, shown in this 1894 reconstruction, reached the peak of its political influence in the 5th and 4th centuries BC. Of central importance was the Oracle of Apollo, whose utterances influenced the decisions of city-states such as Athens and Sparta. Rich gifts dedicated to the god were placed by the states in treasuries that lined the Sacred Way.

TIMELINE

Detail of the Parthenon frieze

462 Ephialtes's reforms pave the way for radical democracy in Athens

431–404 Peloponnesian War, ending with the fall of Athens and start of 33-year period of Spartan dominance

c.424 Death of Herodotus, historian of the Persian Wars

475 BC	450 BC	425 BC

478 With the formation of the Delian League, Athens takes over leadership of Greek cities

451–429 Perikles rises to prominence in Athens and launches a lavish building programme

447 Construction of the Parthenon begins

Bust of Herodotus, probably of Hellenistic origin

Gold Oak Wreath from Vergína
By the mid-4th century BC, Philip II of Macedon dominated the Greek world through diplomacy and warfare. This wreath comes from his tomb.

WHERE TO SEE
CLASSICAL GREECE
Athens is dominated by the Acropolis and its religious buildings, including the Parthenon, erected as part of Perikles's mid 5th-century BC building programme *(pp94–9)*. The Marmaria, just outside the sanctuary at Delphi, features the remains of the unique circular *tholos (p230)*. In the Peloponnese, the town of Messene dates from 396 BC *(p201)*; the best-preserved theatre is at Epidaurus *(pp184–5)*. Philip II's tomb can be seen at Vergína in Macedonia *(p242)*.

Votive of the Rhodians

Stoa of the Athenians

Sacred Way

Athenian Treasury

Slave Boy *(400 BC)*
Slaves were fundamental to the Greek economy and used for all types of work. Many slaves were foreign; this boot boy came from as far as Africa.

Athena Lemnia
This Roman copy of a statue by Pheidias (c.490–c.430 BC), the sculptor-in-charge at the Acropolis, depicts the goddess protector of Athens in an ideal rather than realistic way, typical of the Classical style in art.

387 Plato founds Academy in Athens

Sculpture of Plato

337 Foundation of the League of Corinth legitimizes Philip II's control over the Greek city-states

359 Philip II becomes King of Macedon

400 BC	375 BC	350 BC

399 Trial and execution of Socrates

371 Sparta defeated by Thebes at Battle of Leuktra, heralding a decade of Theban dominance in the area

338 Greeks defeated by Philip II of Macedon at Battle of Chaironeia

336 Philip II is assassinated at Aigai and is succeeded by his son, Alexander

Hellenistic Greece

Alexander the Great of Macedon fulfilled his father Philip's plans for the conquest of the Persians. He went on to create a vast empire that extended to India in the east and Egypt in the south. The Hellenistic period

Alexander the Great was extraordinary for the dispersal of Greek language, religion and culture throughout the territories conquered by Alexander. It lasted from after Alexander's death in 323 BC until the Romans began to dismantle his empire, early in the 2nd century BC. For Greece, Macedonian domination was replaced by that of Rome in AD 168.

Relief of Hero-Worship (c.200 BC)
The worship of heroes after death was a feature of Greek religion. Alexander, however, was worshipped as a god in his lifetime.

Pélla was the birthplace of Alexander and capital of Macedon.

The **Mausoleum** of Halicarnassus was one of the Seven Wonders of the Ancient World.

Issus, in modern Turkey, was the site of Alexander's victory over the Persian army in 333 B

BLACK SEA

• Pélla

• Athens

Mausoleum of Halicarnassus

• Issus

MEDITERRANEAN SEA

AS MIN

Ishtar Ga Babyl

Ammon • **Lighthouse at Alexandria**

Alexander died in Babylon in 323 BC

EGYPT

RED SEA

ARA

Alexander Defeats Darius III
This Pompeiian mosaic shows the Persian leader overwhelmed at Issus in 333 BC. Macedonian troops are shown carrying their highly effective long pikes.

Terracotta Statue
This 2nd-century BC statue of two women gossiping is typical of a Hellenistic interest in private rather than public individuals.

The **Ammon** oracle declared Alexander to be divine.

Alexandria, founded by Alexander, replaced Athens a the centre of Greek culture.

KEY

— — — Alexander's route

▢ Alexander's empire

▢ Dependent regions

TIMELINE

333 Alexander the Great defeats the Persian king, Darius III, and declares himself king of Asia

323 Death of Alexander, and of Diogenes

301 Battle of Ipsus, between Alexander's rival successors, leads to the break-up of his empire into three kingdoms

268–261 Chremonidean War, ending with the capitulation of Athens to Macedon

325 BC | **300 BC** | **275 BC** | **250 B(**

322 Death of Aristotle

331 Alexander founds Alexandria after conquering Egypt

287–275 "Pyrrhic victory" of King Pyrros of Epirus who defeated the Romans in Italy but suffered heavy losses

Diogenes, the Hellenistic philosopher

Fusing Eastern and Western Religion
This plaque from Afghanistan shows the Greek goddess Nike and the Asian goddess Cybele in a chariot pulled by lions.

WHERE TO SEE HELLENISTIC GREECE

The royal palace at Pélla (p243), capital of Macedon and birthplace of Alexander, and the palace of Palatítsia (p242) are exceptional. Pélla has outstanding mosaics, one of which depicts Alexander. Goldwork and other finds are in the museum at Pélla and the Archaeological Museum at Thessaloníki (pp246–7). In Athens, the Stoa of Attalos (p90) in the Greek Agora was given by Attalos of Pergamon (ruled 159 to 138 BC). The Tower of the Winds (pp86–7) in the Roman Agora, built by the Macedonian astronomer Andronikos Kyrrestes, incorporates a water clock.

Susa, capital of the Persian Empire, was captured in 331 BC. A mass wedding of Alexander's captains to Asian brides was held in 324 BC.

Alexander chose his wife, Roxane, from among Sogdian captives in 327 BC.

Roxane
Alexandropolis

SOGDIANI

Taxil

BACTRIA

PERSIA

War elephant

Susa

Sculpture from Persepolis

GEDROSIA

INDIA

Beas

ARABIAN SEA

Battle elephants were used against the Indian King Poros in 326 BC.

Alexander's army turned back at the River Beas.

The **Persian religious** centre of Persepolis, in modern Iran, fell to Alexander in 330 BC.

Alexander's army suffered heavy losses in the Gedrosia desert.

ALEXANDER THE GREAT'S EMPIRE

In forming his empire Alexander covered huge distances. After defeating the Persians in Asia he moved to Egypt, then returned to Asia to pursue Darius, and then his murderers, into Bactria. In 326 BC his troops revolted in India and refused to go on. Alexander died in 323 BC in Babylon.

The Death of Archimedes
Archimedes was the leading Hellenistic scientist and mathematician. This mosaic from Renaissance Italy shows his murder in 212 BC by a Roman.

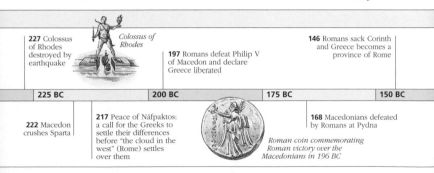

227 Colossus of Rhodes destroyed by earthquake

Colossus of Rhodes

197 Romans defeat Philip V of Macedon and declare Greece liberated

146 Romans sack Corinth and Greece becomes a province of Rome

| 225 BC | 200 BC | 175 BC | 150 BC |

222 Macedon crushes Sparta

217 Peace of Náfpaktos: a call for the Greeks to settle their differences before "the cloud in the west" (Rome) settles over them

168 Macedonians defeated by Romans at Pydna

Roman coin commemorating Roman victory over the Macedonians in 196 BC

Roman Greece

Mark Antony

After the Romans gained final control of Greece, with the sack of Corinth in 146 BC, Greece became the cultural centre of the Roman Empire. The Roman nobility sent their sons to be educated in the schools of philosophy in Athens (see p57). The end of the Roman civil wars between leading Roman statesmen was played out on Greek soil, finishing in the Battle of Actium in Thessaly in 31 BC. In AD 323 the Emperor Constantine founded the new eastern capital of Constantinople; the empire was later divided into the Greek-speaking East and the Latin-speaking West.

ROMAN PROVINCES, AD 211

Mithridates
In a bid to extend his territory, this ruler of Pontus, on the Black Sea, led the resistance to Roman rule in 88 BC. He was forced to make peace three years later.

Bema, or raised platform, where St Paul spoke

Roman basilica

Bouleuterion

Springs of Peirene, the source of water

Notitia Dignitatum *(AD 395) As part of the Roman Empire, Greece was split into several provinces. The proconsul of the province of Achaïa used this insignia.*

RECONSTRUCTION OF ROMAN CORINTH
Corinth *(see pp162–6)* was refounded and largely rebuilt by Julius Caesar in 46 BC, becoming the capital of the Roman province of Achaïa. The Romans built the forum, covered theatre and basilicas. St Paul visited the city in AD 50–51, working as a tent maker.

Baths of Eurycles

TIMELINE

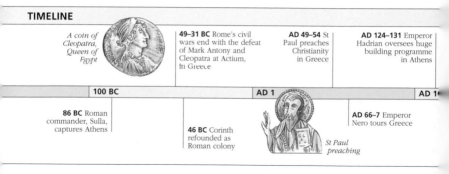

A coin of Cleopatra, Queen of Egypt

49–31 BC Rome's civil wars end with the defeat of Mark Antony and Cleopatra at Actium, in Greece

AD 49–54 St Paul preaches Christianity in Greece

AD 124–131 Emperor Hadrian oversees huge building programme in Athens

100 BC

AD 1

AD 1

86 BC Roman commander, Sulla, captures Athens

46 BC Corinth refounded as Roman colony

St Paul preaching

AD 66–7 Emperor Nero tours Greece

Mosaic *(AD 180)*
*This highly
sophisticated
Roman mosaic of
Dionysos riding
on a leopard comes
from the House of
Masks, on Delos.*

Temple of
Octavia

Odeion or Roman
covered theatre

Greek open-air
theatre

Archaic
Greek
Temple of
Apollo

**Arch of
Galerius**
*This arch at
Thessaloníki
commemorates the
Emperor Galerius's
victory over the
Persians. The carved
panel shows Galerius
in his chariot.*

WHERE TO SEE ROMAN GREECE

In Athens, the Roman Agora, Hadrian's library nearby *(p85)* and the Arch of Hadrian *(p111)*, which leads from the Roman into the old Greek city *(pp90–1)*, are examples of Roman architecture. The Temple of Olympian Zeus *(p111)* and the Theatre of Herodes Atticus *(p100)* are also in Athens. The triumphal arch of Galerius in Thessaloníki *(p244)* commemorates the Emperor Galerius's victories over the Persians in AD 297. The museum at Corinth *(p166)* contains fine Roman mosaics and other artifacts.

Apollo Belvedere
*Much Greek sculpture
is known to us only
through Roman copies
of Greek originals, like
this statue of Apollo.*

---

170 Pausanias completes
guide to Greece for
Roman travellers

267 Goths
pillage Athens

323 Constantine becomes sole
emperor of Roman Empire
and establishes his capital
in Constantinople

395 Goths devastate Athens
and Peloponnese

390 Emperor
Theodosius I makes
Christianity state religion

AD 200	AD 300

*Coin of the
Roman Emperor
Galerius*

293 Under Emperor
Galerius, Thessaloníki
becomes second city to
Constantinople

393 Olympic Games banned

395 Death of Theodosius I; formal
division of Roman Empire into
Latin West and Byzantine East

Byzantine and Crusader Greece

Byzantine court dress arm band

Under the Byzantine Empire, which at the end of the 4th century succeeded the old Eastern Roman Empire, Greece became Orthodox in religion and was split into administrative *themes*. When the capital, Constantinople, fell to the Crusaders in 1204 Greece was again divided, mostly between the Venetians and the Franks. Constantinople and Mystrás were recovered by the Byzantine Greeks in 1261, but the Turks' capture of Constantinople in 1453 was a significant part of the demise of the Byzantine Empire. It left a legacy of hundreds of churches and a wealth of religious art.

BYZANTINE GREECE IN THE 10TH CENTURY

Chapel

Watch-tower of Tsimiskís

Refectory

Two-Headed Eagle
The double-headed eagle was an omnipresent symbol of the power of the Byzantine Empire in this era.

GREAT LAVRA

This monastery is the earliest (AD 963) and largest of the religious complexes on Mount Athos *(see pp252–4)*. Many parts of it have been rebuilt, but its appearance remains essentially Byzantine. The monasteries became important centres of learning and religious art.

Defence of Thessaloníki
The fall of Thessaloníki to the Saracens in AD 904 was a blow to the Byzantine Empire. Many towns in Greece were heavily fortified against attack from this time.

TIMELINE

578–86 Avars and Slavs invade Greece

Gold solidus of the Byzantine Empress Irene, who ruled AD 797–802

400	600	800

529 Aristotle's and Plato's schools of philosophy close as Christian culture supplants Classical thought

680 Bulgars cross Danube and establish empire in northern Greece

726 Iconoclasm introduced by Pope Leo III (abandoned in 843)

841 Parthenon becomes a cathedral

Constantine the Great

The first eastern emperor to recognize Christianity, Constantine founded the city of Constantinople in AD 324. Here he is shown with his mother, Helen.

Cypress tree of Agios Athanásios

Christ Pantokrátor

This 14th-century fresco of Christ as ruler of the world is in the Byzantine city and monastic centre of Mystrás.

WHERE TO SEE BYZANTINE AND CRUSADER GREECE

In Athens, both the Benáki (pp78–9) and the Byzantine (p76) museums contain sculpture, icons, metalwork and textiles. The medieval city of Mystrás (pp192–3) has a castle, palaces, houses and monasteries. The churches of Thessaloníki (p248) and the monasteries of Dafní (pp152–3) and Osios Loúkas (pp222–3) contain fine Byzantine mosaics and frescoes, as do the monasteries of Mount Athos (pp252–4). Chlemoútsi (p169), built in 1223, is one of Greece's oldest Frankish castles. There are important fortresses at Acrocorinth (p166) and Monemvasía (pp186–8).

Fortified walls

Chapel of Agios Athanásios, founder of Great Lávra

Combined library and treasury

The katholikón, the main church in Great Lávra, has the most magnificent post-Byzantine murals on Mount Athos.

1054 Patriarch of Constantinople and Pope Leo IX excommunicate each other

Frankish Chlemoútsi Castle

1081–1149 Normans invade Greek islands and mainland

1354 Ottoman Turks enter Europe via southern Italy and Greece

1390–1450 Turks gain power over much of mainland Greece

1000 | **1200** | **1400**

Basil the Bulgar Slayer, Byzantine emperor (lived 956–1025)

1204 Crusaders sack Constantinople. Break-up of Byzantine Empire as result of occupation by Franks and Venetians

1210 Venetians win control over Crete

1261 Start of intellectual and artistic flowering of Mystrás; Constantinople re-occupied by Byzantines

1389 Venetians in control of much of Greece and the islands

Venetian and Ottoman Greece

Venetian lion of St Mark

Following the Ottomans' momentous capture of Constantinople in 1453, and their conquest of almost all the remaining Greek territory by 1460, the Greek state effectively ceased to exist for the next 350 years. Although the city became the capital of the vast Ottoman Empire, it remained the principal centre of Greek population and the focus of Greek dreams of resurgence. The small Greek population of what today is modern Greece languished in an impoverished and underpopulated backwater, but even there rebellious bands of brigands and private militias were formed. The Ionian Islands, Crete and a few coastal enclaves were seized for long periods by the Venetians – an experience more intrusive than the inefficient tolerance of the Ottomans, but one which left a rich cultural and architectural legacy.

GREECE IN 1493

■ Areas occupied by Venetians

■ Areas occupied by Ottomans

Cretan Painting
This 15th-century icon is typical of the style developed by Greek artists in the School of Crete, active until the Ottomans took Crete in 1669.

Battle of Lepanto *(1571)*
The Christian fleet, under Don John of Austria, decisively defeated the Ottomans off Náfpaktos, halting their advance westwards (see p225).

ARRIVAL OF TURKISH PRINCE CEM ON RHODES

Prince Cem, Ottoman rebel and son of Mehmet II, fled to Rhodes in 1481 and was welcomed by the Christian Knights of St John. In 1522, however, Rhodes fell to the Ottomans after a siege.

TIMELINE

1453 Mehmet II captures Constantinople which is renamed Istanbul and made capital of the Ottoman Empire

1503 Ottoman Turks win control of the Peloponnese apart from Monemvasía

1571 Venetian and Spanish fleet defeats Ottoman Turks at the Battle of Lepanto

1500	1550	1600

1460 Turks capture Mystrás

Cretan chain mail armour from the 16th century

1456 Ottoman Turks occupy Athens

1522 The Knights of St John forced to cede Rhodes to the Ottomans

Shipping

Greek merchants traded throughout the Ottoman Empire. By 1800 there were merchant colonies in Constantinople and as far afield as London and Odessa. This 19th-century embroidery shows the Turkish influence on Greek decorative arts.

The Knights of St John defied the Turks until 1522.

The massive fortifications eventually succumbed to Turkish artillery.

The Knights supported Turkish rebel, Prince Cem.

WHERE TO SEE VENETIAN AND OTTOMAN ARCHITECTURE

Náfplio *(pp182–3)* contains many examples of the Venetian presence, especially the Naval Warehouse (now a museum) and the Palamídi fortress *(p183)*. Following a pattern familiar throughout the Balkan states, enormous efforts were made after Independence to remove or disguise all Ottoman buildings. However, in Athens there are small but well-preserved Ottoman quarters in the Pláka district, and the Tzistarákis Mosque (now the Ceramics Museum, *p86*) is also Ottoman. The White Tower in Thessaloníki *(p244)* was built by the Turks in the 15th century. In Kavála *(p255)*, there is an aqueduct built in the reign of Suleiman the Magnificent, and in Ioánnina *(p210)* the Aslan Pasha Mosque.

Dinner at a Greek House in 1801
Nearly four centuries of Ottoman rule profoundly affected Greek culture, ethnic composition and patterns of everyday life. Greek cuisine incorporates Turkish dishes still found throughout the old Ottoman Empire.

1687 Parthenon seriously damaged during Venetian artillery attack on Turkish magazine

1715 Turks reconquer the Peloponnese

Ali Pasha (1741–1822), a governor of the Ottoman Empire

1814 Britain gains possession of Ionian Islands

1650	1700	1750	1800

1684 Venetians reconquer the Peloponnese

Parthenon blown up

1778 Ali Pasha becomes Vizier of Ioánnina and establishes powerful state in Albania and northern Greece

1801 Frieze on Parthenon removed by Lord Elgin

1814 Foundation of *Filikí Etaireía*, Greek liberation movement

The Making of Modern Greece

Flag with the symbols of the *Filiki Etaireía*

The Greek War of Independence marked the overthrow of the Ottomans and the start of the "Great Idea", an ambitious project to bring all Greek people under one flag *(énosis)*. The plans for expansion were initially successful, and during the 19th century the Greeks succeeded in doubling their national territory and reasserting Greek sovereignty over many of the islands. However, an attempt to take Asia Minor by force after World War I ended in disaster. In 1922 millions of Greeks were expelled from Smyrna in Turkish Anatolia, ending thousands of years of Greek presence in Asia Minor.

THE EMERGING GREEK STATE

Greece in 1832

Areas gained 1832–1923

Klephts (mountain brigands) were the basis of the Independence movement.

Massacre at Chíos
This detail of Delacroix's shocking painting Scènes de Massacres de Scio *shows the events of 1822, when Turks took savage revenge for an earlier killing of Muslims.*

Weapons were family heirlooms or donated by philhellenes.

Declaration of the Constitution in Athens
Greece's Neo-Classical parliament building in Athens was the site of the Declaration of the Constitution in 1843. It was built as the Royal Palace for Greece's first monarch, King Otto, during the 1830s.

TIMELINE

1824 The poet Lord Byron dies of a fever at Mesolóngi

1831 President Kapodístrias assassinated

1832 Great Powers establish protectorate over Greece and appoint Otto, Bavarian prince, as king

1834 Athens replaces Náfplio as capital

German archaeologist Heinrich Schliemann

1830	1840	1850	1860	1

1827 Battle of Navaríno

1828 Ioánnis Kapodístrias becomes first president of Greece

King Otto (ruled 1832–62)

1862 Revolution drives King Otto from Greece

1874 Heinri Schliema begi excavation Mycen

1821 Greek flag of independence raised on 25 March; Greeks massacre Turks at Tripolitsá in Morea

1864 New constitution makes Greece a "crowned democracy"; Greek Orthodoxy made the state religion

Life in Athens
By 1836 urban Greeks still wore a mixture of Greek traditional and Western dress. The Ottoman legacy had not totally disappeared and is visible in the fez worn by men.

FLAG RAISING OF 1821 REVOLUTION

In 1821, the Greek secret society *Filikí Etaireía* was behind a revolt by Greek officers which led to anti-Turk uprisings throughout the Peloponnese. Tradition credits Archbishop Germanós of Pátra with raising the rebel flag near Kalávryta *(see p168)* on 25 March. The struggle for independence had begun.

WHERE TO SEE 19TH-CENTURY GREECE

Independence was proclaimed at the Moní Agías Lávras, near Kalávryta *(p168)*. Lord Byron died at Mesolóngi *(p225)*. Ioánnis Kapodístrias was assassinated at the church of Agios Spyrídon in Náfplio *(p182)*. Pýlos is the site of the battle of Navaríno *(p200)*.

Corinth Canal
This spectacular link between the Aegean and Ionian seas opened in 1893 (see p167).

Eleonthérios Venizélos
This great Cretan politician and advocate of liberal democracy doubled Greek territory during the Balkan Wars (1912–13) and joined the Allies in World War I.

1893 Opening of Corinth Canal

1896 First Olympics of modern era, held in Athens

1908 Crete united with Greece

1917 King Constantine resigns; Greece joins World War I

1919 Greece launches offensive in Asia Minor

1922 Turkish burning of Smyrna signals end of the "Great Idea"

1880	1890	1900	1910	1920

Spyrídon Loúis, marathon winner at the first modern Olympics

1899 Arthur Evans begins excavations at Knosós

1912–13 Greece extends its borders during the Balkan Wars

1920 Treaty of Sèvres gives Greece huge gains in territory

1923 Population exchange agreed between Greece and Turkey at Treaty of Lausanne. Greece loses previous gains

Twentieth-Century Greece

The years after the 1922 defeat by Turkey were terrible ones for Greek people. The influx of refugees contributed to the political instability of the interwar years. The dictatorship of Metaxás was followed by invasion in 1940, then Italian, German and Bulgarian occupation and, finally, Civil War between 1946 and 1949, with its legacy of division. After experiencing the Cyprus problem of the 1950s and the military dictatorship of 1967 to 1974, Greece is now an established democracy and a member of the European Economic and Monetary Union.

1947 Internationally acclaimed Greek artist, Giánnis Tsaroúchis, holds his first exhibition of set designs, in the Romvos Gallery, Athens

1938 Death of sculptor Giannoúlis Chalepás, best known for his *Sleeping Girl* funerary

1946 Government institutes "White Terror" against Communists

1957 Mosaics found by chance at Philip II's 300 BC palace at Pélla

1945 Níkos Kazantzákis publishes *Zorba the Greek*, later made into a film

1933 Death of Greek poet Constantine (C P) Cavafy

1967 Right-wing colonels form Junta, forcing King Constantine into exile

1925	1935	1945	1955	1965

1925	1935	1945	1955	1965

1939 Greece declares neutrality at start of World War II

1951 Greece enters NATO

1955 Greek Cypriots start campaign of violence in Cyprus against British rule

1963 Geórgios Papandréou's centre-left government voted into power

1932 Aristotle Onassis purchases six freight ships, the start of his shipping empire

1948 Dodecanese becomes part of Greece

1960 Cyprus declared independent

1925 Mános Chatzidákis, who wrote music for the film *Never on Sunday,* is born

ΟΙ ΗΡΩΙΔΕΣ ΤΟΥ 1940

1940 Italy invades Greece. Greek soldiers defend northern Greece. Greece enters World War II

1946–9 Civil War between Greek government and the Communists who take to the mountains

1944 Churchill visits Athens to show his support for Greek government against Communist Resistance

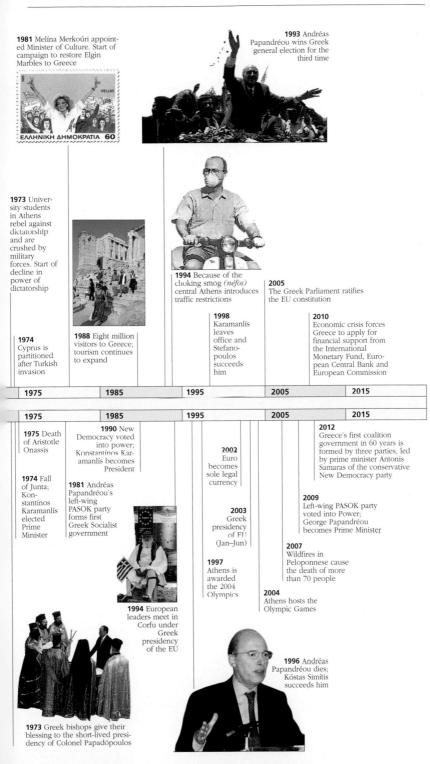

1981 Melína Merkoúri appointed Minister of Culture. Start of campaign to restore Elgin Marbles to Greece

1993 Andréas Papandréou wins Greek general election for the third time

1973 University students in Athens rebel against dictatorship and are crushed by military forces. Start of decline in power of dictatorship

1974 Cyprus is partitioned after Turkish invasion

1988 Eight million visitors to Greece; tourism continues to expand

1994 Because of the choking smog *(néfos)* central Athens introduces traffic restrictions

1998 Karamanlís leaves office and Stefanopoulos succeeds him

2005 The Greek Parliament ratifies the EU constitution

2010 Economic crisis forces Greece to apply for financial support from the International Monetary Fund, European Central Bank and European Commission

| 1975 | 1985 | 1995 | 2005 | 2015 |

| 1975 | 1985 | 1995 | 2005 | 2015 |

1975 Death of Aristotle Onassis

1974 Fall of Junta; Konstantínos Karamanlís elected Prime Minister

1990 New Democracy voted into power; Konstantínos Karamanlís becomes President

1981 Andréas Papandréou's left-wing PASOK party forms first Greek Socialist government

1994 European leaders meet in Corfu under Greek presidency of the EU

2002 Euro becomes sole legal currency

2003 Greek presidency of EU (Jan–Jun)

1997 Athens is awarded the 2004 Olympics

2004 Athens hosts the Olympic Games

1996 Andréas Papandréou dies; Kóstas Simítis succeeds him

2012 Greece's first coalition government in 60 years is formed by three parties, led by prime minister Antonis Samaras of the conservative New Democracy party

2009 Left-wing PASOK party voted into Power; George Papandréou becomes Prime Minister

2007 Wildfires in Peloponnese cause the death of more than 70 people

1973 Greek bishops give their blessing to the short-lived presidency of Colonel Papadópoulos

ATHENS AND MAINLAND GREECE THROUGH THE YEAR

Predominantly rural, Greece is deeply attached to its locally produced food and wine, and chapels dotting the countryside serve as the focus for culinary, as well as religious, celebrations. Festivals of the Orthodox Church are deeply identified with Greekness, no more so than on 25 March, a date which

May Day wild flower wreath

commemorates both the Feast of the Annunciation and the start of the Independence uprising in 1821. Summer festivals are celebrated widely in rural villages, and expatriate Greeks return from across the globe. Organized arts events are a more recent phenomenon, paralleling the rise of tourism.

SPRING

Spring is a glorious time in Greece. The lowland landscape, parched for much of the year, luxuriates in a carpet of green, and wild flowers abound. But the

25 March, Independence Day

weather does not stabilize until late spring, with rainy or blustery days common in March and April. Artichokes ripen in March, and May sees the first strawberries. The fishing season lasts to the end of May, overlapping with the start of the tourist season. Spring festivities focus on Easter.

MARCH

Apókries, Carnival Sunday *(first Sun before Lent)*. Carnivals take place for three weeks leading up to this climax of pre-Lenten festivities. There are parades and costume balls in many large

cities, and the port of Pátra *(see p169)* hosts one of the most exuberant celebrations.
Katharí Deftéra, Clean Monday *(immediately after "Cheese Sunday" – seven Sundays before Easter).* Kites are flown in the countryside.
Independence Day and **Evangelismós** *(25 Mar)*. A national holiday, with parades and dances nation-wide celebrating the 1821 revolt against the Ottoman Empire. The religious festival, one of the most important for the Orthodox Church, marks the Angel Gabriel's announcement to the Virgin Mary that she was to become the Holy Mother.

CELEBRATING EASTER IN GREECE

Greek Orthodox Easter can fall up to three weeks either side of Western Easter. It is the most important religious festival in Greece and Holy Week is a time for Greek families to reunite. It is also a good time to visit Greece, to see the processions and church services and to sample the Easter food. The ceremony and symbolism is a direct link with Greece's Byzantine past, as well as with earlier and more primitive beliefs. The festivities reach a climax at midnight on Easter Saturday. As priests intone "Christ is risen", fireworks are lit, the explosions ushering in a Sunday devoted to feasting, music and dance. Smaller, more isolated towns, such as Andrítsaina and Koróni in the Peloponnese, and Polýgyros (the capital of Chalkidikí), are particularly worth visiting during Holy Week for the Friday and Saturday night services.

Priests in their richly embroidered Easter robes

Christ's bier, *decorated with flowers and containing His effigy, is carried in solemn procession through the streets at dusk on Good Friday.*

Candle lighting *takes place at the end of the Easter Saturday mass. In pitch darkness, a single flame is used to light the candles held by worshippers.*

Banners raised during a workers' May Day rally in Athens

APRIL

Megáli Evdomáda, Holy Week *(Apr or May)*, including *Kyriakí ton Vaíon* (Palm Sunday), *Megáli Pémpti* (Maundy Thursday), *Megáli Paraskeví* (Good Friday), *Megálo Sávvato* (Easter Saturday), and the most important date in the Orthodox calendar, *Páscha* (Easter Sunday).

Agios Geórgios, St George's Day *(23 Apr)*. One of the most important feast days in the Orthodox calendar, commemorating the patron saint of shepherds, and traditionally marking the start of the grazing season. Celebrations are nationwide, and are particularly festive at Aráchova, near Delphi *(see p221)*.

MAY

Protomagiá, May Day, *(1 May)*. Also known as Labour Day, this is given over to a national holiday. Traditionally, families go to the countryside and pick wild flowers, which are made

Firewalkers in a Macedonian village, 21 May

into wreaths with garlic. These are then hung on doors, balconies, fishing boats and even car bonnets to ward off evil. In major towns and cities across the country, there are also parades and workers' rallies to mark Labour Day, usually led by the Communist Party.

Agios Konstantínos kai Agía Eléni *(21 May)*. A celebration throughout Greece for Constantine and his mother, Helen, the first Orthodox Byzantine rulers *(see p37)*. Firewalking ceremonies may be seen in some Macedonian villages.

Análipsi, Ascension *(40 days after Easter; usually late May)*. This is another important religious feast day.

The procession of candles *in the very early hours of Easter Day, here at Lykavittós Hill in Athens, celebrates Christ's resurrection.*

Easter biscuits *celebrate the end of Lent. Another Easter dish,* magirítsa *soup, is made of lamb's innards and is eaten in the early hours of Easter Sunday.*

Egg loaves, *made of sweet plaited dough, contain eggs with shells dyed red to symbolize the blood of Christ. Red eggs are also given separately as presents.*

Lamb roasting *is traditionally done in the open air on giant spits over charcoal, for lunch on Easter Sunday. The first retsina wine from the previous year's harvest is opened. After lunch young and old join hands to dance, Greek-style.*

SUMMER

Warm days in early June signal the first sea-baths for Greeks (traditionally after Análipsi, Ascension Day). The peak tourist season begins, and continues until late August; after mid-July it can be difficult to find hotel vacancies in the more popular resorts. June sees the arrival of cherries, plums and apricots, and honey can start to be collected from hives.

Beehives for summer honey production, near Mount Parnassus

The last green leaf vegetables are soon totally replaced by tomatoes, melons and cucumbers. By July much of the Aegean is buffeted by the notorious *meltémi*, a high-pressure northerly wind, which – though more severe on the islands – can be felt along the mainland coast.

Various cultural festivals – programmed with an eye on the tourist audience, but no less impressive for that – are hosted in major cities and resorts. Outdoor cinemas are also well attended *(see p119)*. Urban Greeks retreat to mountain villages, often the venues for musical and religious fairs.

Consecrated bread, baked for festivals

JUNE

Pentikostí, Pentecost or Whit Sunday *(seven weeks after Orthodox Easter)*. This impor-

tant Orthodox feast day is celebrated throughout Greece.
Agíou Pnévmatos, Feast of the Holy Spirit or Whit Monday *(the following day)*. A national holiday.
Athens Festival *(mid-Jun to mid-Sep)*. A cultural festival encompassing a mix of modern and ancient theatre, ballet, opera, classical music and jazz. It takes place at various venues, including the Herodes Atticus Theatre *(see p119)* and the Lykavittós Theatre *(see p72)*. The Herodes Atticus Theatre, on the slopes of the Acropolis, hosts performances of ancient tragedies, concerts by international orchestras and ballet. The Lykavittós Theatre, spectacularly situated on Lykavittós Hill, with extensive views across Athens, hosts performances of modern music – jazz and folk – as

Herodes Atticus Theatre

well as drama and dance.
Epidaurus Festival *(Jun-Aug)*. Affiliated to the Athens Festival, though sited 150 km (90 miles) from the capital at the Epidaurus Theatre *(see p184)* in the Peloponnese, this festival includes open-air performances of Classical drama.
Agios Ioánnis, St John's Day *(24 Jun)*. A day celebrated throughout Greece commemorating the birth of St John the Baptist. However, it is on the evening of the 23rd that bonfires are lit in most areas, and May wreaths consigned to the flames. Older children jump over the fires. This is an equivalent celebration to midsummer's eve.
Agioi Apóstoloi Pétros kai Pávlos, Saints Peter and Paul *(29 Jun)*. A widely celebrated name day for Pétros and Pávlos.

JULY

Agía Marína *(17 Jul)*. This day is widely celebrated in rural areas, with feasts to honour the saint, an important protector of crops.
Ioánnina's Cultural Summer *(through Jul and Aug)*. A wide range of music, arts and cultural events.
Profítis Ilías, the Prophet Elijah *(18–20 Jul)*. Widely celebrated at hill-top shrines, the best known being Mount Taÿgetos, near the town of Spárti. Name day for Ilías.
Agía Paraskeví *(26 Jul)*. There are many big village festivals on this day, but it is particularly celebrated in the Epirus region.

Agios Panteleímon *(27 Jul)*. As a doctor-saint, he is celebrated as the patron of many hospitals, and as a popular rural saint he is celebrated in the countryside. Name day for Pantelís and Panteleímon.

AUGUST

Metamórfosi, Transfiguration of Christ *(6 Aug)*. For the Orthodox church this is an important feast day. Name day for Sotíris and Sotiría.
Koímisis tis Theotókou,

Strings of tomatoes hanging out to dry in the autumn sunshine

Assumption of the Virgin Mary *(15 Aug)*. A national holiday, and an important and widely celebrated feast day. This is traditionally a day when Greeks return to celebrate in their home villages. It is also a name day for Mary, María,

Girl in national dress for 15 August festivities

Pános and Panagiótis.
Pátra Summer Festival *(Aug–Sep)*. This festival offers events such as Classical drama and art exhibitions, as well as music concerts in the Roman theatre.
Vlachopanagía *(19 Aug)*. This is a day of celebration in many Vlach villages located in the mountainous Epirus region.
Apotomí Kefalís Ioánnou Prodrómou, beheading of John the Baptist *(29 Aug)*. The occasion for festivals at the many country chapels that bear his name.

AUTUMN

By september most village festivals have finished. The sea is at its warmest for swimming and, though the crowds have gone, most facilities are still available. There is a second, minor blooming of wild flowers, and the fine, still days of October are known as the "little summer of St Dimítrios", randomly punctuated by stormy weather. Grapes, and the fat peaches *germádes*, are virtually the only fruit to ripen since the figs of August, and strings of onions, garlic and tomatoes are hung up to dry for the winter. The

hills echo with the sound of the September quail shoot and dragnet fishing resumes.

SEPTEMBER

Génnisis tis Theotókou, birth of the Virgin Mary *(8 Sep)*. An important religious feast day in the calendar of the Orthodox church.
Ypsosis tou Timíou Stavroú, Exaltation of the True Cross *(14 Sep)*. This is an important Orthodox feast day and, although it is almost autumn, it is regarded as the last of Greece's major outdoor summer festivals.

OCTOBER

Agios Dimítrios *(26 Oct)*. This marks the end of the grazing season, when sheep are brought down from the hills. Celebrations for Dimítrios are particularly lively in Thessaloníki, where he is the patron saint. Name day for Dimítris and Dímitra.
Ochi Day *(28 Oct)*. A national holiday, with patriotic parades in cities and plenty of dancing. It commemorates the Greek reply to the 1940 ultimatum from Mussolini calling for Greek surrender: an emphatic no *(óchi)*.

Ceremonial dress on Ochi Day

NOVEMBER

Ton Taxiarchón Archangélou Michaïl kai Gavriíl *(8 Nov)*. Ceremonies at the many rural monasteries and churches named after Archangels Gabriel and Michael. It is also name day for Michális and Gavriíl.
Eisódia tis Theotókou, Presentation of the Virgin in the Temple *(21 Nov)*. An important feast day in the Orthodox calendar, celebrated throughout Greece.
Agios Andréas, St Andrew's Day *(30 Nov)*, Pátra. A long liturgy is recited for Pátra's patron saint in the opulent cathedral named after him.

Celebrating the Assumption of the Virgin Mary, 15 August

View over a snow-covered Herodes Atticus Theatre, Athens

WINTER

Many mountain villages assume a ghostly aspect in winter, with their seasonal inhabitants returned to the cities. Deep snow accumulates at higher altitudes and skiing can begin; elsewhere, rain falls several days of the week. Fishing is in full swing, and at the markets kiwi fruits and exotic greens abound. Cheese shops display a full range of goat and sheep products, and olives are pressed for oil. The major festivals cluster to either side of the solstice. New Year and Epiphany are the most fervently celebrated festivals during winter.

DECEMBER

Agios Nikólaos, St Nicholas's Day *(6 Dec)*. The patron saint of seafarers, travellers, children and orphans is

Women playing cards on Gynaikokratía day, Thrace

celebrated at seaside churches. Name day for Nikólaos and Nikolétta.
Christoúgenna, Christmas *(25 Dec)*. A national holiday and, though less significant than Easter, it still constitutes an important religious feast day.
Sýnaxis tis Theotókou, meeting of the Virgin's entourage *(26 Dec)*. A religious celebration and national holiday.

Branch of olives

JANUARY

Agios Vasíleios, also known as *Protochroniá*, or New Year *(1 Jan)*. A national holiday. Gifts are exchanged on this day and the traditional new year greeting is *Kalí Chroniá*.
Theofánia, or Epiphany *(6 Jan)*. A national holiday and an important feast day. Blessing of the waters ceremonies take place by rivers and coastal locations throughout Greece. Youths dive to recover a cross that is thrown into the water by a priest.

Gynaikokratía *(8 Jan)*, Thrace. Matriarchy is celebrated by women and men swapping roles for the day in some villages of Thrace.

FEBRUARY

Ypapantí, Candlemas *(2 Feb)*. An Orthodox feast day all over Greece, at a quiet time, prior to pre-Lenten carnivals.

Diving for a cross at a blessing of the waters ceremony, 6 January

NAME DAYS

Most Greeks do not celebrate birthdays past the age of about 12. Instead they celebrate their name day, or *giortí*, the day of the saint after whom they were named when baptized. Children are usually named after their grandparents, though in recent years it has become fashionable to give children names deriving from Greece's history and mythology. When someone celebrates their name day you may be told, *Giortázo símera* (I'm celebrating today), to which the traditional reply is *Chrónia pollá* (many years). Friends tend to drop in, bearing small gifts, and are given cakes and sweet liqueurs in return.

The Climate of Mainland Greece

Summer visitors

The mainland climate varies most between the coastal lowlands and the mountainous inland regions. The mountains of western Greece and the Peloponnese get heavy snow in winter, rain during autumn and spring, and hot days in summer. The Ionian coast has milder temperatures, but is the wettest part of Greece. In Macedonia and Thrace rainfall is spread more evenly across the year, with the North Aegean exerting a moderating influence on coastal temperatures. Around Athens, temperatures are hot in summer and rarely drop below freezing in winter, when rainfall is at its greatest.

NORTHERN GREECE

°C (F)			
26 (79)	38 (100)	28 (82)	
17 (63)			16 (61)
4 (39)		7 (45)	-4 (25)

8 hrs	12 hrs	6 hrs	4 hrs
41 mm	22 mm	57 mm	44 mm
month	Apr	Jul	Oct	Jan

CENTRAL AND WESTERN GREECE

°C (F)			
27 (81)	40 (104)	33 (91)	
15 (59)			16 (61)
2 (36)		5 (41)	-6 (21)

8 hrs	11 hrs	5 hrs	3 hrs
80 mm	19 mm	80 mm	84 mm
month	Apr	Jul	Oct	Jan

NORTHERN GREECE

CENTRAL AND WESTERN GREECE

THE PELOPONNESE

ATHENS AND AROUND ATHENS

ATHENS

THE PELOPONNESE

°C (F)			
25 (77)	36 (97)	28 (82)	
11 (52)			15 (59)
1 (34)		4 (39)	-4 (25)

8 hrs	12 hrs	7 hrs	4 hrs
62 mm	20 mm	82 mm	127 mm
month	Apr	Jul	Oct	Jan

ATHENS AND AROUND ATHENS

Average monthly maximum temperature

Average monthly minimum temperature

Average daily hours of sunshine

Average monthly rainfall

°C (F)			
26 (79)	39 (102)	30 (86)	
19 (66)			18 (64)
6 (45)		11 (52)	1 (34)

8 hrs	12 hrs	7 hrs	4 hrs
23 mm	6 mm	51 mm	62 mm
month	Apr	Jul	Oct	Jan

ANCIENT GREECE

Gods, Goddesses and Heroes

The Greek myths that tell the stories of the gods, goddesses and heroes date back to the Bronze Age when they were told aloud by poets. They were first written down in the early 6th century BC and have lived on in Western literature. Myths were closely bound up with Greek religion and gave meaning to the unpredictable workings of the natural world. They tell the story of the creation and the "golden age" of gods and mortals, as well as the age of semi-mythical heroes, such as Theseus and Herakles, whose exploits were an inspiration to ordinary men. The gods and goddesses were affected by human desires and failings and were part of a divine family presided over by Zeus. He had many offspring, both legitimate and illegitimate, each with a mythical role.

Hades and Persephone *were king and queen of the Underworld (land of the dead). Persephone was abducted from her mother Demeter, goddess of the harvest, by Hades. She was then only permitted to return to her mother for three months each year.*

Zeus was the father of the gods and ruled over them and all mortals from Mount Olympos.

Eris was the goddess of strife.

Clymene, a nymph and daughter of Helios, was mother of Prometheus, creator of mankind.

Poseidon, *one of Zeus's brothers, was given control of the seas. The trident is his symbol of power, and he married the sea-goddess Amphitrite, to whom he was not entirely faithful. This statue is from the National Archaeological Museum in Athens (see pp68–71).*

Hera, sister and wife of Zeus, was famous for her jealousy.

Athena was born from Zeus's head in full armour.

Paris was asked to award the golden apple to the most beautiful goddess.

Paris's dog helped him herd cattle on Mount Ida where the prince grew up.

Dionysos, *god of revelry and wine, was born from Zeus's thigh. In this 6th-century BC cup painted by Exekias he reclines in a ship whose mast has become a vine.*

A DIVINE DISPUTE

This vase painting shows the gods on Mount Ida, near Troy. Hera, Athena and Aphrodite, quarrelling over who was the most beautiful, were brought by Hermes to hear the judgment of a young herdsman, the Trojan prince, Paris. In choosing Aphrodite, he was rewarded with the love of Helen, the most beautiful woman in the world. Paris abducted her from her husband Menelaos, King of Sparta, and thus the Trojan War began (*see pp54–5*).

◁ Frieze from the Archaeological Museum, Delphi

Artemis, *the virgin goddess of the hunt, was the daughter of Zeus and sister of Apollo. She can be identified by her bow and arrows, hounds and group of nymphs with whom she lived in the forests. Although sworn to chastity, she was, in contrast, the goddess of childbirth.*

Happiness, here personified by two goddesses, waits with gold laurel leaves to garland the winner. Wreaths were the prizes in Greek athletic and musical contests.

Helios, the sun god, drove his four-horse chariot (the sun) daily across the sky.

Hermes was the gods' messenger.

Aphrodite, the goddess of love, was born from the sea. Here she has her son Eros (Cupid) with her.

Apollo, *son of Zeus and brother of Artemis, was god of healing, plague and also music. Here he is depicted holding a lyre. He was also famous for his dazzling beauty.*

THE LABOURS OF HERAKLES

Herakles (Hercules to the Romans) was the greatest of the Greek heroes, and the son of Zeus and Alkmene, a mortal woman. With superhuman strength he achieved success, and immortality, against seemingly impossible odds in the "Twelve Labours" set by Eurystheus, King of Mycenae. For his first task he killed the Nemean lion, and wore its hide ever after.

Killing the Lernaean hydra *was the second labour of Herakles. The many heads of this venomous monster, raised by Hera, grew back as soon as they were chopped off. As in all his tasks, Herakles was helped by Athena.*

The huge boar *that ravaged Mount Erymanthus was captured next. Herakles brought it back alive to King Eurystheus who was so terrified that he hid in a storage jar.*

Destroying the Stymfalian birds *was the sixth labour. Herakles rid Lake Stymfalía of these man-eating birds, which had brass beaks, by stoning them with a sling, having first frightened them off with a pair of bronze castanets.*

The Trojan War

Ajax carrying the body of the dead Achilles

The story of the Trojan War, first narrated in the *Iliad*, Homer's 8th-century BC epic poem, tells how the Greeks sought to avenge the capture of Helen, wife of Menelaos, King of Sparta, by the Trojan prince, Paris. The Roman writer Virgil takes up the story in the *Aeneid*, where he tells of the sack of Troy and the founding of Rome. Archaeological evidence of the remains of a city identified with ancient Troy in modern Turkey suggests that the myth may have a basis in fact. Many of the ancient sites in the Peloponnese, such as Mycenae and Pylos, are thought to be the cities of some of the heroes of the Trojan War.

Achilles binding up the battle wounds of his friend Patroklos

GATHERING OF THE HEROES

When Paris *(see p52)* carries Helen back to Troy, her husband King Menelaos summons an army of Greek kings and heroes to avenge this crime. His brother, King Agamemnon of Mycenae, leads the force; its ranks include young Achilles, destined to die at Troy.

At Aulis their departure is delayed by a contrary wind. Only the sacrifice to Artemis of Iphigéneia, the youngest of Agamemnon's daughters, allows the fleet to depart.

FIGHTING AT TROY

The *Iliad* opens with the Greek army outside Troy, maintaining a siege that has already been in progress for nine years. Tired of fighting, yet still hoping for a decisive victory, the Greek camp is torn apart by the fury of Achilles over Agamemnon's removal of his slave girl Briseis. The hero takes to his tent and refuses adamantly to fight.

Deprived of their greatest warrior, the Greeks are driven back by the Trojans. In desperation, Patroklos persuades his friend Achilles to let him borrow his armour. Achilles agrees and Patroklos leads the Myrmidons, Achilles's troops, into battle. The tide is turned, but Patroklos is killed in the fighting by Hector, son of King Priam of Troy, who mistakes him for Achilles. Filled with remorse at the news of his friend's death, Achilles returns to battle, finds Hector, and kills him in revenge.

King Priam begging Achilles for the body of his son

PATROKLOS AVENGED

Refusing Hector's dying wish to allow his body to be ransomed, Achilles instead hitches it up to his chariot by the ankles and drags it round the walls of Troy, then takes it back to the Greek camp. In contrast, Patroklos is given the most elaborate funeral possible with a huge pyre, sacrifices of animals and Trojan prisoners and funeral games. Still unsatisfied, for 12 days Achilles drags the corpse of Hector around Patroklos's funeral mound until the gods are forced to intervene over his callous behaviour.

PRIAM VISITS ACHILLES

On the instructions of Zeus, Priam sets off for the Greek camp holding a ransom for the body of his dead son. With the help of the god Hermes he reaches Achilles's tent undetected. Entering, he pleads with Achilles to think of his own father and to show mercy. Achilles relents and allows Hector to be taken back to Troy for a funeral and burial.

Although the Greek heroes were greater than mortals, they were portrayed as fallible beings with human emotions who had to face universal moral dilemmas.

Greeks and Trojans, in bronze armour, locked in combat

ACHILLES KILLS THE AMAZON QUEEN

Penthesileia was the Queen of the Amazons, a tribe of warlike women reputed to cut off their right breasts to make it easier to wield their weapons. They come to the support of the Trojans. In the battle, Achilles finds himself face to face with Penthesileia and deals her a fatal blow. One version of the story has it that as their eyes meet at the moment of her death, they fall in love. The Greek idea of love and death would be explored 2,000 years later by the psychologists Jung and Freud.

An early image of the Horse of Troy, from a 7th-century BC clay vase

Achilles killing the Amazon Queen Penthesileia in battle

THE WOODEN HORSE OF TROY

As was foretold, Achilles is killed at Troy by an arrow in his heel from Paris's bow. With this weakening of their military strength, the Greeks resort to guile.

Before sailing away, they build a great wooden horse, in which they conceal some of their best fighters. The rumour is put out that this is a gift to the goddess Athena and that if the horse enters Troy, the city can never be taken. After some doubts, but swayed by supernatural omens, the Trojans drag the horse inside the walls. That night, the Greeks sail back, the soldiers creep out of the horse and Troy is put to the torch. Priam, with many others, is murdered. Among

the Trojan survivors is Aeneas who escapes to Italy and founds the race of Romans: a second Troy. The next part of the story (the *Odyssey*) tells of the heroes' adventures on their way home to Greece.

DEATH OF AGAMEMNON

Klytemnestra, the wife of Agamemnon, had ruled Mycenae in the ten years that he had been away fighting in Troy. She was accompanied by Aigisthos, her lover. Intent

on vengeance for the death of her daughter Iphigéneia, Klytemnestra receives her husband with a triumphal welcome and then brutally murders him, with the help of Aigisthos. Agamemnon's fate was a result of a curse laid on his father, Atreus, which was finally expiated by the murder of both Klytemnestra and Aigisthos by her son Orestes and daughter Elektra. In these myths, the will of the gods shapes and overrides that of heroes and mortals.

GREEK MYTHS IN WESTERN ART

From the Renaissance onwards, the Greek myths have been a powerful inspiration for artists and sculptors. Kings and queens have had themselves portrayed as gods and goddesses with their symbolic attributes of love or war. Myths have also been an inspiration for artists to paint the nude or Classically draped figure. This was true of the 19th-century artist Lord Leighton, whose depiction of the human body reflects the Classical ideals of beauty. His tragic figure of Elektra is shown here.

Elektra mourning the death of her father Agamemnon at his tomb

Greek Writers and Philosophers

Playwrights Aristophanes and Sophocles

The literature of Greece began with long epic poems, accounts of war and adventure, which established the relationship of the ancient Greeks to their gods. The tragedy and comedy, history and philosophical dialogues of the 5th and 4th centuries BC became the basis of Western literary culture. Much of our knowledge of the Greek world is derived from Greek literature. Pausanias's *Guide to Greece*, written in the Roman period and used by Roman tourists, is a key to the physical remains.

Hesiod with the nine Muses who inspired his poetry

EPIC POETRY

As far back as the 2nd millennium BC, before even the building of the Mycenaean palaces, poets were reciting the stories of the Greek heroes and gods. Passed on from generation to generation, these poems, called *rhapsodes,* were never written down but were changed and embellished by successive poets. The oral tradition culminated in the *Iliad* and *Odyssey (see pp54–5),* composed around 700 BC. Both works are traditionally ascribed to the same poet, Homer, of whose life nothing reliable

is known. Hesiod, whose most famous poems include the *Theogony*, a history of the gods, and the *Works and Days*, on how to live an honest life, also lived around 700 BC. Unlike Homer, Hesiod is thought to have written down his poems, although there is no firm evidence available to support this theory.

PASSIONATE POETRY

For private occasions, and particularly to entertain guests at the cultivated drinking parties known as *symposia*, shorter poetic forms were developed. These poems were often full of passion, whether love or hatred, and could be personal or, often, highly political. Much of this poetry, by writers such as Archilochus, Alcaeus, Alcman, Hipponax and Sappho, survives only in quotations by later writers or on scraps of papyrus that have been preserved by chance from private libraries in Hellenistic and Roman Egypt. Through these fragments we can gain glimpses

of the life of a very competitive elite. Since *symposia* were an almost exclusively male domain, there is a strong element of misogyny in much of this poetry. In contrast, the fragments of poems discovered by the authoress Sappho, who lived on the island of Lésvos, are exceptional for showing a woman competing in a literary area in the male-dominated society of ancient Greece, and for describing with great intensity her passions for other women.

HISTORY

Until the 5th century BC little Greek literature was composed in prose – even early philosophy was in verse. In the latter part of the 5th century, a new tradition of lengthy prose histories, looking at recent or current events, was established with Herodotus's account of the great war between Greece and Persia (490–479 BC). Herodotus put the clash between Greeks and Persians into a context, and included an ethnographic account of the vast Persian Empire. He attempted to record objectively what people said about the past. Thucydides took a narrower view in his account of the long years of the Peloponnesian War between Athens and Sparta (431–404 BC). He concentrated on the political history, and his aim was to work out the "truth" that lay behind the events of the war. The methods of Thucydides were adopted by later writers of Greek history, though few could match his acute insight into human nature.

Herodotus, the historian of the Persian wars

An unusual vase-painting of a *symposion* for women only

The orator Demosthenes in a
Staffordshire figurine of 1790

ORATORY

Public argument was basic to
Greek political life even in
the Archaic period. In the
later part of the 5th century
BC, the techniques of per-
suasive speech began to be
studied in their own right.
From that time on some
orators began to publish
their speeches. In particular,
this included those wishing
to advertise their skills in
composing speeches for the
law courts, such as Lysias
and Demosthenes. The texts
that survive give insights into
both Athenian politics and
the seamier side of Athenian
private life. The verbal
attacks on Philip of Macedon
by Demosthenes, the 4th-
century BC Athenian
politician, became models
for Roman politicians seeking to defeat their oppo-
nents. With the 18th-century
European revival of interest
in Classical times, Demosthenes again became a
political role model.

DRAMA

Almost all the surviving
tragedies come from the
hands of the three great 5th-
century BC Athenians:
Aeschylus, Sophocles and
Euripides. The latter two
playwrights developed an
interest in individual psy-
chology (as in Euripides's
Medea). While 5th-century
comedy is full of direct
references to contemporary
life and dirty jokes, the
"new" comedy developed
in the 4th century BC is
essentially situation comedy
employing character types.

Vase painting of two costumed
actors from around 370 BC

GREEK PHILOSOPHERS

The Athenian Socrates was recognized in
the late 5th century BC as a moral arbiter.
He wrote nothing himself but we know of
his views through the "Socratic dialogues",
written by his pupil, Plato, examining the
concepts of justice, virtue and courage.
Plato set up his academy in
the suburbs of Athens.

His pupil, Aristotle, founded the Lyceum,
to teach subjects from biology to ethics, and
helped to turn Athens into one of the first
university cities. In 1508–11 Raphael painted
this vision of Athens in the Vatican.

Aristotle, author of the *Ethics*, had
a genius for scientific observation.

Euclid laid
the rules of
geometry
in around
300 BC.

Plato saw "the
seat of ideas"
in heaven.

Epicurus
advocated
the pursuit
of pleasure.

Socrates taught by debating his ideas.

Diogenes, the Cynic, lived like a beggar.

Temple Architecture

Temples were the most important public buildings in ancient Greece, largely because religion was a central part of everyday life. Often placed in prominent positions, temples were also statements about political and divine power. The earliest temples, in the 8th century BC, were built of wood and sun-dried bricks. Many of their features were copied in marble buildings from the 6th century BC onwards.

Pheidias, sculptor of the Parthenon, at work

TEMPLE CONSTRUCTION

This drawing is of an idealized Doric temple, showing how it was built and used.

The cella, or inner sanctum, housed the cult statue.

The pediment, triangular in shape, often held sculpture.

The cult statue was of the god or goddess to whom the temple was dedicated.

**Fluting on t
columns** was carved
situ, guided by that on t
top and bottom drum

A ramp led up to the temple entrance.

The stepped platform was built on a stone foundation.

The column drums were initially carved with bosses for lifting them into place.

TIMELINE OF TEMPLE CONSTRUCTION

700 First temple of Poseidon, Ancient Isthmia (Archaic; *see p167*) and first Temple of Apollo, Corinth (Archaic; *see p162*)

550 Second temple of Apollo, Corinth (Doric; *see p162*)

520 Temple of Olympian Zeus, Athens, begun (Doric; completed Corinthian 2nd century AD; *see p111*)

6th century Temple of Artemis, Ancient Brauron (Doric; *see pp146–7*)

Detail of the Parthenon pediment

7th century Temple of Hera, Olympia (Doric; *see p170*)

460 Temple of Zeus, Olympia (Doric; *see p171*)

447–405 Temples of the Acropolis, Athens: Athena Nike (Ionic), Parthenon (Doric), Erechtheion (Ionic) *(see pp94–9)*

445–425 Temple of Apollo, Bassae (Doric with Ionic; *see p177*)

440–430 Temple of Poseidon, Soúnio (Doric; *see pp148–9*)

4th century Temple of Apollo, Delphi (Doric; *see p229*); Temple of Athena Aléa, Tegéa (Doric and 1st Corinthian capital; *see p177*)

700 BC	600 BC	500 BC	400 BC	300 BC

The gable ends of the roof were surmounted by statues, known as *akroteria*, in this case of a Nike or "Winged Victory". Almost no upper portions of Greek temples survive.

The roof was supported on wooden beams and covered in rows of terracotta tiles, each ending in an upright *akroterion*.

Stone blocks were smoothly fitted together and held by metal clamps and dowels: no mortar was used in the temple's construction.

The ground plan was derived from the megaron of the Mycenaean house: a rectangular hall with a front porch supported by columns.

Caryatids, *or figures of women, were used instead of columns in the Erechtheion at Athens' Acropolis. In Athens' Agora (see pp90–91), tritons (half-fish, half-human creatures) were used.*

THE DEVELOPMENT OF TEMPLE ARCHITECTURE

Greek temple architecture is divided into three styles, which evolved chronologically, and are most easily distinguished by the column capitals.

Doric *temples were surrounded by sturdy columns with plain capitals and no bases. As the earliest style of stone buildings, they recall wooden prototypes.*

Triangular pediment filled with sculpture

Guttae imitated the pegs for fastening the wooden roof beams.

Triglyphs resembled the ends of cross beams.

Metopes could contain sculpture.

Doric capital

Ionic *temples differed from Doric in their tendency to have more columns, of a different form. The capital has a pair of volutes, like rams' horns, front and back.*

Akroteria, at the roof corners, could look Persian in style.

The frieze was a continuous band of decoration.

The Ionic architrave was subdivided into projecting bands.

The Ionic frieze took the place of Doric *triglyphs* and *metopes*.

Ionic capital

Corinthian *temples in Greece were built under the Romans and only in Athens. They feature columns with slender shafts and elaborate capitals decorated with acanthus leaves.*

The pediment was decorated with a variety of mouldings.

Akroterion in the shape of a griffin

The cella entrance was at the east end.

The entablature was everything above the capitals.

Acanthus leaf capital

Vases and Vase Painting

Donkey cup

The history of Greek vase painting continued without a break from 1000 BC to Hellenistic times. The main centre of production was Athens, which was so successful that by the early 6th century BC it was sending its high-quality black- and red-figure wares to every part of the Greek world. The Athenian potters' quarter of Kerameikós can still be visited today *(see pp88–9)*. Beautiful works of art in their own right, the painted vases are the closest we can get to the vanished paintings with which ancient Greeks decorated the walls of their houses. Although vases could break during everyday use (for which they were intended) a huge number still survive intact or in reassembled pieces.

This 6th-century BC black-figure vase *shows pots being used in an everyday situation. The vases depicted are* hydriai. *It was the women's task to fill them with water from springs or public fountains.*

The white-ground lekythos *was developed in the 5th century BC as an oil flask for grave offerings. They were usually decorated with funeral scenes, and this one, by the Achilles Painter, shows a woman placing flowers at a grave.*

The naked woman holding a *kylix* is probably a flute-girl or prostitute.

THE SYMPOSION
These episodes of mostly male feasting and drinking were also occasions for playing the game of *kottabos*. On the exterior of this 5th-century BC *kylix* are depictions of men holding cups, ready to flick out the dregs at a target.

THE DEVELOPMENT OF PAINTING STYLES
Vase painting reached its peak in 6th- and 5th-century BC Athens. In the potter's workshop, a fired vase would be passed to a painter to be decorated. Archaeologists have been able to identify the varying styles of many individual painters of both black-figure and red-figure ware.

The body of the dead man is carried on a bier by mourners.

The geometric design is a prototype of the later "Greek-key" pattern.

Chariots and warriors form the funeral procession.

Geometric style *characterizes the earliest Greek vases, from around 1000 to 700 BC, in which the decoration is in bands of figures and geometric patterns. This 8th-century BC vase, placed on a grave as a marker, is over 1 m (3 ft) high and depicts the bier and funeral rites of a dead man.*

Eye cups *were given an almost magical power by the painted eyes. The pointed base suggests that they were passed around during feasting.*

This kylix is being held by one handle by another woman feaster, ready to flick out the dregs at a *kottabos* target.

The rhyton, *such as this one in the shape of a ram's head, was a drinking vessel for watered-down wine. The scene of the symposion around the rim indicates when it would have been used.*

This drinker holds aloft a branch of a vine, symbolic of Dionysos's presence at the party.

Striped cushions made reclining more comfortable.

The drinking horn shape was copied in the pottery *rhyton*.

VASE SHAPES

Almost all Greek vases were made to be used; their shapes are closely related to their intended uses. Athenian potters had about 20 different forms to choose from. Below are some of the most commonly made shapes and their uses.

The amphora *was a two-handled vessel used to store wine, olive oil and foods preserved in liquid such as olives. It also held dried foods.*

This krater *with curled handles or "volutes" is a wide-mouthed vase in which the Greeks mixed water with their wine before drinking it.*

The hydria *was used to carry water from the fountain. Of the three handles, one was vertical for holding and pouring, two horizontal for lifting.*

The lekythos *could vary in height from 3 cm (1 in) to nearly 1 m (3 ft). It was used to hold oil both in the home and as a funerary gift to the dead.*

The oinochoe, *the standard wine jug, had a round or trefoil mouth for pouring, and just one handle*

The kylix, *a two-handled drinking cup, was one shape that could take interior decoration.*

Black-figure style *was first used in Athens around 630 BC. The figures were painted in black liquid clay on to the iron-rich clay of the vase which turned orange when fired. This vase is signed by the potter and painter Exekias.*

Red-figure style *was introduced in c.530 BC. The figures were left in the colour of the clay, silhouetted against a black glaze. Here a woman pours from an* oinochoe *(wine jug).*

ATHENS
AREA BY AREA

Athens at a Glance

Athens has been a city for 3,500 years but its greatest glory was during the Classical period of ancient Greece from which so many buildings and artifacts still survive. The 5th century BC in particular was a golden age, when Perikles oversaw the building of the Acropolis. Within the Byzantine Empire and under Ottoman rule, Athens played only a minor role. It returned to prominence in 1834, when it became the capital of Greece. Today it is a busy and modern metropolitan centre.

The **Kerameikós** *quarter* (see pp88–9) *was once the potters' district of ancient Athens and site of the principal cemetery, whose grave monuments can still be seen. Tranquil and secluded, it lies off the main tourist track.*

SEE ALSO

- *Where to Stay* pp264–7
- *Where to Eat* pp284–8
- *Getting Around Athens* pp324–7

The **Agora** (see pp90–91), *or market place, was the ancient centre of commercial life. The Stoa of Attalos was reconstructed in 1953–6 on its original, 2nd-century BC foundations. It now houses the Agora Museum.*

The **Tower of the Winds** (see pp86–7) *stands beside the Roman forum, but this small, octagonal building is Hellenistic in style. The tower – built as a water clock, with a compass, sundials and weather vane – has a relief on each side depicting the wind from that direction.*

The **Acropolis** (see pp94–101) *has dominated Athens for over 2,000 years. From the scale of the Parthenon to the delicacy of the Erechtheion, it is an extraordinary achievement.*

| 0 metres | 500 |
| 0 yards | 500 |

◁ **The Parthenon on the Acropolis, viewed from the Hephaisteion**

The National Archaeological Museum (see pp68–71) *houses some of the treasures from one of the greatest Western civilizations. This is the Plaque of Ninnion, dating from the 4th century BC, which depicts the Eleusinian Mysteries* (see p156).

CENTRAL ATHENS NORTH
(see pp66–81)

The Museum of Cycladic Art (see pp74–5) *holds an unrivalled collection of Cycladic artifacts. This marble figurine with crossed-arm pose is typical of the style.*

CENTRAL ATHENS SOUTH
(see pp82–113)

The Benáki Museum (see pp78–9), *formed from a private collection, is a treasure house of antiquities, jewellery, Greek art, icons, folk costumes and Byzantine relics, such as this gold-plated incense holder.*

Panagía Gorgoepíkoös (see p105), *or Little Cathedral, is one of the best-preserved Byzantine buildings in Athens. You can spot ancient carved reliefs reused in the walls of this tiny church.*

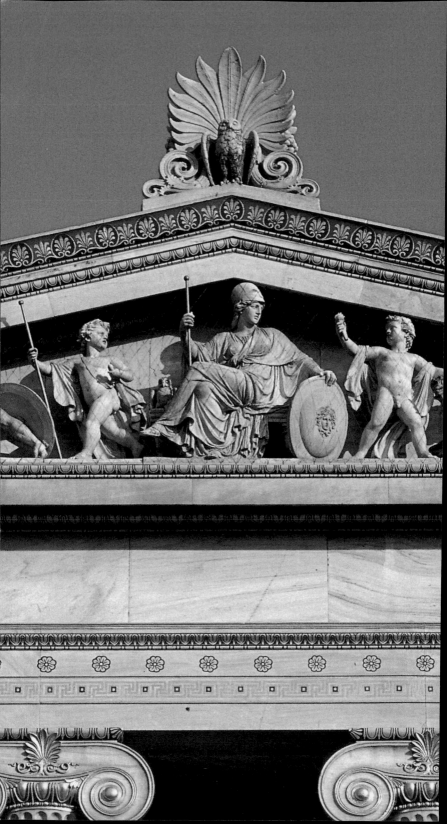

CENTRAL ATHENS NORTH

Inhabited for 7,000 years, Athens was the birthplace of European civilization. It flourished in the 5th century BC when the Athenians controlled much of the eastern Mediterranean. The buildings from this era, including those in the ancient Agora and on the Acropolis, lie largely in the southern part of the city. The northern half has grown since the early 1800s when King Otto made Athens the new capital of Greece. When the king's architects planned the new, European-style city, they included wide, tree-lined avenues, such as Panepistimíou and Akadimías, that were soon home to many grand

Icon of the Archangel Michael, from the Byzantine Museum

Neo-Classical public buildings and mansion houses. Today, these edifices still provide elegant homes for all the major banks, embassies and public institutions, such as the University and the Library.

The chic residential area of Kolonáki is located in the north of the city centre, as is the cosmopolitan area around Patriárchou Ioakeím and Irodótou. These streets have excellent shopping and entertainment venues. Most of Athens' best museums, including the National Archaeological Museum, are also found in this area of the city. For information on getting around Athens, see pages 324–7.

SIGHTS AT A GLANCE

Museums and Galleries
Benáki Museum pp78–9 ❿
Byzantine Museum ❼
Museum of the City
  of Athens ⓬
Museum of Cycladic Art
  pp74–5 ❽
National Archaeological
  Museum pp68–71 ❶
National Gallery of Art ❺
National Historical
  Museum ⓭
Theatrical Museum ⓫
War Museum ❻

Squares, Parks and Gardens
Exárcheia and Stréfi Hill ❷
Lykavittós Hill ❸
Plateía Kolonakíou ❾

Churches
Kapnikaréa ⓮

Historic Buildings
Gennádeion ❹

KEY
Ⓜ Metro station

◁ **The elegant façade of the Neo-Classical University building** *(see p81)*

National Archaeological Museum ❶
Εθνικό Αρχαιολογικό Μουσείο

Hellenistic bronze head from Delos

Opened in 1891, this superb museum, often known simply as the National Museum, brought together a collection that had previously been stored all over the city. Additional wings were added in 1939. The priceless collection was then dispersed and buried underground during World War II to protect it from possible damage. The museum reopened in 1946, but it took a further 50 years of renovation and reorganization finally to do justice to its formidable collection. With the combination of such unique exhibits as the Mycenaean gold, along with the unrivalled amount of sculpture, pottery and jewellery on display, this is without doubt one of the world's finest museums.

Neo-Classical entrance to the National Archaeological Museum on Patission

GALLERY GUIDE
On the ground floor, Mycenaean, Neolithic and Cycladic finds are followed by Geometric, Archaic, Classical, Roman and Hellenistic sculpture. Smaller collections of bronzes, Egyptian artifacts, the Eléni Stathátou jewellery collection and the Karapános collection are also on the ground floor. The first floor houses a collection of pottery.

Bronze collection

Dipýlon Amphora
This huge Geometric vase was used to mark an 8th-century BC woman's burial and shows the dead body surrounded by mourning women. It is named after the location of its discovery near the Dipýlon Gate in Athens' Kerameikós (see pp88–9).

Sculpture garden and café

Main entrance hall

Harp Player
The minimalist Cycladic style of sculpture flourished in the 3rd millennium BC and originated in the Cyclades. The simple lines and bold forms of the marble figurines influenced many early 20th-century artists, including the British sculptor Henry Moore.

Entrance

Ground floor

★ **Mask of Agamemnon**
Found at Mycenae by Schliemann, this gold death mask was originally thought to have belonged to the legendary king Agamemnon. It dates from the mid-1600s BC.

VISITORS' CHECKLIST

44 Patission, Exárcheia.
Map 2 E2.
Tel 210 821 7724.
M Omónoia.
◯ 8am–3pm Tue–Sun,
1:30–8pm Mon.
www.namuseum.gr

ʏρtian lection

Thíra Frescoes

Eléni Stathátou jewellery collection

The Pottery Collection contains a vast display of vases.

Carapános ollection

Stairs to first floor

★ **Youth of Antikýthira**
This fine Hellenistic bronze statue was discovered off the island of Antikýthira in 1900. Larger than life, it is approximately 2m (7 ft) tall.

Aphrodite and Pan
This marble sculpture of Aphrodite, Eros and the goat-footed Pan was found on Delos and dates from c.100 BC.

The Courtyard
has stairs leading to a basement café and shop.

KEY TO FLOORPLAN

▢ Neolithic and Cycladic Art
▢ Mycenaean Art
▢ Geometric and Archaic Art
▢ Classical Sculpture
▢ Roman and Hellenistic Sculpture
▢ Other collections
▢ Thíra Frescoes
▢ Pottery Collection
▢ Temporary exhibitions
▢ Non-exhibition space

STAR EXHIBITS

★ Mask of Agamemnon

★ Youth of Antikýthira

Exploring the National Archaeological Museum's Collection

Displaying its treasures in chronological order, the museum presents an impressive and thorough overview of Greek art through the centuries. Begin-

ning with early Cycladic figurines and continuing through the Greek Bronze Age, the exhibits end with the glories of Hellenistic period bronzes and a collection of busts of Roman emperors. High points in between include the numerous gold artifacts found at Mycenae, the elegant Archaic *koûroi* statues and the many examples of fine Classical sculpture.

Mycenaean head of a sphinx

NEOLITHIC AND CYCLADIC ART

The dawning of Greek civilization (3500–2900 BC) saw primitive decorative vases and figures. This collection also contains terracotta figurines, jewellery and a selection of weapons.

Neolithic clay vases with simple painted decoration

The vibrant fertility gods and goddesses, such as the *kourotróphos* (nursing mother) with child, are particularly well preserved. Of exceptional importance are the largest known Cycladic marble figurine, from Amorgós, and the earliest known figures of musicians – the *Flute Player* and *Harp Player*, both from Kéros. Later finds from Mílos, such as the painted vase with fishermen, reveal the changes in pot shapes and colour that took place in the late Cycladic Bronze Age.

MYCENAEAN ART

It is not difficult to understand the allure of the museum's most popular attraction, the Hall of Mycenaean Antiquities, with its dazzling array of 16th-century BC gold treasures. Other exhibits in the collection include frescoes, ivory sculptures and seal rings made out of precious stones.

From the famous shaft graves *(see p180)* came a procession of daggers, cups, seals and rings as well as a number of regal death masks, including the justly famous *Mask of Agamemnon*. Two superb *rhytons*, or wine jugs, are also on display: one in the shape of a bull's head, made in silver with gold horns, and one in gold shaped like a lion's head. Equally rich finds from sites other than Mycenae have since been made. These include two gold bull cups found at Vafeió, in Crete, a gold phial entwined with dolphins and octopuses (excavated from a royal tomb at Déntra), clay tablets with the early Linear B script from the Palace of Nestor *(see p201)* and a magnificent sword from the Tomb of Stáfylos on the island of Skópelos.

Mycenaean bronze dagger, inlaid with gold

THE DEVELOPMENT OF GREEK SCULPTURE

Sculpture was one of the most sophisticated forms of Greek art. We are able to trace its development from the early *koûroi* to the great works of named sculptors such as Pheidias and Praxiteles in Classical times. Portraiture only began in the 5th century BC; even then most Greek sculptures were of gods and goddesses, heroes and athletes and idealized men and women. These have had an enormous influence on Western art down the centuries.

The Volomándra Koúros *was discovered in Attica and dates from the mid-6th century BC. The highly stylized* koúroi *(statues of naked youths) first appear in the mid-7th century BC. Derived from Egyptian art, these figures share a common pose and proportions. Clothed* kórai *are the female counterpart.*

The Marathon Boy *(340 BC), like many other Greek bronzes, was found on the sea floor. The dreamy expression and easy pose of the figure are characteristic of the works of Praxiteles, the leading late Classical sculptor. An example of the "heroic nude", it shows a great naturalism and perfect balance.*

GEOMETRIC AND ARCHAIC ART

Famed for its monumental burial vases, such as the *Dipýlon Amphora*, the Geometric period developed a more ornate style in the 7th century BC with the introduction of mythological and plant and animal motifs. By the 6th century BC the full artistry of the black-figure vases had developed. Two rare examples from this period are a *lekythos* depicting Peleus, Achilles and the centaur Cheiron, and the sculptured heads known as *aryballoi*.

Warrior from Boiotia, early 7th century BC

CLASSICAL SCULPTURE

The collection of Classical sculpture contains both fine statues and a selection of grave monuments, mostly from the Kerameikós. These include the beautiful *stele* (*c*.410 BC) of Hegeso (*see p88*). Classical votive sculpture on display includes parts of a statue of the goddess

This "valedictory stele" (*mid-4th century BC*) *shows a seated woman bidding farewell to her family. The figures express a dignified suffering found in many Greek funerary reliefs.*

Hera, from the Argive Heraion in the Peloponnese, and many statues of the goddess Athena, including the Roman *Varvakeion Athena*, a reduced copy of the original ivory and gold statue from the Parthenon (*see p99*).

ROMAN AND HELLENISTIC SCULPTURE

Although a large number of Greek bronzes were lost in antiquity, as metal was melted down in times of emergency for making weapons, the museum has some excellent pieces on display. These include the famous bronzes *Poseidon* and the *Horse with the Little Jockey*, both found at Cape Artemísion on Évvoia, and the *Youth of Antikýthira*, found in the sea off that island. Another of the best-known sculptures is the *Marathon Boy*.

OTHER COLLECTIONS

The museum also houses several smaller collections, many donated by private individuals. Among these is the glittering **Eléni Stathátou jewellery collection**, which covers the Bronze Age through to the Byzantine period. The **Karapános collection**, which is composed mainly from discoveries made at the site at Dodóni (*see p211*), contains many fine bronzes, including *Zeus Hurling a Thunderbolt*. Also on display are small decorative and votive pieces, and strips of lead inscribed with questions for the oracle at Dodóni.

Gold Hellenistic ring from the Eléni Stathátou collection

Other collections include the **Egyptian collection** and the **Bronze collection** which comprises many small pieces of statuary and decorative items discovered on the Acropolis.

THIRA FRESCOES

Two of the famous frescoes discovered at Akrotíri on the island of Thíra (Santoríni) in 1967, and originally thought to be from the mythical city of Atlantis, are displayed in the museum. The rest are on Santoríni. Dating from 1500 BC, they confirm the sophistication of late Minoan civilization. The colourful, restored images depict boxer boys, and animals and flowers symbolizing spring time.

POTTERY COLLECTION

The strength of this vast collection lies not only in its size, but in the quality of specific works, representing the flowering of Greek ceramic art. The real gems belong to the 5th century BC when red-figure vases and white-ground *lekythoi* became the established style (*see p60*) and were produced in vast numbers. Expressive painting styles and new designs characterize this period. The most poignant pieces are by the "Bosanquet Painter" and the "Achilles Painter" who portrayed young men by their graves.

Hellenistic bronze known as the *Horse with the Little Jockey*

View northeast to Lykavittós Hill from the Acropolis

Exárcheia and Stréfi Hill ❷

Εξάρχεια
Λόφος Στρέφη

Map 2 F2 & 3 A2. **M** Omónoia.

Until recently, the area around Plateía Exarcheíon was renowned as a hotbed of anarchist activity. Prior to the invasion of students, Exárcheia was a very attractive area and the 19th-century Neo-Classical buildings still stand as testament to this. Today, the area is picking up again and although parts of it are still rather run-down, an influx of gentrification has brought many fashionable cafés, bars and *ouzerí* to the area. Themistokléous, which leads off the square down to Omónoia, is pleasant to wander along; the local food stores and small boutiques make a refreshing change from the noisy bars. Plateía Exarcheíon is especially lively at night when the outdoor cafés and the open-air cinema, the Riviera, in the streets that climb towards Stréfi, attract many visitors.

Every year a demonstration takes place on 17 November, marking the date in 1973 when many students were killed by the Junta *(see p43)* during a sit-in.

The nearby park of Stréfi Hill, with its intriguing maze of paths, is quiet and peaceful by day but comes to life at night when its cafés are full. Stréfi Hill is one of the many green areas in Athens that provide welcome relief from the noise and grime of the city, particularly in the oppressive heat of summer.

The restaurant on Lykavittós Hill, overlooking Athens

Lykavittós Hill ❸

Λόφος Λυκαβηττού

Map 3 B4. **Funicular:** *from Ploutárchou, 8:45am–12:45pm Mon–Wed & Fri–Sun, 10:30am–12:45pm Thu.*

The peak of Lykavittós (also known as Lycabettus) reaches 277 m (910 ft) above the city, and is its highest hill. It can be climbed on foot by various paths or by the easier, albeit vertiginous, ride in the funicular from the corner of Ploutárchou. On foot, it should take about 45 minutes. The hill may derive its name from a combination of the words *lýki* and *vaino*, meaning "path of light". The ancient belief was that this was the rock once destined to be the Acropolis citadel, accidentally dropped by the city's patron goddess, Athena. Although it is without doubt the most prominent hill in Athens, surprisingly little mention is made of Lykavittós in Classical literature; the exceptions are passing references in Aristophanes's *Frogs* and Plato's *Kritías*. This landmark is a favourite haunt for many Athenians, who come for the panoramic views of the city from the observation decks that rim the summit.

The small whitewashed chapel of **Agios Geórgios** crowns the top of the hill. It was built in the 19th century on the site of an older Byzantine church, dedicated to Profítis Ilías (the Prophet Elijah). Both saints are celebrated on their name days (Profítis Ilías on 20 July and Agios Geórgios on 23 April). On the eve of Easter Sunday, a spectacular candlelit procession winds down the peak's wooded slopes *(see p45)*.

Lykavittós Hill is also home to a summit restaurant and café and the open-air **Lykavittós Theatre**, where contemporary jazz, pop and dance performances are held annually during the Athens Festival *(see p46)*.

Gennádeion ❹
Γεννάδειον

American School of Classical Studies,
Souidías 54, Kolonáki. **Map** 3 C4.
Tel *210 723 6313*. Ⓜ *Evangelismós.*
🚍 *3, 7, 8, 13*. ◯ *8:30am–9pm
Mon–Fri, 9am–2pm Sat.* ◉ *Aug,
main public hols.*

The Greek diplomat and
bibliophile Ioánnis
Gennádios (1844–1932)
spent a lifetime accumulat-
ing rare first editions and
illuminated manuscripts. In
1923, he donated his collection to the American School
of Classical Studies. The
Gennádeion building, named
after him, was designed and
built between 1923 and 1925
by the New York firm Van
Pelt and Thompson to house
the collection. Above its
façade of Ionic columns is an
inscription which translates as
"They are called Greeks who
share in our culture" – from
Gennádios's dedication speech
at the opening in 1926.

Researchers need special
permission to gain access to
over 70,000 rare books and
manuscripts and no items are
allowed to be removed from
the library. Casual visitors
may look at selected exhibits
that are on show, and books,
posters and postcards are for
sale at the souvenir stall.

Exhibits in the main reading
room include 192 Edward
Lear sketches purchased in
1929. There is also an eclectic
mix of Byron memorabilia,
including the last known
portrait of the poet made
before his death in Greece in
1824 *(see p149)*.

The imposing Neo-Classical
façade of the Gennádeion

National Gallery of Art ❺
Εθνική Πινακοθήκη

Vasiléos Konstantínou 50, Ilísia.
Map / C1. **Tel** *210 723 5937*.
Ⓜ *Evangelismós.* 🚍 *3, 13*.
◯ *9am–3:30pm Mon & Thu–Sun,
2–9pm Wed.* ◉ *main public hols.*
🖼 ♿ www.nationalgallery.gr

Opened in 1976, the National
Gallery of Art is housed in a
modern low-rise building
which contains a permanent
collection of European and
Greek art. The ground floor
stages travelling exhibitions
and opens out on to a sculpture garden. The first floor,
with the exception of five
impressive works by El Greco
(1541–1614), is devoted to a
minor collection of non-Greek,
European art. Alongside
works of the Dutch, Italian
and Flemish schools, there
are studies, engravings and
paintings by Rembrandt,
Dürer, Brueghel, Van Dyck,
Watteau, Utrillo, Cézanne and
Braque, among others. These

include Caravaggio's *Singer*
(1620), Eugène Delacroix's
Greek Warrior (1856) and
Picasso's Cubist-period *Woman
in a White Dress* (1939).

A changing display of Greek
modern art from the 18th to
the 20th century is featured
on the second floor. The 19th
century is represented mainly
by numerous depictions of
the War of Independence and
seascapes, enlivened by portraits such as Nikólaos Gýzis's
The Loser of the Bet (1878),
Waiting (1900) by Nikifóros
Lýtras and *The Straw Hat* (1925)
by Nikólaos Lýtras. There are
many fine works by major
Greek artists including Chatzimichaïl, Chatzikyriákos-Gkíkas,
Móralis and Tsaroúchis.

War Museum ❻
Πολεμικό Μουσείο

Corner of Vasilisis Sofías & Rizári,
Ilísia. **Map** 7 C1. **Tel** *210 725 2975*.
Ⓜ *Evangelismós.* 🚍 *3, 7, 8, 13*.
◯ *9am–2pm Tue–Sat, 9:30am–2pm
Sun.* ◉ *main public hols.* ♿
www.warmuseum.gr

The War Museum
was opened in
1975 after the
fall of the mili-
tary dictator-
ship *(see p43)*.
The first nine
galleries are
chronologi-
cally ordered,
and contain
battle scenes,
armour and
plans from as far

**Spartan bronze
helmet**

back as ancient Mycenaean
times through to the more
recent German occupation of
1941. Other galleries contain a
miscellany of items including a
selection of different uniforms
and Turkish weapons.

There is a fine display of
paintings and prints of leaders
from the Greek War of Independence *(see pp40–41)*,
such as General Theódoros
Kolokotrónis (1770–1843).
His death mask can also be
seen in the museum. A sizeable collection of fine oils
and sketches by the artists
Floras-Karavías and Argyrós
vividly captures the hardships
of the two world wars.

Modern sculpture outside the National Gallery of Art

Museum of Cycladic Art ❽
Μουσείο Κυκλαδικής Τέχνης

Opened in 1986, this modern museum offers the world's finest collection of Cycladic art. It was initially assembled by Nicholaos and Dolly Goulandrís and has expanded with donations from other Greek collectors. The museum now has an excellent selection of ancient Greek and Cypriot art, the earliest from about 5,000 years ago. The

Cycladic marble head Cycladic figurines, dating from the 3rd millennium BC, have never enjoyed quite the same level of popularity as Classical sculpture. However, the haunting simplicity of these marble statues has inspired many 20th-century artists and sculptors, including Picasso, Modigliani and Henry Moore.

LOCATOR MAP

KEY

- ▨ Non-exhibition space
- ▨ Cycladic art
- ▨ Ancient Greek art
- ▨ Ancient Cypriot art
- ▨ Daily life in antiquity
- ▨ Temporary exhibitions

Terracotta Figurine
This elegant figure of a woman is one of many that were thought to have been produced at Tanágra, in Boiotia, Central Greece. It dates from 330–320 BC.

Second floor

Bronze Askos
This elegant Hellenistic bronze wine jar dates from the 2nd century BC. The jar is so named because of its resemblance to the shape of a goat skin, or askos.

First floor

Main entrance

Ground floor

GALLERY GUIDE

In the main building, the Cycladic collection is on the first floor. Ancient Greek art is on the second, and the third shows Ancient Cypriot art. The fourth floor houses objects from everyday life in antiquity. Temporary exhibitions are held on the ground floor and in the Stathátos Mansion.

Red-Figure Kylix
This 5th-century BC drinking cup depicts a boxing match between two young male athletes, supervised by their instructor.

Third floor

Fourth floor

VISITORS' CHECKLIST

Neofýtou Doúka 4, Kolonáki (entrance to Stathátos Mansion at Irodótou 1). **Map** 7 B1.
Tel 210 722 8321. 3, 7.
10am–5pm Mon, Wed, Fri & Sat, 10am–8pm Thu, 11am–5pm Sun. main public hols. limited. **www**.cycladic.gr

★ **White Lekythos**
This fine clay lekythos (funerary vase) is an example of white-ground vase painting (see p60) and was used to contain embalming oil. It depicts a mourning woman taking offerings to a grave, and dates from c.450 BC.

Stairs and lifts connecting all floors

★ **Cycladic Figurine**
This "Folded Arm" figurine of a woman is 39 cm (15 in) tall. It has only four toes on each foot and a swollen abdomen, likely indicating pregnancy.

Entrance to main building via walkway

The first and ground floors house temporary exhibitions.

The original porch is the entrance to the Stathátos Mansion.

STATHATOS MANSION
This wing of the Museum of Cycladic Art was opened in 1992. It is housed in this elegant Neo-Classical building, once the home of Otto and Athína Stathátos. It was designed and built by the architect Ernst Ziller in 1895.

STAR EXHIBITS

★ Cycladic Figurine
★ White Lekythos

A 14th-century icon of St Michael in the Byzantine Museum

Byzantine Museum ❼
Βυζαντινό Μουσείο

Vasilíssis Sofías 22, Plateía Rigílis, Kolonáki. **Map** 7 B1. **Tel** 210 729 4926. **M** Evangelismós. **🚌** 3, 8, 7, 13. **🕙** 8:30am–3pm Tue–Sun. **⬤** main public hols. **🏷 ♿** ground floor only. **🖥** www.byzantinemuseum.gr

Originally called the Villa Ilissia, this elegant Florentine-style mansion was built between 1840 and 1848 by Stamátis Kleánthis for the Duchesse de Plaisance (1785–1854). This eccentric woman, wife of one of Napoleon's generals, was a key figure in Athens society during the mid-19th century and a dedicated philhellene.

Collector Geórgios Sotiríou converted the house into a museum in the 1930s with the help of architect Aristotélis Záchos. They transformed the entrance into a monastic court, incorporating a copy of a fountain from a 4th-century mosaic in Dafní *(see pp152–3)*.

Following extensive renovations, the museum reopened with a modern open-plan, split-level exhibition space built underground, below the courtyard. The museum's collection is now divided into two sections and laid out in chronological order: section one, *From the Ancient World to Byzantine*, traces the rise of Christianity, while section two, *The Byzantine World*, runs from the 6th century AD up until the fall of Constantinople in 1453.

Section one is dominated by fragments of ornamental stone carvings and mosaics taken from basilicas, sarcophagi, and early religious sculpture such as the *Shepherd Carrying a Lamb* and *Orpheus Playing a Lyre*, both of which illustrate the way in which the Christian church absorbed and adapted pagan symbols. Section two presents an array of icons, frescoes and precious ecclesiastical artifacts. Fine pieces to watch out for include the Treasury of Mytilene (a horde of 7th century gold and silver jewellery, coins and goblets discovered in a sunken ship), the Double-sided Icon of St George and the Mosaic Icon of the Virgin (both dating from the 13th century). There are also some magnificent frescoes that were rescued from the Church of the Episkopi and are cleverly displayed in the positions they would have been in in the church, which was based on a cross plan with a dome and narthex.

In summer, there are often concerts in the courtyard. Year-round, there are frequent guided tours free of charge. Call to find out what's on.

Funerary stele showing Orpheus with his lyre

The *Episkepsis*, from the Byzantine Museum, depicting the Virgin and Child

ICONS IN THE ORTHODOX CHURCH

The word icon simply means "image" and has come to signify a holy image through association with its religious use. Subjects range from popular saints such as St Andrew and St Nicholas to lesser-known martyrs, prophets and archangels. The image of the Virgin and Child is easily the most popular and exalted. Icons are a prominent feature in the Greek Orthodox religion and appear in many areas of Greek life. You will see them in taxis and buses, on boats and in restaurants, as well as in homes and churches. An icon can be in fresco, a mosaic, or made from bone or metal. The most common form is a portable painting, in wax-based paints applied to wooden boards treated with gesso. The figures are arranged so that the eyes are clearly depicted and appear to be looking directly at the viewer of the icon. These works, often of great artistic skill, are unsigned, undated and share a rigid conformity, right down to details of colour, dress, gesture and expression *(see pp20–21)*. The icon painter is careful to catch every detail of a tradition that stretches back hundreds of years.

Puppet Theatre from the Theatrical Museum

Museum of Cycladic Art ❽

See pp74–5.

Plateía Kolonakíou ❾
Πλατεία Κολωνακίου

Kolonáki. **Map** 3 B5. 🚌 *3, 7, 8, 13.*

Kolonáki Square and its neighbouring side streets are the most chic and sophisticated part of Athens. The area is often missed by those who restrict themselves to the ancient sites and the popular flea markets of Monastiráki. Also known as Plateía Filikís Etaireías, the square is named after a small ancient column *(kolonáki)* found in the area. Celebrated for its designer boutiques and fashionable bars and cafés, smart antique shops and art galleries, sumptuous *zacharoplasteía* (pastry shops) and *ouzerí*, it revels in its status as the city's most fashionable quarter *(see p116)*. The lively pavement cafés around the square each attract a particular devoted clientele. At one there may be rich kids drinking *frappé* (iced coffee) perched on their Harley Davidson motorbikes. Another, such as the *Lykóvrissi*, will be full of an older crowd of intellectuals sipping coffee and discussing the ever-popular subject of politics.

Benáki Museum ❿

See pp78–9.

Theatrical Museum ⓫
Μουσείο και Κέντρο Μελέτης του Ελληνικού Θεάτρου

Akadimias 50, Athens. **Map** 2 F4. *Tel 210 362 9430.* Ⓜ *Panepistímio.* 🚌 *3, 8, 13.* ◯ *10am–3pm Mon–Fri, 10am–1pm Sun.* ◯ *Aug, 17 Nov, main public hols.* ♿ *limited.* 📷

Housed in the basement of a fine Neo-Classical building, this small museum traces Greek theatrical history from Classical times to present day. There are displays of original posters, programmes, costumes and designs from productions by influential directors such as Károlos Koun. There is also a colourful puppet theatre. The dressing rooms of famous Greek actresses such as Eléni Papadáki and Elli Lampéti have been recreated to give an insight into their lives.

Perikles, from the Theatrical Museum

Museum of the City of Athens ⓬
Μουσείο της Πόλεως των Αθηνών

Paparrigopoúlou 7, Plateía Klafthmónos, Sýntagma. **Map** 2 E5. *Tel 210 323 1397.* Ⓜ *Panepistímio.* 🚌 *1, 2, 4, 5, 9, 11, 12, 15, 18.* ◯ *9am–4pm Mon & Wed–Fri, 10am–3pm Sat–Sun.* ◯ *main public hols.* 📷

King Otto and Queen Amalía *(see p40)* lived here from 1831 until their new palace, today's Voulí parliament building *(see p112)*, was completed in 1838. It was joined to the neighbouring house to create what was known as the Old Palace.

The palace was restored in 1980 as a museum devoted to royal memorabilia, furniture and family portraits, maps and prints. It offers a delightful look at life during the early years of King Otto's reign.

Exhibits include the manuscript of the 1843 Constitution, coats of arms from the Frankish (1205–1311) and Catalan (1311–88) rulers of Athens, and a scale model of the city as it was in 1842, made by architect Giánnis Travlós (1908–1985). The museum also has a fine art collection, including Nikólaos Gýzis's *The Carnival in Athens* (1892) and a selection of watercolours by the English artists Edward Dodwell (1767–1832), Edward Lear (1812–88) and Thomas Hartley Cromek (1809–73).

Upstairs sitting room recreated in the Museum of the City of Athens

Benáki Museum ⑩
Μουσείο Μπενάκη

This outstanding museum was founded in 1931 by Antónis Benákis (1873–1954), the son of Emmanouïl, a wealthy Greek who made his fortune in Egypt. Housed in an elegant Neo-Classical mansion, which was once the home of the Benákis family, the collection contains a diverse array of Greek arts and crafts, paintings and jewellery, local costumes and political memorabilia that spans over 5,000 years, from the Neolithic era to the 20th century.

Flag of Hydra
The imagery symbolizes the island of Hydra's supremacy in sea warfare as it was Greece's most powerful naval community.

Lecture hall

Bridal Cushion
This ornate embroidered cushion comes from Epirus and dates from the 18th century. It depicts a bridal procession, with ornamental flowers in the background.

Second floor

Roof garden

Auditorium

★ Detail of Wood Decoration
This intricately painted and carved piece of wooden panelling comes from the reception room of a mansion in Kozáni, in western Macedonia. It dates from the 18th century.

Atrium

Silver Ciborium
Used to contain consecrated bread, this elegant piece of ecclesiastical silverware is dated 1667 and comes from Edirne, in Turkey.

KEY TO FLOORPLAN

- ☐ Ground floor
- ☐ First floor
- ☐ Second floor
- ☐ Third floor
- ☐ Non-exhibition space

Entrance

Ship Pendant
This early 17th-century gold pendant is enamelled with blue and green and set with pearls. It comes from the island of Pátmos and is thought to be Venetian.

Third floor

VISITORS' CHECKLIST

Corner of Koumpári & Vasilísis
Sofías, Sýntagma.
Map 7 A1.
Tel 210 367 1000.
Ⓜ *Sýntagma.* 🚍 *3, 7, 8, 13.*
◯ 9am–5pm Mon, Wed, Fri
& Sat, 9am–midnight Thu,
9am–3pm Sun.
● 1 Jan, 25 Mar, Good Fri am,
Easter Sun, 1 May, 25, 26 Dec.
🎫 (free Thu). 📷 🚻 🍴 🛍
www.benaki.gr

GALLERY GUIDE

The ground floor collection is arranged into different periods and ranges from Neolithic to late-Byzantine art and Cretan icon painting. The first floor exhibits are organized geographically and are from Asia Minor, mainland Greece and the Greek islands. There is also a collection of ecclesiastical silverware and jewellery. The second floor displays items relating to Greek spiritual, economic and social life, and the third floor concentrates on the Greek War of Independence (see pp40–41) and modern political and cultural life.

First floor

Ground floor

★ Icon of St Anne with the Virgin
A product of the Cretan School, this icon of St Anne was painted in the 15th century. St Anne is carrying the Virgin Mary as a child, who is holding a white lily, symbol of purity.

Bowl from Paphos
Dating from the 13th century AD, this colourful bowl originates from Cyprus. The dancing figure is holding rattles.

★ El Faiyûm Portrait
This Hellenistic portrait of a man, painted on linen, dates from the 3rd century AD.

STAR EXHIBITS

- ★ El Faiyûm Portrait
- ★ Icon of St Anne with the Virgin
- ★ Detail of Wood Decoration

Neo-Classical façade of the National Historical Museum

National Historical Museum ⑬

Εθνικό Ιστορικό Μουσείο

Stadíou 13, Sýntagma. **Map** 2 F5. *Tel* 210 323 7617. Ⓜ Sýntagma. 🚌 1, 2, 4, 5, 9, 10, 11, 18. ☐ 9am–2pm Tue–Sun. 🔴 main public hols. 🎫 free Sun. www.nhmuseum.gr

Designed by French architect François Boulanger (1807–75), this museum was originally built as the first home of the Greek parliament. Queen Amalía laid the foundation stone in 1858, but it was 13 years later that it became the first permanent site of the Greek parliament. The country's most famous prime ministers have sat in the imposing chamber of the Old Parliament of the Hellenes, including Chárilaos Trikoúpis and Theódoros Deligiánnis, who was assassinated on the steps at the front of the building in 1905. The parliament moved to its present-day site in the Voulí building on Plateía Syntágmatos *(see p112)* after the Voulí was renovated in 1935.

In 1961, the building was opened as the National Historical Museum, owned by the Historical and Ethnological Society of Greece. Founded in 1882, the purpose of the society is to collect objects that illuminate the history of

Statue of General Theódoros Kolokotrónis

modern Greece. The museum covers all the major events of Greek history from the Byzantine period to the 20th century in a chronological display. Venetian armour, traditional regional costumes and jewellery and figureheads from the warships used during the Revolution in 1821 are just some examples of the many exhibits on show.

The collection also focuses on major parliamentary figures, philhellenes and leaders in the War of Independence, displaying such items as Byron's sword, the weapons of Theódoros Kolokotrónis (1770–1843), King Otto's throne and the pen that was used by Elefthérios Venizélos to sign the Treaty of Sèvres in 1920. The revolutionary memoirs of General Makrigiánnis (1797–1864) can also be seen. Among the numerous paintings on view is a fine rare woodcut of the *Battle of Lepanto* (1571), the work of Bonastro.

Outside the building is a copy of Lázaros Sóchos's statue of Kolokotrónis on horseback, made in 1900, the original of which is in Náfplio *(see pp182–3)*, the former capital of Greece. A dedication on the statue reads (in Greek): "Theódoros Kolokotrónis 1821. Ride on, noble commander, through the centuries, showing the nations how slaves may become free men."

Kapnikaréa ⑭

Καπνικαρέα

Corner of Ermoú & Kalamiótou, Monastiráki. **Map** 6 D1. *Tel* 210 322 4462. Ⓜ Monastiráki. ☐ 8am–2pm Mon, Wed; 8am–12:30pm & 5–7pm Tue, Thu, Fri; 8–11:30am Sun. 🔴 main public hols.

This charming 11th-century Byzantine church was rescued from demolition in 1834, thanks to the timely intervention of King Ludwig of Bavaria. Stranded in the middle of a square between Ermoú and Kapnikaréa streets, it is surrounded by the modern office blocks and shops of Athens' busy garment district.

Traditionally called the Church of the Princess, its foundation is attributed to Empress Irene, who ruled the Byzantine Empire from AD 797 to 802. She is revered as a saint in the Greek church for her efforts in restoring icons to the Empire's churches.

The true origins of the name "Kapnikaréa" are unknown, although according to some sources, the church was named after its founder, a "hearth-tax gatherer" *(kapnikaréas)*. Hearth tax was imposed on buildings by the Byzantines.

Restored in the 1950s, the dome of the church is supported by four Roman columns. Frescoes by Fótis Kóntoglou (1895–1965) were painted during the restoration, including one of the Virgin and Child. Much of Kóntoglou's work is also on display in the National Gallery of Art *(see p73)*.

The dome and main entrance of the Byzantine Kapnikaréa

Athenian Neo-Classical Architecture

Neo-Classicism flourished in the 19th century, when the architects who were commissioned by King Otto to build the capital in the 1830s turned to this popular European style. Among those commissioned were the Hansen brothers, Christian and Theophil, and also Ernst Ziller. As a result of their planning, within 50 years a modern city had emerged, with elegant administrative

National Bank, built in the 1890s

buildings, squares and tree-lined avenues. In its early days Neo-Classicism had imitated the grace of the buildings of ancient Greece, using marble columns, sculptures and decorative detailing. In later years, it evolved into an original Greek style. Grand Neo-Classicism is seen at its best in the public buildings along Panepistimíou; its domestic adaptation can be seen in the houses of Pláka.

Schliemann's House *(also known as Ilíou Mélathron, the Palace of Ilium, or Troy) was built in 1878 by Ziller. The interior is decorated with frescoes and mosaics of mythological subjects. It is now home to the Numismatic Museum* (**Map** 2 F5).

The National Library *was designed by Danish architect Theophil Hansen in 1887 in the form of a Doric temple with two side wings. Built of Pentelic marble, it houses over half a million books, including many illuminated manuscripts and rare first editions* (**Map** 2 F4).

The National Theatre *was built between 1882 and 1890. Ernst Ziller used a Renaissance-style exterior with arches and Doric columns for George I's Royal Theatre. Inspired by the Public Theatre of Vienna, its interior was very modern for its time* (**Map** 2 D3).

Athens Academy *was designed by Theophil Hansen and built between 1859 and 1887. Statues of Apollo and Athena, and seated figures of Socrates and Plato, convey a Classical style, as do the Ionic capitals and columns. Inside the building, the Academy hall has beautiful frescoes that depict scenes from the myth of Prometheus* (**Map** 2 F4).

The University of Athens *was designed by Christian Hansen. This fine building, completed in 1864, has an Ionic colonnade and a portico frieze depicting the resurgence of arts and sciences under the reign of King Otto. A symbol of wisdom, the Sphinx is connected with Athens through the Oedipus legend (see p221). Oedipus, who solved the riddle of the Sphinx, later found sanctuary in enlightened Athens. Other statues on the façade include Patriarch Gregory V, a martyr of the War of Independence* (**Map** 2 F4).

CENTRAL ATHENS SOUTH

Southern Athens is dominated by the Acropolis and is home to the buildings that were at the heart of ancient Athens. Pláka and Monastiráki still revel in their historical roots as the oldest inhabited areas of the city, and are full of Byzantine churches and museums. Nestling among the restored Neo-Classical houses are grocery stores, icon painters

Relief from Panagía Gorgoepíkoös

and open-air tavernas. In the busy streets of Monastiráki's flea market, food vendors, gypsies and street musicians provide the atmosphere of a Middle Eastern bazaar. Southeast of Plateía Syntágmatos are the National Gardens, the city centre's tree-filled park. For information on getting around Athens, see pages 324–7.

SIGHTS AT A GLANCE

Museums and Galleries
Greek Folk Art Museum ⑰
Ilías Lalaoúnis Jewellery Museum ⑧
Jewish Museum of Greece ⑱
Kanellópoulos Museum ⑨
Kyriazópoulos Folk Ceramic Museum ①
Municipal Art Gallery ④
Museum of Greek Popular Musical Instruments ⑪
University of Athens Museum ⑩

Ancient Sites
Acropolis pp94–101 ⑦
Ancient Agora pp90–91 ⑥
Kerameikós pp88–9 ⑤
Temple of Olympian Zeus ⑲
Tower of the Winds pp86–7 ②

Churches
Agios Nikólaos Ragavás ⑭
Mitrópoli ⑬
Panagía Gorgoepíkoös p105 ⑫
Russian Church of the Holy Trinity ⑳

Historic Districts
Anafiótika ⑮

Markets
Flea Market ③

Squares and Gardens
National Gardens ㉒
Plateía Lysikrátous ⑯
Plateía Syntágmatos ㉑

Historic Buildings and Monuments
Kallimármaro Stadium ㉔
Presidential Palace ㉓

Cemeteries
First Cemetery of Athens ㉕

KEY

▪ Street-by-Street: Monastiráki *pp84–5*	🚋 Tram stop
▪ Street-by-Street: Central Pláka *pp102–103*	Ⓜ Metro
	ℹ Tourist information

0 metres   500
0 yards   500

◁ **The remaining columns of the ancient Temple of Olympian Zeus**

Street-by-Street: Monastiráki

This old area of the city takes its name from the little sunken monastery in Plateía Monastirakíou. The former heart of Ottoman Athens, Monastiráki is still home to the bazaar and market stalls selling everything from junk to jewellery. The Fethiye Mosque and the Tzistarákis Mosque, home of the Kyriazópoulos Museum, stand as reminders of the area's Ottoman past. Roman influences are also strong in Monastiráki. The area borders the Roman Agora and includes the remains of Emperor Hadrian's library and the unique Tower of the Winds, a Hellenistic water clock. Monastiráki mixes the atmospheric surroundings of ancient ruins with the excitement of bargaining in the bazaar.

Flea Market
Plateía Avissynías is the heart of the flea market, which extends through the surrounding streets. It is particularly popular on Sundays ❸

KEY

- - - Suggested route

STAR SIGHTS

★ Tower of the Winds

0 metres   50
0 yards   50

Ifaístou is named after Hephaistos, the god of fire and metal craftsmanship. Areos is named after Ares, the war god.

Monastiráki metro station

The Fethiye Mosque is situated in the corner of the Roman Agora. It was built by the Turks in the late 15th century to mark Mehmet the Conqueror's visit to Athens.

Ancient Agora ↗
(see pp90–91)

LOCATOR MAP
*See Athens Street Finder
maps 2, 6*

Pantánassa church belonged to the monastery (monastiráki) which gave the area its name. Also known as the church of the Dormition of the Virgin, it is thought to have been built in the 10th century. It is situated opposite the metro station, on the east side of Plateía Monastirakíou.

Kyriazópoulos Folk Ceramic Museum

Housed in the old Tzistarákis Mosque, this museum is part of the Museum of Greek Folk Art. Originally opened in 1974, it contains around 800 fine ceramics originating from all over Greece ❶

Pláka *(see
pp102–3)* ➤

Hadrian's Library was built in the years following AD 132. It measured 118 m (387 ft) by 78 m (256 ft). Smaller rooms and a garden with a pool were contained in the complex, in addition to the vast library itself.

★ Tower of the Winds

This unusual, octagonal structure was built as a water clock and weather vane by the astronomer Andrónikos Kyrrestes in the 1st century BC ❷

Kyriazópoulos Folk Ceramic Museum ❶

Μουσείο Ελληνικής Λαϊκής Τέχνης, Συλλογή Κεραμικών Β. Κυριαζοπούλου

Tzistarákis Mosque, Areos 1, Monastiráki. **Map** 6 D1. **Tel** 210 324 2066. M Monastiráki. ○ 9am–3pm Mon & Wed–Sun. ● main public hols. 🎫 www.melt.gr

This colourful collection of ceramics was donated to the Greek Folk Art Museum in 1974 by Professor Vasíleios Kyriazópoulos. Now an annexe of the Folk Art Museum, the Kyriazópoulos Folk Ceramic Museum is housed in the imposing Tzistarákis Mosque (or the Mosque of the Lower Fountain). Of the hundreds of pieces on display, many are of the type still used today in a traditional Greek kitchen, such as terracotta water jugs from Aígina, earthenware oven dishes from Sífnos and storage jars from Thessaly and Chíos. There are also some ceramic figures and plates, based on mythological and folk stories, crafted by Minás Avramídis and Dimítrios Mygdalinós who came from Asia Minor in the 1920s.

The mosque itself is of as much interest as its contents. It was built in 1759 by the newly appointed Turkish *voivode* Tzistarákis. The *voivode* was the civil governor who possessed complete powers over the law courts and the police. He collected taxes for his own account, but also had to pay for the sultan's harem and the treasury. His workmen dynamited the 17th column of the Temple of Olympian Zeus (*see p111*) in order to make lime to be used for the stucco work on the mosque. Destruction of ancient monuments was forbidden by Turkish law and this act of vandalism was the downfall of Tzistarákis. He was exiled the same year. The mosque has been well restored after earthquake damage in 1981.

Ceramic of a young girl from Asia Minor

Tower of the Winds ❷

Αέρηδες

Within Roman Agora ruins, Pláka. **Map** 6 D1. **Tel** 210 324 5220. M Monastiráki. ○ Apr–Oct: 8am–7pm daily; Nov–Mar: 8:30am–3pm daily. ● main public hols. 🎫 ♿

The remarkable Tower of the Winds is set within the ruins of the Roman Agora. Constructed from marble in the 2nd century BC by the Syrian astronomer Andrónikos Kyrrestes, it was built as a combined weather vane and water clock. The name comes from the external friezes, personifying the eight winds. Sundials are etched into the walls beneath each relief.

The tower is well preserved, standing today at over 12 m (40 ft) high with a diameter of 8 m (26 ft). Still simply called Aérides ("the winds") by Greeks today, in the Middle Ages it was thought to be either the school or prison of Socrates, or even the tomb of Philip II of Macedon (*see p242*). It was at last correctly identified as the Horologion (water clock) of Andrónikos in the 17th century. All that remains today of its elaborate water clock are the origins of a complex system of water pipes and a circular channel cut into the floor which can be seen inside the tower.

The west and southwest faces of the Tower of the Winds

The west- and north-facing sides each contain a hole which lets light into the otherwise dark interior of the tower.

Northwest entrance

Reservoir

This interior floorplan of the tower shows the compass direction of the building's eight sides. External friezes personify each of the eight winds.

NORTH

Boreas blows the cold north wind through a large conch shell.

NORTHWEST

Skiron scatters glowing ashes from a bronze vessel.

WEST

Zephyros is a semi-naked youth scattering flowers.

For hotels and restaurants in this region see pp264–7 and pp284–8

Flea Market ❸
Παζάρι

From Plateía Monastirakíou to Plateía Avyssinías, Monastiráki. **Map** 5 C1.
M *Monastiráki.* ☐ *8am–2pm Sun.*

A banner welcomes visitors to Athens' famous flea market, past the ubiquitous tourist trinket shops of Adrianoú and Pandrósou streets. For the locals, the true heart of the market lies just west of Plateía Monastirakíou, in Plateía Avyssinías and its warren of surrounding streets.

On Sunday mornings when the shops are closed, the market itself bursts into action. Traders set out their bric-a-brac on stalls and the pavement and many bargains

Shoppers browsing in Athens' lively flea market

can be found, especially the colourful handwoven woollen cloths and the many bangles and beads sold by hippies. More expensive items are also on sale, including brassware, leatherware and silverware.

During the week the shops in the surrounding area are

open and filled with much the same as the Sunday stalls. Individual shops each have their own specialities, so hunt around before making a purchase. You can buy almost anything, from antiques and old books to taverna chairs and army surplus gear.

The southwest wind, *Lips, heralds a swift voyage. The reliefs show that each wind was given a personality according to its characteristics, and each promises different conditions. Gentle Zephyros and chilly Boreas, mentioned in Western literature and represented in art and sculpture, are the best known of these.*

Whirling dervishes *used the tower as a monastery in the mid-18th century. The dervishes were a Muslim order of ascetics. The tower's occupants became a popular attraction for Grand Tour visitors who came to witness the weekly ritual of a frenzied dance, which is known as the* sema.

Relief carving of mythological figure

Metal rod casting shadow

Lines of sundial carved into wall of tower

SOUTHWEST	SOUTH	SOUTHEAST	EAST	NORTHEAST

Lips holds the *aphlaston* (or stern ornament) of a ship as he steers.

Notos is the bearer of rain, emptying a pitcher of water.

Euros is a bearded old man, warmly wrapped in a cloak.

Apeliotes is a young man bringing fruits and corn.

Kaïkias empties a shield full of icy hailstones on those below.

Miss T K, by Giánnis Mitarákis, in the Municipal Art Gallery

Municipal Art Gallery ❹

Πινακοθήκη του Δήμου Αθηναίων

Peiraios 51, Plateía Koumoundoúrou, Omónoia. **Map** 1 C4. **Tel** 210 324 3022. **M** Omónoia. ◯ 10am–2pm & 5–9pm Tue–Sat, 10am–2pm Sun. ⬤ 3 Oct, main public hols. 🎫 ♿

This little-visited museum has one of the finest archive collections of modern Greek art. Designed by architect Panagiótis Kálkos in 1872, the home of the museum is the old Neo-Classical Foundling Hospital. It was built to cope with the city's population explosion towards the end of the 19th century; unwanted babies were left outside the main entrance to be cared for by hospital staff.

The Municipality of Athens has been amassing the collection since 1923. It now offers a fine introduction to the diverse styles of modern Greek artists. Many paintings are passionate reflections on the Greek landscape, such as Dímos Mpraésas's (1878–1967) landscapes of the Cyclades, or Konstantínos Parthénis's (1882–1964) paintings of olive and cypress trees.

There are also portraits by Giánnis Mitarákis and still lifes by Theófrastos Triantafyllídis. Paintings such as Nikólaos Kartsonákis's *Street Market* (1939) also reveal the folk roots that are at the heart of much modern Greek art.

Kerameikós ❺

Κεραμεικός

This ancient cemetery has been a burial ground since the 12th century BC. The Sacred Way led from Eleusis *(see pp156–7)* to Kerameikós and the Panathenaic Way set out from the Dípylon Gate here to the Acropolis *(see pp94–7)*. Most of the graves remaining today are along the Street of the Tombs. The sculptures excavated in the early 1900s are in the National Archaeological Museum *(see pp68–71)* and the Oberlander Museum; however, plaster copies of the originals can be seen *in situ.*

Grave Stele of Hegeso
This is from the family burial plot belonging to Koroibos of Melite. It shows his wife, Hegeso, admiring her jewels with a servant and dates from the late 5th century BC.

Precinct of Aristion

STREET OF THE TOMBS

The Precinct of Lysimachides contains a marble dog, originally one of a pair.

The Sanctuary of Hekate was sacred to the ancient goddess of the underworld. It contained an altar and votive offerings.

South terrace

Oberlander Museum

★ **Tomb of Dionysios of Kollytos**
This fine tomb belongs to a rich treasurer. A bull often represents the god Dionysos.

STAR MONUMENTS

- ★ Tomb of Dionysios of Kollytos
- ★ Stele of Demetria and Pamphile

STREET OF THE TOMBS

Most of the monuments in the Street of the Tombs date from the 4th century BC. The different styles, from the lavish *stelae* (relief sculptures) to the simple *kioniskoi* (small columns), all reveal the dignity that is typical of Greek funerary art.

LOCATOR MAP

Stele of Dexileos
Dexileos was a young man killed in 394 BC during the Corinthian War. The son of Lysanias, he is seen on the relief slaying an enemy.

This tumulus was the burial place of an old Attic family dating from the 6th century BC.

Tomb of Hipparete

River Eridanos

The Sacred Way led from the Sacred Gate to Ancient Eleusis *(see pp156–7).*

Sacred Gate, Acropolis

South Hill

Loutrophoros of Hegetor
The farewell scene depicted on this two-handled vase is typical of the less ornate style of commemorative funerary art.

★ Stele of Demetria and Pamphile
This moving sculpture shows the seated Pamphile with her sister Demetria behind her. This was one of the last ornate stelae to be made in the late 4th century BC.

🎦 Oberlander Museum
This museum is named after Gustav Oberlander (1867–1936), a German-American industrialist whose donations helped fund its construction in the 1930s. In Gallery 1, some large fragments from grave *stelae* found incorporated into the Dípylon and Sacred Gates are exhibited. These include a marble sphinx (c.550 BC) that once crowned a grave *stele*. Galleries 2 and 3 offer an array of huge Proto-geometric and Geometric amphorae and black-figure *lekythoi* (funerary vases). The most moving exhibits come from children's graves and include pottery toy horses and terracotta dolls. There are also examples of some of the 7,000 *ostraka* (voting tablets) *(see pp90–91)* found in the bed of the river Eridanos. Among the superb painted pottery, there is a red-figure *hydria* (water vase) of Helen of Troy and a *lekythos* of Dionysos with satyrs.

Winged sphinx from grave stele

Geometric funerary amphora from the Oberlander Museum

Ancient Agora 6

Αρχαία Αγορά

Voting lot

The Agora, or market–place, formed the political heart of ancient Athens from 600 BC. Democracy was practised in the *Bouleuterion* (Council) and the law courts, and in open meetings. Socrates was indicted and executed in the state prison here in 399 BC. The theatres, schools and stoas filled with shops also made this the centre of social and commercial life. Even the city mint that produced Athens' silver coins was here. The American School of Classical Studies began excavations of the Ancient Agora in the 1930s, and since then the vast remains of a complex array of public buildings have been revealed.

View across the Agora from the south showing the reconstructed Stoa of Attalos on the right

The Panathenaic Way was named after the Great Panathenaia festival which took place every four years.

Library of Pantainos

Monopteros temple

Triton statues

Temple of Ares

Altar of the twelve gods

Stoa of Zeus Eleutherios

Hellenistic temple

Temple of Apollo Patroös

Odeion of Agrippa
This statue of a triton (half-god, half-fish) once adorned the façade of the Odeion of Agrippa. It dates from AD 150 and is now in the Agora museum.

RECONSTRUCTION OF THE ANCIENT AGORA

This shows the Agora as it was in c.AD 200, viewed from the northwest. The main entrance to the Agora at this time was via the Panathenaic Way, which ran across the site from the Acropolis in the southeast to the Kerameikós in the northwest.

0 metres

0 yards   5

Stoa of Attalos
This colonnaded building was reconstructed in the mid-20th century as a museum to house finds from the Ancient Agora site.

Statue of Hadrian
Hadrian was Emperor of Rome from AD 117–38. Athens was under his authority. The statue dates from the 2nd century AD.

Southeast temple
The middle stoa housed shops.
Altar of Zeus
Southwest temple
Heliaia
Southwest fountain

Latrines
The Tholos was the Council headquarters.

Bouleuterion or Council chamber

Monument of the Eponymous Heroes

Metroön
Arsenal

Ostrakon condemning a man named Hippokrates to exile

🖼 **Stoa of Attalos**
This fine building was rebuilt between 1953 and 1956, helped by a huge donation from John D Rockefeller, Jr. An impressive two-storey stoa, or roofed arcade, founded by King Attalos of Pergamon (ruled 159–138 BC), it dominated the eastern quarter of the Agora until it was burnt down by the Heruli tribe in AD 267. Reconstructed using the original foundations and ancient materials, it now contains a museum whose exhibits reveal the great diversity and sophistication of ancient life. Artifacts include rules from the 2nd-century AD Library of Pantainos, the text of a law against tyranny from 337 BC, bronze and stone lots used for voting and a *klepsýdra* (water clock) used for timing speeches. *Ostraka* (voting tablets on which names were inscribed) bear such famous names as Themistokles and Aristeides the Just, the latter banished, or "ostracized", in 482 BC. More everyday items, such as terracotta toys and portable ovens, and hobnails and sandals found in a shoemaker's shop, are equally fascinating. Also on display are some beautiful black-figure vases and an unusual oil flask moulded into the shape of a kneeling boy.

Oil flask in the Archaic style

Hephaisteion
This temple, also known as the Theseion, is the best-preserved building on the site. It was built c.449–440 BC.

Acropolis 🄮
Ακρόπολη

In the mid-5th century BC, Perikles persuaded the Athenians to begin a grand programme of new building work in Athens that has come to represent the political and cultural achievements of Greece. The work transformed the Acropolis with three contrasting temples and a monumental gateway. The Theatre of Dionysos on the south slope was developed further in the 4th century BC, and the Theatre of Herodes Atticus was added in the 2nd century AD.

LOCATOR MAP

★ Porch of the Caryatids
These statues of women were used in place of columns on the south porch of the Erechtheion. The originals, four of which can be seen in the Acropolis Museum (see p100), have been replaced by casts.

An olive tree now grows where Athena first planted her tree in a competition against Poseidon.

The Propylaia was built in 437–432 BC to form a new entrance to the Acropolis *(see p96)*.

★ Temple of Athena Nike
This temple to Athena of Victory is on the west side of the Propylaia. It was built in 426–421 BC (see p96).

The Beulé Gate was the first entrance to the Acropolis *(see p96).*

Pathway to Acropolis from ticket office

STAR SIGHTS

★ Parthenon

★ Porch of the Caryatids

★ Temple of Athena Nike

Theatre of Herodes Atticus
Also known as the Odeion of Herodes Atticus, this superb theatre was originally built in AD 161. It was restored in 1955 and is used today for outdoor concerts (see p97).

◁ The Porch of the Caryatids on the Erechtheion

★ **Parthenon**
Although few sculptures are left on this famous temple to Athena, some can still be admired, such as this one from the east pediment (see pp98–9).

VISITORS' CHECKLIST

Dionysíou Areopagítou (main entrance), Pláka. **Map** 6 D2. **Tel** 210 321 0219. Ⓜ Acrópoli. 🚌 230, 231. ◐ Apr–Oct: 8am–8pm daily (to 2:30pm Sat & Sun); Nov–Mar: 8:30am–3pm daily. ● 1 Jan, 25 Mar, Easter Sun,1 May, 25 & 26 Dec. 🎫 (free Sun, Nov–Mar). 📷 ♿ **www**.culture.gr

Two Corinthian columns
are the remains of choregic monuments erected by sponsors of successful dramatic performances *(see p97)*.

Panagía Spiliótissa
is a chapel set up in a cave in the Acropolis rock *(see p97)*.

Theatre of Dionysos
This figure of the comic satyr, Silenus, can be seen here. The theatre visible today was built by Lykourgos in 342–326 BC (see p97).

Sanctuary of Asklepios

Stoa of Eumenes

The Acropolis rock
was an easily defended site. It has been in use for nearly 5,000 years.

TIMELINE

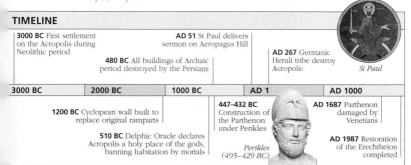

3000 BC First settlement on the Acropolis during Neolithic period

AD 51 St Paul delivers sermon on Aeropagus Hill

480 BC All buildings of Archaic period destroyed by the Persians

AD 267 Germanic Heruli tribe destroy Acropolis

St Paul

3000 BC	2000 BC	1000 BC	AD 1	AD 1000

1200 BC Cyclopean wall built to replace original ramparts

447–432 BC Construction of the Parthenon under Perikles

AD 1687 Parthenon damaged by Venetians

510 BC Delphic Oracle declares Acropolis a holy place of the gods, banning habitation by mortals

Perikles (495–429 BC)

AD 1987 Restoration of the Erechtheion completed

Exploring the Acropolis

Relief of Mourning Athena

Once through the first entrance, the Beulé Gate, straight ahead is the Propylaia, the grand entrance to the temple complex. Before going through here, it is worth exploring the Temple of Athena Nike, on the right. Beyond the Propylaia are the Erechtheion and the Parthenon *(see pp98–9)* which dominate the top of the rock. There are also stunning views of Athens itself from the Acropolis. Access to all the temple precincts is banned to prevent damage. On the south slope of the Acropolis are the two theatres, once used for drama festivals in honour of the god Dionysos. The striking Acropolis Museum and the hills immediately to the west are covered on pages 100–101.

View of the Acropolis from the southwest

⋔ Beulé Gate

The gate is named after the French archaeologist Ernest Beulé who discovered it in 1852. It was built in AD 267 after the raid of the Heruli, a Germanic people, as part of the Roman Acropolis fortifications. It incorporates stones from the *choregic* monument *(see p109)* of Nikias that was situated near the Stoa of Eumenes. Parts of the original monument's dedication are still visible over the architrave. There is also an inscription identifying a Roman, Flavius Septimius Marcellinus, as donor of the gateway. In 1686, when the Turks destroyed the Temple of Athena Nike, they used the marble to build a bastion for artillery over the gate.

⋔ Temple of Athena Nike

This small temple was built in 426–421 BC to commemorate the Athenians' victories over the Persians. The temple frieze has representative scenes from the Battle of Plataéa (479 BC).

Designed by Kallikrates, the temple stands on a 9.5-m (31-ft) bastion. It has been used as both observation post and an ancient shrine to the goddess of Victory, Athena Nike, of whom there is a remarkable sculpture situated on the balustrade. Legend records the temple site as the place where King Aegeus stood waiting for his son Theseus to return from his mission to Crete to slay the Minotaur. Theseus had promised to swap his ships' black sails for white on his return but in the melee of the victorious battle had forgotten his promise. When King Aegeus saw the black sails he presumed his son to be dead and threw himself into the sea.

Built of Pentelic marble, the temple has four Ionic columns 4 m (13 ft) high at each portico end. It was reconstructed in 1834–8, after being destroyed in 1686 by the Turks. On the point of collapse in 1935, it was again dismantled and reconstructed according to information resulting from more recent research.

⋔ Propylaia

Work began on this enormous entrance to the Acropolis in 437 BC. Although the outbreak of the Peloponnesian War in 432 BC curtailed its completion, its architect Mnesikles created a building admired throughout the ancient world. The Propylaia comprises a rectangular central building divided by a wall into two porticoes. These were punctuated by five entrance doors, rows of Ionic and Doric columns and a vestibule with a blue-coffered ceiling decorated with gold stars. Two wings flank the main building. The north wing was home to the *pinakothíki*, an art gallery.

During its chequered history – later as archbishop's residence, Frankish palace, and Turkish fortress and armoury – parts of the building have been accidentally destroyed; it even suffered the misfortune of being struck by lightning in 1645, and later the explosion of the Turkish gunpowder store *(see p98)*.

⋔ Erechtheion

Built between 421 and 406 BC the Erechtheion is situated on the most sacred site of the Acropolis. It is said to be

The eastern end of the Erechtheion

The remains of the Theatre of Dionysos

where Poseidon left his trident marks in a rock, and Athena's olive tree sprouted, in their battle for possession of the city. Named after Erechtheus, one of the mythical kings of Athens, the temple was a sanctuary to both Athena Polias, and Erechtheus-Poseidon.

Famed for its elegant and extremely ornate Ionic architecture and caryatid columns in the shape of women, this extraordinary monument is built on different levels. The large rectangular cella was divided into three rooms. One contained the holy olive wood statue of Athena Polias. The cella was bounded by north, east and south porticoes. The south is the Porch of the Caryatids, the maiden statues which are now in the Acropolis Museum.

The Erechtheion complex has been used for a range of purposes, including a harem for the wives of the Turkish disdar (commander) in 1463. It was almost completely destroyed by a Turkish shell in 1827 during the War of Independence (see pp40–41). Restoration work here has caused heated disputes: holes have been filled with new marble, and copies have been made to replace original features that have been removed to the safety of the museum.

⋔ Theatre of Herodes Atticus

This small Roman theatre seats 5,000 spectators and is still in use today (see p119). Built by the Roman consul Herodes Atticus between AD 161 and 174, in memory of his wife, the shape was hollowed

out of the rocks on the southern slope of the Acropolis. The semicircular orchestra in front of the stage was repaved with alternating blue and white marble slabs in the 1950s. Behind the stage, its distinctive colonnade once contained statues of the nine Muses. The whole theatre was originally enclosed by a cedar-wood roof that gave better acoustics and allowed for all-weather performances.

⋔ Theatre of Dionysos

D. Areopagitou, Makrygiánni. **Tel** 210 322 4625.
⬤ Apr–Oct: 8am–7pm daily; Nov–Mar: 8:30am–2:30pm daily. 📷

Cut into the southern cliff face of the Acropolis, the Theatre of Dionysos is the birthplace of Greek tragedy, and was the first theatre built of stone. Aeschylus, Sophocles, Euripides and Aristophanes all had their plays performed here,

Throne from the Theatre of Dionysos

during the dramatic contests of the annual City Dionysia festival, when it was little more than a humble wood-and-earth affair. The theatre was rebuilt in stone by the Athenian statesman Lykourgos between 342–326 BC, but the ruins that can be seen today are in part those of a much bigger structure, built by the Romans, which could seat 17,000. They used it as a gladiatorial arena, and added a marble balustrade with metal railings to protect spectators. In the 1st century AD, during Emperor Nero's reign, the orchestra was given its marble flooring, and in the 2nd century AD the front of the stage was decorated with reliefs showing Dionysos's life. Above the theatre there is a cave sacred to the goddess Artemis. This was converted into a chapel in the Byzantine era, dedicated to **Panagía i Spiliótissa** (Our Lady of the Cave), and was the place where mothers brought their sick children. Two large Corinthian columns nearby are the remains of choregic monuments erected to celebrate the benefactor's team winning a drama festival. The Sanctuary of Asklepios to the west, founded in 420 BC, was dedicated to the god of healing. Worshippers seeking a cure had to take part in purification rites before they could enter the temple precincts.

Interior of the Panagía i Spiliótissa chapel, above the Theatre of Dionysos

The Parthenon
Ο Παρθενώνας

One of the world's most famous buildings, this temple was begun in 447 BC. It was designed by the architects Kallikrates and Iktinos, primarily to house the 12 m (40 ft) high statue of Athena Parthenos (Maiden), sculpted by Pheidias. Taking nine years to complete, the temple was dedicated to the goddess in 438 BC. Over the centuries, it has been used as a church, a mosque and an arsenal, and has suffered severe damage. Built as an expression of the glory of ancient Athens, it remains the city's emblem to this day.

View of the Parthenon today, from the west

The west cella was used as a treasury.

Akroterion

The external frieze consisted of triglyphs and metopes.

Marble walls concealed the cellas, or inner rooms.

Parthenon Frieze
The frieze, designed by Pheidias, ran around the inner wall of the Parthenon. The metopes (sections of the frieze) depicted the Great Panathenaia festival, honouring Athena.

RECONSTRUCTION OF THE PARTHENON

This reconstruction, from the southeast, shows the Parthenon as it was in the 5th century BC. It was 70 m (230 ft) long and 30 m (100 ft) wide. The entablature of this peripteral temple (with a single row of columns around the edge) was painted in blue, red and gold.

Each column was constructed from fluted drums of marble. The fluting was added once the columns were in place.

The Elgin Marbles *(see p100)* were taken largely from the internal frieze.

VEDUTA DEL CAST. D'ACROPOLIS DALLA PARTE DI TRAMONTANA

Explosion of 1687
During the Venetian siege of the Acropolis, General Francesco Morosini bombarded the Parthenon with cannon-fire. The Turks were using the temple as an arsenal at the time and the ensuing explosion demolished much of it, including the roof, the inner structure and 14 of the outer columns.

Statue of Athena
The huge chryselephantine (ivory and gold) statue of Athena, patron goddess of Athens, was the focus of the Parthenon. No trace of it remains today, but this smaller Roman copy can be seen in the National Archaeological Museum (see pp68–71).

THE ILLUSION OF PERFECTION

Every aspect of the Parthenon was built on a 9:4 ratio to make the temple completely symmetrical. The sculptors also used visual trickery to counteract the laws of perspective. The illustration below is exaggerated to show the techniques they employed.

The base of the temple is higher in the middle than at the edges.

Entasis (a bulge in the middle) makes each column look straight.

Each column leans inwards slightly.

The internal columns were in two rows and Doric in style.

The roof was made from Pentelic marble tiles supported on wooden rafters.

Northeast Corner
This corner shows the remains of the pediment sculptures and the vertical carvings of the triglyphs alternating with the faded metope carvings.

The steps curved upwards slightly at the centre to make them appear level from a distance.

Entrance

View of the East Cella
The cella was the inner room of the temple. In the case of the Parthenon, there were two – east and west. The east cella contained the enormous cult statue of Athena and the offerings bestowed upon it. The west cella was the back room, reserved for the priestess.

Around the Acropolis

The Moscho-phoros (Calf-Bearer)

The area around the Acropolis was the centre of public life in Athens. In addition to the Agora in the north *(see pp90–91)*, political life was largely centred on the Pnyx and the Areopagos, the hills lying to the west of the Acropolis: the Assembly met on the former and murder trials were heard by a council of ex-magistrates on the latter. Other ancient remains and the glittering Acropolis Museum, located at the foot of the Acropolis provide a fascinating insight into what daily life was like in ancient Athens.

Excavation site at the Acropolis Museum

Acropolis Museum

Dionysiou Areopagitou 15, Acrópoli.
Tel *210 900 0900.* Ⓜ *Acrópoli.*
⭘ *8am–8pm Tue–Sun (to 10pm Fri).*
www.theacropolismuseum.gr

After decades of planning and delays, the Acropolis Museum opened in the historic Makrigiánni district, southeast of the Acropolis. The museum had been planned since the late 1970s to replace the old Acropolis Museum, situated next to the Parthenon, which was always considered too small and dilapidated to really do justice to the sculptures and architectural pieces found on the Acropolis hill. Today, the €130-million, multi-storey, all-glass show-piece designed by Bernad Tschumi, is undoubtedly a more fitting home for the hill's stunning treasures.

Tschumi had the added challenge of constructing the building over excavations of an early Christian settlement.

Concrete pillars and a glass walkway allow the building to hover over the ruins, which are on view in the lobby near the entrance.

The rest of the collection is installed in chronological order and begins with finds from the slopes of the Acropolis. These include statues and reliefs from the Sanctuary of Asklepios.

The **Archaic Collection** is set out in a magnificent double-height gallery. Fragments of painted pedimental statues include mythological scenes of Herakles grappling with various monsters and the more peaceful votive statue of the *Moschophoros*, or Calf-Bearer, portraying a young man carrying a calf on his shoulders (c.570 BC).

The sky-lit **Parthenon Gallery** on the top floor is the high-light. Here, arranged around an indoor court and looking out on to the Parthenon, the remaining parts of the Parthe-non frieze are displayed in the order in which they would have graced the Parthenon (there are significant blank spaces left for those held in London). The sculptures depict the Panathenaic pro-cession, including the chariot and *apobates* (slaves riding chariot horses) and a sacrifi-cial cow being led by youths.

On the level below, the **post-Parthenon Collection** comprises sculptures from the Temple of Athena Nike, and architectural features from the Propylaia and the Erechtheion, including the original four caryatids from the south porch.

THE ELGIN MARBLES

These famous sculptures, also called the Parthenon Marbles, are held in the British Museum in London. They were acquired by Lord Elgin in 1801–3 from the occupying Turkish authorities. He sold them to the British nation for £35,000 in 1816. There is great controversy surrounding the Marbles. While some argue that they are more care-fully preserved in the British Museum, the Greek government does not accept the legality of the sale and many believe they belong in Athens. A famous supporter of this cause was the Greek actress and politi-cian, Melína Merkoúri, who died in 1994.

The newly arrived Elgin Marbles at the British Museum, in a painting by A Archer

Areopagus Hill

There is little left to see on this low hill today, apart from the rough-hewn, slippery steps and what are thought to be seats on its summit. The Areopagus was used by the Persians and Turks during their attacks on the Acropolis citadel, and played an important role as the home of the Supreme Judicial Court in the Classical period. It takes its name, meaning the "Hill of Ares", from a mythological trial that took place here when the god Ares was acquitted of murdering the son of Poseidon. The nearby **Cave of the Furies** inspired the playwright Aeschylus *(see p57)* to set Orestes's trial here in his play *Eumenides* (The Furies). The hill also achieved renown in AD 51, when St Paul delivered his sermon "On an unknown God" and gained his first convert, Dionysios the Areopagite, who subsequently became the patron saint of Athens.

The Asteroskopeíon on the Hill of the Nymphs

Pnyx Hill

If Athens is the cradle of democracy, Pnyx Hill is its exact birthplace. During the 4th and 5th century BC the *Ekklesia* (citizens' assembly) met here to discuss and vote upon all but the most important matters of state, until it lost its powers during Roman rule. In its heyday, 6,000 Athenians gathered 40 times a year to listen to speeches and take vital political decisions. Themi-stokles, Perikles and Demosthenes all spoke from the *bema* (speaker's platform) that is still visible today. Carved out of the rock face, it formed the top step of a platform that doubled as a primitive altar to the god Zeus. There are also the remains of the huge retaining wall which was built

to support the semicircular terraces that placed citizens on a level with the speakers. It completely surrounded the auditorium which was 110 m (358 ft) high.

Agios Dimítrios

Dionysíou Areopagítou, south slope of Acropolis. ☐ *daily.* ✦ *except Sun.*
This Byzantine church is often called Agios Dimítrios Loum-pardiáris, after an incident in 1656. The Turkish *disdar* (commander) at the time, Yusuf Aga, laid plans to fire a huge cannon called Loumpárda, situated by the Propylaia *(see p96)*, at worshippers in the church as they celebrated the feast day of Agios Dimítrios. However, the night before the feast, lightning struck the Propylaia, miraculously killing the commander and his family.

Cross from Agios Dimítrios church

Filopáppos Hill

The highest summit in the south of Athens, at 147 m (482 ft), offers spectacular views of the Acropolis. It has always played a decisive defensive role in Athens' history – the general Demetrios Poliorketés built an important fort here overlooking the strategic Piraeus road in 294 BC, and Francesco Morosini bombarded the Acropolis from here in 1687. Popularly called Filopáppos

Hill after a monument still on its summit, it was also known to the ancient Greeks as the Hill of Muses or the Mouseíon, because the tomb of Musaeus, a disciple of Orpheus, was traditionally held to be located here.

Built between AD 114–16, the Monument of Philopappus was raised by the Athenians in honour of Caius Julius Antiochus Philopappus, a Roman consul and philhellene. Its unusual concave marble façade, 12 m (40 ft) high, contains niches with statues of Philopappus and his grand-father, Antiochus IV. A frieze around the monument depicts the arrival of Philopappus by chariot for his inauguration as Roman consul in AD 100.

Hill of the Nymphs

This 103-m (340-ft) high tree-clad hill takes its name from dedications found carved on rocks in today's Observatory Garden. The Asteroskopeíon (Observatory), built in 1842 by the Danish architect Theophil Hansen, with funds from philanthropist Baron Sína, occupies the site of a sanctuary to nymphs associated with childbirth. The modern church of Agía Marína nearby has similar associations of childbirth; pregnant women used to slide effortlessly down a smooth rock near the church, in the hope of an equally easy labour.

The Monument of Philopappus, AD 114–116

Street-by-Street: Central Pláka

Pláka is the historic heart of Athens. Even though only a few houses date back further than the Ottoman period, it remains the oldest continuously inhabited area of the city. One explanation of its name comes from the word *pliaka* (old), which was used to describe the area by Albanian soldiers in the service of the Turks who settled here in the 16th century. Despite the crowds of tourists and the many Athenians who come to eat in the tavernas or browse in antique shops, it still retains the feel of a residential neighbourhood.

Mitrópoli
Athens' cathedral was built in the second half of the 19th century **13**

★ Panagía Gorgoepíkoös
This tiny 12th-century church, also known as the Little Cathedral, has some beautiful carvings **12**

Museum of Greek Popular Musical Instruments
A range of folk instruments is displayed in this museum which was opened in 1991 **11**

Thoukydídou
is named after the historian Thucydides (c.460–400 BC).

Monastiráki
(see pp84–5)

Acropolis
(see pp94–101)

University of Athens Museum
Occupying the university's original home, this museum has memorabilia from the university's early days, including these old medical artifacts **10**

Ancient Agora
(see pp90–91)

Kanellópoulos Museum
Privately owned, this museum has exquisite works of art from all areas of the Hellenic world **9**

Plateía
Syntágmatos
(see p112)

Greek Folk Art Museum
*Offering the best of Greek folk art,
this has everything from shadow
puppets to terracotta ornaments* ⑰

LOCATOR MAP
See Street Finder maps 5–6

NIKODIMOU

YPEREIDOU

THOUKYDIDOU

CHATZIMICHALI

CEKROPOS

KYDATHINAION

ADRIANOU

IPODON

THESPIDOS

SOTIROS

ADRIANOU

0 metres   50

0 yards   50

**Agios Nikólaos
Ragavás**
*This 11th century,
Byzantine chapel is
a popular location
for weddings* ⑭

Plateía Lysikrátous
*Named after the monu-
ment in its centre, this
square was a favourite
haunt of the poet Byron* ⑯

KEY

– – – Suggested route

STAR SIGHT

★ Panagía
Gorgoepíkoös

Anafiótika
*The whitewashed houses and winding
streets resembling a Cycladic village
were built in the 19th century by
settlers from the island of Anáfi* ⑮

Ilías Lalaoúnis Jewellery Museum

Μουσείο Κοσμήματος Ηλία Λαλαούνη

Karyatidon & P. Kallisperi 12, Acrópoli. **Map** 6 D3. **Tel** *210 922 1044.* M *Acrópoli.* ○ *9am–3pm Wed–Sat, 11am–4pm Sun.* ● *main public hols.* 🏛 🅾 *by prior written permission only.* ♿ 📷

Situated just below the Theatre of Dionysos, this small museum is a delight for anyone interested in decorative arts. The permanent collection comprises over 4,000 pieces spanning 60 years of jewellery making by designer Ilías Lalaoúnis, who is credited with the revival of Greek jewellery making in the 1950s.

Kanellópoulos Museum

Μουσείο Κανελλοπούλου

Corner of Theorías & Pános 12, Pláka. **Map** 6 D2. **Tel** *210 324 4447.* M *Monastiráki.* ○ *8:30am–3pm Tue–Sun, noon–3pm Good Fri.* ● *1 Jan, 25 Mar, Easter Sun, 25, 26 Dec.* 🏛 🅾

In an immaculately restored Neo-Classical town house, this museum contains a varied collection of artifacts from all over the Hellenistic world. On display are 6th-century BC helmets, 5th-century BC gold Persian jewellery and Attic vases. Also on view are Cycladic figurines, some unusual terracotta figures of actors in their theatrical masks and a fine 2nd-century AD El Faiyûm portrait of a woman.

A huge block of stone that fell from the walls of the Acropolis can still be seen as an exhibit on the ground floor.

Sculpture of a triton from the Kanellópoulos Museum

Rempétika musicians, Museum of Greek Popular Musical Instruments

University of Athens Museum

Μουσείο Ιστορίας του Πανεπιστημίου Αθηνών

Thólou 5, Pláka. **Map** 6 E2. **Tel** *210 368 9502.* M *Monastiráki.* ○ *Apr–Oct: 5–9pm Mon & Wed, 9:30am–2:30pm Tue, Thu & Fri; Nov–Mar: 9:30am–2:30pm Mon–Fri.* ● *main public hols.* **www**.history-museum.uoa.gr

This three-storey house was the first home of the University of Athens. It opened on 3 May 1837 with 52 students and 33 professors in its first year. In November 1841 the University moved to its new quarters, and from 1922 the building was home to many immigrant families. While they were there, a taverna known as the "Old University" was opened on the ground floor.

In 1963 the building was declared a National Monument. Later reacquired by the university, the old building was opened as a museum in 1974. Today, the "Old University", as it is still known, has an eclectic collection of memorabilia such as corporeal body maps, anatomical models, scientific instruments and medicine jars.

Museum of Greek Popular Musical Instruments

Μουσείο Ελληνικών Λαϊκών Μουσικών Οργάνων

Diogénous 1–3, Pláka. **Map** 6 D1. **Tel** *210 325 0198.* M *Monastiráki.* ○ *10am–2pm Tue–Sun, noon–6pm Wed.* ● *17 Nov, main public hols.* **www**.instruments-museum.gr

Cretan musicologist Phoebus Anogianákis donated over 1,200 musical instruments to the Greek State in 1978. In 1991 this study centre and museum was opened, devoted to the history of popular Greek music, including Anogianákis's collection. The museum traces the development of different styles of island music and the arrival of *rempétika* (Greek "blues") from Smyrna in 1922.

Instruments from all over Greece are displayed, with recordings and headphones. The basement contains church and livestock bells, as well as water whistles, wooden clappers and flutes. Elsewhere there are wind instruments including *tsampoúna* (bagpipes made from goatskin) and string instruments such as the Cretan *lýra*.

Panagía Gorgoepíkoos ⑫
Παναγία η Γοργοεπήκοος

Bas-relief from south façade

This domed cruciform church is built entirely from Pentelic marble, now weathered to a rich corn-coloured hue. Dating from the 12th century, it measures only 7.5 m (25 ft) long by 12 m (40 ft) wide. The size of the church is in scale with Athens when it was just a village in the 12th century. Adorned with friezes and bas-reliefs taken from earlier buildings, the exterior mixes the Classical and Byzantine styles. Although dedicated to Panagía Gorgoepíkoos (the Madonna who Swiftly Hears) and Agios Elefthérios (the saint who protects women in childbirth), it is often affectionately known as the Mikrí Mitrópoli (Little Cathedral).

VISITORS' CHECKLIST

Plateía Mitropóleos, Pláka.
Map 6 E1. M *Monastiráki.*
⬭ *7am–7pm daily.* ✞

The south façade of the church, dwarfed by the giant Mitrópoli

Allegorical Animals
This 12th-century bas-relief detail is one of a pair from the west façade.

Four brick pillars replaced the original marble ones in 1834.

The floor is lower than ground level by about 30 cm (12 in).

Fragments of Classical buildings made from Pentelic marble were combined with Byzantine sections in the style of a Classical frieze.

Main entrance

Lintel Frieze
This relief depicting the months of the year dates from the 4th century BC. The central cross was added in the 12th century.

Modern mosaics above the main entrance to Athens' cathedral, Mitrópoli

Mitrópoli ⓭
Μητρόπολη

Plateía Mitropóleos, Pláka. **Map** 6 E1.
Tel *210 322 1308.* Ⓜ *Monastiráki.*
◯ *7am–7pm daily.*

Work began in 1840 on this huge cathedral, using marble from 72 demolished churches for its walls. The cornerstone was laid in a ceremony by King Otto and Queen Amalía on Christmas Day 1842. It took another 20 years to finish the building, using three different architects (François Boulanger, Theophil Hansen and Dimítrios Zézos) which may account for its slightly ungainly appearance. On 21 May 1862, it was formally dedicated to Evangelismós Theotókou (the Annunciation of the Virgin) by the king and queen. At 40 m (130 ft) long, 20 m (65 ft) wide and 24 m (80 ft) high, it is the largest church in Athens.

The cathedral is the official seat of the Bishop of Athens, and remains a popular city landmark that has been used for ceremonial events from the coronations of kings to the weddings and funerals of the rich and famous.

Inside, there are the tombs of two saints murdered by the Ottoman Turks: Agía Filothéi and Gregory V. The bones of Agía Filothéi, who died in 1589, are still visible in a silver reliquary. Her charitable works included the ransoming of Greek women enslaved in Turkish harems. Gregory V, Patriarch of Constantinople, was hanged and thrown into the Bosphorus in 1821. His body was rescued by Greek sailors and taken to Odessa. It was eventually returned to Athens by Black Sea (Pontic) Greeks 50 years later.

Agios Nikólaos Ragavás ⓮
Άγιος Νικόλαος ο Ραγκαβάς

Corner of Prytaneíou & Epichármou, Pláka. **Map** 6 E2. *Tel* *210 322 8193.* Ⓜ *Monastiráki.* ▦ *1, 2, 4, 5, 9, 10, 11, 12, 15, 18.* ◯ *8am–noon, 5–8pm daily.* ♿ *limited.*

This typical 11th-century Byzantine church, rebuilt in the 18th century and restored to some of its former glory in the late 1970s, incorporates marble columns and other remains of ancient buildings in its external walls. It is one of the favourite parish churches of Pláka, frequently used for colourful Greek weddings which spill out on to the street at weekends. It was the first church in Athens to have a bell after the War of Independence (1821), and the first to ring out after the city's liberation from the Germans on 12 October 1944.

Anafiótika ⓯
Αναφιώτικα

Map 6 D2. Ⓜ *Monastiráki.*

Nestling beneath the northern slopes of the Acropolis, this area is one of the oldest settlements in Athens. Today, its white-washed houses, cramped streets, lazy cats and pots of basil on windowsills

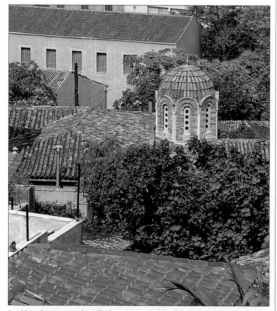

Looking down on Agios Nikólaos Ragavás church from Anafiótika

◁ View from Anafiótika towards the Ancient Agora

still give it the atmosphere of a typical Cycladic village. Its first residents were refugees from the Peloponnesian War *(see p30)*. By 1841, it had been colonized by workmen from Anáfi, in the Cyclades, who eventually gave the area its name. Part of the influx of island craftsmen, who helped to construct the new city following Independence, ignored an 1834 decree declaring the area an archaeological zone, and completed their houses overnight, installing their families by morning. By Ottoman law, this meant the authorities were powerless to knock the new houses down.

The area is bounded by two 17th-century churches: Agios Geórgios tou Vráchou to the east, which has a tiny courtyard filled with flowers, and Agios Symeón to the west, which contains a copy of a miraculous icon, originally brought from Anáfi.

Akrokérama, or terracotta sphinxes, on a roof in Anafiótika

Plateía Lysikrátous ⑯
Πλατεία Λυσικράτους

Lysikrátous, Sélley & Epimenídou, Pláka. **Map** 6 E2. 🚌 *1, 5, 9, 10.*

Situated in the east of the Pláka district, this square is named after the monument of Lysikrates that dominates it. Despite Lord Elgin's attempts to remove it to England, the elegant structure is the city's only intact choregic monument. These monuments were built to commemorate the victors at the annual choral and dramatic festival at the Theatre of Dionysos *(see p100).* They take their name from the rich sponsor *(choregos)* who produced the winning team. Built in 334 BC, this is the earliest known example where Corinthian

capitals are used externally. Six columns rise in a circle to a marble dome, decorated with an elegant finial of acanthus leaves which supported the winner's bronze trophy. It bears the inscription "Lysikrates of Kikynna, son of Lysitheides, was choregos; the tribe of Akamantis won the victory with a chorus of boys; Theon played the flute; Lysiades, an Athenian, trained the chorus; Evainetos was archon". The Athenians elected nine magistrates known as archons each year, and referred to the year by the name of one of them, the "eponymous archon." A frieze above this inscription, probably the theme of the winners' performance, depicts a battle between Dionysos, the god of theatre, and Tyrrhenian pirates. Surrounded by satyrs, the god transforms them into dolphins and their ship's mast into a sea serpent.

Capuchin friars converted the monument into a library. Grand tour travellers, such as Chateaubriand (1768–1848) and Byron *(see p149),* stayed at their convent, which was founded on the site in 1669.

The monument of Lysikrates, named after the *choregos* of the winning team of actors

Byron was inspired while staying there and wrote some of his poem, *Childe Harold,* sitting in the monument during his final visit to Athens in 1810.

Not far from the monument is the beautifully restored 11th-century Byzantine church of Agía Aikateríni (St Catherine). In 1767 it was given to the monastery of St Catherine of Mount Sinai. It was renovated, but in 1882 the monastery was forced to exchange it for land elsewhere and it became a local parish church.

ICON PAINTERS IN PLAKA

Pláka is littered with small artists' studios where icons are still painted using traditional methods. The best are situated just south of Plateía Mitropóleos, among the ecclesiastical shops selling vestments and liturgical objects, on Agías

Filothéis and Apóllonos streets. In some workshops, painters still use the Byzantine method of painting in egg-based tempera on specially treated wood. Customers of all religions can order the saint of their choice in a variety of different sizes. A medium-sized icon depicting a single saint, 25 cm by 15 cm (10 in by 6 in) and copied from a photograph, takes about one day to complete.

Ornate embroidery from Ioánnina, Epirus, on display in the Greek Folk Art Museum

Greek Folk Art Museum ⑰
Μουσείο Ελληνικής Λαϊκής Τέχνης

Kydathinaíon 17, Pláka. **Map** 6 E2.
Tel 210 321 3018. Ⓜ Acrópoli.
🚌 2, 4, 9, 10, 11, 12, 15.
🚋 1, 5. ○ 9am–3pm Tue–Sun.
● main public hols. 🈲
🚻 limited. 📷 www.melt.gr

Greek folk art, including some embroidery and costumes from the mainland and Aegean islands, fills five floors in this fascinating museum. The collection also covers the renaissance of decorative crafts in the 18th and 19th centuries, to reveal a rich heritage of traditional techniques in skills such as weaving, woodcarving and metalwork.

The ground floor has an extensive collection of fine embroidery work, showing a wide range of techniques.

Displays on the mezzanine floor include ceramics, metalwork and woodcarving. The ceramics range from architectural works, such as chimneys, to decorative or practical pieces such as household pots. Made from terracotta and faïence,

Decorative plate from Rhodes

they include both glazed and unglazed pieces. The metalwork on view includes examples made from copper, iron, bronze, steel and pewter. Many are covered with intricate decoration. The woodcarving products are equally impressive in their decoration, often being inlaid with mother-of-pearl, ivory or silver. The wood used varies widely, from walnut to fragrant cedar and wild olive. Also on the mezzanine are disguise costumes. Their origin is thought to be in the ancient Greek drama festivals in honour of Dionysos which made use of overtly expressive masks.

The puppets from the Karagkiózis theatre *(see p151)* amused the audience by satirizing topical political and social life.

The first floor houses popular paintings, including works by Theófilos Chatzimichaïl *(see p218)*. There is an excellent collection of silverware on the second floor of the museum, with displays of various ecclesiastical items such as chalices and crosses, as well as secular pieces, such as ornate weaponry and delicate jewellery. Examples of traditional weaving and stone-carving can be found on the third floor. The range of materials used for weaving includes lamb's wool, goat's hair, silk and plant fibres. Traditional costumes are also on show on this floor. The decorations and design, which are frequently elaborate, vary according to the geographical region. Costumes from many different areas are on display.

Jewish Museum of Greece ⑱
Εβραϊκό Μουσείο της Ελλάδας

Níkis 39, Sýntagma. **Map** 6 F2.
Tel 210 322 5582. Ⓜ Sýntagma.
🚌 1, 2, 4, 5, 9, 10, 11, 12, 15, 18.
○ 9am–2:30pm Mon–Fri, 10am–2pm Sun. ● main public hols & Jewish festivals. 🚻 📷 📷
www.jewishmuseum.gr

This small museum traces the history of Greece's Jewish communities which date back to the 3rd century BC. The exhibits present a revealing portrait of the Sephardic Jews, who fled Spain and Portugal in the 15th century, to settle throughout Greece in the religiously tolerant years of the Ottoman Empire.

Reconstruction of the ark from Pátra

Among the examples of traditional costumes and religious ceremonial instruments, one item of particular interest is the reconstruction of the *ehal*. This is the ark containing the Torah from the Pátra synagogue, which dates from the 1920s. It was rescued by Nikólaos Stavroulákis, founder of the museum, who has also written several books about the Greek Jews, on sale in the museum bookshop.

Moving displays of documentation record the German occupation of Greece during World War II when 87 per cent of the Jewish population here was wiped out. Over 45,000 Greeks from Thessaloníki alone were sent to Auschwitz and other concentration camps during a period of five months in 1943.

Hadrian's Arch, next to the Temple of Olympian Zeus

Temple of Olympian Zeus ⓭
Ναός του Ολυμπίου Διός

Corner of Amalías & Vasilíssis Olgas, Pláka. **Map** 6 F3. *Tel* 210 922 6330. Ⓜ Acrópoli. 🚌 2, 4, 11. ⏰ 8:30am–7pm daily (Nov–Mar: to 3pm). ⬤ main public hols. 🎫 (free Sun, Nov–Mar.) 📷 ♿ limited.

The temple of Olympian Zeus is the largest in Greece, exceeding even the Parthenon in size. Work began on this vast edifice in the 6th century BC, in the reign of the tyrant Peisistratos, who allegedly initiated the building work to gain public favour. Although there were several attempts over many years to finish the temple, it was not completed until 650 years later.

The Roman Emperor Hadrian dedicated the temple to Zeus Olympios during the Panhellenic festival of AD 132, on his second visit to Athens. He also set up a gold and ivory inlaid statue of the god inside the temple, a copy of the original by Pheidias at Olympia *(see pp170–72)*. Next to it he placed a huge statue of himself. Both these statues have since been lost.

Only 15 of the original 104 Corinthian columns remain, each 17 m (56 ft) high – but enough to give a sense of the enormous size of this temple, which would have been approximately 96 m (315 ft) long and 40 m (130 ft) wide.

Corinthian capitals were added to the simple Doric columns by a Roman architect in 174 BC.

The temple is situated next to Hadrian's Arch, built in AD 131. It was positioned deliberately to mark the boundary between the ancient city and the new Athens of Hadrian.

The Russian Church of the Holy Trinity

Russian Church of the Holy Trinity ⓴
Ρωσική εκκλησία Αγίας Τριάδας

Filellínon 21, Pláka. **Map** 6 F2. *Tel* 210 323 1090. Ⓜ Sýntagma. 🚌 1, 2, 4, 5, 9, 10, 11, 12, 15, 18. ⏰ 7:30–10am Mon–Fri, 7–11am Sat & Sun. ⬤ main public hols. ♿ limited.

Still in use by the Russian community, this was once the largest church in the city. Built in 1031 by the Lykodímou family (also called Nikodímou), it was ruined by an earthquake in 1701. In 1780 the Turkish governor, Hadji Ali Haseki, partly demolished the church to use its materials for the defensive wall that he built around the city. During the siege of the city in 1827, it received more damage from Greek shells fired from the Acropolis.

The church remained derelict until the Russian government restored it 20 years later. It was then reconsecrated as the Church of the Holy Trinity.

A large cruciform building, its most unusual feature is a wide dome, 10 m (33 ft) in diameter. Its interior was decorated by the Bavarian painter Ludwig Thiersch. The separate belltower also dates from the 19th century, its bell a gift from Tsar Alexander II.

The remaining Corinthian columns of the Temple of Olympian Zeus

The Tomb of the Unknown Soldier in Plateía Syntágmatos

Plateía Syntágmatos ㉑
Πλατεία Συντάγματος

Sýntagma. **Map** 6 F1. ⊞ *1, 5, 9, 10, 12, 15, 18.* Ⓜ *Sýntagma.*

This square (also known as Sýntagma Square) is home to the Greek parliament, in the Voulí building, and the Tomb of the Unknown Soldier, decorated with an evocative relief depicting a dying Greek hoplite warrior. Unveiled on 25 March 1932 (National Independence Day), the tomb is flanked by texts from Perikles's famous funeral oration. The other walls that enclose the square are covered in bronze shields celebrating military victories since 1821.

The National Guard (*évzones*) are on continuous patrol in front of the tomb, dressed in their famous uniform of kilt and pom-pom clogs. They are best seen at the changing of the guard, every Sunday at 11am.

National Gardens ㉒
Εθνικός Κήπος

Borders Vasilíssis Sofías, Iródou Attikoú, Vasilíssis Olgas & Vasilíssis Amalías, Sýntagma. **Map** 7 A1. Ⓜ *Sýntagma.* ⊞ *1, 3, 5, 7, 8, 10, 13, 18.* Ⓞ *dawn–dusk.* **Botanical Museum, zoo, cafés** Ⓞ *8am–7pm daily (Nov–Mar: to 3pm).*

Behind the Voulí parliament building, this 16-ha (40-acre) park, cherished by all Athenians and formerly known as the "Royal Gardens", was renamed the National Gardens by decree in 1923. Queen Amalía ordered the creation of the park in the 1840s; she even used the fledgling Greek navy to bring 15,000 seedlings from around the world. The gardens were landscaped by the Prussian horticulturalist Friedrich Schmidt, who travelled the world in search of rare plants.

Although the gardens have lost much of their original grandeur, they remain one of the most peaceful spots in the city. Shady paths meander past small squares, park benches and ponds filled with goldfish. A huge feral cat population is also resident in the park. Remains of Roman mosaics excavated in the park and an old aqueduct add atmosphere. Modern sculptures of writers, such as Dionýsios Solomós, Aristotélis Valaorítis and Jean Moreas, can be found throughout the park. There is also a small **Botanical Museum** to visit, a ramshackle zoo, and cafés. South of the park lies the **Záppeion**

exhibition hall, an impressive building in use today as a conference centre. It was donated by Evángelos and Konstantínos Záppas, cousins who made their fortunes in Romania. Built by Theophil Hansen, architect of the Athens Academy (*see p81*), between 1874 and 1888, it also has its own gardens. The elegant café next door to the Záppeion is a pleasant place to relax and refresh after a walk around these charming, peaceful gardens.

The tranquil National Gardens

Presidential Palace ㉓
Προεδρικό Μέγαρο

Iródou Attikoú, Sýntagma. **Map** 7 A2. Ⓜ *Sýntagma.* ⊞ *3, 7, 8, 13.* Ⓞ *to the public.*

This former royal palace was designed and built by Ernst Ziller (*see p81*) in c.1878. It was occupied by the Greek Royal Family from 1890 until the hasty departure of King Constantine in 1967. It is still guarded by the *évzones* whose barracks are at the top of the street. After the abolition of the monarchy, it became the official residence of the President of Greece and he still uses it today when hosting dignitaries. Its well-maintained gardens can just be seen through the iron railings.

Voulí parliament building in Plateía Syntágmatos, guarded by *évzones*

For hotels and restaurants in this region see pp264–7 and pp284–8

Kallimármaro Stadium 🄬

Καλλιμάρμαρο Στάδιο

Archimídous 16, Pagkráti.
Map 7 B3. **Tel** 210 752 2985.
🚇 3, 4, 11. ⬤ 8am–7pm daily
(Nov–Feb: to 5pm).

This huge marble structure set
in a small valley by Ardittós
Hill occupies the exact site
of the original Panathenaic
Stadium built by Lykourgos
in 330–329 BC. It was first
reconstructed for gladiatorial
contests during Hadrian's
reign (AD 117–138), then
rebuilt in white marble by the
wealthy Roman benefactor
Herodes Atticus for the Panathenaic Games in AD 144.
Neglected for many years, its
marble was gradually quarried
for use in new buildings.

In 1895 Geórgios Avéroff
gave four million drachmas in
gold for the restoration of the
stadium in time for the start
of the first modern Olympic
Games on 5 April 1896. Designed by Anastásios Metaxás,
the present structure is a faithful replica of Herodes Atticus's

Some of the ornate tombs in the First Cemetery of Athens

stadium, as described in the
Guide to Greece by Pausanias
(see p56). Built in white Pentelic marble, it is 204 m (669 ft)
long and 83 m (272 ft) wide
and seats up to 60,000. Between 1869 and 1879 architect
Ernst Ziller excavated the site.
His finds included a double-
headed statue of Apollo and
Dionysos, one of many used
to divide the stadium's running
track down its length. The statue is on show in the National
Archaeological Museum *(see
pp68–71)*. During the 2004
Olympics, Kallimármaro
hosted the marathon finish.

First Cemetery of Athens 🄬

Πρώτο Νεκροταφείο
Αθηνών

Entrance in Anapáfseos, Méts.
Map 7 A4. **Tel** 210 923 6118. 🚇 2,
4. ⬤ 7am–sunset daily. ♿ limited.

Athens' municipal cemetery,
which is not to be confused
with the Kerameikós, the
ancient cemetery *(see p88–9)*,
is a peaceful place, filled with
pine and olive trees and the
scent of incense burning at
the well-kept tombs.

Fine examples of 19th-
century funerary art range
from the flamboyance of some
of the marble mausoleums
to the simplicity of the Belle
Epoque *Kimoméni* or *Sleeping
Girl (see p42)*. Created by
Giannoúlis Chalepás, this
beautiful tomb is found to the
right of the main cemetery
avenue where many of
Greece's foremost families
are buried.

Among the notable 19th-
and 20th-century figures with
tombs here are Theódoros
Kolokotrónis *(see p80)*, British
philhellene historian George
Finlay (1799–1875), German
archaeologist Heinrich
Schliemann *(see p180)*, the
Nobel Prize-winning poet
Giórgos Seféris (1900–71)
and the actress and politician
Melína Merkoúri (1922–94).

In addition to the large
number of tombs for famous
people that are buried here,
the cemetery contains a
moving, single memorial to
the 40,000 Athenians who
perished through starvation
during World War II.

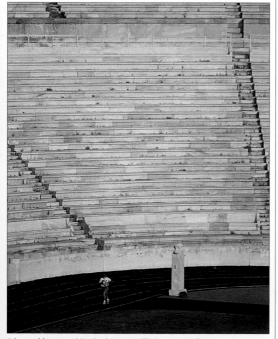

A lone athlete exercising in the vast Kallimármaro Stadium

SHOPPING IN ATHENS

Shopping in Athens offers many delights. There are street markets, quiet arcades, traditional arts and crafts shops, and designer fashion boutiques to rival Paris and New York. Most Athenians go to the triangle which is formed by Omónoia, Sýntagma and Monastiráki squares to buy everyday household items, clothes and shoes. For leather goods, bargain hunters should head for Mitropóleos, Ermoú, Aiólou and nearby streets. Along the smarter Stadíou and Panepistimíou, there are world-class jewellers and large clothing stores. The maze of arcades in the centre also houses smart leather-goods shops, booksellers, cafés and *ouzerís*. The most stylish shopping is to be found in Kolonáki where some of the city's most expensive art galleries and antique shops are clustered among the foreign and Greek designer outlets selling the latest fashions. Around Athinás, Monastiráki and Pláka there is an eclectic mix of aromatic herb and spice stores, religious retailers selling icons and church candlesticks, second-hand bookshops with rare posters and prints, and catering stores packed with household goods such as pots and pans.

Colourful
shadow
puppet

OPENING HOURS

Shops generally open from 8am–2pm or 9am–3pm, Monday to Saturday. On Tuesdays, Thursdays and Fridays there is late shopping from 5:30–9pm. The exceptions are department stores, tourist shops, supermarkets, florists and *zacharoplasteía* (cake shops) which often open for longer. Many shops close every year throughout August, the time when many Greeks take their holidays.

DEPARTMENT STORES AND SUPERMARKETS

The main stores are **Attica** and **Notos Galleries**. They stock a wide range of beauty

Notos Galleries, one of the largest department stores in Athens

products, clothes, gifts, and household goods. Attica is not as big as Notos Galleries but it is more exclusive. **Carrefour Marinopoulos** is a supermarket chain as is **AB Vassilópoulos**, which is located in the city centre. Situated close to the Olympic Station, **The Mall Athens** and **Golden Hall** are two of the city's largest covered shopping complexes, filled with outlets and restaurants. The Mall Athens also has several cinemas.

MARKETS

Athens is famous for its flea markets. **Monastiráki** market starts early in the morning every Sunday, when dealers set out their wears along Adrianoú and neighbouring streets. Hawkers of *salépi* (a drink made from sesame seeds) and gypsy clarinet players weave through the crowds.

The commercial tourist and antique shops of Pandrósou and Ifaístou, which collectively refer to themselves as "Monastiráki Flea Market", are open every day. Friday, Saturday and Sunday mornings are the best times to visit Plateía Avissynías. For food, the **Central Market** (Varvakios Agorá), which takes place every day except Sunday, is excellent, as are the popular *laïkés agorés* (street markets) selling fruit and vegetables, which occur daily in different areas. A centrally located *laïki agorá* is the one on **Xenokrátous** in Kolonáki, and takes place each Friday.

Greeks buy in bulk and stallholders will find it strange if you buy small quantities of less than half a kilo (1 lb) of a fruit or vegetable. In most cases you will be given a bag to serve yourself – do not be afraid to touch, smell and even taste.

ART AND ANTIQUES

As authentic Greek antiques become increasingly hard to find, many shops are forced

Shoppers in Adrianoú at the centre of Monastiráki Flea Market

to import furniture, glassware and porcelain from around the globe. Fortunately, however, there are still reasonable buys in old Greek jewellery, brass and copperware, carpets and embroidery, engravings and prints. Some can be found at **Antiqua**, just off Plateía Syntágmatos. Kolonáki is a prime area for small, exclusive stores around Sólonos, Skoufá and their side streets. Try the **Athens Design Centre** for bowls, platters and vases painted in bright colours, and **Serafetinídis** for excellent antique kilims and carpets. Kolonáki is also the art centre with well-established galleries selling paintings and prints. The **Zoumpouláki Gallery** specializes in art and antiques.

Monastiráki also has many antique shops. Look out for **Skoutis** – a store selling 19th-century jewellery and costumes. Try **Martínos** for beautiful, ornate icons and silverware and the **Athens Gallery**, which specializes in fine art and sculpture.

Antique jewellery and ornaments for sale in Monastiráki

TRADITIONAL FOLK ART AND CRAFTS

Affordable popular folk art, crafts and souvenirs are plentiful in Monastiráki and Pláka. There are innumerable stores filled with ecclesiastical ephemera and cramped icon painters' studios. Many shops stock elegant wood carvings, rustic painted wooden trays and richly coloured *flokáti* rugs (see p209). **Amorgós** is packed with fine wood

The famous shoemaker and poet Stávros Melissinós

carvings and puppets, as seen in the Karagkiózis theatre in Maroúsi (see p151). Among the more unusual shops offering unique services is **Melissinós Art** in Psyrrí. This self-styled poet sandal-maker makes a wide variety of sturdy sandals and leather goods and is famous for handing out translations of his work as a parting gift.

Hellenic Art & Design sells a variety of affordable everyday objects designed by artists living in Greece. Beautiful carved shepherds' crooks from Epirus as well as a large variety of finely crafted ceramics can be found at the fascinating **Centre of Hellenic Tradition**.

JEWELLERY

Athens is justly famed for its jewellery stores. There is no shortage in Monastiráki and Pláka, which are full of small shops selling gold and silver. **Maris**, in Pláka, has a large selection of good-value classic and contemporary jewellery. Exclusive jewellers, such as **Anagnostópoulos**, can be found in Voukour-estíou. Window displays also dazzle at the designer of world-class fame **Zolótas**, whose own pieces copy museum treasures. Another famous name is that of the designer Ilías Lalaoúnis, whose collections, inspired by Classical and other archaeological

sources, such as the gold of Mycenae, are eagerly sought by the rich and famous. At the **Ilías Lalaoúnis Jewellery Museum** over 3,000 of his designs are exhibited, and there is also a workshop where you can watch the craftsmen demonstrate the skills of the goldsmith and buy some of the jewellery.

MUSEUM COPIES

Museum shops provide some of the better buys in the city. Well-crafted, mostly tasteful copies draw on the wide range of ancient and Byzantine Greek art. They come in all shapes and sizes, from a life-size Classical statue to a simple Cycladic marble bowl. Many fine reproductions of the exhibits in the **Benáki Museum** (see pp78–9) can be bought from a collection of silverware, ceramics, embroidery and jewellery in the museum shop.

The **Museum of Cycladic Art** (see pp74–5) has some fine Tanagran and Cycladic figurines, bowls and vases for sale. There is a large selection of reproduction statues and pottery at the **National Archaeological Museum** (see pp68–71) souvenir shop. Apart from the museums, the Pláka shop **Orpheus** offers good quality marble and pottery copies of Classical Greek works as well as glittering Byzantine icons.

Display of reproduction red- and black-figure vases for sale

Períptero in Kolonáki selling English and Greek newspapers

BOOKS, NEWSPAPERS AND MAGAZINES

All the *periptera* (kiosks) in the city centre sell foreign newspapers and magazines. English publications include the weekly *Athens News* and the monthly magazine *Odyssey (see p313)*. Athens' wealth of bookshops includes many selling foreign language publications. For foreign books, go to the huge branches of **Eleftherou-dákis** or **Papasotiriou** on Panepistimíou, with specialist floors concentrating on English and Greek fiction, academic genres and children's books. Try **Politeia** for books on history, archaeology and classics, and **Libro** for fiction and non-fiction books and stationery.

One of the many designer stores to be found in Kolonáki

CLOTHES & ACCESSORIES

Although there are some famous Greek designers, such as **Parthénis** whose hallmark is black and white minimalism, most fashion stores concentrate on imported clothes. However, there are plenty of high-quality clothes: every

designer label can be found in the city's main fashion centre, Kolonáki. There are branches of such famous names as **Gucci**, **Ralph Lauren** and **Max Mara**. Such upmarket stores as **Sótris**, **Bettina**, **Free Shop** and **Stamatópoulos** typify the area's urban chic. For good-quality high-street fashion there is the Spanish chain **Zara**.

KITCHENWARE

Cavernous catering stores in the side streets around the Central Market specialize in classic Greek kitchen- and tableware. There are tiny white cups and copper saucepans used to make Greek coffee, long rolling pins for making filo pastry, and metal olive oil pourers. **Kotsóvolos** in Stadíou has a huge range of cheap and cheerful equipment, including traditional *kantária* (wine-measuring jugs), used to serve retsina in restaurants, round *tapsiá* (metal roasting dishes), and *saganákia* (two-handled pans) used for frying cheese. **Notos Home** in Omónoia stocks a good selection of kitchenware as well as furniture and other life-style products.

FOOD AND DRINK

There are myriad gourmet treats in Athens, including unusual *avgotáracho* (smoked cod roe preserved in beeswax), herbs and spices, cheeses and wines. The bakeries and *zacharoplasteía* (patisseries) are irresistible, brimming with delicious breads and biscuits, home-made ice cream and yoghurt. **Aristokratikón**, off Plateía Syntágmatos, sells luxurious chocolates and marzipan. One of Athens' best patisseries, **Afoi Asimakópouloi**, is full of decadent *mpaklavás* and crystallized fruits. **Loumidis**, near Omónoia, is the best place to buy freshly ground coffee.

The Central Market on Athinás is one of the most enticing places for food shopping. It is surrounded by stores packed with cheeses, olives, pistachio nuts, dried fruits and pulses such as *fáva* (yellow split peas) and *gígantes* (butter beans). You will find a range of herbs and spices at **Bahar**, in particular dried savory and sage, lemon verbena and saffron. **Green Farm** is one of a new generation of organic supermarkets.

Two enterprising *cáves* (wine merchants), **The Winebox** in Xenokratous and **Cellier** in Kriezótou, offer a broad range of wines and spirits from various small Greek wineries. **Vrettós** in Pláka has an attractive and varied display of own-label spirits and liqueurs.

A crammed Athenian kitchenware store

DIRECTORY

DEPARTMENT STORES AND SUPERMARKETS

AB Vassilópoulos
Spýrou Merkouri 38,
Pagkrati. **Map** 7 C2.
Tel 210 725 8913.
One of several branches.

Attica
Panepistimíou 9,
Sýntagma. **Map** 2 F5.
Tel 211 180 2600.

Carrefour Marinopoulos
Kanari 9, Kolonáki. **Map** 3 A5. *Tel 210 362 4907.*

Golden Hall
Kifisías 37a, Maroúsi.
Tel 210 680 3450.

Notos Galleries
Stadíou and Aiólou,
Omónoia. **Map** 2 E4.
Tel 210 324 5811.

The Mall Athens
Andrea Papandreou 35,
Maroúsi.
Tel 210 630 0000.

MARKETS

Central Market (Varvakios Agorá)
Athinás, Omónoia.
Map 1 D4.

Monastiráki
Adrianoú & Pandrósou,
Pláka. **Map** 6 E1.

Xenokrátous
Xenokrátous, Kolonáki.
Map 3 C5.

ART AND ANTIQUES

Antiqua
Amaliás 2, Sýntagma.
Map 4 F2.
Tel 210 323 2220.

Athens Design Centre
Valaoritou 4, Kolonáki.
Map 2 F5.
Tel 210 361 0194.

Athens Gallery
Pandrósou 14,
Pláka. **Map** 6 D1.
Tel 210 324 6942.

Martínos
Pandrósou 50, Pláka.
Map 6 D1.
Tel 210 321 3110.

Serafetinídis
Pat. Ioakeim 21, Kolonáki.
Map 3 B5.
Tel 210 721 4186.

Skoutis
Dimokritou 10,
Kolonáki. **Map** 3 A5.
Tel 210 361 3557.

Zoumpouláki Gallery
Plateía Kolonakiou 20,
Kolonáki. **Map** 3 A5.
Tel 210 360 8278.

TRADITIONAL FOLK ART AND CRAFTS

Amorgós
Kódrou 3, Pláka. **Map** 6 E1.
Tel 210 324 3836.

Centre of Hellenic Tradition
Mitropóleos 59 (Arcade) –
Pandrósou 36, Monastiráki.
Map 6 D1.
Tel 210 321 3023.

Hellenic Art & Design
Chairefontos 10, Pláka.
Map 6 E2.
Tel 210 322 3064.

Melissinós Art
Ag. Theklas 2, Psyrrí.
Map 2 D5.
Tel 210 321 9247.

JEWELLERY

Anagnostópoulos
Voukourestíou 8, Kolonáki.
Map 2 F5.
Tel 210 360 4426.

Ilías Lalaoúnis Jewellery Museum
Karyatidon & P. Kallisperi
12, Akropoli. **Map** 6 D3.
Tel 210 922 1044.

Márls
Ifaistou 5, Pláka.
Map 6 D1.
Tel 210 321 9082.

Zolótas
Stadiou 9 & Kolokotroni,
Kolonáki. **Map** 2 F5.
Tel 210 322 1222.

MUSEUM COPIES

Orpheus
Pandrósou 28B, Pláka.
Map 6 D1.
Tel 210 324 5034.

BOOKS, NEWSPAPERS AND MAGAZINES

Eleftheroudákis
Panepistimíou 11,
Kolonáki. **Map** 2 F5.
Tel 210 325 8440.

Libro
Pat. Ioakeim 8, Kolonáki.
Map 3 B5.
Tel 210 724 7116.

Papasotiriou
Panepistimíou 37,
Kolonáki. **Map** 2 E4.
Tel 210 574 0888.

Politeia
Asklipiou 1–3 &
Akadímias, Pefkakia.
Map 2 F4.
Tel 210 360 0235.

CLOTHES & ACCESSORIES

Bettina
Anagnostopoúlou 29,
Kolonáki. **Map** 3 A5.
Tel 210 339 2094.

Free Shop
Voukourestiou 50,
Kolonáki.
Map 3 A5.
Tel 210 364 1308.

Gucci
Tsakálof 27, Kolonáki.
Map 3 A5.
Tel 210 360 2519.

Max Mara
Akadímias 14, Kolonáki.
Map 3 A5.
Tel 210 360 2142.

Parthénis
Dimokrítou 20, Kolonáki.
Map 3 A5.
Tel 210 363 3158.

Ralph Lauren
Voukourestíou 11,
Kolonáki. **Map** 3 A5.
Tel 210 361 7122.

Sótris
Anagnostopoúlou 30,
Kolonáki. **Map** 3 A4.
Tel 210 363 9281.
One of two branches.

Stamatópoulos
Pat. Ioakeim 17, Kolonáki.
Map 3 B5.
Tel 210 323 6966.

Zara
Skoufa 22, Kolonáki.
Map 3 A5.
Tel 210 363 6340.
One of several branches.

KITCHENWARE

Kotsóvolos
Stadíou and
Dragatsaniou. **Map** 2 E4.
Tel 210 289 9600.

Notos Home
Plateía Kotzia, Omónoia.
Map 2 D4.
Tel 210 374 3000.

FOOD & DRINK

Afoi Asimakópouloi
Chariláou Trikoúpi 82,
Exárcheia.
Map 3 A3.
Tel 210 361 0092.

Aristokratikón
Voulis 7, Sýntagma.
Map 2 E5.
Tel 210 322 0546.

Bahar
Evripídou 31, Omónoia.
Map 2 D4.
Tel 210 321 7225.

Cellier
Kriezótou 1, Kolonáki.
Map 3 A5.
Tel 210 361 0040.

Green Farm
Dimokrítou 13, Kolonáki.
Map 3 A5.
Tel 210 361 4001.

Loumidis
Aiolou 106, Omónoia.
Map 2 E4.
Tel 210 321 1461.

The Winebox
Xenokrátous 25,
Kolonáki.
Map 3 C5.
Tel 210 725 4710.

Vrettós
Kydathinaíon 41, Pláka.
Map 6 E2.
Tel 210 323 2110.

ENTERTAINMENT IN ATHENS

Athens excels in the sheer variety of its open-air summer entertainment. Visitors can go to outdoor showings of the latest film releases, spend lazy evenings in garden bars with the heady aroma of jasmine, or attend a concert in the atmospheric setting of the Herodes Atticus Theatre, which sits beneath the Acropolis.

The Mousikís Mégaron Concert Hall has given the city a first-class classical concert venue and draws some of the best names in the music world. For most Athenians,

Athens listings magazine

however, entertainment means late-night dining in tavernas, followed by bar- and club-hopping until the early hours. There is also an enormous number of large discotheques, music halls and intimate *rempétika* clubs, playing traditional Greek music, throughout Athens. Whatever your musical taste, there is something for everyone in this lively city. Sports and outdoor facilities are also widely available, in particular watersports, which are within easy reach of Athens along the Attic coast.

LISTINGS MAGAZINES

The most comprehensive Greek weekly listings magazine is *Athinorama*, which is published on Thursdays. It lists events and concerts, and the latest bars and clubs. The English language publications such as the weekly *Athens News* and the bimonthly *Odyssey* also have listings sections. All publications are generally available at kiosks.

BOOKING TICKETS

Although it is necessary to book tickets in advance for the summer Athens Festival *(see p46)* and for concerts at the Mégaron Concert Hall, most theatres and music clubs sell tickets at the door on the day of the performance. However,

there is also a central ticket office (Ticket Services, Panepistimiou 39, Tel: 210 723 4567), open daily from 10am to 4pm, where tickets can be purchased for the various events of the summer Athens Festival *(see p46)*.

THEATRE AND DANCE

There are many fine theatres scattered around the city centre, often hidden in converted Neo-Classical mansion houses or arcades. Numerous popular revues that combine an entertaining mixture of contemporary political satire and comedy are regularly performed in theatres such as the **Lampéti**.

Some excellent productions of 19th-century Greek and European plays are staged at the **National Theatre**. Playhouses such as the

Ibsen at the Evros Theatre, Psyrrí

Evros, **Athinón**, **Alfa** and **Vrettánia** also mount Greek-language productions of works by well-known 19th– and 20th-century playwrights such as Ibsen.

The major classical venues, including the National Theatre, put on contemporary dance and ballet as well as plays and operas. The **Dóra Strátou Dance Theatre** on Filopáppos Hill performs traditional regional Greek dancing nightly between May and September.

The Dóra Strátou Dance Theatre performing traditional Greek dancing outdoors

The doorway to the outdoor Dexamení cinema

CINEMA

Athenians love going to the cinema, especially from late May to September when the warm weather means that local open-air cinemas are open. All foreign-language films are subtitled, with the exception of children's films which are usually dubbed. The last showing is always at 11pm, which makes it possible to dine before seeing a movie.

The city centre has several excellent, large-screen cinemas showing the latest international releases. **Ideál**, **Elly** and **Astor Nescafé** are large, comfortable, indoor cinemas equipped with Dolby Stereo sound systems. The **Attikon Cinemax Class** and **Astı** tend to show a comprehensive range of art-house and cult movies.

Athenians like to hang out at the bars and tavernas next to open-air cinemas, such as **Dexamení** in Kolonáki, the **Riviéra** in Exarcheía or **Ciné Paris** in Pláka, before catching the last performance. The acoustics are not always perfect but the relaxed atmosphere, in the evening warmth, with street noises, typically cats and cars, permeating the soundtrack, is an unforgettable experience. These cinemas seem more like clubs, with tables beside the seats for drinks and snacks. The outdoor

Thiseíon cinema comes with the added attraction of a stunning view of the Acropolis.

CLASSICAL MUSIC

The annual Athens Festival, held throughout the summer, attracts the major international ballet and opera companies, orchestras and theatrical troupes to the open-air **Herodes Atticus Theatre**, which seats 5,000 people, and to other venues around the city. This has always been the premier event of the classical music calendar. In 1991, the **Mousikís Mégaron Concert Hall** was inaugurated, providing a year-round venue for opera, ballet and classical music performances. This majestic marble building contains two recital halls with superlative acoustics, an exhibition space, a shop and a restaurant. The Olympia Theatre is home to the **Lyrikí Skiní** (National Opera), and stages excellent ballet productions as well as opera.

Details of concerts held at cultural centres such as the **French Institute** can be found in listings magazines and newspapers.

TRADITIONAL GREEK MUSIC

The lively Greek music scene thrives in a variety of venues throughout central Athens. The large music halls of Syngróu advertise on omnipresent billboards around the city. **Posidonio**, **Athinón Arena** and **Stavros tou Notou** attract the top stars and their loyal fans. The more old-fashioned venues in Pláka, such as **Zoom** and **Mostroú**, offer more intimate surroundings for the haunting sounds of *rempétika* music, which draws its inspiration and defiant stance from the lives of the urban poor. **Rempétiki Istoría** and **Taksími** are two of the places at which you can hear genuine bouzouki (Greek mandolin) music. Both bars have well-known bouzouki players, and reasonable prices.

Accordionist in Plateía Kolonakíou

Mpoémissa attracts a much younger crowd, more concerned with dancing the night away than with the authenticity of the music.

A classical concert at the Herodes Atticus Theatre

ROCK AND JAZZ MUSIC

International acts usually perform at large stadiums or the open-air **Lykavittós Theatre** as part of the annual Athens Festival. The **Gagarin 205 Live Music Space**, a successfully converted cinema, also attracts the very cream of foreign and Greek rock bands. Greek bands can be enjoyed at the **An Club**, which offers patrons the intriguing prospect of Greek rock-and-roll dinner dancing.

The city's premier jazz venue is the **Half Note Jazz Club**. The club is housed in a former stonemason's workshop and is located opposite the First Cemetery. The Half Note is a cosy and popular venue, presenting the best of foreign contemporary jazz.

Alternatively, **Six d.o.g.s** is a cultural centre featuring a project space, a bar, a café and an area for live music and theatrical performances by young Greek artists.

Live music in one of the city's popular rock clubs

NIGHTCLUBS

Athens is a hive of bars and nightclubs that come and go at an alarming rate. The up-and-coming areas of town are Gazi and, closer to the centre of town, Psyrrí, where there are a number of trend-setting bar-restaurants: the best, such as **Gazarte** and **Hoxton**, also have dance floors. Large clubs such as **B.e.d. Club** and **Villa Mercédes** offer special DJ nights and are good spots for dinner or for clubbing late at night.

Marathon runner in Athens retracing the path of his ancestors

SPORT

Most taxi drivers will reel off their favourite football team to passengers before they have had a chance to mention their destination. Such is the Athenian passion for football that the two main rival teams, Panathenaïkós and Olympiakós, are always the subject of fervent debate. Each team is backed by a consortium of private companies, each of which also owns a basketball team of the same name. Football matches are played every Wednesday and Sunday during the September to May season. The basketball teams play weekly, in what is the latest popular national sport.

Lack of adequate parkland within the city means that joggers are a rare sight, despite the annual **Athens Open Marathon** every October. The athletes run from Marathon to the Kallimármaro Stadium in the centre of Athens (see p113). The **Olympiakó Stadium** in Maroúsi seats 80,000 and was built in 1982. Its glass roof was designed by Spanish architect Santiago Calatrava for the 2004 Olympic Games. The Panathenaïkós football team are based here. It has excellent facilities for all sports and includes an indoor sports hall, swimming pools and tennis courts in its 100 ha (250 acres) of grounds. The **Karaïskáki Stadium** in Néo Fáliro is the home of the Olympiakós football team. There are also facilities there for many other sports including

volleyball and basketball. Another famous event is the **Acropolis Rally**, a celebration of vintage cars, held around the Acropolis every spring. It attracts some 50 to 100 cars.

Outside the city centre, there are more facilities on offer, including bowling at the **Bowling Centre of Piraeus** and golf at the fine 18-hole **Glyfáda Golf Course**, which is located close to the airport. Tennis courts are available for hire at various places, including the **Politia Tennis Club**.

Proximity to the Attic coast means that a large variety of watersports is on offer. Windsurfing and water-skiing are widely available on most beaches. **Naftikos Omilos Vouliagmenis** offers water-skiing lessons for all ages and levels. One of the most renowned scuba-diving clubs is the **Aegean Dive Centre**, which has lessons for all levels.

Basketball, an increasingly popular national sport among the Greeks

DIRECTORY

THEATRE AND DANCE

Alfa
Patisíon 37 & Stournári,
Exárcheia. **Map** 2 E2.
Tel 210 523 8742.

Athinón
Voukourestíou 10,
Kolonáki. **Map** 2 E5.
Tel 210 331 2343.

Dóra Strátou Dance Theatre
Filopáppou Hill,
Filopáppou.
Map 5 B4.
Tel 210 921 4650.

Lampéti
Leof Alexándras 106,
Exárcheia. **Map** 4 D2.
Tel 210 645 7086.

National Theatre
Agíou Konstantínou 22,
Omónoia.
Map 1 D3.
Tel 210 528 8173.

Vrettánia
Panepistimíou 7,
Sýntagma. **Map** 2 E4.
Tel 210 322 1579.

CINEMA

Asti
Korai 4, Exárcheia.
Map 2 E4.
Tel 210 322 1925.

Astor Nescafé
Stadiou 28,
Kolonáki. **Map** 2 E5.
Tel 210 323 1297.

Attikon Cinemax Class
Stadiou 19, Kolonáki.
Map 2 E5.
Tel 210 322 8821.

Cine Paris
Kydathinaion 22, Pláka.
Map 6 E2.
Tel 210 322 2071.

Dexamení
Plateía Dexamenís,
Dexamení. **Map** 3 B5.
Tel 210 362 3942.

Elly
Akadimias 64,
Omónoia. **Map** 2 E3.
Tel 210 363 2789.

Ideál
Panepistimíou 46,
Omónoia. **Map** 2 E4.
Tel 210 382 6720.

Riviéra
Valtetsiou 46,
Exárcheia. **Map** 2 F3.
Tel 210 384 4827.

Thiseíon
Apostólou Pávlou 7,
Thiseío. **Map** 5 B2.
Tel 210 347 0980.

Village Cinemas
Tel 801 100 9191.
www.villagecinemas.gr

CLASSICAL MUSIC

French Institute
Sína 31, Kolonáki.
Map 3 A4.
Tel 210 339 8600.

Herodes Atticus Theatre
Dionysíou Areopagítou,
Acropolis. **Map** 6 C2.
Tel 210 324 1807.

Lyrikí Skiní, Olympia Theatre
Akadimías 59,
Omónoia. **Map** 2 F4.
Tel 210 361 2461.

Mousikís Mégaron Concert Hall
V Sofías & Kókkali,
Stégi Patrídos. **Map** 4 E4.
Tel 210 728 2333.

TRADITIONAL GREEK MUSIC

Athinón Arena
Peiraios 166, Gazi.
Map 1 A5.
Tel 210 347 1111.

Mostroú
Mnisikléous 22,
Pláka. **Map** 6 D1.
Tel 210 322 5558.

Mpoémissa
Solomoú 13–15,
Exárcheia. **Map** 2 D2.
Tel 210 383 8803.

Posidonio
Poseidónos 18, Ellinikó.
Tel 210 894 1033.

Rempétiki Istoría
Ippokrátous 181,
Neápoli.
Map 3 C2.
Tel 210 642 4937.

Stavros tou Notou
Frantzi & Thirápou 37,
Néos Kósmos.
Tel 210 922 6975.

Taksími
C. Trikoúpi & Isávron 29,
Neápoli.
Map 3 A2.
Tel 210 363 9919.

Zoom
Kydathinaíon 39,
Pláka. **Map** 6 E2.
Tel 210 322 5920.

ROCK, JAZZ AND ETHNIC MUSIC

An Club
Solomoú 13–15,
Exárcheia.
Map 2 E2.
Tel 210 330 5056.

Gagarin 205 Live Music Space
Liosíon 205,
Attiki.
Map 1 C1.
Tel 210 854 7600.

Half Note Jazz Club
Trivonianoú 17,
Mets.
Map 6 F4.
Tel 210 921 3310.

Lykavittós Theatre
Lykavittós Hill.
Map 3 B4.
Tel 210 722 7209.

Six d.o.g.s
Avramiotou 6–8,
Monastiráki.
Map 2 D5.
Tel 210 321 0510.

NIGHTCLUBS

B.e.d Club
Poseidonos 58, Glyfáda.
Tel 210 894 1620.

Gazarte
Voutadon 32–34, Gazi.
Map 1 A5.
Tel 210 346 0347.

Hoxton
Voutádon 42, Gazi.
Map 1 A5.
Tel 210 341 3395.

Villa Mercédes
Andronikou and
Tzaféri 11, Rouf.
Tel 210 342 2606.

SPORT

Aegean Dive Centre
Zamanou 53 &
Pandhoras, Glyfáda.
Tel 210 894 5409.
www.adc.gr

Bowling Centre of Piraeus
Profitis Ilías,
Kastélla.
Tel 210 412 7077.

Glyfáda Golf Course
Panopis 15 & Kypros,
Glyfáda.
Tel 210 894 6459.

Karaïskáki Stadium
Néo Fáliro.
Tel 210 481 2736.

Naftikos Omilos Vouliagmenis
Lemos Vouliagmenis.
Tel 210 896 2416.
www.nov.gr

Olympiakó Stadium
Leof Kifisías 37, Maroúsi.
Tel 210 683 4060.

Politia Tennis Club
Aristotelous 18, Politia.
Tel 210 620 0003.
www.politiatennisclub.gr

ATHENS STREET FINDER

Map references given for sights in Athens refer to the maps on the following pages. References are also given for Athens hotels *(see pp264–7)*, Athens restaurants *(see pp284–8)* and for useful addresses in the *Survival Guide* section *(see pp302–27)*. The first figure in the reference tells you which Street Finder map to turn to, and the letter and number refer to the grid reference. The map below shows the area of Athens covered by the eight Street Finder maps (the map numbers are shown in black). The symbols used for sights and features are listed in the key below.

SCALE OF KEY

0 kilometres   1

0 miles   0.5

KEY

Major sight	Funicular	Post office
Place of interest	Taxi rank	Railway line
Other sight	Parking	Pedestrianized street
M Metro station	Tourist information	
Railway station	Hospital with casualty unit	
Main coach or bus station	Police station	SCALE OF MAP PAGES
Trolleybus terminus	Church	0 metres 250
Tram stop	Synagogue	0 yards 250

Street Finder Index

Name	Ref
ros Konstanto-poulou	8 F4
saiou	7 C4
savron	3 A2
siodou	7 B2
vykou	7 B2

J

lewish Museum	6 F2

K

Kairi	2 D5
Kaisareias	4 F3
Kaisareias	8 E5
Kakourgo Dikeiou	2 D5
Kalaischrou	6 E3
Kalamida	2 D5
Kalamiotou	2 E5
Kalchantos	8 F4
Kalkon	6 D5
Kallergi	1 C3
Kallidromiou	2 F1
Kalliga	3 B1
Kallikratous	3 A3
Kallimachou	7 C2
allimarmaro Stadium	7 B3
Kallirois	5 A4
Kallisperi	6 D3
Kallisthenous	5 A3
Kalogrioni	6 D1
altezon	1 A2
alvou	3 B1
alypsous	1 A4
Kamaterou	2 D2
anari	3 A5
anari	8 D5
anellopoulos Museum	6 D2
aningos,	2 E3
aningos, Plateia	2 E3
apetan Petroutsou	4 F2
aplanon	2 F4
apnikarea	6 E1
apnikareas	6 D1
apno	2 D2
apodistriou	2 E2
apsali	3 B5
arachristos	4 D4
araiskaki	1 C5
araiskaki, Plateia	1 C3
aratza	5 C4
area	6 F4
arer	6 E4
aritsi, Plateia	2 E5
arneadou	3 C5
arodistriou	5 A5
arolou	1 C3
arori	2 D5
artali	4 F4
aryatidon	6 D3
arydi	5 A1
assianis	3 C2
atsantoni	3 A1
atsikogianni	1 C5
avalotti	6 D3
edrinou	4 E1
ekropos	6 E2
elsou	6 F5
ennenty	8 E3
erameikos	1 B5
erameikou	1 A4
erameon	1 B2
erasountos	4 F4
eratsiniou	1 A3
erkinis	4 E2
afas	2 E3
Ikis	1 A1
monos	1 A2
ou Petzoglou	8 E2
outacheias	8 E4
Kirras	4 F1
Kisamou	8 E5
Kitsiki Nikolaou, Plateia	3 C4
Klada	6 D5
Kladou	6 D1
Klafthmonos, Plateia	2 E4
Kleanthi	7 B2
Kleious	1 A1
Kleisouras	8 E1
Kleisovis	2 E3
Kleisthenous	2 D4
Kleitomachou	7 A3
Kleitou	2 E4
Kleomenous	3 B4
Kleomvrotou	1 A4
Klepsydras	6 D2
Kodratou	1 B2
Kodrika	2 D5
Kodrou	6 E1
Koimiseos Theotokou	8 F3
Kokkali	4 E4
Kokkini	6 E4
Kolchidos	4 F1
Koletti	2 F3
Kolofontos	8 D2
Kolokotroni	2 E5
Kolokynthous	1 B3
Kolonakiou, Pl	3 B5
Kolonou	1 B3
Komninon	3 B2
Koniari	4 D3
Kononos	8 D2
Konstantinou Lourou	4 E4
Konstantinou-poleos, Leof	1 A3
Kontogoni	3 C1
Kontoliou	8 D5
Korai	2 E4
Korai	7 C5
Kordeliou	8 E5
Korinis	1 C4
Korinthou	1 A1
Kornarou	6 E1
Koromila	5 C5
Koronaiou	4 F5
Koroneias	4 E2
Koronis	3 A3
Korytsas	8 F5
Koryzi	6 E4
Kosma Aitolou	4 D2
Kosma Melodou	3 B3
Kotopouli, M	2 D3
Kotyaiou	4 E3
Kotzia, Plateia	2 D4
Koukakiou, Plateia	5 C4
Kouma	3 A1
Koumanoudi	3 B1
Koumoundourou	2 D3
Koumpari	7 A1
Kountourioti, Plateia	5 B5
Kountouriotou	2 F2
Koutsikari	4 E1
Kraterou	4 F5
Kraterou	8 F1
Kratinou	2 D4
Kriezi	1 C5
Kriezotou	2 F5
Krinis	8 F5
Krisila	7 B4
Kritis	1 C1
Kritonos	8 D1
Kropias	1 B1
Krousovou	8 E1
Ktisiou	7 C2
Ktisiviou	7 B3
Kydantidon	5 A3
Kydathinaion	6 E2
Kymaion	5 A1
Kynaigeirou	1 B2
Kyniskas	7 A4
Kyprou, Leof	8 D5
Kyriazopoulos Folk Ceramic Museum	6 D1
Kyrillou Loukareos	4 D2
Kyrinis	3 C2
Kyvellis	2 E1

L

Name	Ref
Lachitos	4 E4
Laertou	8 E4
Lakedaimonos	4 F1
Lamachou	6 F2
Lamias	4 F2
Lampardi	3 C2
Lampelet	1 B1
Lamprou Katsoni	3 C2
Lampsakou	4 E4
Laodikeias	4 F5
Larissa	1 B1
Larissis	1 B1
Larisis, Plateia	1 C1
Laskareos	3 B2
Laspa	3 B2
Lassani	6 D5
Lavragka	1 B2
Lazaion	5 C4
Lefkippou	8 D4
Lefkotheas	8 D4
Lekka	2 E5
Lempesi	6 E3
Lenorman	1 A1
Leocharous	2 E5
Leokoriou	1 C5
Leonida Drossi	3 C1
Leonidou	1 A4
Leonnatou	1 B3
Lepeniotou	1 C5
Leventi	3 B5
Levidou	8 E2
Limpona	2 D5
Liosion	1 C1
Litous	8 F5
Livini	4 D2
Livvis	4 F5
Lofos Ardittou	7 A3
Lofos Finopoulou	3 B1
Lomvardou	3 B1
Longinou	6 F4
Lontou	2 F3
Louizis Riankour	4 F2
Louka	1 C5
Loukianou	3 B5
Lydias	8 F3
Lykavittos Hill	3 B3
Lykavittou	3 A5
Lykavittou, Plateia	3 A4
Lykeiou	7 B1
Lykofronos	7 B5
Lykomidon	5 B1
Lykourgou	2 D4
Lysikratous	6 E2
Lysikratous, Pl	6 E2
Lysimachias	6 D5
Lysimachou	7 C5
Lysippou	7 B3

M

Madritis, Plateia	7 D1
Maiandrou	4 E5
Maiandroupoleos	4 F1
Mainemenis	4 F1
Makedonias	2 D1
Makedonon	4 E3
Makri	6 E3
Makris	8 E5
Makrygianni	6 E3
Makrynitsas	4 F1
Malamou	6 F4
Mamouri	1 C1
Manis	2 F3
Manoliasis	8 E2
Manou	8 D3
Mantineias	8 F5
Mantzakou	3 A2
Mantzarou	3 A4
Marasli	3 C5
Marathonos	1 B3
Marikas Iliadi	4 E3
Marinou Charvouri	6 F4
Markidi	4 F2
Markou Evgenikou	3 C2
Markou Mousourou	7 A3
Markou Mpotsari	5 C4
Marni	1 C3
Massalias	2 F4
Matrozou	5 B5
Mavili, Plateia	4 E3
Mavrikiou	3 B2
Mavrokordatou	2 E3
Mavrokordatou, Plateia	2 D2
Mavromataion	2 E1
Mavromichali	2 F3
Megalou Alexandrou	1 A4
Megalou Spilaiou	4 E2
Meintani	5 C5
Melanthiou	2 D5
Meleagrou	7 B2
Melidoni	1 B5
Melissou	7 C4
Menaichmou	6 E4
Menandrou	1 C4
Menedimou	1 B1
Menekratous	6 F5
Menonos	6 F5
Merlie Oktaviou	3 A3
Merlin	3 A5
Mesogeion	8 D3
Mesolongiou	2 F3
Mesolongiou	8 E5
Mesolongiou, Plateia	8 D3
Messapiou	5 A4
Metagenous	6 E5
Metaxourgeiou, Plateia	1 B3
Meteoron	7 A5
Methonis	2 F2
Metonos	1 C4
Metsovou	2 F1
Mexi Ventiri	4 D5
Miaouli	2 D5
Michail Karaoli	8 F2
Michail Mela	4 D3
Michail Psellou	3 A1
Michail Voda	2 D1
Michalakopoulou	4 E5
Mikras Asias	4 F4
Mileon	4 F2
Milioni	3 A5
Miltiadou	2 D5
Mimnermou	7 B2
Miniati	7 A3
Mirtsiefsky	5 A4
Misaraliotou	6 D3
Misountos	8 E3
Misthou	8 D2
Mitromara	6 D3
Mitroou	6 D1
Mitropoleos	6 D1
Mitropoleos, Plateia	6 E1
Mitropoli	6 E1
Mitsaion	6 D3
Mnisikleous	6 D1
Momferratou	3 B1
Monastiraki	2 D5
Monastirakiou, Plateia	2 D5
Monastiriou	1 A3

MAINLAND GREECE

Mainland Greece at a Glance

The unique attraction of the mainland lies in the
wealth of ancient remains, set in landscapes of great
natural beauty. Classical sites are most notable in the
south, around Athens, and the coasts of Attica and
the Peloponnese, while Macedonian remains can be
seen in the temperate northeast. Byzantine
monasteries and churches
are found all over the
country, particularly on the
holy peninsula of Mount
Athos which is governed
by its 20 monasteries.

The Metéora area
(see pp216–17) *combines
extraordinary sandstone
pinnacles with some of the
first medieval monasteries
in Greece, perched on the
rocky peaks.*

NORTHERN GREECE
(see pp232–57)

Delphi (see
pp228–31) *is
home to the
evocative ruins
of an ancient
religious complex
and theatre
situated on
Mount Parnassus.*

CENTRAL AND WESTERN GREE
(see pp202–31)

Ancient Olympia (see
pp170–73) *was, from
the 8th century BC to
the 4th century AD, the
site of the Panhellenic
Games, forerunner of
today's Olympics. One
of the best-preserved
buildings is the Temple
of Hera* (left), *dating
from around the 6th
century BC.*

THE PELOPONNESE
(see pp158–201)

Mystrás (see pp192–3) *is one of
the best-preserved Byzantine
complexes in Greece, exemplified
by this church of Agía Sofía. It
is a medieval city, and held out
against the Ottomans
until 1460.*

0 kilometres   50

0 miles   25

The Máni peninsula
*(see pp194–9) is dotted
with tower houses.*

◁ **Moní Spiliótissa, near the Zagorian village of Arísti in Western Greece**

Thessaloníki's *Archaeological Museum (see pp246–7) has spectacular gold finds from the tombs of the Macedonian kings, and this bronze head from around AD 235 of Alexander Severus.*

Osios Loúkas *monastery (see pp222–3) is beautifully set in a flowering orchard. The octagonal design of the 11th-century dome was widely copied. Its plain exterior conceals the gold ground mosaics inside.*

Mount Athos has, since 1060, been entirely occupied by monks *(see pp252–4).*

Ancient Corinth (see pp162–6), *capital of the Roman province of Achaia, was renowned for its luxury and elegance, exemplified by this ornate capital.*

The Monastery of Dafní (see pp152–3) *is a famous work of Byzantine architecture with outstanding medieval mosaics decorating the interior of the church.*

AROUND ATHENS *(see pp140–57)*

Athens

Mycenae (see pp178–80), *one of Greece's oldest sites, dates back to 1550 BC; the Lion Gate was the entrance to the citadel. Mycenae was possibly ruled by Agamemnon.*

Epidaurus *(see pp184–5)* has one of the best-preserved theatres In Greece.

Monemvasía (see pp186–8) *means "one way in", a reference to the strategic advantage of this heavily fortified Byzantine seaport. Its former role as the main port of Byzantine Greece is reflected in the buildings of the old town.*

AROUND ATHENS

ATTICA

T*he area around Athens, known as Attica, is the spiritual heart-land of ancient and modern Greece. Its archaeological sites have attracted generations of scholars and plunderers alike, and its mountains and coastline have provided important refuge in times of strife. Today the golden beaches along the eastern coast attract those simply wishing to escape the bustle of modern Athens.*

The land of Attica was the basis of Athenian wealth. The fine marble from the quarries on Mount Ymittós and Mount Pentéli was used for the temples and sculptures of ancient Athens. The silver from Lávrio financed their construction, and the produce from the local agricultural areas fed the population.

Waiting for a ferry in Piraeus

Attica has witnessed many significant historical events. The plain of Marathon was the site of one of the greatest battles in Greek history. Piraeus, now Greece's largest and busiest port, was also the port of ancient Athens. The Classical temples at less-known archaeological sites around the countryside, such as Eleusis, Ramnoús and Brauron, offer a rural retreat from the overcrowding and pollution of the city. At Soúnio, the majestic, well-preserved Temple of Poseidon on the cape has been a beacon for mariners for centuries.

The Byzantine era also left a great legacy of fine architecture to the region. Two of the best examples of this are the imposing monasteries of Dafní and Kaisarianí, with their ornate mosaics and elegant stonework.

South of Athens, the summer heat of the Attic plain is ideal for growing crops. Grapes are a speciality in the Mesógeia (Midland) region, which produces some of the finest retsina in the country. North of Athens, the pine-forested Mount Párnitha provides interesting walks and offers superb views over the city from the summit.

The peaceful ruins of the Parthenon of the Bear Maidens at Ancient Brauron

◁ The Christ Pantokrátor figure in the dome of the *katholikón* of the Monastery of Dafní

Around Athens

Beyond the endless urban sprawl of Athens, the region around
the city, known as Attica, offers the diversity of wild mountains,
Byzantine monasteries and churches, evocative archaeological sites
and sandy beaches. Not surprisingly, such easy accessibility to the
coast and countryside has led to overcrowding in Athens' suburbs,
and pollution around Piraeus and Ancient Eleusis. The hills
of Mount Párnitha and Ymittós are rich in wildlife, with deserted trails,
caves and icy spring water. In the summer months, Athenians move
out to the Attic Coast, where the well-kept beaches have every kind
of watersport facility, and there are bars and clubs. Towards the
cape at Soúnio there are countless fish tavernas by the sea and
quiet rocky coves ideal for snorkelling.

**Boats moored in Mikrolímano
harbour, Piraeus**

SEE ALSO

- **Where to Stay** pp267–8
- **Where to Eat** pp288–9

KEY

═══	Dual-carriageway
───	Major road
═══	Minor road
───	Scenic route
───	Main railway
───	Minor railway
───	Regional border

GETTING AROUND

Athens' international airport, Elefthérios, serves the region.
There are two routes out of Athens to southeast Attica: the
popular coastal road from Piraeus to Soúnio, and the inland
road, via Korópi and Markópoulo, to the east-coast towns of
Pórto Ráfti and Lávrio. This is also the way for the turn-off to
the port of Rafína, where there are ferry connections to Evvoia
and the Cyclades. Frequent buses from Athens link all the
towns in the area. Mount Párnitha and northern Attica are
best reached by taking the 1 (E75) national road.

The Temple of Poseidon on the cape at Soúnio

LOCATOR MAP

SIGHTS AT A GLANCE

0 kilometres	10
0 miles	5

a Oropou
ΝΤ ❶
ΌΣ
  Aghii
  Apostoli
  Kalamos
  81
        ❷ RAMNOÚS
  Kapandriti
  Lake Marathónas
  1
  E75   Ag. Marina
      ❸ MARATHÓNAS
T T I C A
  Ekali   Schinias
  83
⓭ KIFISIÁ
  🏛
  oussi   Nea Makri
  Pendeli   Zoumberi
  Pallini   Máti
              ❹ RAFÍNA
  54
ΜΟΝΙ   ATTICA
ΚAISARIANÍS ⓫ ZOOLOGICAL   Loutsa
⓬   Spata PARK
nittós
  ❿ PAIANÍA
  89   ANCIENT
        ❺ BRAURON
oli   Vravróna
  Koropi
        ❻ PÓRTO RÁFTI
  Markópoulo
  Kaliva
  Thorikou   Kaki Thalassa
Vári
gméni
iza Agia Marina
  91 Keratea
  Lagonissi
              89
  COAST
  Anávysos
              Makrónisos
        LÁVRIO ❼
Palia Fokea
  91
        ❽ SOÚNIO

The *katholikón* of Moní Kaisarianís

View of the Enkoimitírion at Oropós

Ancient Oropós ❶
Ωρωπός

Kálamos, Attica. **Road map** D4.
Tel 22960 22426. 🚌 Kálamos.
⬜ daily. ⚫ main public hols. 🏛

The peaceful sanctuary of
Oropós nestles on the left
bank of the Cheímarros, a
small river surrounded by
pine trees and wild thyme
bushes. It is dedicated to
Amphiáraos, a hero credited
with healing powers whom,
according to mythology,
Zeus rescued when he was
wounded in battle. It is said
that the earth swallowed up
Amphiáraos while he was
riding his chariot, and that he
then miraculously reappeared
through the sacred spring at
this site. In ancient times visitors would throw coins into
the spring in the hope of
being granted good health.

The Amphiaraion
sanctuary came to
prominence as a
healing centre in
the 4th century BC,
when its Doric
temple and sacri-
ficial altar were
built, attracting the
sick from all over
Greece. Houses
erected during the
Roman period,
when the area
became a popular
spa centre, are still
visible on the right
bank of the river.
The Enkoimitírion
was the site's most
interesting building.
It was a long stoa, the
remains of which are still
visible today, where the
patients underwent
treatment by *enkoimisis*.
This gruesome ritual
entailed the sacrifice
of a goat in whose
bloody hide the
patient would then
spend the night. The
next morning, priests
would prescribe
medicines based on
their interpretations
of the dreams of the patient.
Above the Enkoimitírion are
the remains of an impressive
theatre, which has a well-
preserved *proskenion* (stage)
and five sculpted marble
thrones, once reserved for the
use of priests and guests of
honour. On the right bank of
the valley, opposite the altar,
is a water clock dating from
the 4th century BC.

**Marble throne from
the theatre at Oropós**

Ramnoús ❷
Ραμνούς

Attica. **Road map** D4. **Tel** 22940
63477. 🚌 ⬜ daily (Sanctuary of
Nemesis only). ⚫ main public hols.
🏛 ♿

Ramnoús is a remote but
beautiful site, overlooking
the gulf of Evvoia. It is home
to the only Greek sanctuary
dedicated to the goddess of
vengeance, Nemesis. The
sanctuary was demolished
when the Byzantine Emperor
Arcadius decreed in AD 399
that all temples left standing
should be destroyed. Thus
only the remains of this
sanctuary can be seen today.
Within its compound, two
temples are preserved side
by side. The smaller and
older Temple of Themis
dates from the 6th
century BC. Used as
a treasury and
storehouse in
ancient times, its
impressive poly-
gonal walls are all
that now survive.
Within the cella,
some important
statues of the
goddess and her priestess,
Aristonoë, were uncovered.
They can now be seen in the
National Archaeological
Museum *(see pp68–71)*.
The larger Temple of Nemesis
dates from the mid-5th century
BC. It is very similar in design
to the Hephaisteion in Athens'
Agora *(see pp90–91)* and the
Temple of Poseidon at Soúnio
(see p148). Built in the Doric

The remains of the Temple of Nemesis at Ramnoús

For hotels and restaurants in this region see pp267–8 and pp288–9

style, the temple contained a statue of Nemesis by Agorakritos, a disciple of Pheidias *(see p98)*. The statue has been partially reconstructed from fragments, and the head is now in the British Museum.

The quayside at the port of Rafína

Marathónas ❸
Μαραθώνας

Attica. **Road map** D4. **Tel** 22940 55155. 🚌 **Site & Museum** ◯ Tue–Sun. ⬤ main public hols. 🏛

The Marathon Plain is the site of the great Battle of Marathon, where the Athenians defeated the Persians. The burial mound of the Athenians lies 4 km (2 miles) from the modern town of Marathónas. This tumulus is 180 m (590 ft) in circumference and 10 m (32 ft) high. It contains the ashes of the 192 Athenian warriors who died in the battle. The spot was marked by a simple *stele* of a fallen warrior, Aristion, by the sculptor Aristocles. The original is now in the National Archaeological Museum *(see pp68–71)* in Athens. There is a copy at the site, inscribed with an epigram by the ancient poet Simonides: "The Athenians fought at the front of the Greeks at Marathon, defeating the gold-bearing Persians and stealing their power."

In 1970 the burial mound of the Plataians and royal Mycenaean tombs were found nearby in the village of Vraná. The Plataians were the only other Greeks who sent warriors in time to assist the Athenians already at the battle. The **Marathon Museum** displays archaeological finds from these local sites. There are also some beautiful

Plate discovered in the tomb of Plataians

Egyptian-style statues from the 2nd century AD, found on the estate of Herodes Atticus, on the Marathon Plain. This wealthy benefactor was born and bred in this area. He is known for erecting many public buildings in Athens, including the famous theatre located on the southern slope of the Acropolis *(see p100)* that was named in his honour.

Environs

Just 8 km (5 miles) west of Marathónas is **Lake Marathónas**, which is crossed by a narrow causeway. This vast expanse of water is manmade. The impressive dam, made from white Pentelic marble, was built in 1926. It created an artificial lake that was Athens' sole source of water until 1956. The lake is fed by the continuous streams of the Charádras and Varnávas which flow down from Mount Párnitha *(see p151)* and makes a good setting for a picnic.

Rafína ❹
Ραφήνα

Attica. **Road map** D4. 🏠 8,600. 🚤 🚌

The charm of Rafína is its lively fishing port, packed with caïques and ferries. After Piraeus it is the main port in Attica. Frequent buses from Athens bring passengers for the regular hydrofoil and ferry connections to the Cyclades and other Aegean islands.

One of the administrative *demes* (regions) of ancient Athens, Rafína is a longestablished settlement. Although there is little of historical or archaeological interest, the town offers a selection of excellent fish restaurants and tavernas. Choose one by the waterside to sit and watch the hustle and bustle of this busy port.

Environs

North of Rafína, a winding road leads to the more picturesque resort of **Máti**. Once a quiet hamlet, it is packed today with trendy cafés and bars, apartment blocks and summer houses owned by Athenians.

THE BATTLE OF MARATHON

When Darius of Persia arrived at the Bay of Marathon with his warships in 490 BC, it seemed impossible that the Greeks could defeat him. Heavily outnumbered, the 10,000 Greek hoplites had to engage 25,000 Persian warriors. Victory was due to the tactics of the commander Miltiades, who altered the usual battle phalanx by strengthening the wings with more men. The Persians were enclosed on all sides and driven back to the sea. Around 6,000 Persians died and only 192 Athenians. The origins of the marathon run also date from this battle. News of the victory was relayed by a runner who covered the 41 km (26 miles) back to Athens in full armour before dying of exhaustion.

Vase showing Greek hoplites fighting a Persian on horseback

Ancient Brauron ❺
Βραυρώνα

Situated near modern Vravrona, Brauron is one of the most evocative sites near Athens. Although little remains of its former architectural glory, finds in the museum reveal its importance as the centre of worship of Artemis, goddess of childbirth and protectress of animals *(see p53)*. Legend relates that it was founded by Orestes and Iphigéneia, the children of Agamemnon, who introduced the cult of Artemis into Greece. Evidence of Neolithic and Mycenaean remains have been found on the hill above the site, but the tyrant Peisistratos brought Brauron its fame in the 6th century BC when he made the worship of Artemis Athens' official state religion.

0 metres   30
0 yards   30

KEY TO THE SANCTUARY OF ARTEMIS

① Temple of Artemis
② Chapel of Agios Geórgios
③ Sacred House
④ Tomb of Iphigéneia
⑤ Parthenon of the Bear Maidens
⑥ Dormitories
⑦ Stoa
⑧ Stone Bridge

The Parthenon of the Bear Maidens at Brauron

Exploring Ancient Brauron

The centre of this compact site lies just north of the prehistoric acropolis. The 5th-century BC Doric **Temple of Artemis**, of which only the foundations remain, formed the focal point of the sanctuary to the goddess. Beside the temple stands a late Byzantine chapel, dedicated to **Agios Geórgios**.

From here a path leads southeast to the oldest cult site in the sanctuary. This is said to be the **Tomb of Iphigéneia**,

the high priestess of Artemis. Next to it are the foundations of the **Sacred House**, which was used as a home by the cult's priestesses. The most extensive remains at the site are to the northeast, at the **Parthenon of the Bear Maidens**. This courtyard may have been the place where young girls performed the

bear dance. Surrounded by a late 5th-century BC **stoa**, the courtyard had rooms behind that were used as dining areas and **dormitories**. Only the foundations remain, but the stone sleeping couches and bases of statues can still be seen. There is also a 5th-century BC **stone bridge** to the west.

BRAURONIA CEREMONY

Held every four years in the spring, the Brauronia festival was celebrated in atonement for the killing of one of Artemis's sacred pet bears. Although little is known about the mysterious rites today, Aristophanes mentions the "bear dance" that initiates had to perform in his play *Lysistrata*. Disguised as bears and adorned with saffron-coloured robes, young girls, aged between 5 and 10, performed a dance honouring this sacred animal.

Relief showing pilgrims approaching the altar of Artemis at the Brauronia ceremony

The small Byzantine chapel of Agios Geórgios

Mycenaean vase from the
Brauron Museum, 1200–1100 BC

🛈 Brauron Museum

This fascinating museum
has a wealth of finds
from the site. In
Room 1, there are
cases filled with
assorted votive
offerings such as
miniature vases and
jewellery. In Room 2
are the serene statues
of árktoi ("bear
maidens"). Room 3
has a fine votive
relief of the gods
Zeus, Leto, Apollo
and Artemis, and
the remains of an
altar. Rooms 4
and 5 offer a variety of prehistoric and Mycenaean finds,
including some ornate
Geometric vases.

Statue of a
bear maiden

RETSINA

Although many Greeks prefer drinking whisky to wine these
days, retsina is still favoured by millions of tourists. Around
16 million bottles were drunk in 1994, and 50 per cent of
them were exported around the world. The
unique, distinctive flavour comes from the
Aleppo pine resin which is added in small
quantities to the grape juice during fermen-
tation. This method has been used since
antiquity to preserve and flavour wine in
Greece. Since entry into the EEC (now
called the EU) in 1981, traditional
production areas have had their own
appellations. Aficionados agree that some
of the best retsina comes from the
Meságeia appellation in Attica, where the
Savatiano grape is cultivated. Kourtákis,
the largest producers of retsina, have
their vineyards in Markópoulo and Koropí.

Collection of
pine resin

Pórto Ráfti ❻
Πόρτο Ράφτη

Attica. **Road map** D4. 👥 3,300. 🚌

Pórto Ráfti takes its name from
Ráfti island which is visible just
off the headland. On the island
is a colossal marble statue of
a seated female, made in the
Roman period, known as "the
tailor" (ráftis). It was most likely
built to be used as a beacon for
shipping and would have lit up
the harbour. Pórto Ráfti has one
of the best natural harbours in
Greece, although the town
itself has never developed
into an important seafaring
port. In April 1941, during
World War II, 6,000 New
Zealand troops were
successfully evacuated from
the beach. Today it is primarily
a pleasant holiday resort, with
tavernas and bars. The area is
rich in archaeological history.

Many Mycenaean tombs have
been found south of the bay
of Pórto Ráfti, at Peratí, a port
that flourished in the 7th and
6th centuries BC.

Environs

The remains of a fortress that
was built during the
Chremonidean War (268–261
BC) between Egypt and
Macedon can be seen on the
southern **Koróni** headland.
The northern coastline of
Peratí is pockmarked with
unexplored caves, and attracts
many people who come to
swim in the clear water and
fish off the craggy rocks.
  Markópoulo, a thriving
market town and viticultural
centre 8 km (5 miles) inland,
is famous for its tavernas.
Spicy sausages are for sale
in the butchers' shops and
the bakeries are fragrant with
the smell of fresh bread.

Pórto Ráfti harbour with Ráfti island in the background

One of the many 19th-century Neo-Classical buildings in Lávrio

Lávrio ❼
Λαύριο

Attica. **Road map** D4. 🏠 8,800.
🚌 🚢 🛥 Thu.

Lávrio was famous for its silver mines in ancient times. They were used as a source of revenue for the Athenian state and financed Perikles's programme of grand public buildings in Athens in the 5th century BC (see p30). They also enabled the general Themistokles to construct a fleet capable of beating the Persians at the Battle of Salamis in 480 BC. It was this excellent naval fleet which established Athens as a naval power. Before their final closure in the 20th century, the mines were also exploited by French and Greek companies for other minerals such as manganese and cadmium.

Originally worked by slaves, over 2,000 mine shafts have been discovered in the surrounding hills, and some are now open to visitors as the **Mineralogical Museum**. It is the only such museum in Greece. Traces of ore and minerals in the rock face can be seen on tours of the old mines. Since their closure the area has suffered high unemployment. The old Neo-Classical houses and empty harbourfront warehouses indicate the former prosperity of the town. Makrónisos, the narrow island opposite the port, was used as a prison for political detainees during the Civil War (see p42).

🏛 **Mineralogical Museum**
Leof Andréa Kordelá. **Tel** 22920 26270. ◯ 10am–noon Wed, Sat & Sun. 🅿 🔥

Soúnio ❽
Σούνιο

9 km (5.5 miles) from Lávrio, Attica.
Road map D4. **Tel** 22920 39363. 🚌 to Lávrio. ◯ 9am–sunset daily. 🅿 🛈

The Temple of Poseidon, built on a site set back from sheer cliffs tumbling into the Aegean Sea at Soúnio (Cape Sounion), was ideally located for worship of the powerful god of the sea. Its brilliant white marble columns have been a landmark for ancient and modern mariners alike.

The present temple, built in 444 BC, stands on the site of older ruins. An Ionic frieze, made from 13 slabs of Parian marble, is located on the east side of the temple's main approach path. It is very eroded but is known to have depicted scenes from the mythological battle of the Lapiths and centaurs, and also the adventures of the hero Theseus, who was thought

The Doric columns of the Temple of Poseidon

to be the son of Poseidon, according to some legends.

Local marble, taken from quarries at nearby Agriléza, was used for the temple's 34 slender Doric columns, of which 15 survive today. The temple also possesses a

The ruins of the Temple of Poseidon on Soúnio

For hotels and restaurants in this region see pp267–8 and pp288–9

unique design feature which helps combat the effects of sea-spray erosion: the columns were cut with only 16 flutings instead of the usual 20, thus reducing the surface area exposed to the elements.

When Byron carved his name on one of the columns in 1810, he set a dangerous precedent for vandalism at the temple, which is now covered with scrawled signatures.

A waterside restaurant at Várkiza, along the Attic coast

Attic Coast **9**
Παραλία Αττικης

Attica. **Road map** D4.

The coastal strip from Piraeus to Soúnio is often called the "Apollo Coast" after a small Temple of Apollo discovered at Vouliagméni. It is covered with beaches and resort towns that are always very busy at weekends, and particularly so in the summer holiday season.

One of the first places along the coast from Piraeus is the tiny seaside resort of **Palaió Fáliro** which is home to the Phaleron War Cemetery. In this quiet spot is the Athens Memorial, erected in May 1961 to 2,800 British soldiers who died in World War II.

Noisy suburbs near Athens airport, like **Glyfáda** and **Álimos** (famous as the birthplace of the ancient historian Thucydides), are very commercialized with a large number of marinas, hotels and shopping malls.

At chic **Vouliagméni**, with its large yacht marina, luxury

---

hotels line the promontory. A short walk northwards away from the coast, beside the main road, is the enchanting Vouliagméni Lake. This unusual freshwater lake lies beneath low, limestone cliffs. The stunning stretch of warm, sulphurous water has been used for years to bring relief to sufferers of rheumatism. There are changing rooms and a café close by.

At **Várkiza**, the wide bay is filled with windsurfers. By the main road there is a luxury club-restaurant, *Island*. Open throughout the summer season, it serves cocktails and Mediterranean cuisine and attracts a glamorous crowd. From Várkiza, a road snakes inland to **Vári**, renowned for

its restaurants serving meat dishes. The Vári cave is located about 2 km (1 mile) north of the village. Inside is a freshwater spring and some fine stalactites have developed. Some minor Classical ruins remain in the caves, although many have been removed. There is unrestricted access and no admission charge.

From Várkiza to Soúnio, the coastal road is lined with quiet bathing coves, fish tavernas and luxury villas. **Anávysos** is a thriving market town surrounded by vineyards and fields. In its harbour, caïques sell locally caught fish every day, and there is a small street market every Saturday, with stalls piled high with seasonal fruit and vegetables.

Colourful stall of local produce in Anávysos

Sculpture in the gardens of the Vorrés Museum

Paianía ❿
Παιανία

Attica. **Road map** D4. 🏛 *9,700*. 🚌
🚇 *Tue*.

Just east of Athens, Paianía is
a town of sleepy streets and
cafés. In the main square, the
church of **Zoödóchou Pigís**
has some fine modern
frescoes by the 20th-century
artist Fótis Kóntoglou. The
birthplace of the orator
Demosthenes (384–322 BC),
Paianía is more famous today
for the **Vorrés Museum**. Set in
beautiful gardens, this features
private collector Ion Vorrés's
eclectic array of ancient and
modern art. The museum is
divided into two sections,
encompassing 3,000 years of
Greek history and heritage.
The first is housed in what

was the collector's
private home: two
traditional village
houses filled with
ancient sculptures,
folk artifacts, cer-
amics, Byzantine
icons, seascapes
and furniture. The
second section,
housed in a
specially built
modern building,
offers a unique
overview of
contemporary
Greek art since
the 1940s, with
many excellent
works by more
than 300 different
painters and
sculptors,
encompassing
every major art movement
from Photo-Realism to Pop Art.

🏛 **Vorrés Museum**
Diadóchou Konstantínou 1. *Tel 210
664 4771*. ◻ *10am–2pm Sat & Sun.*
● *Aug & main public hols.* 📷 ♿

Environs
Above Paianía, the **Koutoúki
Cave** is hidden in the foothills
of Mount Ymittós. It was found
in 1926 by a shepherd looking
for a goat which had fallen into
the 12,200 sq m (130,000 sq ft)
cave. There are tours every
half hour, with son et lumière
effects lighting up the stalagmites and stalactites. The temperature inside is 17°C (62°F).

🛖 **Koutoúki Cave**
4 km (2.5 miles) W of Paianía. *Tel
210 664 2108*. ◻ *9am–3pm Mon–
Fri, 9:30am–2:30pm Sat–Sun.* 📷

Attica Zoological
Park ⓫
Αττικό Ζωολογικό Πάρκο

Yalou, Spata. **Road map** D4.
Tel 210 663 7424. 🚌 *319*.
◻ *9am–sunset daily.* 📷 📷

Attica Zoological Park is an
increasingly popular attraction
just a short drive east of
Athens. The zoo has over 300
species of animal, from white
lions and tigers to yellow
anacondas and pygmy hippos.
It also has one of the largest
bird collections in the world.
In Cheetah Land, visitors can
walk through a special tunnel
within the cheetah enclosure.

Moní Kaisarianís ⓬
Μονή Καισαριανής

5 km (3 miles) E of Athens, Attica.
Road map D4. *Tel 210 723 6619*.
🚌 *to Kaisarianís.* ◻ *8:30am–3pm
Tue–Sun.* ● *main public hols.* 📷

Moní Kaisarianís was founded
in the 11th century. In 1458,
when Sultan Mehmet II conquered Athens, the monastery
was exempted from taxes in
recognition of the abbot's gift
to the sultan of the keys of
the city. This led to great
prosperity until 1792, when it
lost these privileges and went
into decline. The complex was
used briefly as a convent after
the War of Independence,
until 1855. Its buildings were
eventually restored in 1956.
The small *katholikón* is
dedicated to the Presentation
of the Virgin. All the frescoes

Moní Kaisarianís, hidden in the hills around Mount Ymittós

For hotels and restaurants in this region see pp267–8 and pp288–9

date from the 16th and 17th centuries.

Just above the monastery, the source of the River Ilissós has been visited since antiquity, its water is reputed to cure sterility. Before the Marathon dam was built (see p145), the spring was Athens' main source of water.

Kifisiá 🔞
Κηφισιά

12 km (7.5 miles) NE of Athens, Attica. **Road map** D4. 🏛 40,000. 🚇 M Kifisiá.

Kifisiá has been a favourite summer retreat for many Athenians since Roman times. Once the exclusive domain of rich Greeks, it is congested today with apartment blocks and shopping malls. Traces of its former tranquillity can still be seen by taking a ride in a horse-drawn carriage. These wait by the metro station offering drives down shady streets lined with mansions and villas, built in a bizarre variety of period styles such as Alpine chalet and Gothic Neo-Classicism.

The **Goulandrís Natural History Museum**, which opened in 1974, is housed in one of these villas. Its large collection covers all aspects of Greece's varied wildlife and minerals. There are 200,000 varieties of plants in the herbarium, and over 1,300 examples of taxidermy; the stuffed creatures are carefully displayed in their natural habitats.

The tiny chapel of Agía Triáda on the hillside of Mount Párnitha

Clam shell outside the Goulandrís Natural History Museum, Kifisiá

🏛 Goulandrís Natural History Museum
Levidou 13. **Tel** 210 801 5870. 🕐 9am–2:30pm Mon–Sat, 10am–2:30pm Sun. 🔴 main public hols. 🖼

Environs
In Maroúsi, a suburb of Kifisiá, is the small **Spathári Museum of Shadow Theatre**, which is devoted to the fascinating history of the Karagkiózis puppet theatre. Shadow theatre came to Greece from the Far East, via players who used to travel throughout the Ottoman Empire performing for the aristocracy in the 18th century. It was soon transformed into a popular folk art by entertainers who would travel around Greece with their makeshift theatres. The name Karagkiózis refers to the indomitable and impoverished Greek character who is tormented by the other standard theatrical characters such as the rich Pasha and tough guy Stávrakas. The museum displays the history of two generations of the Spathári family, who were the leading exponents of this dying art, along with their home-made sets and puppets.

Puppet from the Museum of Shadow Theatre

🏛 Spathári Museum of Shadow Theatre
Mesogion & Ipirou 27, Maroúsi. **Tel** 210 612 7245. 🕐 9am–2pm Mon–Fri & 6–8pm Wed, 10am–1pm Sun. 🔴 main public hols.

Mount Párnitha 🔞
Ορος Πάρνηθα

Attica. **Road map** D4. 🚌 to Aharnés, Thrakomakedónes & Agía Triáda.

In ancient times, Mount Párnitha sheltered wild animals. Today, this rugged range, which extends nearly 25 km (16 miles) from east to west, is rich in less dangerous fauna. Tortoises can be seen in the undergrowth and birds of prey circle the summit of Karampóla at 1,413 m (4,635 ft). Wild flowers are abundant, particularly in autumn and spring when cyclamen and crocus carpet the mountain. There are spectacular views of alpine scenery, all within an hour's drive of the city. At the small town of **Acharnés**, a cable car ascends to a casino perched at over 900 m (3,000 ft).

Still little used by hikers, the mountain has plenty of demanding trails. The most popular walk leads from Thrakomakedónes, in the foothills of the mountain, to the Báfi refuge. This uphill march takes about two hours, and offers superb views of the surrounding mountain scenery. Starting with thorny scrub typical of the Mediterranean maquis, it follows well-trodden paths to end among alpine firs and clear mountain air. Once at the Báfi refuge, it is worth walking on to the Flampoúri refuge which has some dramatic views.

Monastery of Dafní ⓯
Μονή Δαφνίου

The monastery of Dafní was founded in the 5th century AD. Named after the laurels *(dáfnes)* that used to grow here, it was built with the remains of an ancient sanctuary of Apollo, which had occupied this site until it was destroyed in AD 395. In the early 13th century, Otto de la Roche, the first Frankish Duke of Athens, bequeathed it to Cistercian monks in Burgundy. Greek Orthodox monks took the site in the 16th century, erecting the elegant cloisters just south of the church. Following earthquake damage in 2000, the beautiful gold-leaf Byzantine mosaics in the *katholikón* (main church) have undergone major restoration.

Fresco detail

Aerial view of the monastery complex

The Gothic exonarthex was built almost 30 years after the main church.

Cloisters
This arcade was built in the 16th century. On the other side of the courtyard, above a similar arcade, are the monks' cells.

The symmetry of the design makes Dafní one of the most attractive examples of Byzantine architecture in Attica.

KEY TO MOSAICS IN THE KATHOLIKON

Esonarthex
Exonarthex
Entrance

WALLS
1 Resurrection
2 Adoration of the Magi
4 Archangel Gabriel
5 Archangel Michael
6 Nativity of the Virgin
8 St John the Baptist
9 Entry into Jerusalem
12 Dormition of the Virgin
13 Last Supper
14 Washing of the Feet
15 Betrayal by Judas
16 Prayer of Sts Anne and Joachim
17 Blessing of the Priests
18 Presentation of the Virgin
20 St Thomas

CEILING AND DOME
3 Nativity
7 Annunciation
10 Christ Pantokrátor
11 Transfiguration
19 Baptism

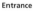

Entrance

★ Christ Pantokrátor
The Pantokrátor ("Almighty") gazes sternly down from the dome of the katholikón. *Around the central figure are images of the 16 prophets.*

VISITORS' CHECKLIST

10 km (6 miles) NW of Athens,
Attica. **Road map** D4.
Tel 210 581 1558.
8am–8pm daily.

The dome is 8 m (26 ft) in diameter and 16 m (52 ft) high at the centre.

Nave

The Transfiguration
This is in the northwest corner under the dome. Elijah and Moses are on either side of Christ and the apostles Peter, James and John are below.

The Windows
Elaborate three-tiered brickwork surrounds each of the windows.

Ticket office and museum

STAR MOSAICS

★ Christ Pantokrátor

★ Esonarthex Mosaics

★ Esonarthex Mosaics
These mosaics include depictions of the Last Supper *and the* Washing of the Feet. *The finest is the* Betrayal *by Judas.* Christ stands unmoved as Judas kisses Him.

Piraeus ⑯
Πειραιάς

Waiting for a ferry

One of the biggest Mediterranean ports, Piraeus is also one of the largest cities in Greece. It has been the port of Athens since ancient times. The Long Walls between Piraeus and Athens were started in 480 BC by Themistokles. However, Sulla destroyed the walls in 86 BC and by the Middle Ages Piraeus was little more than a fishing village. When Athens became the Greek capital in 1834, Piraeus was once again revitalized, with Neo-Classical buildings and factories. In 1923, 100,000 refugees came here from Asia Minor, bringing their culture and contributing to the cosmopolitan feel of this port city.

Small boats moored in peaceful Mikrolímano harbour

View across Kentrikó Limáni with ferries in the foreground

Exploring Piraeus

After the Junta *(see p43)* razed many irreplaceable public buildings in the town centre in the early 1970s, civic pride re-emerged with a vengeance. Beside the Municipal Theatre, there are elegant open-air restaurants and fountains in the shade of Neo-Classical façades. On the streets behind the main banks and ticket offices that rim the **Kentrikó Limáni** (the main ferry port), there are smart restaurants and shops, as well as some fine examples of Neo-Classical architecture, such as the **Town Hall**. For information on ferry departures from Kentrikó Limáni, see page 323.

South of the railway station around Navarínou lies the lively market area, including fishmongers', fruit and vegetable stalls, ships' chandlers and hardware stores. On Sunday mornings there is also a bustling flea market, which

is centred on the antique shops around Plateía Ippodameías, and also on Alipédou and Skylítsi streets.

There are two harbours in Piraeus, situated east of Kentrikó Limáni. **Pasalimáni** (Pasha's Port, also known as Limáni Zéas) was once used to harbour the Ottoman fleet. Today it is filled with luxurious yachts. Once known simply as Zéa, Pasalimáni used to be one of Themistokles's major naval ports, with dry docks for 196 triremes. Marína Zéas, the mouth of Pasalimáni, is a jetty used as a dock for hydrofoils to the Argo-Saronic islands. The second harbour, **Mikrolímano** (Little

Harbour) houses many colourful fishing caïques. It is popular for its waterside fish restaurants and has a more relaxing ambience than the larger harbour.

On the coastal road between Pasalimáni and Mikrolímano, smart bars and clubs occupy the renovated Neo-Classical mansions in the gentrified **Kastélla** neighbourhood. Even traditionally working-class areas, such as Drapetsóna (the most important manufacturing centre in the country), are now popular for their late-night restaurants.

🎭 Municipal Theatre

Agiou Konstantínou 2. *Tel 210 412 0333.* ☐ *Tue–Sun.*
The Neo-Classical façade of this imposing building is one of the delights of Piraeus. Designed by Ioánnis Lazarímos (1849–1913), who based his plans on the Opéra Comique in Paris, it has seating for 800, making it one of the largest modern theatres in Greece. It took nearly ten years to complete and was finally

Façade of the Municipal Theatre

inaugurated on 9 April 1895. Today, it is the home of both the **Municipal Art Gallery** and also the **Pános Aravantinoú Museum of Stage Decor**. The Museum of Stage Decor has displays of set designs by the stage designer Pános Aravantinoú (who worked with the Berlin opera in the 1920s), as well as general ephemera from the Greek opera.

Archaeological Museum

Chariláou Trikoúpi 31. **Tel** 210 452 1598. ◯ 8:30am–3pm Tue– Sun. ● main public hols. 🖾 ♿
This museum is home to some stunning bronzes. Found by workmen in 1959, large statues of Artemis with her quiver, Athena with her helmet decorated with owls, and Apollo reveal the great expressiveness of Greek sculpture. The Piraeus *koúros* of Apollo, dating from 520 BC, is the earliest full-size bronze

to be discovered. There is also a seated cult statue of the earth goddess Cybele and a fine collection of Greek and Roman statues and grave stelae. Near the museum are the remains of the 2nd-century BC **Theatre of Zéa**; the remains include a well-preserved orchestra.

Statue of Athena in the Archaeological Museum

Hellenic Maritime Museum

Aktí Themistokléous, Freatýda. **Tel** 210 451 6264. ◯ 9am–2pm Tue–Sat (from 9:30am Sun). ● main public hols, Aug. 🖾
On the quayside of Marína Zéas, an old submarine marks the entrance to this fascinating museum. Its first room is built around an original section of Themistokles's Long Walls. More than 2,000 exhibits, such as models of triremes, ephemera from naval battleships and paintings of Greek *trechantíri* (fishing caïques), explore the world of Greek seafaring. From early

voyages around the Black Sea by trireme to 20th-century emigration to the New World by transatlantic liner, the museum unravels the complexities of Greek maritime history. Exhibits include models of ships, maps, flags, uniforms and pictures. The War of Independence is well documented with information and memorabilia about the generals who served in it. The old naval ship *Averof*, which was the flagship of the Greek fleet until 1951, has been fully restored and is berthed nearby. As part of the museum, the ship is also open to visitors.

PIRAEUS CITY CENTRE

Archaeological Museum ④
Hellenic Maritime Museum ⑥
Kastélla ⑧
Mikrolímano ⑦
Municipal Theatre ②
Pasalimáni ⑤
Theatre of Zéa ③
Town Hall ①

0 metres 500
0 yards 500

Key to Symbols *see back flap*

Ancient Eleusis ⑰
Αρχαία Ελευσίνα

Eleusis was an ancient centre of religious devotion that culminated in the annual Eleusinian Mysteries. These attracted thousands of people from around the Greek-speaking world, for whom the only initial requirement for becoming a *mystes* (or initiate) was to be neither a murderer nor a barbarian. Both men and women were freely admitted. Existing from Mycenaean times, the sanctuary was closed by the Roman Emperor Theodosius in AD 392, and was finally abandoned when Alaric, king of the Goths, invaded Greece in AD 396, bringing Christianity in his wake.

Anaktoron
This small rectangular stone edifice had a single entrance. It was considered the holiest part of the site. Meaning "palace", it existed long before the Telesterion, which was built around it.

Telesterion
Designed by Iktinos, this temple was built in the 5th century BC. It was constructed to hold several thousand people at a time.

4th-century BC shops and bouleuterion (council chamber)

THE ELEUSINIAN MYSTERIES

Perhaps established by 1500 BC and continuing for almost 2,000 years, these rites centred on the myth of the grieving goddess Demeter, who lost her daughter Persephone (or Kore) to Hades, god of the Underworld, for nine months each year *(see p52)*. Participants were sworn to secrecy, but some evidence of the details of the ceremony does exist. Sacrifices were made before the procession from the Kerameikós *(see pp88–9)* to Eleusis. Here the priestesses would reveal the vision of the holy night, thought to have been a fire symbolizing life after death for the initiates.

A priestess with a *kiste mystika* (basket)

Temple of Kore hewn out of rock

Roman houses

ANCIENT ELEUSIS

This reconstruction is of Eleusis as it was in Roman times (c.AD 150) when the Mysteries were still flourishing. The view is from the east. Although there is little left today, it is still possible to sense the awe and mystery that the rites of Eleusis inspired.

Ploutonion
This cave is said to be where Persephone was returned to earth. It was a sanctuary to Hades, god of the Underworld and the abductor of Persephone.

Greater Propylaia
Built from Pentelic marble in the 2nd century AD by the Roman Emperor Antoninus Pius, this was modelled on the Propylaia of Athens' Acropolis.

One of a pair of triumphal arches

Temple of Artemis Propylaia

Well of Kallichoron
Demeter is believed to have grieved for Persephone here.

Lesser Propylaia
This fragment shows sheaves of grain and poppies, which were used to make kykeon, the drink of the initiates.

Relief from the Telesterion, now in the museum

◉ Eleusis Museum
This small museum, south of the Telesterion, has five rooms. The entrance hall contains a copy of the famous relief from the Telesterion showing Triptólemos receiving grain from Demeter. Also in this room are a large 7th-century BC amphora and a copy of the Ninnion votive painting, one of the few remaining representations of the Eleusinian Mysteries. The other rooms are arranged on the left of the hall. In the first of these there is an elegant 6th-century BC *kouros* and a 2nd-century BC Roman statue of Dionysos. In the second room there are two models of the site. The third room has a Classical period terracotta sarcophagus and a large caryatid from the Lesser Propylaia carrying a *kiste mystika* basket on her head. The last room has a variety of pottery fragments, including examples of unusual terracotta containers that were used to carry foodstuffs in the annual *kernoforía* procession.

Fleeing maiden

THE PELOPONNESE

PELOPONNESE

*O*ne of the primary strongholds and battlefields of the 1821–31 Revolution, the Peloponnese is the kernel from which the modern Greek state grew. This enormous peninsula, which falls short of being an island by the mere 6-km (4-mile) width of the Corinth isthmus, also has some of the most spectacularly varied scenery and monuments on the mainland.

The name "Peloponnese" means "island of Pelops", who in legend was fed to the gods by Tantalos, his father. Resurrected, he went on to sire the Atreid line of kings, whose semi-mythical misadventures and brooding citadels were given substance by the discovery of remains at Mycenae. Today the ancient and medieval sites of the Argolid region, to the south of Corinth, contrast with the elegantly Neo-Classical town of Náfplio.

In the west lies Ancient Olympia, the athletic and religious nexus of the ancient world and inspiration for the games' revival in modern times. The lush coastal plain of Ileía, heart of an early medieval Crusader principality, spawned Frankish-Byzantine architecture, most famously at Chlemoútsi.

Leonidas statue, Spárti town

More purely Byzantine art adorns the churches of Mystrás, Geráki and the remote Máni region, whose warlike medieval inhabitants claimed to be descended from the warriors of ancient Sparta. Imposing Venetian fortifications at the beach-fringed capes of Methóni, Koróni and Monemvasía allowed the Venetians to play a role here after most of their other Aegean possessions were lost to the Ottomans.

In Arcadia, at the centre of the Peloponnese, lushly cultivated valleys rise to conifer-draped mountains and deep gorges such as the Loúsios; cliff-side monasteries and sombre hilltowns, like Stemnítsa, are a world apart from the popular Mediterranean image of Greece.

Restaurant terrace overlooking the sea, Monemvasía

◁ Náfplio, seen from the stairs leading to the town's Venetian citadel, Palamídi

Exploring the Peloponnese

Ancient and medieval ruins are abundant on the Peloponnese, and provide the main focus of sightseeing. Though there are few highly developed resorts away from the Argolid and Ileía, such areas as the Loúsios Gorge and Kalógria attract thousands of trekkers and naturalists. A rural economy is still paramount inland, with Pátra being the only large city. The landscape is dominated by forested mountains and the west coast, between Pátra and Methóni, boasts some of the finest beaches in the Mediterranean.

Karýtaina village, Loúsios Gorge

GETTING AROUND

Major roads link Athens and Pátra via Corinth. Secondary roads are more interesting, if dangerously narrow. Buses link major towns with their surrounding villages, but it is not so easy to get from one major town to another. There is only one train line from Athens to the Peloponnese, and it goes as far as Kiato, north of Corinth; from there, you'll have to travel by bus to other destinations. The Rio-Antirio bridge crosses the Gulf of Corinth in the north to link the Peloponnese with mainland Greece. Ferries and hydrofoils *(see p323)* serve various points on the east coast, such as Monemvasía and Neápoli.

SIGHTS AT A GLANCE

**Gýtheio harbour,
Inner Máni**

LOCATOR MAP

SEE ALSO

- **Where to Stay** pp268–70
- **Where to Eat** pp289–91

KEY

	Dual-carriageway
	Road under construction
	Major road
	Minor road
	Scenic route
	Main railway
	Regional border
△	Summit

0 kilometres   20

0 miles   20

Ancient Corinth ➊
Αρχαία Κόρινθος

Ancient Corinth derived its prosperity from its position on a narrow isthmus between the Saronic and Corinthian gulfs. Transporting goods across this isthmus, even before the canal *(see p167)* was built, provided the shortest route from the eastern Mediterranean to the Adriatic and Italy. Founded in Neolithic times, the town was razed in 146 BC by the Romans, who rebuilt it a century later. Attaining a population of 750,000 under the patronage of the emperors, the town gained a reputation for licentious living which St Paul attacked when he came here in AD 52. Excavations have revealed the vast extent of the city, destroyed by earthquakes in Byzantine times. The ruins constitute the largest Roman township in Greece.

LOCATOR MAP

The bema (platform) was where St Paul was accused of sacrilege by the Jews of Corinth.

Bouleuterion

The agora was the hub of Roman civic life.

South stoa

★ **Lechaion Way**
This marble-paved road linked the port of Lechaion with the city, ending at a still-surviving stairway and an imposing propylaion (entrance).

The Peirene fountain's springs still supply the local modern village.

Basilica

RECONSTRUCTION OF ANCIENT CORINTH (C.AD 100)

Bouleuterion

South stoa

Bema

Agora

Peirene fountain

Basilica

Lechaion Way

Temple of Apollo

Northwest stoa

Glauke fountain

Temple of Octavia

Odeion

Theatre

Temple of Octavia

These three ornate Corinthian columns, topped by a restored architrave, are all that remain of a temple, standing on a platform, dedicated to the sister of the Emperor Augustus.

VISITORS' CHECKLIST

7 km (4 miles) SW of modern Corinth, Peloponnese. **Road map** C4. *Tel* 27410 31207. 🚌 **Site & Museum** ☐ Apr–Oct: 8am–8pm daily; Nov–Mar: 8:30am–3pm daily. ● 1 Jan, 25 Mar, Good Fri am, Easter Sun, 1 May, 25, 26 Dec. 🎫 📷 ♿ limited. **Acrocorinth:** 4 km (2.5 miles) S of Ancient Corinth. *Tel* 27410 31266. ☐ 8am–8pm daily (to 3pm Nov–Mar). 🍴

Acrocorinth
(see p166)

The museum contains artifacts from the site (see p166).

Odeion

This was one of several buildings endowed by Herodes Atticus, the wealthy Athenian and good friend of the Emperor Hadrian.

The theatre was modified in the 3rd century AD so water could be piped in and mock sea battles staged.

The Glauke fountain's four cisterns were hewn from a cubic monolith and filled by an aqueduct from the hills.

The northwest stoa had two series of columns, the outer being Doric and the inner Ionic.

★ Temple of Apollo

The most striking structure of the lower city, this temple was one of the few buildings preserved by the Romans when they rebuilt the site in 46 BC. At the southeast corner an ingenious stepped ramp leads to the temple terrace.

STAR SIGHTS

★ Temple of Apollo

★ Lechaion Way

The surviving Doric columns of the Temple of Apollo, Ancient Corinth ▷

Exploring Acrocorinth and the Museum

Excavations of recent years have yielded numerous artifacts now on view in the museum, and have revealed the vast extent of the ancient city which included the summit of Acrocorinth. Altogether, the ruins constitute the largest Roman township in Greece, since few earlier structures were restored after the Romans destroyed the town in 146 BC. Acrocorinth became one of medieval Greece's most important fortresses and can now be reached by a road which climbs the western face of the hill from the lower town.

⋔ Acrocorinth

Acrocorinth, 4 km (2 miles) above the main city, has been held and refortified by every occupying power in Greece since Roman times. Entry is on the west, where the peak's natural defences are weakest, through three successive gateways from different eras. The lowest is mostly Turkish; the middle, Frankish; and the third and highest, Byzantine, though it and two adjacent towers incorporate abundant ancient masonry. Beyond sprawls a 24-ha (60-acre) terraced wilderness of minaret stumps, Muslim tombs, and lonely mosques or chapels – all that remains of the town abandoned almost two hundred years ago, when its last defenders, the Turks, were defeated.

The lower elevation at the southwest corner of the 5-km (3-mile) circuit of walls sports a Venetian tower, while the true, northeast summit bears the scant foundations of an Aphrodite temple, attended in antiquity by 1,000 sacred

Mosaic of Bacchus (Dionysos), 2nd century AD, in the museum

prostitutes. It was against such practices that St Paul wrote his two "letters to the Corinthians". Today its attraction is one of the most sweeping views in the whole of Greece, up to 60 km (37 miles) in all directions from the Geráneia range in the northeast to the peaks of Zíria in the southwest. Towards Zíria, a prominent nearby hill, Penteskoúfi, was fortified by the Franks during the 13th century.

Acrocorinth could withstand lengthy sieges owing to the presence of the upper Peirene spring, on the southeast side of the ramparts. A stairway descends to a vaulted, subterranean chamber pool; in dry seasons the water recedes to expose a column supporting an ornate Hellenistic pediment.

▮ Museum

The site museum, just south of the odeion, ranks among Greece's best provincial collections. All periods of the ancient town's history are represented, though the Roman gallery in the west wing is particularly rich. Here pride of place goes to 2nd-century AD mosaics lifted from the floors of nearby villas: a head of Bacchus (Dionysos) set in a circular geometric pattern, a nude shepherd playing his flute to three cows, and a goat napping under a tree. The north doorway is flanked by two columns in the shape of Phrygian prisoners, shown with their arms crossed, their tunics and long hair seeming to prefigure medieval art. Also housed in the west wing are some of the 274 objects stolen from the museum in 1990 and recovered nine years later in Miami. The east gallery features older artifacts. Attic ware from the 5th century BC (see pp60–61), including the famous "Owl" vase, is rarer than the 7th- and 6th-century BC pottery, some painted with fantastic beasts, for which Corinth was noted.

At the shrine of Asklepios, just within the northern boundary of the ancient city walls, votive offerings in the shape of afflicted body parts were found and are on display in a back room, the precursors of the *támmata* or metal *ex votos* left in modern Orthodox churches. Other oddities include a 6th-century marble sphinx and Hellenistic pediments with lion-head spouts.

Stone reliefs in the central courtyard include depictions of the Labours of Herakles (see p53), one of which was performed nearby at the sanctuary of Neméa.

The entrance to Acrocorinth, with its three gateways

Ships passing through the Corinth Canal with the road bridge overhead

Corinth Canal ❷
Διώρυγα της Κορίνθου

Peloponnese. **Road map** C4.
🚌 Loutráki.

Stormy cape Matapan, or
Taínaro *(see p199)*, the
southernmost point of the
Peloponnese, was one of the
dreaded capes of antiquity;
rather than risk sailing around
it, boats would be unloaded
on one shore of this isthmus,
dragged the 6 km (4 miles)
across on the *díolkos* (paved
slipway), and then refloated.

The traffic enriched Corinth
and inspired plans for a canal.
Emperor Nero began construction, but the project was only
completed between 1882 and
1893. The 23-m (75-ft) wide
canal is obsolete in an age of
giant container ships which
easily weather the cape, but
small freighters squeezing
through are regularly seen
from the road bridge above.

Environs
Near the southern end of the
canal is the site of **Ancient
Isthmia**, once the major local
religious centre (devoted to
Poseidon) and location of the

biennial Isthmian Games.
Today only foundations of
Poseidon's temple (7th
century BC) and the remains
of a starting gate for track
events in the adjacent,
vanished stadium are traceable.

The site museum stresses
finds from Kechriés, Corinth's
eastern port; unique exhibits
include panels of painted
glass or stone embedded
in a resin matrix. They
were intended to decorate
an Isis temple but were
never used owing to an
earthquake in AD 375.

🏛 Ancient Isthmia
Southern end of Corinth Canal.
Site & Museum *Tel* 27410 37244.
⬜ 8:30am–3pm Tue–Sun.
⬤ main public hols. 📷 ♿

Heraion of Perachóra ❸
Ηραίον της Περαχωρας

13 km (8 miles) W of Loutráki,
Peloponnese. **Road map** C4. 🚌

Probably founded during the
8th century BC, the Heraion of
Perachóra (a nearby village)
was primarily a religious centre.
Only foundations and column
stumps remain of the Archaic
temple of Hera Limenia, plus
an altar and a Classical stoa,
but the site has an incompar-
able setting, above a tiny
cove on the south shore of
Cape Melangávi, close to a
19th-century lighthouse.

Scenic Vouliagméni Lake,
3 km (2 miles) east, is fringed
by Aleppo pines, with the best
swimming and a selection of
tavernas at its west end.

Ancient Neméa ❹
Αρχαία Νεμέα

5 km (3 miles) NE of Neméa,
Peloponnese. **Road map** C4.
Tel 27460 22739. 🚌
Site ⬜ 8:30am–3pm Mon–Fri.
Museum ⬜ 8:30am–3pm Tue–Sun.
⬤ main public hols. 📷 ♿

Evocatively occupying an
isolated rural valley, the site of
Ancient Neméa is a local landmark, with the Doric columns
of its 4th-century Zeus temple
plainly visible from afar. Below
them lie the broken remains of
column drums toppled by van-
dals between the 4th and 13th
centuries AD. At the west end
of the temple's complete floor,
the deep *adyton* (underground
crypt) has been exposed.

A short walk to the southwest, under a giant modern
shelter, is a Hellenistic bath-
house, which is now open
to the public after extensive
excavations. The digs revealed
the plunge-pool and feed
system and also uncovered the
Byzantine village, which took
root here in the 4th century,
including graves, kilns and a
basilica built above the ancient
pilgrims' inn.

The **museum** has interesting
reconstructions and old
engravings. The Hellenistic
stadium, 400 m (1,300 ft) to the
southeast, has the earliest
known vaulted entrance tunnel.

Three Doric columns of the Temple of Zeus, Ancient Neméa

View of the Sanctuary of Hera at Perachóra, Cape Melangávi

The peaks of Mount Chelmós, seen from the southeast at dawn

Mount Chelmós **⑤**

Όρος Χελμός

Peloponnese. **Road map** C4.
🚌 to Kalávryta.

Rising to 2,355 m (7,729 ft),
Mount Chelmós is the
third highest point of the
Peloponnese, its foothills
cloaked in extensive forests
and divided by deep gorges.
The most famous of these is
Mavronéri, where the waterfall cascading from the remote
north face of the summit is
claimed to be the source of
the mythical river Styx.

Overlooking the wooded
Feneoú valley, on the
southeastern slopes, stands
the remote monastery of
Agíou Georgíou Feneoú,
originally founded in 1693,
though mostly dating to the
mid-18th century. The
katholikón, with its high
dome and transept, offers
unusual frescoes. A stairway
leads to a "secret" school,
which functioned during
the Ottoman years.

Moní Agías Lávras, 6 km
(4 miles) from Kalávryta,
played a pivotal role in the
Greek Revolution. The Archbishop of Pátra raised the
standard of revolt here on
25 March 1821, the banner
now being the centrepiece
of a nationalist shrine in the
upstairs treasury *(see pp40–41)*.

Founded in 961, Agías Lávras
has been rebuilt after its
destruction by the Germans in
1943. On the day before their
arrival, the Germans had set
fire to the town of Kalávryta,
where they perpetrated one
of their worst occupation atroc-
ities, massacring 1,436 men
and boys in reprisal for local
resistance. The cathedral clock
is permanently stopped at the
time the killing began.

The **Cave of the Lakes**, near
Kastriá, was known in ancient
times but was lost until its
rediscovery in 1964. Groups
can visit the first 350 m
(1,150 ft) of the cave, down
to the second of 15 lakes.
The massive stalactite-hung
caverns were formed by an
underground river, which
still flows during the winter.

🏞 Cave of the Lakes
16 km (10 miles) S of Kalávryta.
Tel 26920 31633. ◯ 9am–4:30pm
daily (to 5:30pm Sat & Sun). 🖼

Old steam locomotive at Diakoftó

Kalávryta-Diakoftó Railway **⑥**

Οδοντωτός Σιδηρόδρομος
Καλαβρύτων–Διακοφτού

Peloponnese. **Road map** C4.
Tel 26920 22245. 🚂 several daily
(9am–4pm) Kalávryta–Diakoftó–
Kalávryta. 🖼

The most enjoyable narrow-
gauge railway in Greece was
engineered between 1889 and
1896 by an Italian company
to bring ore down from the
Kalávryta area. Over 22 km
(14 miles) of track were laid,
over 6 km (4 miles) of which
relies on a third rail (a "rack
and pinion" system), engaged
where grades are up to one
in seven. Two of the original
steam locomotives, replaced in
1959, are displayed at Diakoftó.
For a good view of the mechanism, travel by the driver.

En route there are 14 tunnels
and many bridges over the
Vouraïkós Gorge.
The single station
of Méga Spílaio,
with two modest
hotels, is roughly
halfway. The
station is the start
of a 45-minute trail
up to **Moní Méga
Spílaio**, which is
believed to be the
oldest monastery
in Greece.

Pátra ●
Πάτρα

Peloponnese. **Road map** C4. 🏛
231,000. 🚇 🚌 🚕 ℹ️ *Filodimenos
26 (2610 620353).* ⭕ 8am–3pm daily.

Greece's third largest city and
second port is no beauty.
Tower blocks dominate the
few elegantly arcaded streets
of this planned Neo-Classical
town. Where Pátra excels is
in its celebration of carnival –
the best in Greece – for
which the city's large gay
community and student
body both turn out in force.

On the ancient acropolis
the originally Byzantine
kástro bears marks of every
subsequent era. The vast
bailey, filled with gardens and
orchards, often hosts public
events, as does the nearby
brick Roman odeion.

At the southwest edge of
town, the mock-Byzantine
basilica of **Agios Andréas**
stands where St Andrew was
supposedly martyred, and
houses his skull and a
fragment of his cross.

Environs
Founded in 1861, the **Achaïa
Clauss Winery** was Greece's
first commercial winery
and is now one of the
largest vintners in Greece.
It produces 30 million litres
(7 million gallons) a year, with
grapes gathered from across
the country. Tours include a
visit to the Imperial Cellar,
where Mavrodaphne, a fortified
dessert wine, can be tasted

🏛 Achaïa Clauss Winery
Petroto, 6 km (4 miles) SE of Pátra.
***Tel** 2610 580102.* ⭕ Apr–Sep:
10am–6pm daily; Oct–Mar: 9am–
5pm daily. ⬤ main pub hols. ♿ 📷

Kalógria ●
Καλόγρια

Peloponnese. **Road map** B4.
🚌 to Lápas. ℹ️ Lápas town hall
26930 31234).

The entire lagoon-speckled
coast, from the Araxos river
mouth to the Kotýchi lagoon,
ranks as one of the largest wetlands in Europe. Incorporating
the Strofiliá marsh and a 2,000-
ha (5,000-acre) umbrella pine

Sandy beaches of Kalógria

dune-forest, the area enjoys
limited protection as a reserve.
Development is confined to a
zone between the Prokópos
lagoon and the excellent, 7-km
(4 mile) beach of Kalógriá. The
dunes also support Aleppo
pines and valonea oaks, while
bass, eels and water snakes
swim in the marsh channels.

Migratory populations of
ducks, including pintails and
coots, live at Kotýchi, while
marsh harriers, owls, kestrels
and falcons can be seen all
year round. A **Visitor Centre**
at Lápas runs nature trails
through the dunes nearby.

ℹ️ Visitor Centre
Kotýchion Strofiliás. ***Tel** 26930
31651.* ⭕ 9am–3pm Mon–Fri.
⬤ main public hols. ♿ 📷

Chlemoútsi Castle ●
Χλεμούτσι

Kástro, Peloponnese. **Road map** B4.
⭕ daily.

The most famous Frankish
castle in Greece, known also
as "Castel Tornesi" after the
gold *tournois* coin minted
here in medieval times, was
erected between 1219 and 1223
to defend thriving Glaréntza
port (Kyllíni) and the principality capital of Andreville
(Andravída). To bolster the
weak natural defences, exceptionally thick walls and a
massive gate were built; much
of the rampart catwalk can
still be followed. The magnificent hexagonal keep has
echoing, vaulted halls; a plaque
by the entry commemorates
the 1428–32 residence of
Konstantínos Palaiológos, the
last Byzantine emperor, while
he was governor of Ileía.

Steps lead to a roof for views
over the Ionian islands and
the coastal plain. Chlemoútsi
is now being reconstructed,
with the enormous fan-shaped
courtyard already used for
summer concerts.

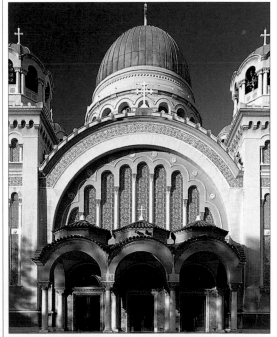

The modern Byzantine-style basilica of Agios Andréas, Pátra

Ancient Olympia ⑩
Ολυμπία

At the confluence of the rivers Alfeiós and Kládeos, the Sanctuary of Olympia enjoyed over 1,000 years of esteem as a religious and athletics centre. Though the sanctuary flourished in Mycenaean times (see pp26–7), its historic importance dates to the coming of the Dorians and their worship of Zeus, after whose abode on Mount Olympos the site was named. More elaborate temples and secular buildings were erected as the sanctuary acquired a more Hellenic character, a process completed by 300 BC. By the end of the reign of Roman Emperor Hadrian (AD 117–38), the sanctuary had begun to have less religious and political significance.

Aerial view south over the Olympia site today

The Temple of Hera, begun in the 7th century BC, is one of the oldest temples in Greece.

The Philippeion, commissioned by Philip II, honours the dynasty of Macedonian kings.

Decorative window
This window is part of Pheidias's work-shop where a huge statue of Zeus (see p241) was made.

Olympia Museum (see p172)

Main entrance

The Heroön housed an altar dedicated to an unknown hero.

```
0 metres          50
0 yards           50
```

Palaestra
This was a training centre for wrestlers, boxers and long-jumpers. Much of the colonnade which surrounded the central court has been reconstructed.

Stadium Entrance
Late in the 3rd century BC, the stadium entrance acquired a vaulted ceiling, part of which survives. The existing stadium was the third laid out at Olympia.

VISITORS' CHECKLIST

Peloponnese. **Road map** B4.
Tel 26240 22742. 🚌 🚊
Site ☐ Apr–Oct: 1:30–8pm
Mon, 8am–8pm Tue–Sun;
Nov–Mar: 10:30am–5pm
Mon, 8:30am–3pm Tue–Sun.
⬤ main public hols. 📷 📷 📷
♿ **Museum of the History of the Olympic Games**
Tel 26240 29119. ☐ same
hours as site. 📷 ♿ limited.
📧 http://odysseus.culture.gr

The Treasuries, which stored votive offerings from their donor city-states, looked like miniature temples.

The Metroön was a Doric shrine to the pre-Olympian goddess Rhea.

South Hall

Altar of Oaths

The Bouleuterion, or council house, was the seat of the Olympic Senate.

Sanctuary entrance

The Leonidaion, with its clover-shaped water-garden, accommodated distinguished guests.

RECONSTRUCTION OF OLYMPIA (AD 100)
This shows Olympia as it was under the Romans. At that time the worship of Zeus predominated; the games were dedicated to him, and his temple (containing a huge statue of the god) was at the heart of the Olympian enclosure.

Temple of Zeus
Though only column bases and tumbled sections remain, they clearly indicate the grandeur of this 5th-century BC Doric temple.

Exploring the Olympia Archaeological Museum

Archaic clay head of Hera

The Olympia Archaeological Museum, built opposite the excavation site to display its many treasures, officially opened in 1982 and is one of the richest museums in Greece. Except for the central hall, devoted solely to the pediment and metope sculptures from the Zeus temple, and the corner room dedicated to the games, the exhibits are arranged chronologically over 12 rooms, proceeding clockwise from the entrance hall from prehistory, through the Classical period, to the Romans.

Prehistoric, Geometric and Archaic Galleries

To the left of the entrance hall, room 1 contains finds from the Prehistoric period including pottery and 7th-century BC bronze reliefs. There is also a model of the early Helladic Pelopian Tumulus. Exhibits in room 2 include a bronze tripod cauldron, elongated male figures upholding cauldron handles and griffin-headed cauldron ornaments, popular in the 7th century BC. There are also bronze votive animals from the Geometric period, found in the area surrounding the altar of Zeus. Room 3 has lavishly painted terracotta architectural members from various buildings in the sanctuary.

Classical Galleries

Weapons and helmets made by pilgrims and athletes at Olympia were favourite offerings to Zeus. Two famous helmets used in the Persian Wars *(see p29)* are shown in room 4: an Assyrian helmet, and that of Miltiades, victor at the Battle of Marathon *(see p145)*. This room also contains a 5th-century BC Corinthian terracotta of *Zeus and Ganymede*, the most humanized of the portrayals of Zeus.

The central hall houses surviving relief statuary from the Temple of Zeus. Unusually, both pediments survive, their compositions carefully balanced though not precisely symmetrical. The more static east pediment tells of the chariot race between local king Oinomaos and Pelops, suitor for the hand of the king's daughter Hippodameia. Zeus stands between the two contestants; a soothsayer on his left foresees Oinomaos's defeat. The two local rivers are personified in the corners. The western pediment, a metaphor for the tension between barbarism and civilization, portrays the mythological *Battle of the Lapiths and the Centaurs*. The centaurs, invited to the wedding of Lapith king Peirithous, attempt, while

Zeus and Ganymede, in terracotta

drunk, to abduct the Lapith women. Apollo, god of reason, is central, laying a reassuring hand on Peirithous's shoulder as the latter rescues his bride from the clutches of the centaur chief. Theseus is seen to the left of Apollo preparing to dispatch another centaur, while the Lapith women watch from the safety of the corners. The interior metopes, far less intact, depict the *Twelve Labours of Herakles*, a hero mythically associated with the sanctuary.

In its own niche, the fragmentary 5th-century BC *Nike* (room 6), by the sculptor Paionios, was a thanksoffering from Messene and Náfpaktos, following their victory over Sparta during the Peloponnesian War *(see p30)*. A plaster reconstruction allows visualization of the winged goddess on the back of an eagle as she descends from heaven to proclaim victory.

The more complete *Hermes*, by Praxiteles, also has a room to itself (room 8), and shows the nude god carrying the infant Dionysos to safety, away from jealous Hera. The arm holding the newborn deity rests on a tree-trunk

Statue of *Hermes* by Praxiteles

hung with Hermes' cape; Dionysos reaches for a bunch of grapes in the elder god's now-vanished right hand. Room 7 is devoted to Pheidias's workshop and the tools and materials used to create his gold and ivory statue of Zeus.

Hellenistic and Roman Galleries

Room 9 contains late-Classical and Hellenistic finds including the terracotta sima of the Leonidaion. Rooms 10 and 11 are devoted to a series of statues of Roman emperors and generals and a marble bull dedicated by Regilla, wife of Herodes Atticus. Displays in room 12 include glass from the late-Roman cemetery at Frangonisi, Miraka, in which athletes and sanctuary officials were buried.

The Origins of the Olympic Games

The establishment of the Olympic Games in 776 BC is traditionally treated as the first certain event in Greek history. Originally, men's sprinting was the only event and competitors were local; the first recorded victor was Koroivos, a cook from nearby Elis. During the 8th and 7th centuries BC, wrestling, boxing, equestrian events and boys' competitions were added. The elite of

Title page of 1896 Games brochure

many cities came to compete and provided victory trophies, although, until the Romans took charge in 146 BC, entry was restricted to Greeks. Local cities disputed control of the games, but a sacred truce guaranteed safe conduct to spectators and competitors. Part of a pagan festival, the Christians did not approve of the games and they were banned by Theodosius I in AD 393.

The ancient pentathlon *consisted of sprinting, wrestling, javelin- and discus-throwing and the long jump (assisted by swinging weights). From 720 BC, athletes competed naked and women were excluded from spectating.*

Wrestling and boxing *are depicted on this 6th-century BC amphora. The boxers are shown wearing* himantes, *an early type of boxing glove made of leather straps wrapped around the hands and wrists.*

The Olympic revival *came in 1896, when the first modern games were held in Athens (see p113). They were organized by the Frenchman Baron Pierre de Coubertin.*

TIMELINE

Discus thrower

470–456 BC Temple of Zeus constructed; Olympia at its zenith

AD 393 Games forbidden by Emperor Theodosius I

1875 Systematic German excavations begin, continuing to the present

1896 Modern games revived

3000 BC	2000 BC	1000 BC	AD 1	AD 1000

3rd millennium BC Site of Olympia first inhabited

776 BC First recorded games

AD 67 Nero competes, unfairly rescheduling the games, and "wins" most prizes

AD 600 Alfeiós River begins to bury the site in silt

AD 551 Earthquake destroys much of site

Loúsios Gorge ⓫
Φαράγγι του Λούσιου

Walkers in the gorge

Although merely a tributary of the Alfeiós River, the Loúsios stream in its upper reaches boasts one of the most impressive canyons in Greece. Scarcely 5 km (3 miles) long, the Loúsios Gorge is nearly 300 m (985 ft) deep at the narrowest, most spectacular portion. Because of its remote mountain setting near the very centre of the Peloponnese, the Loúsios region was one of the strongholds of the revolutionaries during the Greek War of Independence *(see pp40–41)*. Medieval monasteries and churches cling to the steep cliffs of the gorge, and hiking trails have been marked, connecting some of the area's highlights. The picturesque villages *(see p176)* of the canyon's east bank make suitable touring bases.

TRIPOLI

Dimitsána is the best place to join the path.

ZATUNA

Palaiochóri

LOUSIOS GORGE

Loúsios

Néa Moní Filosófou
Situated on the west bank amid the narrows, this 17th-century monastery was renovated and restaffed by a caretaker monk. Frescoes in the church date from 1693 and illustrate many seldom-depicted biblical episodes, such as the Gadarene Swine.

★ Ancient Gortys
The Asklepieion, or therapeutic centre, of Ancient Gortys occupies a sunken excavation on the west bank. It includes the foundations of a 4th-century BC temple to Asklepios, the god of healing.

Agios Andréas, an 11th-century chapel, stands just below the Loúsios narrows.

Kókkoras Bridge
This restored medieval bridge once carried the age-old road linking the regions of Arcadia and Ileía. Anglers fish for trout here in the icy river water.

STAR SIGHTS

★ Moní Aimyalón

★ Ancient Gortys

★ Moní Agíou Ioánnou Prodrómou

Wooded flanks of the Loúsios Gorge, viewed from the south

VISITORS' CHECKLIST

Peloponnese. **Road map** C4.
🚌 *Dimitsána*. **All monasteries**
🔘 *dawn–dusk (often closed for
1–2 hours at midday)*. **Moní
Aimyalón** 🔘 *daily*. **Néa Moní
Filosófou** 🔘 *daily*. **Ancient
Gortys** 🔘 *daily*. 🔘 *main public
hols*. **Trekking** *Take walking shoes
and maps; paths are not always
robust or clearly marked. Do not
enter the gorge after heavy rain.*

ZIGOVISTI

**Paleá Moní
Filosófou**, dat-
ing to 960, is the
oldest monastery
of the area. It is
now in ruins.

★ Moní Aimyalón
*Founded in 1605, Moní Aimyalón
is tucked into a side canyon, above
garden plots. A passage partly hewn
through the rock leads to its barrel-
vaulted church with excellent
frescoes from 1608.*

KEY

🅿	Parking
═══	Minor road
– –	Footpath

TRIPOLI

Stemnítsa *(see p176)* is
a charming village and
a good place to hike
out to, having passed
through the gorge.

ELLINIKO

★ Moní Agíou Ioánnou Prodrómou
*Wedged into a palisade on
the canyon's east flank, this
12th-century monastery is the
most spectacular sight of the
Loúsios. There is room for only
a dozen monks in the tiny,
frescoed church whose shape
is dictated by the cliff face.*

0 kilometres 1

0 miles 0.5

Exploring Around the Loúsios Gorge

Overlooking the gorge are some of the most beautiful hill-towns in the Arcadia region, making good bases for exploring the area. The best-marked trail is between Néa Moní Filosófou and Moní Prodrómou (take water and food). Dimitsána has one bus service daily to Trípoli, while two weekday buses between Andrítsaina and Trípoli can be picked up below Karýtaina. Getting around by car is best, though taxis are available. Winters can be chilly and wet, with snow chains required.

Bridge over the Alfeiós River, below Karýtaina, complete with chapel

The narrow streets of Dimitsána

Dimitsána

Spread along an airy ridge with the River Loúsios on three sides and glorious views down the valley, Dimitsána stands on the Classical site of Ancient Teuthis. The town boasts four belfries; that of **Agía Kyriakí** is illuminated at night, while the three-level **Pyrsogiannítiko** bell tower was erected by skilled Epirot masons in 1888.

Two clerics involved in the 1821 revolution against Turkish rule *(see pp40–41)* were born here. The birthplace of Archbishop Germanós of Pátra, who helped instigate the revolution, is marked by a plaque near the summit of westerly Kástro hill. A plaque dedicated to Patriarch Gregory V stands in the market; he was hanged in Istanbul when news of the revolt reached the sultan.

Dimitsána's mansions date from its heyday as a trade centre in the 18th century. There were 14 powder factories here during the War of Independence – the town's **Water Mill Museum** has exhibits on powdermaking.

> 🏛 **Water Mill Museum**
> Dimitsána. *Tel 27950 31630.*
> ⭘ 10am–5pm Wed–Mon.
> ⬤ main public hols.

Stemnítsa

Situated in a large hollow, the village of Stemnítsa forms a naturally hidden fortress. In medieval times, Stemnítsa was one of Greece's main metalworking centres. Today, it boasts a well-respected school for gold- and silversmiths. A **Folk Museum** re-creates workshops of indigenous craftsmen and local house interiors, and hosts a gallery of weaponry, textiles and ceramics belonging to the Savvopoúlou family.

Among a number of magnificent medieval churches, those of **Treís Ierárches**, near the Folk Museum, and 10th-century **Profítis Ilías**, up on Kástro hill, have frescoes in excellent condition. Also at Kástro, the 12th-century **Panagía Mpaféro** has an unusual portico, while the **Moní Zoödóchou Pigís**, on the northerly hillside, was where the revolutionary chieftains held their first convention during the War of Independence; it is for this reason that Stemnítsa was called the first capital of Greece.

> 🏛 **Folk Museum**
> Stemnítsa. *Tel 27950 81252.*
> ⭘ 10am–1pm & 5–8pm daily.
> ⬤ Wed (Oct–Jun), main public hols.

Karýtaina

In a strategic position on a bend of the Alfeiós, Karýtaina is now a virtual ghost town of less than 200 inhabitants. It has a 13th-century **Kástro**, dating to the time when the town was the seat of a Frankish barony. The castle was the hideout of Theódoros Kolokotrónis, who survived a long Turkish siege here in 1826. Nearby, the **Panagía tou Kástrou** boasts restored 11th-century column capitals with intricate reliefs.

Environs

East of Karýtaina, a bridge over the Alfeiós dates to 1439; four of six original arches survive, with a tiny chapel built into one pier.

The town of Dimitsána, seen from the east

Andrítsaina ⑫
Ανδρίτσαινα

Peloponnese. **Road map** C4.
🏠 *900.* 🚌

Despite its current role as the gateway to the Temple of Bassae, the sleepy town of Andrítsaina is hardly touched by tourism. Tavernas and shops around its central square, home to a lively morning produce market, make few concessions to modernity in either their cuisine or their vivid displays. These are echoes of the 18th century, when this was a major market centre. Downhill from the 18th-century fountain of Traní, a **Folk Museum** features local rag-rugs, traditional dress and metalware.

🏛 **Folk Museum**
Andrítsaina. ◯ *daily.*
● *main public hols.*

Environs
The 5th-century BC **Temple of Bassae** graces a commanding knoll, occupying the most remote site of any major ancient sanctuary. Today it hides under an enormous tent, until 50 million euros (£33 million) can be raised to re-install the architraves. Without them, winter frost damages the temple's colonnades, now reinforced by scaffolding.

Below Bassae lies the modern village of Figaleía, named after the ancient town to the west. The citizens of Ancient Figaleía built the temple in thanks to Apollo Epikourios for stopping a plague. A path descends to the gorge of the Nédas

🏛 **Temple of Bassae**
14 km (9 miles) S of Andrítsaina. **Tel**
26260 22275. ◯ Apr–Oct: 8:30am–
8pm daily (to 3pm Nov–Mar). 🔲 ♿

Ancient Tegéa ⑬
Τεγέα

Peloponnese. **Road map** C4.
Tel 27150 56540. 🚌 **Site** ◯ daily.
Museum ◯ 8:30am–3pm Tue–Sun.
● main public hols. ♿

South of modern Trípoli, the remains of the ancient city of Tegéa lie near the village of Aléa. The most impressive

Typical street-café scene at the traditional town of Andrítsaina

ruin is the 4th-century BC Doric temple of Athena Aléa, with its massive column drums, the second largest temple in the Peloponnese after Olympia's Temple of Zeus (*see p171*). The site **museum** has sculpture from the city, including a number of fragments of the temple pediment.

Argos ⑭
Άργος

Peloponnese. **Road map** C4.
🏠 *20,000.* 🚌

One of the oldest settlements in Greece, modern Argos is a busy, rather shabby market town, with its open-air fairground next to a restored Neo-Classical marketplace. To the east of the central square, the **Archaeological Museum** exhibits local finds from all eras. Highlights include a bronze helmet and breast-plate, and an Archaic pottery fragment showing Odysseus blinding Polyphimos, as well as a *krater* (bowl) from the 7th century BC.

The most visible traces of Ancient Argos lie on the way to Trípoli, where Roman baths and an amphitheatre are dwarfed by the size of one of the largest and most steeply raked theatres in the Greek world. From here a path climbs Lárisa hill, one of Argos's two ancient acropoleis.

🏛 **Archaeological Museum**
E of Plateía Agíou Pétrou. **Tel** 27510
68819. ◯ 8:30am–3pm Tue–Sun.
● main public hols. 🔲 ♿

Environs
Heading south of Ancient Argos, past the theatre, a minor road leads to the village of **Ellinikó** on the outskirts of which stands an intact pyramidal building. Dating from the 4th century BC, the structure is thought to have been a fort guarding the road to Arcadia.

Lérna, further south, is a 2200-BC palace dubbed the "House of the Tiles" for its original terracotta roofing. It now shelters under a modern protective canopy. Adjacent Neolithic house foundations and two Mycenaean graves, inside the palace foundations, suggest two millennia of habitation. Settlers were attracted by springs which powered watermills and still feed a deep seaside pond. This was the home of the legendary nine-headed serpent Hydra, which Herakles killed as one of his Labours (*see p53*).

Seating in the ancient theatre of Argos, seen from the stage

Mycenae ⑮
Μυκήναι

The fortified palace complex of Mycenae, uncovered by the archaeologist Heinrich Schliemann *(see p180)* in 1874, is one of the earliest examples of sophisticated citadel architecture. The term "Mycenaean", more properly late Bronze Age, applies to an entire culture spanning the years 1700–1100 BC. Only the ruling class inhabited this hilltop palace, with artisans and merchants living just outside the city walls. It was abandoned in 1100 BC after a period of great disruption in the region.

Secret Stairway
A flight of 99 steps drops to a cistern deep beneath the citadel. A torch is needed to see your way down the steps. Linked to a spring outside, the cistern provided water in times of siege.

Northeast gate

Lion Gate
The Lion Gate was erected in the 13th century BC, when the walls were realigned to enclose Grave Circle A. It takes its name from the lions carved above the lintel.

Artisans' workshops

The megaron was the social heart of the palace.

MYCENAE TODAY

Secret Stairway
Royal Palace
Grave Circle A
Klytemnestra's Tomb

Lion Gate
Path to the Treasury of Atreus
Grave Circle B

Bastion

RECONSTRUCTION OF MYCENAE
This illustration shows Mycenae as it was in the time of the House of Atreus and the 1250 BC Trojan War *(see pp54–5)*. Most tombs lie outside the walls *(see p180)*.

Royal Palace

Situated at the acropolis summit, only the floors remain of this central structure. Burn-marks dating to its destruction in 1200 BC are still visible on the stone.

The "Cyclopean" walls, up to 14 m (46 ft) wide, were unbreachable. Later Greeks imagined that they had been built by giants.

The houses of Mycenae yielded a number of tablets inscribed with an archaic script, known as Linear B, deciphered by Michaïl Ventrís in 1952.

The House of Tsoúntas, named after its discoverer, was a minor palace.

Klytemnestra, after murdering her husband, Agamemnon

THE CURSE OF THE HOUSE OF ATREUS

King Atreus slaughtered his brother Thyestes's children and fed them to him; for this outrage the gods laid a curse on Atreus and his descendants *(see p180).* Thyestes's surviving daughter, Pelopia, bore her own father a son, Aigisthos, who murdered Atreus and restored Thyestes to the throne of Mycenae. But Atreus also had an heir, the energetic Agamemnon, who seized power.

Agamemnon raised a fleet to punish the Trojan Paris, who had stolen his brother's wife, Helen. He sacrificed his daughter to obtain a favourable wind. When he returned he was murdered by his wife, Klytemnestra, and her lover – none other than Aigisthos. The murderous pair were in turn disposed of by Agamemnon's children, Orestes and Elektra.

Great ramp

Grave Circle A

This contained six royal family shaft graves containing 19 bodies. The 14 kg (31 lb) of gold funerary goods are on display in Athens (see p70).

Exploring the Tombs of Mycenae

Mycenae's nobles were entombed in shaft graves, such as Grave Circle A *(see p179)* or, later, in *tholos* ("beehive") tombs. The *tholos* tombs, found outside the palace walls, were built using successive circles of masonry, each level nudged steadily inward to narrow the diameter until the top could be closed with a single stone. The entire structure was then buried, save for an entrance approached by a *dromos* or open-air corridor.

The entrance to the Treasury of Atreus, with a gap over its lintel

Treasury of Atreus

The Treasury of Atreus *(see p179)* is the most outstanding of the *tholos* tombs. Situated at the southern end of the site, the tomb dates from the 14th century BC and is one of only two double-chambered tombs in Greece. It has a 36-m (120-ft) *dromos* flanked by dressed stone and a small ossuary (the second chamber) which held the bones from previous

burials. A 9-m (30-ft) long lintel stone stands over the entrance; weighing almost 120 tonnes (264,550 lb), it is still not known how it was hoisted into place, and is a tribute to Mycenaean building skills.

The treasury is also known as the Tomb of Agamemnon. However, the legendary king and commander of the Trojan expedition *(see pp54–5)* could not have been buried here, as the construction of the tomb predates the estimated period of the Trojan War by more than 100 years.

Tomb of Klytemnestra

Of the other *tholos* tombs only the so-called Tomb of Klytemnestra, which is situated just west of the Lion Gate, is as well preserved as that of Atreus. It is a small, single-chambered sepulchre with narrower and more steeply inclined walls, but the finely masoned *dromos* and similar triangular air hole over the entrance (which also relieved pressure on the lintel) date it to the same period.

HEINRICH SCHLIEMANN

Born in Mecklenburg, Germany, Heinrich Schliemann (1822–90) was self-educated and by the age of 47 had become a millionaire, expressly to fund his archaeological digs. Having discovered Troy and demonstrated the factual basis of Homer's epics, he came to Mycenae in 1874 and commenced digging in Grave Circle A. On discovering a gold death mask which had preserved the skin of a royal skull, he proclaimed: "I have gazed upon the face of Agamemnon!" Although archaeologists have since dated the mask to 300 years earlier than any historical Trojan warrior, the discovery corroborated Homer's description of "well-built Mycenae, rich in gold".

TREASURY OF ATREUS

Unlike their Greek contemporaries who would cremate their dead, the Mycenaeans buried their deceased in tombs. In the Treasury of Atreus, a Mycenaean king was buried with his weapons and enough food and drink for his journey through the Underworld.

Tholos, made of 33 rows of stone

Doorway

Dromos, with walls lined with water-proofing clay

Resting-place of the king's body

Ossuary

Earth mound covering the entire chamber

Ancient Tiryns ⑯
Τίρυνθα

4 km (2 miles) NW of Náfplio, Peloponnese. **Road map** C4. **Tel** 27520
22657. ⬛ ⬜ *Apr–Oct: 8am–8pm
daily; Nov–Mar: 8:30am–3pm daily.* 📷

The 13th-century BC citadel
of Tiryns confirms Homer's
epithet "mighty-walled". A
700-m (2,300-ft) circuit of
Cyclopean walls (named
after the giants who could be
imagined manoeuvering the
huge blocks into place) attains
a thickness of 8 m (26 ft).
The fortifications, over double
their present height, were
necessarily stronger than those
of Mycenae since Tiryns was
not on a naturally strong site.

**Excavated ruins of the Cyclopean
walls, Tiryns**

The bluff on which it stood
was only 18 m (59 ft) higher
than the surrounding plain
which, in ancient times, was a
salt marsh.

An inclined ramp to the east,
designed with sharp turns to
expose attackers' unshielded
sides, leads to the massive
middle gate, the lintel of which
has long been missing. At the
southern end of the complex,
beyond and beneath the
vanished inner gate, a gallery
with a pointed corbel ceiling
has had its walls polished by
the fleeces of sheep which
have sheltered here for centuries. On the west side, a
stone stairway between inner
and outer walls, leading to a
postern gate, has been completely preserved. The lower,
northern acropolis was the
last to be enclosed and was
used to protect commoners,
animals and (as at Mycenae)
a water supply.

Environs
The early 13th-century
Byzantine church of
the Panagías rears up
startlingly in the
cemetery at **Agía
Triáda**, a village which
is 5 km (3 miles) north
of Tiryns. The walls
are constructed of
ancient masonry to
shoulder height;
above that, at the
southeast corner of
the building, the
builders have inserted
an entire Classical
grave *stele*.

Further north, the
Argive Heraion was the
Archaic and Classical religious
centre of the Argolid. The
most impressive remains are
those of a late 5th-century BC
temple. Home to the priestesses of Hera, and a huge
ivory-and-gold cult statue of
the goddess, the temple was
flanked by stoas, identifiable
by remaining column stumps.
Above the temple is the ledge
where the Achaian leaders
swore loyalty to Agamemnon
before sailing for Troy. To
the west, complete with drain-
gutter, stands the "Peristyle
Building" where *symposia*
were hosted.

🏛 **Argive Heraion**
10 km (6 miles) N of Tiryns.
⬜ *8:30am–3pm daily.*

Náfplio ⑰

See pp182–3.

Epidaurus ⑱

See pp184–5.

Tower of Theseus, Ancient Troezen

Ancient Troezen ⑲
Τροιζήνα

60 km (37 miles) E of Náfplio,
Peloponnese. **Road map** D4.
⬜ *unrestricted access.*

Near the modern village
of Troizína are the sparse
ruins of ancient Troezen, the
legendary birthplace of the
hero Theseus and the setting
for Euripides' incestuous tragedy *Hippolytus*. Remains from
many eras are scattered over a
wide area; most conspicuous
are three Byzantine chapels
known as *Episkopí*, from the
time when this was the seat
of the Bishops of Damála.

The town was built on a
high bluff isolated by two
ravines; the westerly Damála
Gorge is sheer, and half an
hour's walk up it a natural
rock arch called the "Devil's
Bridge" spans the canyon.
Near the lower end of the
gorge stands the "Tower of
Theseus", Hellenistic at its
base, medieval higher up.

Foundations of the Argive Heraion, seen at dawn

Náfplio ⑰
Ναύπλιο

With its marble pavements, looming castles and remarkably homogenous architecture, Náfplio is the most elegant town in mainland Greece. It emerged from obscurity in the 13th century and endured many sieges during the struggles between Venice and Turkey for the ports of the Peloponnese. The medieval quarter, to the west, is mostly a product of the second Venetian occupation (1686–1715). From 1829 until 1834, the town was the first capital of liberated Greece.

View over Náfplio from the stairway to the Palamídi fortress

Exploring Náfplio

Defended to the south by the Akronafplía and Palamídi fortresses and to the north by Boúrtzi castle, Náfplio occupies the northern side of a peninsula at the head of the Argolic Gulf. Since the Venetian period, **Plateía Syntágmatos** has been the hub of public life, and still looks much as it did three centuries ago when a couple of mosques were erected by the victorious Ottomans. One stands at the east end of the square and now houses a cinema;

President Kapodístrias

Vouleftikó Mosque, to the south, was where the Greek parliament (*voulí*) first met. West of the bus station, **Agios Geórgios** cathedral was built as a mosque during the first Ottoman occupation (1540–1686). Also converted is the **Catholic church**, another early mosque near the top of Potamiánou, which contains a monument honouring fallen philhellenes, including George Washington's nephew. Four Turkish fountains survive from the second Turkish occupation (1715–1822). The most famous are the scroll-arched one behind the "Cinema" Mosque and another opposite **Agios Spyrídon** on Kapodistríou; this is near where President Kapodístrias was assassinated on 9 October 1831. There are less elaborate Ottoman fountains up the steps at number 9 Tertsétou, and at the corner of Potamiánou and Kapodistríou.

📷 Archaeological Museum

Plateía Syntágmatos. **Tel** 27520 27502. ☐ 8:30am–3pm Tue–Sun. ♿
Exhibits here largely centre on Mycenaean artifacts from various local sites, including Tiryns (*see p181*). Noteworthy are a Neolithic *thylastro* (baby-bottle), a late Helladic octopus vase, a full set of bronze Mycenaean armour and a complete Mycenaean boar's tusk helmet. There is also a large selection of Prehistoric, Archaic and Classical pottery.

📷 Folk Art Museum

Vas. Alexandrou 1. **Tel** 27520 28379. ☐ 9:30am–2:30pm Mon–Sat, 10am–3pm Sun. 📷 ♿
This award-winning museum, established in a former mansion by the Peloponnesian Folklore Foundation, focuses on textiles. Regional costumes are exhibited across two floors with Queen Olga's stunning blue and white wedding gown taking pride of place on the first floor. Also on the first floor are paintings by major Greek artists Giánnis Tsaroúchis and Theófilos Chatzimichaïl (*see p218*). On the second floor are guns and an impressive grandfather clock decorated with revolutionary scenes.

⚓ Boúrtzi

NW of harbour.
This island fortress acquired its appearance during the second Venetian occupation, and until 1930 had the dubious distinction of being the local executioner's residence. It defended the only navigable passage in the bay; the channel could

The fortified isle of Boúrtzi, north of Náfplio harbour

be closed off by a chain extending from the fortress to the town.

♦ Akronafplía

W of Palamídi.
🕐 *unrestricted access.*
Akronafplía, also known as Its Kale ("Inner Castle" in Turkish), was the site of the Byzantine and early medieval town, and contains four Venetian castles built in sequence from west to east. The most interesting

Palamídi fortress seen from the isle of Boúrtzi

relic is the Venetian Lion of St Mark relief over the 15th-century gate just above the Catholic church. The western-most "Castle of the Greeks" was Náfplio's ancient acropolis, now home to the clocktower, a major landmark.

♦ Palamídi

Polyzoïdou. *Tel* 27520 28036. 🕐 *Apr–Oct: 8am–7:30pm; Nov–Mar: 8:30am–2:30pm daily.* 🔲 *main public hols.* 🎫
Palamídi, named after the Homeric hero Palamedes, the son of Náfplios and Kliméni, is a huge Venetian citadel built between 1711 and 1714. It was designed to withstand all contemporary artillery, though

it fell to the Ottomans in 1715 after a mere one-week siege, and to the Greek rebels led by Stáïkos Staïkópoulos on 30 November 1822, after an 18-month campaign.

The largest such complex in Greece, Palamídi consists of a single curtain wall enclosing seven self-sufficient forts, now named after Greek heroes; the gun slits are aimed at each other as well as outward, in case an enemy managed to penetrate the defences. Fort Andréas was the Venetian

Detail above fountain, Agía Moní

headquarters, with a Lion of St Mark in relief over its entrance. The Piazza d'Armi, from where Náfplio assumes toy-town dimensions below you, offers arguably the best views in the country. At the summit, an eighth fort, built by the Ottomans, looks south towards Karathóna beach.

Environs

The 12th-century convent of **Agía Moní** nestles 4 km (2 miles) outside Náfplio; the octagonal dome-drum rests on four columns with Corinthian capitals. Just outside the walls, in an orchard, the Kánathos fountain still springs from a niche decorated with animal reliefs; this was ancient Amymone, where the goddess Hera bathed each year to renew her virginity.

NAFPLIO TOWN CENTRE

Agios Geórgios ④
Agios Spyrídon ⑤
Akronafplía ⑦
Archaeological Museum ①
Catholic Church ⑥
Folk Art Museum ③
Plateía Syntágmatos ②

Boúrtzi
PLATEIA IATROU
BOUBOULINAS
Agia Moni
VAS. OTHONOS
VAS. OLGAS
AKTI MIAOULI
VAS. ALEXANDROU
IPSILANDOU
Folk Art Museum ③
Archaeological Museum
AMALIAS
PLATEIA SYNTAGMATOS ① ②
War Museum
PLATEIA TRIONNA-VARHON
PLATEIA KAPODISTRIOU
VAS. KONSTANTINOU
STAIKOPOLOU
Bus Station
PLAPOUTA
Tourist information 100m (110 yards)
ZYGOMALA
FETHINIS ANDSTASIS
POTAMIANOU KOKKINOU
TERZAKI
Agios Spyrídon ⑤
KAPODISTRIOU PAPANIKOLAOU
Agios Geórgios ④
PLATEIA STAIKOPOULOU
Catholic Church ⑥
FOTOMARA
Clock Tower
⑦
Akronaflía Fortress
Palamídi

0 metres 200
0 yards 200

Key to Symbols *see back flap*

Epidaurus ⑱
Επίδαυρος

Though most renowned for its magnificent theatre, the Sanctuary of Epidaurus was an extensive thera-peutic and religious centre, dedicated to the healing god Asklepios. A mortal physician deified by Zeus after his death for retrieving a patient from the underworld, Asklepios was depicted in his temple here clutching a staff and flanked by a dog and a serpent – common symbols of natural wisdom. This sanctuary was active from the 6th century BC until at least the 2nd century AD, when the traveller-historian Pausanias recorded a visit.

Dusk over Epidaurus during a modern production at the theatre

The Theatre
Designed by Polykleitos the Younger late in the 4th cen-tury BC, the theatre is well known for its near-perfect acoustics which are endlessly demonstrated by tour group leaders. Owing to the sanc-tuary's relative remoteness, its masonry was never pilfered, and it remained undiscovered until the 1970s. It has the only circular *orchestra* (stage) to have survived from antiquity, though the altar that once stood in the centre has now gone. Two side corridors, or *paradoi*, gave the actors access to the stage; each had a monu-mental gateway whose pillars have

now been re-erected. Behind the *orchestra* and facing the auditorium stand the remains of the *skene*, the main reception

Foundations of the *tholos* building in the Asklepieion

hall, and the *proskenion* which was used by performers as an extension of the stage. Today, the theatre is still the venue for a popular summer festival of ancient drama.

The Asklepieion
Most of the Asklepieion, or Sanctuary of Asklepios, is being re-excavated and many of its monuments are off-limits. One of the accessible sites is the *propylaia*, or monumental gate-way, at the north edge of the sanctuary, its original entrance. Also preserved are a ramp and some buckled pavement from the Sacred Way which led north from the gateway to the coastal town of ancient Epidaurus. At the northwestern end of the

RECONSTRUCTION OF THE THEATRE
Surrounding the central *orchestra*, the north-facing *cavea* (cavity) of the theatre is 114 m (374 ft) across and is divided into blocks by 36 staircases.

Parados

Skene

Proskenion

The orchestra, 20 m (66 ft) in diameter, is the stage on which the actors performed.

The top 21 tiers were added in the Roman period.

A paved depression, 2 m (6 ft) wide, collected rainwater.

Diazoma (walkway)

The lower 34 rows are original, dating to the 4th century BC.

Overview of today's site showing the stadium at the bottom (west)

sanctuary stand the remains of the *tholos* (a circular building of uncertain function, also designed by Polykleitos) whose concentric passages are thought to have been used either as a pit for sacred serpents, or possibly as the locale for rites by the cult's priests. Patients slept in the *enkoimitírion* – a hall north of the *tholos* where they would await a diagnostic dream or a visit from the

harmless serpents. Therapeutic mineral springs, which are still on tap beside the museum, also played a part in the curing of patients who were brought here. Only the foundations of Asklepios's temple have survived, lying to the east of the *tholos*.

Another undisturbed point is the late Classical stadium south of the *tholos*. With intact rows of stone benches and a

starting line still visible, this was used during the quadrennial festival in honour of Asklepios. The Romans built an odeion inside the Hellenistic gymnasium, to host the festival's musical contests.

Environs

The adjacent village of Lygourió reflects the importance of the region during Byzantine times. There are three Byzantine churches, the most distinguished being the 14th-century **Koímisis tis Theotókou**, which has superb early medieval frescoes.

THE ORIGINS OF GREEK DRAMA

Greek drama developed from ritual role-play at festivals of Dionysos *(see p52)*. First came group dancing – 6th-century BC Athenian vases show groups elaborately costumed, often as animals. In the late 6th century BC, the first Greek theatres appeared: rectangular (later round) spaces with seats on three sides. Singing and dancing choruses were joined by individual actors, whose masks made visible at a distance the various character roles, all played by just three male actors. The depiction of animal choruses on vases suggests humorous presentation, but the earliest plays in Athens were tragedies, staged in sets of three by a single writer *(see p57)*, in which episodes from epic poems and mythology were acted out. Historical events were rarely dramatized as they

Masks *were worn by actors to express the personality of the characters they played.*

were politically sensitive. Comedy became part of the dramatic festival at Athens only in the 480s BC.

Theatre was mass entertainment and had to cater for large numbers – during the Roman period, the theatre at Epidaurus could hold 13,000 people – but it is uncertain whether women were permitted to attend the performances.

Souvenir statuettes, *such as this terracotta figurine of a sinister character from one of the later comedies, could be bought as mementos after performances.*

The chorus, *though chiefly an impersonal commentator, often spoke directly to the characters, questioning them on the wisdom of their actions.*

Monemvasía ⑳
Μονεμβασία

A fortified town built on two levels on a rock rearing 350 m (1,150 ft) above the sea, Monemvasía well deserves its nickname, "the Gibraltar of Greece". A town of 50,000 in its 15th-century prime, Monemvasía enjoyed centuries of existence as a semi-autonomous city-state, living off the commercial acumen (and occasional piracy) of its fleets and its strategic position astride the sea lanes from Italy to the Black Sea. Exceptionally well defended, it was never taken by force but fell only through protracted siege *(see p188)*. Though the upper town is in ruins, most of the lower town is restored.

Mural above the main entrance to Agía Sofía

Pathway to Upper Town
A paved stair-street zigzags up the cliff face from the lower town to the tower gate of the upper town (see p188).

★ Agía Sofía
Standing at the summit of Monemvasía, this beautiful 13th-century church is the only intact remnant of the upper town (see p188).

Giánnis Rítsos's House
Immediately next to the gate, the birthplace of prominent poet and communist Giánnis Rítsos (1909–90) is marked by a plaque and a bust at the front.

Western gate

The mosque has been refurbished as a museum to display local finds, including some fine marble works.

Panagía Myrtidiótissa
The façade of this 18th-century church sports a Byzantine inscription and a double-headed eagle from an earlier Byzantine church.

STAR SIGHTS
- ★ Agía Sofía
- ★ Walls

"The Gibraltar of Greece"

Monemvasía was severed from the mainland by an earthquake in AD 375, remaining an island until the causeway was built in the 6th century.

VISITORS' CHECKLIST

Peloponnese. **Road map** C5.
800. Main square. Géfira.
27320 61210 *(number for the tourist police, available during summer)*. **Mosque Museum:** *Tel* 27320 61403.
8am–3pm Tue–Sun.
Mon & main public hols.

Agios Nikólaos, begun in 1703, resembles Myrtidiótissa in its masonry, cruciform plan and cement-covered dome.

★ Walls

The 16th-century walls are 900 m (2,953 ft) long and up to 30 m (98 ft) high. Much of the parapet can be walked.

The east gate opens on to a former burial ground known as Lípsoma.

Panagía Chrysafítissa has its bell hanging from a cypress tree.

The sea gate gave access to the sea when the main port was threatened.

Christós Elkómenos

Restored in 1697, this 13th-century cathedral with its Venetian belfry is stark inside; the only decoration is the plaque of two peacocks above the door.

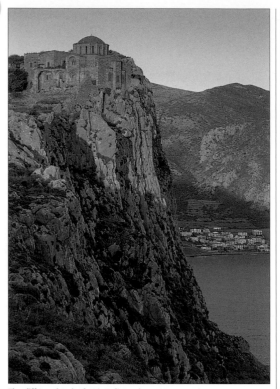

The cliff-top church of Agía Sofía, at dawn, Monemvasía upper town

Exploring the Upper Town

First fortified in the 6th century as a refuge from raiding Avars, the upper town is the oldest part of Monemvasía. Largely in ruins, the area is now under the protection of the Greek archaeological service. Though in medieval times it was the most densely populated part of the peninsula,

Ruins of Monemvasía's 13th-century fortress

the upper town is deserted today, the last resident having departed in 1911.

A path climbs the cliff face above the town's north-western corner, leading to an entrance gate which still has its iron slats. Directly ahead a track leads to the summit's best-preserved building, the church of **Agía Sofía**. It was founded by Emperor Andronikos II (1282–1328) in emulation of Dafní monastery *(see pp152–3)* near Athens. With its 16-sided dome, the church perches on the brink of the northerly cliff and is visible from a considerable distance inland. The west portico is Venetian, while the niche on the south wall dates from its use as a mosque. A few frescoes surviving from the early 14th century are badly faded, but the *Ancient of Days* can be discerned in the sanctuary's vault, as can the *Birth of John the Baptist* in the north vault. Carved ornamentation has fared better, such as the

For hotels and restaurants in this region see pp268–70 and pp289–91

THE SIEGE OF MONEMVASIA

The siege of Monemvasía by the Greeks, early in the War of Independence *(see pp40–41)*, began on 28 March 1821. Due to a Greek ruse, the town's Turkish garrison was badly supplied with food, and reinforcements failed to arrive. By late June, both Christians and Muslims were forced to eat weeds, cats and mice, some even resorting to cannibalism. Turkish civilians in the lower town urged surrender, but the garrison of the upper town refused. The besiegers also seemed set to give up, but one night, the Greek commander inside the town convinced three messengers to swim from the Portello Gate to the revolutionary forces on the mainland, giving them word to persevere. They did, and on 1 August the Turks surrendered, handing over the keys of the city to the Greek Prince Kantakouzinós.

The taking of Monemvasía by Prince Kantakouzinós

marble capitals flanking the south windows, depicting mythical monsters and a richly dressed woman.

To the west are the remains of a 13th-century **fortress**, amid the debris of former barracks, guardrooms and a gunpowder magazine from the Venetian period. A vast **cistern** recalls the times of siege when great quantities of water had to be stored. Food supplies, entirely imported, were more of a problem, as was demonstrated by the siege of 1821.

Agía Paraskeví, viewed from Byzantine Geráki

Geráki ㉑
Γεράκι

Peloponnese. **Road map** C5.
🏛 2,000. 🚌

Occupying a spur of Mount Párnonas, Geráki is like a miniature Mystrás with its *kástro* overlooking the frescoed Byzantine churches on the slopes below. The polygonal **kástro** was built in 1254–5 by the Frank, Jean de Nivelet, though it was ceded in 1262 to the Byzantines, together with Monemvasía and Mystrás. Inside, 13th-century **Agios Geórgios** is a hybrid Franko-Byzantine church, the third

aisle and narthex added after 1262; a carved marble screen and varied frescoes decorate its interior.

Below the west gate, 13th-century **Zoödóchou Pigís** sports a complete Gothic door and south window, while inside later frescoes include *Christ on the Road to Calvary*.

At the base of the hill, the domeless, 14th-century church of **Agía Paraskeví** has a fine *Nativity* in its cross vault, plus a painting of the donor family on the west wall.

Environs
Four more churches stand a short drive to the west in **Geráki** village. Both 12th-century Agios Athanásios and 13th-century Agios Sózon share a cross-in-square plan, with a high dome on four piers. Market edicts of the Roman Emperor Diocletian, inscribed on stone, flank the doorway of barrel-vaulted, 14th-century Agios Ioánnis Chrysóstomos, covered inside with scenes from the life of Christ and the Virgin. Tiny Evangelístria has a Pantokrátor fresco in its dome.

7th-century BC clay head of a woman, from Spárti acropolis

Spárti ㉒
Σπάρτη

Peloponnese. **Road map** C5.
🏛 20,000. 🚌

Though one of the most powerful of the Greek city-states, ancient Sparta was unfortified and has few ruins dating to its heyday. The acropolis lies 700 m (2,300 ft) northwest of the modern town centre. On the western side of the acropolis is the cavity of the Roman theatre, its masonry largely pilfered to build Mystrás, while directly east stands the long, arcaded stoa which once held shops. Of the Artemis Orthia sanctuary just east of town, where Spartan youths were flogged to prove their manhood, only some Roman seating remains. The most interesting finds are on display in the museum.

The highlight of the rich **Archaeological Museum** is the fine collection of Roman mosaics, including two lions rampant over a vase, Arion riding his dolphin, Achilles disguised as a woman on Skýros, and a portrait of Alkibiades. A Classical marble head of a warrior, possibly Leonidas I *(see p224)*, was found on the acropolis, while bas-reliefs of Under-world serpent-deities hail from a sanctuary of Apollo at Amyklés, 8 km (5 miles) south of Spárti. Bizarre ceramic masks are smaller replicas of those used in dances at the Artemis Orthia sanctuary.

🏛 **Archaeological Museum**
Agíou Níkonos 71. **Tel** 27310 28575. ☐ 8am–3pm Tue–Sun.
● main public hols. 🖼 ♿

LIFE IN ANCIENT SPARTA

Rising to prominence around 700 BC, Sparta became one of the most powerful city-states of ancient Greece. Its power was based on rigid social and military discipline, as well as hatred of foreigners, which eventually led to its downfall as it had no allies. The "city" was made up of five villages, where the male citizens lived communally in constant readiness for war. Warriors were selected at the age of seven and subjected to rigorous training – whipping contests, with young boys as the victims, were held in the sanctuary of Artemis Orthia. Sparta was able to support its citizens as professional soldiers because it had conquered neighbouring Messenia, and the enslaved population provided all the food required. Sparta led the Greek forces against the Persians, but ceased to be a major power after defeat by Thebes in 371 BC.

5th-century BC bronze figurine of a Spartan warrior

Mystrás ㉓
Μυστράς

Double-eagle marble plaque, Mitrópoli

Majestic Mystrás occupies a panoramic site on a spur of the severe Taÿgetos range. Founded by the Franks in 1249, it soon passed to the Byzantines, under whom it became a town of 20,000 and, after 1348, the seat of the Despots of Morea. The despotate acted semi-independently and had become the last major Byzantine cultural centre by the 15th century, attracting scholars and artists from Italy and Serbia as well as Constantinople. One result was the uniquely cosmopolitan decoration of the Mystrás churches – their pastel-coloured frescoes, crowded with detail, reflect Italian Renaissance influence.

PLAN OF MYSTRAS

KASTRO

UPPER TOWN

LOWER TOWN

Spárti & Néos Mystrás

0 metres   100
0 yards   100

KEY TO PLAN
① Lower town entrance
② Mitrópoli
③ Moní Perivléptou
④ Moní Pantánassas
⑤ Vrontóchion
⑥ Monemvasía Gate
⑦ Despots' Palace
⑧ Agía Sofía
⑨ Upper town entrance
⑩ Kástro

Exploring Mystrás
Now in ruins, Mystrás consists of a lower and upper town, linked by the Monemvasía Gate. The site can be entered from the castle at the top of the upper town or from the base of the lower town. Allow half a day for exploring the monasteries, churches, palaces and houses which line the narrow, winding streets. An unusual northwest-to-southeast alignment of the churches is dictated by the site's steep topography.

VISITORS' CHECKLIST

5 km (3 miles) W of Spárti, Peloponnese. **Road map** C5. *Tel 27310 83377.* ▦ to Néos Mystrás. ☐ May–Sep: 8am–8pm daily; Oct–Apr: 8:30am–3pm daily. ● 1 Jan, 25 Mar, Good Fri, Easter Sun, 1 May, 25 & 26 Dec. ▦ ▢

courtyard. Like many Balkan cathedrals, it began life in 1291 as a barrel-vaulted nave flanked by two aisles. The domes were added early in the 1400s in a clumsy attempt to equal the architecture of the Pantánassas and Afentikó churches. Frescoes, mostly early 14th century, show the martyrdom of the church's patron (Agios Dimítrios) in the northeast vaulting, while Christ's miracles begin next to these with the *Healing of the Lepers* and continue on the southwest aisle in such scenes as the *Wedding at Cana*. In the narthex is the *Preparation of the Throne of Judgment*, flanked by angels, a theme repeated in the southwest diaconicon (sacristy). The last Byzantine emperor, Konstantínos Palaiológos, was crowned here in 1449; a double-eagle plaque marks the spot.

🛈 Mitrópoli
The Mitrópoli, situated by the lower town entrance, is the oldest church in Mystrás. It is approached through a double

The 14th-century fresco of the *Nativity* in the south vault of Moní Perivléptou

🛈 Moní Perivléptou
Squeezed against the rock face, the 14th-century monastery of Perivléptou has a compact, three-aisled church. Its small dome retains a fresco of the Pantokrátor, flanked by the Virgin and prophets, arranged in diminishing order of importance. The 14th-century frescoes, the most refined in Mystrás, focus on the 12 major church feasts. They include a vivid *Nativity* and *Baptism* in the south vault, the *Transfiguration* and *Entry into Jerusalem*, complete with playing children, in the west aisle, and *Doubting Thomas* and the *Pentecost* in the north vault, decorating the wall over the entrance.

The hillside with remains of Byzantine Mystrás, seen from the south

🏛 Moní Pantánassas

Dating to 1428, Pantánassas was the last church built at Mystrás. With its decorated apses and the brickwork of its arcaded belfry it imitates Afentikó in the Vrontóchion as an eclectic architectural experiment. The highest frescoes, from 1430, are of most merit, particularly a vivid *Raising of Lazarus* in the northeast vault. Both the *Nativity* and the *Annunciation* in the southwest vault feature animals. The southeast aisle displays the *Descent into Hell*, in which Christ raises Adam and Eve from their coffins, opposite a lively *Entry into Jerusalem*.

🏛 Vrontóchion

A 13th-century monastic complex built by Abbot Pachómios, the Vrontóchion was the cultural centre of medieval Mystrás – in the 15th century, the Neo-Platonist philosopher Geórgios Gemistós, or Plethon, 1355–1452) taught here. It has

two churches; the earliest, Agioi Theódoroi, dates from 1295 and has the largest dome at Mystrás, supported on eight arches. Few frescoes survive. The early 14th-century Afentikó (or Panagía Odigítria) is richly frescoed, with six domes. The galleries and two north-side chapels are shut, but in the west gallery dome a *Virgin Orans* (praying) and *Prophets* are visible; in the south vault, a crowded *Baptism* includes water monsters. Above the altar, apostles gesticulate towards the aura of the rising Christ in the *Ascension*. The best-preserved frescoes can be found in the north bay of the narthex.

🏰 Despots' Palace

The Despots' Palace consists of two wings which are currently being reconstructed. The northeast wing was begun by the Franks; the northwest hall, erected after 1348 and a rare example of Byzantine civic

architecture, has the throne room of the rulers of the Cantacuzene and Palaiológos dynasties. The square was a venue for public events under the despots and a marketplace under the Ottomans.

The ruins of the Despots' Palace, viewed from the south

⛰ Kástro

Flanked by sheer ravines to the south and west, and crowning the summit of the upper town, the kástro is reached by a path leading from the upper entrance which stands above the church of Agía Sofía. Built by Guillaume de Villehardouin in 1249, the kástro retains its original Frankish design, though it was greatly altered by the Byzantines and Turks. A double circuit of curtain walls encloses two baileys and a walkway can be taken around most of the structure, affording panoramic views over the lower town.

It was here that the German writer Goethe, in Part Two of *Faust*, set the meeting of Faust and Helen of Troy, revived after 3,000 years.

Afentikó church, part of the Vrontóchion complex

Outer Máni ㉔
Έξω Μάνη

A harsh, remote region, bounded by mountains to the north, the rocky Máni was the last part of Greece to embrace Christianity, doing so in the 9th century with an enthusiasm borne out by dozens of surviving Byzantine chapels. Though well defended against invaders, the area has a history of internal feuding which led to the building of its many tower houses. A ravine at Oítylo divides Inner Máni, to the south *(see pp198–9)*, from the more fertile Outer, or Messenian, Máni which boasts some of the finest country in the Mediterranean.

LOCATOR MAP

from the Turks, the Oítylots were granted passage by the Genoese and, once in Corsica, founded the villages of Paomia and Cargèse. These towns account for the stories of Napoleon's part-Mániot origins.

Environs
From the southwestern corner of Oítylo, a broad path descends west to **Moní Dekoúlou**, nestled in its own little oasis. The 18th-century church features an ornate *témblon* (wooden altar screen) and vivid original frescoes; though they have been preserved by the darkness, a torch is required to see them now. The monastery is only open in the evenings or by prior arrangement with the resident caretakers.

The village of **Néo Oítylo** stands 4 km (2 miles) south of the monastery. Quietly secluded, the village has a pebble beach with fine views.

Oítylo
Though administratively within the region of Lakonía, by tradition the village of Oítylo (pronounced "Itilo") belongs to the Outer Máni. It affords superb panoramic views over Limeníou Bay and across a flanking ravine, traditionally the border betwen the Inner and Outer Máni, to Kelefá Castle *(see p198)*. Its relatively good water supply fosters a lush setting around and below the village, with cypresses and a variety of orchard trees. Unlike most Mániot villages, Oítylo is not in economic decline. Its many fine houses include graceful 19th-century mansions. The village was capital of the Máni between the 16th and 18th centuries, and was the area's most infamous slave-trading centre; both Venetians and Turks were sold to each other here. A plaque in the square, written in French and Greek, commemorates the flight, in 1675, of 730 Oítylots to Corsica – 430 of whom were from the Stefanópoulos clan. Seeking refuge

THE MANIOT FEUDS
By the 15th century, a number of refugee Byzantine families had settled in the Máni, the most powerful forming a local aristocracy known as the Nyklians. Feuding between clans over the inadequate land was rife, though only Nyklians had the right to construct stone towers, which attained four or five storeys and came to dominate nearly every Mániot village.

Once commenced, blood feuds could last months, even years, with periodic truces to tend to the crops. Clansmen fired at each other from facing towers, raising them in order to be able to catapult rocks on to opponents' roofs. The hostilities ended only with the total destruction or submission of the losing clan. Historically, the most important clans were those of Mavromichális at Areópoli, Grigorákis at Gýtheio and Τroupákis at Kardamýli, whose members boasted of never having been completely subjugated by any foreign power. The Ottomans wisely refrained from ruling the Máni directly, but instead quietly encouraged the clans to feud in order to weaken potential rebellions, and appointed a Nyklian chieftain as *bey* (regional lord) to represent the sultan locally. Under the final *bey*, Pétros Mavromichális, the clans finally united, instigating the Greek Independence uprising on 17 March 1821 *(see pp40–41)*.

Pétros Mavromichális

Oítylo viewed from the northwest, looking towards Kelefá Castle

Agios Spyrídon south window, framed with marble reliefs

Kardamýli

Kardamýli was the lair of the Troupákis family, important rivals of the Mavromichális clan. Nicknamed Moúrtzinos or "Bulldogs" for their tenacity in battle, they claimed to be descended from the Byzantine dynasty of Palaiológi. Olive oil *(see p283)* used to be the chief source of income for Kardamýli, but this has now been superseded by tourism.

Inland rises the ancient and medieval acropolis, heralded by twin Mycenaean chamber tombs. In Old Kardamýli (sign posted) are Troupákis-built towers which stand alongside the 18th-century church of **Agios Spyrídon**. This building is made of Hellenistic masonry

and graced by a pointed, four-storey belfry; the south window and doorway are framed by intricate marble reliefs.

Environs

Two paths lead from Kardamýli, one upstream along the **Vyrós Gorge** where two monasteries shelter beneath the cliffs; the other to the villages of Gourniés and Exochóri. A short drive to the south, **Stoúpa** is popular for its two sandy bays; novelist Níkos Kazantzákis (1883–1957) lived here briefly and partly based his Zorba the Greek character on a foreman who worked nearby. The village of **Agios Nikólaos**, a short walk to the south, curls around Outer Máni's most photogenic harbour. It has four tavernas and the closest beach is at Agios Dimítrios, 3 km (2 miles) further south.

Mount Taÿgetos

The distinctive pyramidal summit and knife-edged ridge of Mount Taÿgetos, standing at 2,404 m (7,885 ft), divides the regions of Messinía and Lakonía. Formed of limestone and densely clad in black pine and fir, the range is the

Taÿgetos, seen through the Vyrós Gorge

watershed of the region and offers several days of wilderness trekking to experienced, well-equipped mountaineers.

Anavrytí and Palaiopanagiá, on the east, and Pigádia and Kardamýli, on the west, are the usual trailhead villages. Various traverses can be made by using the Vyrós and Ríntomo gorges which drain west from the main ridge; an unstaffed alpine refuge at Varvára-Deréki, above Palaiopanagiá, is the best starting point for those wanting to head straight for the summit.

The ridge of Mount Taÿgetos with an olive grove in the foreground

Inner Máni
Μέσα Μάνη

Inner, or Lakonian, Máni is divided into two regions – the "Shadowed", western flank and the "Sunward", eastern shore. The former is famous for its numerous caves and churches, the latter for its villages which perch dramatically on crags overlooking the sea. With its era of martial glory over *(see p194)*, Inner Máni is severely depopulated, its only future being as a holiday venue. Retired Athenians of Mániot descent have restored the famous towers as hunting lodges for the brief autumn shoot of quail and turtle dove.

LOCATOR MAP

imperial togas. Until World War II, Gýtheio exported acorns used in leather-tanning, gathered by women and children from nearby valleys.

The town's heart is Plateía Mavromicháli, with the quay extending to either side lined by tiled, 19th-century houses. The east-facing town enjoys sunrises over Cape Maléas and the Lakonian Gulf while snowy Mount Taÿgetos looms beyond a low ridge to the north.

In the bay, and linked to the waterfront by a causeway, lies the islet of Marathonísi, thought to be Homer's Kranaï islet. It was here that Paris of Troy and Helen spent their first night together *(see p52)*. It is dominated by the Tzanetakis tower, a crenellated 18th-century fortress which now houses the **Museum of the Máni**. The subject of the exploration of the Máni in medieval times is covered on the ground floor, while the exhibits of the upper storey place the tower houses in their social context.

Gýtheio
The lively town of Gýtheio is the gateway to the Máni peninsula and one of the most attractive coastal towns in the southern Peloponnese. It was once the naval base of ancient Sparta *(see p189)*, though the main ancient relic is a Roman theatre to the north. The town was wealthy in Roman times when it exported the purple molluscs used for colouring

Environs
Standing 12 km (7 miles) to the southwest, the **Castle of Passavá** was built in 1254 by the Frankish de Neuilly clan to guard a defile between Kelefá and Oítylo. Its name stems from *passe avant*, the clan's motto, though the present building is an 18th-century Turkish construction. The Turks left the castle in 1780 after Tzanetbey Grigorákis avenged the murder of his uncle by massacring 1,000 Muslim villagers inside. Today's overgrown ruins are best approached from the southwest.

Areópoli
The Mavromichális *(see p194)* stronghold of Tsímova was renamed Areópoli, "the city of Ares" (god of war), for its role in the War of Independence *(see p40)*; it was here that the Mániot uprising against the Turks was proclaimed by Pétros Mavromichális. Now the main town of the Máni, its central old quarter features two 18th-century churches: **Taxiarchón** boasts the highest belltower in the Máni, as well as zodiacal apse reliefs, while **Agios Ioánnis**, adorned with naive frescoes, was the chapel of the Mavromichális.

Environs
Ottoman **Kelefá Castle**, standing 10 km (6 miles) north of Areópoli, is the second castle guarding the Máni. It was built in 1670 to command the bays of Oítylo and Liméni and counter the impending Venetian invasion *(see p38)*.

19th-century houses lining the harbour of Gýtheio

Semi-ruined tower houses of Vátheia village, the architectural jewel of the Máni

The bastions of the pentagonal curtain walls are preserved. The castle can be reached from the Areópoli–Gýtheio road (sign posted) and from a footpath from Oítylo.

Pýrgos Diroú Caves
This cave system is one of the largest and most colourful in Greece. During summer, crowds take a 30-minute punt ride along the underground stream which passes through Glyfáda cavern, reflecting the overhanging stalactites. A 15-minute walk then leads to the exit. A nearby chamber, called Alepótrypa cave, is drier and just as spectacular with waterfalls and a lake. Until an earthquake closed the entrance, the cave was home to Neolithic people, and a separate **museum** chronicles their life and death.

The Shadowed Coast
Between Pýrgos Diroú and Gerolimónas lies the 17-km (11-mile) shore of the Shadowed Coast. Once one of the most densely populated regions of the Máni, it is famous for its numerous Byzantine churches built between the 10th and 14th centuries. The ruins of many Mániot tower houses can also be found.

Among the finest churches is 11th-century **Taxiarchón**, at Charoúda, with its interior covered by vivid 18th-century frescoes. Heading south, the road continues to **Agios Theódoros**, at Vámvaka, where the dome is supported by

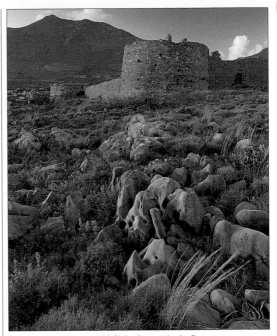

Corner turret of Ottoman Kelefá Castle, near Areópoli

carved beams; birds bearing grapes adorn its marble lintel.

Káto Gardenítsa boasts the 12th-century **Agía Soteíra**, with its frescoed iconostasis and domed narthex, while 12th-century **Episkopí**, near Stavri, has a complete cycle of 18th-century frescoes.

Near Ano Mpoulárioi village, doorless **Agios Panteleímon** offers 10th-century frescoes (the earliest and the most primitive in the Máni), while in the village, the 11th-century **Agios Stratigós** bears a set of 12th- and 13th-century frescoes – the *Acts of Christ* is the most distinguished.

Vátheia, 10 km (6 miles) east of Gerolimónas, is one of the most dramatically located of the villages; overlooking the sea and Cape Taínaro, its bristling tower houses constitute a showpiece of local architectural history.

Tower houses of Vátheia village, viewed from the southeast

For hotels and restaurants in this region see pp268–70 and pp289–91

Koróni 🕸
Κορώνη

Peloponnese. **Road map** C5.
🏛 *1,400.* 🚌

One of the "eyes of Venice" (along with Methóni), Koróni surveys the shipping lanes between the Adriatic and Crete. It stands at the foot of a Venetian castle, begun in 1206, whose walls now shelter the huge **Timíou Prodrómou** convent. A Byzantine chapel and foundations of an Artemis temple stand by the gate of the convent whose cells and chapels command fine views.

The town, lying beneath the castle and divided by stepped streets, dates to 1830. Little has changed here and many houses retain elaborate wrought-iron balconies, horizontal-slat shutters and tile "beaks" on the undulating roofs. A lively seafront is the sole concession to tourism.

Methóni 🕸
Μεθώνη

Peloponnese. **Road map** B5.
🏛 *1,300.* 🚌

Methóni, a key Venetian port, controlled the lucrative pilgrim trade to Palestine after 1209. With the sea on three sides, its rambling **castle** is defended on its landward side by a Venetian moat, bridged by the French in 1828. The structure combines Venetian, Ottoman and even French military architecture. The remains within the walls include two ruined *hammams* (baths), a Venetian church, minaret bases and the main street. Boúrtzi, an islet fortified by the Turks, stands beyond the Venetian sea-gate.

♟ Castle
⏱ 9am–7pm daily (9am–3pm winter).

Pýlos 🕸
Πύλος

Peloponnese. **Road map** C5.
🏛 *2,500.* 🚌

The town of Pýlos, originally known as Avaríno (later Navaríno) after the Avar tribes which invaded the area in the 6th century, is French in design, like Methóni. Life is confined to Plateía Trión Navárchon and the seafront on either side.

To the west, the castle of **Nió**kastro, Ottoman and Venetian in origin, was extensively repaired by the French after 1828; their barracks are now a gallery of antiquarian engravings by the artist René Puaux (1878–1938). An institute of underwater archaeology is situated in the former dungeons of the hexagonal keep. The roof gives views over the outer bailey, immense Navaríno Bay and Sfaktiría island, site of a memorable Athenian victory over the Spartans.

BATTLE OF NAVARINO

An unexpected naval engagement which decided the War of Independence *(see pp40–41)*, the Battle of Navaríno took place on 20 October 1827. Victory here by the French, Russian and English allies over the Ottoman fleet broke the Greek-Ottoman deadlock and resolved the problem of the sultan's refusal of an armistice. The allied fleet of 27 ships, commanded by admirals Codrington, de Rigny and Heyden, entered Navaríno Bay where Ibrahim Pasha's armada of 89 lay anchored. The outnumbered allies merely intended to intimidate Ibrahim into leaving the bay, but were fired upon, and a full-scale battle ensued. By nightfall three-quarters of the Ottoman fleet was sunk, with negligible allied casualties; Greek independence was now inevitable. The admirals are honoured by an obelisk in their namesake square in Pýlos.

Scene from the dramatic *Battle of Navaríno*, painted by Louis Ambroise Garneray (1783–1857)

The fortified islet of Boúrtzi, off the coast at Methóni, with its 16th-century octagonal tower

The arcaded former mosque, now Sotíras church, Pýlos

The perimeter walls are dilapidated, but it is possible to walk along the parapet, starting from the imposing west bastion overlooking the mouth of the bay, and finishing above the east gate. The domed and arcaded church of **Sotíras**, once a mosque, is the only medieval survival in the outer bailey.

⛪ Niókastro

Town centre. **Tel** 27230 22010.
☐ 8:30am–3pm Tue–Sun. ☀ main public hols. 🈂 ♿ limited.

Environs

Boat tours visit a number of memorials on and around **Sfaktiría**, which commemorate those sailors lost in the Battle of Navaríno, foreign philhellenes and revolutionary heroes.

The north end of Navaríno Bay, 11 km (7 miles) north of Pýlos, has excellent beaches, especially **Voïdokoiliá** lagoon, where Telemachos, Odysseus's son, disembarked to seek news of his father from King Nestor. You can walk up the dunes to **Spiliá tou Néstora**, an impressively large cave, which may have been the inspiration for Homer's cave in which Nestor and Neleus kept their cows. A more strenuous path continues to Palaiókastro, the ancient acropolis and Franco Venetian castle, built on Mycenaean foundations.

Nestor's Palace ㉙
Ανάκτορο του Νέστορα

16 km (10 miles) NE of Pýlos, Peloponnese. **Road map** B5. 🚌 **Site** **Tel** 27630 31437. ☐ 8:30am–3pm daily. **Museum Tel** 27630 31358. ☐ 8:30am–3pm Tue–Sun. ☀ main public hols. 🈂 ♿ limited.

Discovered in 1939, the 13th-century BC palace of Mycenaean King Nestor was excavated by Carl Blegen from 1952. Hundreds of tablets in the ancient Linear B script were found, as well as a bathtub and olive oil jugs (the contents of which fuelled the devastating fire of 1200 BC).

13th-century BC bathtub excavated from Nestor's Palace

Today, only waist-high walls and column bases suggest the typical Mycenaean plan of a two-storey complex around a central hall. The **museum**, 3 km (2 miles) away in Chóra, has frescoes from the palace.

Ancient Messene ㉚
Αρχαία Μεσσήνη

34 km (21 miles) NW of Kalamáta, Peloponnese. **Road map** C5. **Tel** 27240 51201. 🚌 **Site** ☐ 8:30am–sunset daily. **Museum** ☐ 8am–2:30pm Tue–Sun. ☀ main public hols. 🈂

Ancient Messene is now confusingly known as Ithómi – named after the mountain that sits overhead. It is an underrated, intriguing site, still undergoing excavation. The city walls are 9 km (6 miles) long and date from the 4th century BC. They enclose a vast area that incorporates the foundations of a Zeus temple, and the acropolis on Mount Ithómi to the northeast. The massive, double Arcadia Gate situated on the north side is flanked by square towers.

The archaeological zone includes the picturesque village of Mavrommáti, whose water is still supplied by the ancient Klepsýdra fountain at the heart of the site. Below the village you will find an odeion (amphitheatre), a *bouleuterion* (council hall), stoas and a monumental stairway, all of which surround the foundations of an Asklepios temple. Just a little way further down the hill from here lies a well-preserved stadium.

Remains of the Arcadia Gate, with its fallen lintel, Ancient Messene

CENTRAL AND WESTERN GREECE

EPIRUS · THESSALY · STEREA ELLADA

*C*entral and Western Greece encompasses many of the lesser-known regions of mainland Greece and is, therefore, little touched by tourism. Though Epirus has produced a distinctive and largely autonomous culture, Stereá Elláda has always been of strategic importance, with the pass at Thermopylae and the Vale of Tempe providing invasion routes into the very heart of Greece.

This region of Greece is dominated by the central plain of Thessaly (the former bed of an inland sea) and the sights of interest lie largely on the periphery. Isolated by the Píndos mountains, the Epirus region, to the west, has the strongest of regional identities, having played a minor role in ancient Greece and maintained a large degree of autonomy under the Turks. The regional capital, Ioánnina, is thus a fascinating mixture of Turkish architecture and the local traditions of silversmithing and wood carving.

Woman from Métsovo, northern Píndos

To the east, the grand Katára Pass, guarded in Ottoman times by the town of Métsovo, cuts through the mountains, providing access to the Byzantine Metéora monasteries which soar on the summits of the area's steeply eroded peaks.

In Stereá Elláda, one of the country's most important ancient sights, the ruins of the Delphic Oracle, stands only a short drive away from the Monastery of Osios Loúkas, perhaps the finest of late Byzantine buildings, decorated with some of the period's greatest mosaics.

While the Gulf of Corinth has many popular resorts, the towns of Lamía, Arta, Tríkala, and Mesolóngi (where the British poet Lord Byron died) make few concessions to tourism and so offer a more accurate picture of life in Greece today: its markets, tavernas, church-going and the evening *vólta*.

Megálo Pápigko, one of the many remote, once-isolated villages of Zagória in the Epirus region

◁ The Byzantine Monastery of Osios Loúkas, with the belltower in the foreground

Exploring Central and Western Greece

Stretching from Attica in the south to Macedonia in the north, the vast expanse of Central and Western Greece has a little of everything, from excellent beaches to the venerable towns of Ioánnina and Métsovo with their craftsmen's guilds and Ottoman heritage. The Pílio offers the best combination of scenery and coastal resorts, while no one should miss the two prime attractions of Ancient Delphi, site of the oracle of Apollo, and the Byzantine splendour of the monasteries of Metéora. Walkers should head north where, in addition to the Víkos Gorge, the Píndos Mountains have several of Greece's highest peaks. The flora and fauna are both splendid here, especially in spring, but wildlife enthusiasts should not miss the wonderful wetlands around Mesolóngi and the beautiful Amvrakikós Gulf, near Arta.

Agíou Nikoláou, one of Metéora's soaring monasteries

SIGHTS AT A GLANCE

Doric columns of the Temple of Apollo, Delphi

LOCATOR MAP

GETTING AROUND

There are domestic airports at Préveza, which receives European charter flights in summer, Larisa and Ioánnina. Internal flights are fairly inexpensive if travelling from another part of Greece, but within the region a car is by far the best way to travel. Central Greece's main roads are generally good, though twisting mountain routes can make journeys longer than they seem on the map. The E55 is a good, fast road, as are the other major E roads which circle the region. Trains serve only a small part of the eastern side of the area, though bus connections are good between major towns, with services to smaller villages.

Terraced bar overlooking the west coast, Párga

SEE ALSO

0 kilometres 25

0 miles 25

Lake Drakolímni, behind the sheer cliffs of Astráka

Píndos Mountains ❶
Οροσειρά Πίνδου

Epirus. **Road map** B2. ✕
🚌 *Ioánnina.* ℹ️ *Dodónis 39,*
Ioánnina (26510 41868).
🕐 *8am–3pm Mon–Fri.*

The Píndos is a vast range stretching from the Greek border with Albania south beyond Métsovo. It extends east into Macedonia, and west towards the Ionian Sea, incorporating two national parks, Greece's second longest gorge and its second highest mountain, Oros Smólikas, standing at 2,640 m (8,660 ft). The Píndos National Park lies just inside western Macedonia, between Métsovo and Vovoúsa, while the Víkos-Aóos National Park is a boot-shaped area encompassing the Víkos Gorge *(see p208)* and the Aóos River.

The peaks are snow-covered from October until May, when the melting snows water the ground, producing swathes of lilac crocus, gentians, grass-of-Parnassus and many species of orchid *(see p23)*. The protection offered by the parks provides the visitor with an increased chance of seeing roe deer, wild boar and the European wild cat, all of which exist in small numbers.

Smólikas is accessible during summertime for those who are well equipped and prepared for camping or staying in mountain huts. Slightly easier to reach from the fascinating Zagorian villages by the Víkos Gorge are Gamíla 2,500 m (8,200 ft) and Astráka 2,440 m (8,000 ft), while the two mountain lakes both called Drakolímni are each worth the effort it takes to get to them. One is below Gamíla, near a sheer drop to the Aóos River, while the other stands beneath Smólikas.

Although there are good walking guides and maps of the area, with mountain huts to stay in and accommodation in some of the larger villages, visitors should not venture into the mountains unless they are experienced walkers. The weather can change quickly, and in many places you will be a long way from any kind of settlement – though this is one of the main attractions of the Píndos Mountains. They show the rugged side of Greece, offering remote valleys and routes where few visitors venture.

WILDLIFE OF THE PINDOS MOUNTAINS

Visitors to the coastal lowlands are often sceptical when told that wolves and bears still survive in Greece. However, despite the severe erosion of their natural habitat over the last 20 years, both European wolves and European brown bears can be found. The Píndos mountains, and particularly the northern regions towards Albania, continue to harbour the greatest numbers of these endangered and now protected creatures.

The silver European wolf, a rare native of the region

They are extremely wary of man, having been persecuted by farmers and goatherds down the centuries. Therefore, visitors should consider themselves very fortunate if they see a bear. Wolves are just as hard to see but more evident, as they can often be heard howling at dawn and dusk, and will even respond to imitations of their howls. They pose no real threat to visitors.

One of the 80 European brown bears of the northern Píndos

Zagória ❷
Ζαγόρια

Epirus. **Road map** B2.

Some of Europe's most spectacular scenery can be found only 25 km (15 miles) north of Ioánnina (see p210), in the area known as Zagória. Though the soil is largely uncultivable, on the forested hillsides some 45 traditional Epirot villages still survive; many of them boast imposing *archontiká* (mansions) dating to prosperous 18th- and 19th-century Ottoman times when Zagória was granted autonomy.

Vlach and Sarakatsan shepherds (see p209) make up most of the settled population. Over the winter months, the shepherds used to turn to crafts, forming into guilds of itinerant masons and woodcarvers, who would travel the Balkans selling their trades. This hard and ancient way of life is under threat, as the villagers, and especially the younger generation, prefer to earn their living from tourism.

A series of arched packhorse bridges are among the most memorable monuments to the skills of the local people and are unique features of the region. Two especially fine examples can be seen at either end of the village of **Kípoi**.

Vítsa village, by the Víkos Gorge

Southwestern Zagória is the busiest area, with a bus from Ioánnina to Monodéndri bringing in walkers and climbers. Some of the villages in the east of the region, such as **Vrysochóri**, were refuges for guerrillas during World War II and therefore burnt by the Germans; they have recovered only slowly.

Near the almost deserted village of **Vradéto**, a 15th-century muletrack zigzags its way up a steep rockface beyond which the path leads to a stunning view of the spectacular Víkos Gorge (see p208). **Monodéndri**, opposite Vradéto, is the usual starting point for the gorge trail, though another path can be taken from **Vítsa**. Nearby are the two villages of **Megálo Pápigko** and **Mikró Pápigko**. They are 4 km (2 miles) apart and their names reflect their sizes, but even "big" Pápigko is no more than a scattering of houses around cobbled streets, with a choice of restaurants, and rooms available in renovated mansions.

Further south, though still surrounded by mountains, is the relatively thriving village of **Tsepélovo**. It has a bus service to Ioánnina and a restored mansion which provides accommodation, as well as a number of *pensions* and tavernas. Its cobbled streets and slate-roofed houses provide a perfect portrait of a Zagorian village.

Packhorse bridge near the village of Kípoi

ZAGORIAN VILLAGES
Scattered across the limestone wilderness of the north Píndos, the villages of Zagória lie to the southwest of the Aóos River between Ioánnina and Kónitsa.

Kónitsa

Aóos

GAMILA ▲ 2,497 m 8,190 ft

Vrysochóri

Kalývia

Megálo Pápigko

ASTRAKA ▲ 2,436 m 7,990 ft

Mikró Pápigko

Víkos

Aristi

Voïdomátis

Víkos Gorge

Z A G O R I A

Elafótopos

Vradéto

Tsepélovo

Monodéndri

Kakaviá

Kalpaki

Vítsa

Kípoi

Negádes

20 (E90)

Ioánnina

KEY

▬▬▬ Major road

▬▬ Minor road

═══ Road in poor condition

- - Scenic footpath

0 kilometres 2

0 miles 2

Víkos Gorge Walk ❸

To trek the length of the Víkos Gorge is to undertake what is arguably the greatest walk in Greece. Carved by the Voïdomátis River, the deeply eroded limestone walls rise to 915 m (3,000 ft). The gorge cuts through the Víkos-Aóos National Park, established in 1975. Cairns and way-marks define the route which snakes through the boulder-strewn ravine bed and continues up through stands of beech, chestnut and maple to

Greek tortoise

the higher ground. Egyptian vultures, are commonly seen circling in the thermals, and lizards and tortoises abound. The walk begins at Mon-odéndri, but landslides and lack of maintenance make the route challenging, and should only be attempted by experienced hikers. There is a shorter 4-km (2-mile) walk between the northern villages of Mikró Pápigko and Víkos.

⑤ Mikró Pápigko

IOANNINA

Víkos

④

Voïdomátis

Megálo Pápigko ⑤
One of the area's protected traditional villages, stone-built Megálo Pápigko stands at 950 m (3,117 ft), beneath the cliffs of Pýrgi.

Rock pinnacle ④
For the Pápigko villages, cross the gorge here beneath a landmark pinnacle of rock. The path branches to the west for Víkos village.

③ 🏠

Agía Triáda ③
After 3 hours you pass the white shrine of Agía Triáda, standing opposite a well.

Z A G O R I A

Oxiá Viewpoint ②
From Monodéndri, a road can be taken to the Oxiá site, one of the area's finest viewpoints, along with Mpelóï opposite.

② ☀ Mpelóï viewpoint

🏠

①

P

• Vítsa

IOANNINA

Monodéndri ①
With its magnificent views over the gorge, this village is the most popular start for the walk. The path is signposted from the church in the lower square.

0 kilometres   5

0 miles   2

KEY

- - Walk route
═══ Minor road
═══ Road in poor condition

🏠 Monastery
☀ Viewpoint
P Parking

TIPS FOR WALKERS

Starting point: Monodéndri.
Getting there: 40 km (25 miles) NW of Ioánnina, by car or bus.
Length: 14 km (8 miles) to Megálo Pápigko.
Difficulty: For experienced hikers only. Hiking equipment required.
Walking time: 6–7 hours.

Métsovo ❹
Μέτσοβο

Epirus. **Road map** B2. 🎿 *3,500.* 🚌
ℹ️ *26560 41233.*

Situated close by the Katára Pass (the route crossing the Píndos Mountains), Métsovo has a vitality unique among Greek mountain towns. It was originally a small village inhabited by Vlach shepherds, but it became one of the region's most important commercial centres after being granted tax privileges in return for guarding the pass during Ottoman times *(see pp38–9)*. Local merchant families invested their new wealth in the town and continue to do so today by providing endowments and grants to encourage industry among the local craftspeople.

One such family was the Tosítsas, and some idea of the size of their wealth can be gained by touring the rebuilt 18th-century **Archontikó Tosítsa**, which has been preserved as a museum. Rising to three floors, the mansion contains an armoury and washroom on the ground floor, with huge wood-panelled reception rooms and

Shepherds' crooks, rugs and silverware in a souvenir shop in Métsovo

bedrooms upstairs, carpeted with beautiful, locally woven *kilim* rugs. Intricate gold- and silverware are on display, as well as collections of Epirot costumes and embroidery. Would-be visitors must wait outside for the half-hourly guided tour.

Another of Métsovo's benefactors was the writer and politician Evángelos Avéroff (1910–90) who founded the **Avéroff Museum**. The core of

Interior of the Archontikó Tosítsa, Métsovo

the gallery is Avéroff's own collection of some 200 paintings and sculptures he acquired over the years, always with the ambition of opening a museum of modern Greek art in his home town. His collection has been expanded to show the work of several dozen Greek artists from the 19th and 20th centuries.

Ancient traditions have survived in the area, from the simple craft of carving shepherds' crooks (from the town's sheep farming days) to embroidery and wine- and cheese making. Some of the older men (and a few women) still wear traditional costumes; you can see them, dressed in black, sitting in the shelters and cafés around the town square. The shelters are needed during winter when the town, at 1,156 m (3,793 ft) becomes a popular ski resort. The rugs on sale in the souvenir shops also reflect this alpine character.

📷 **Archontikó Tosítsa**
Off main thoroughfare. **Tel** 26560 41084. 🕐 *9am–1pm & 4–5:30pm Fri–Wed.* 📷

📷 **Avéroff Museum**
Off central square. **Tel** 26560 41210. 🕐 *10am–4pm Wed–Mon.* 📷
www.averoffmuseum.gr

Environs
Fifteen minutes' walk south, signposted from the centre of town, stands the small and charming 14th-century **Moní Agíou Nikoláou**. Today it is inhabited only by caretakers who are more than happy to show visitors the church's vivid post-Byzantine frescoes, the monks' living quarters and their own supplies of flowers, fruit and vegetables.

VLACH SHEPHERDS

Of unknown origin, the nomadic Vlach shepherds are today centred in the Píndos Mountains, particularly in and around Métsovo. Their language, which has no written form, is a dialect of Latin origin, and it is thought that they might be descended from Roman settlers who moved through Illyria into the northern Balkans. Traditionally, their way of life has been transhumant – spending summers in the mountains before moving down to the plains of Thessaly with their sheep for six months to avoid the worst of the winter snows. It is a hard way of life which is gradually disappearing, and the shepherds who remain can be found in such villages as Métsovo and Vovoúsa in Epirus, and Avdélla, Samarína and Smíxi in western Macedonia – their traditional summer settlements. Their winter homes lie mainly around Kastoriá *(see p240)*.

Zagorian Vlach shepherd

Ioánnina ⑤

Ιωάννινα

Chalice made of Ioánninan silver

The capital of the Epirus region, Ioánnina prospered during Ottoman times (see pp38–9) when its famous craftsmen's guilds, including the silversmiths', were formed. The Turkish influence is most visible in the fortress area which extends on a small headland into Lake Pamvótis (it was once moated on its landward side). Though dating to the 13th century, the area was rebuilt in 1815 by Ali Pasha, the Turkish tyrant most closely associated with it. Inside the fortress precinct a village-like peace reigns, though the bustle of the bazaar and the modern area is a reminder that this is still the region's busiest city.

Aslan Pasha Mosque, housing the Popular Art Museum

artifacts that include items from the site of Dodóni. Among these is a bronze eagle from the 5th century BC, statuettes of young children and lead tablets inscribed with questions for the oracle.

Ioánnina and the isle of Nisí, seen from the north

🔯 Municipal Museum

Aslan Pasha Mosque. *Tel* 26510 26356. ☐ Jun–Aug: 8:30am–7:30pm daily; Sep–May: 8:30am–4:30pm daily. ● main public hols. 🎟
At the northern corner of the fortress, this small museum is housed within the Aslan Pasha Mosque, built by Aslan Pasha in 1618. While the mosque itself, which retains original decoration on its dome, makes a visit worthwhile, the weapons and costumes on display tell something of Ioánnina's recent past. Turkish furniture inlaid with mother-of-pearl can also be found, alongside Jewish rugs and tapestries.

🔯 Byzantine Museum

Inner Fortress. *Tel* 26510 25989. ☐ Jun–Sep: 8am–8pm Tue–Sun, 1:30–8pm Mon; Oct–May: 8am–5pm. ● main public hols. 🎟
This modern museum contains a few items from local archaeological excavations, but the core is an imaginative display of icons from the 16th to the 19th centuries. Silverware, for which the town is renowned, is displayed in a separate annexe, once the treasury, with a reconstruction of a typical silversmith's workshop.

🔯 Archaeological Museum

Plateía 25 Martíou 6. *Tel* 26510 01050. ☐ Apr–Oct: 8am–8pm Tue–Sun, 1:30–8pm Mon; Nov–Mar: 8:30am–3pm Tue–Sun. 🎟 ♿
Set in a small park, this museum displays various

🔯 Popular Art Museum

Michaíl Angélou 42. *Tel* 26510 20515. ☐ 9am–2pm Mon–Fri (5:30–8pm Tue & Wed). ● main public hols. 🎟
Housed in a mansion, this museum has a collection of local crafts. As well as silver-work and traditional costumes, there are woven textiles made by the nomadic, tent-dwelling Sarakatsans who number less than the Vlach tribe (see p209).

ALI PASHA

Ali Pasha was born in Albania in 1741 and, in 1788, was installed at Ioánnina by the Turks as Pasha of Epirus. Though a murderer, he was a great administrator who made the town one of the wealthiest in Greece. His aim was to gain independence from his overlords and by 1820 he had an empire stretching from Albania to the Peloponnese. When news spread of his intention to create a Greco-Albanian state, Sultan Mahmud II of Turkey dispatched troops to put him to death. After a long siege within the fortress at Ioánnina, Ali Pasha agreed to meet the Turkish commander on the island of Nisí where, on 24 January 1822, he was hunted down, trapped and killed.

Tapestry of Ali Pasha (centre), Moní Agíou Panteleímonos, Nisí

🗿 Nisí

15 minutes by boat NE from fortress.
Though its first inhabitants
were the monks who came
here in the early years of the
13th century, the single village
on the isle of Nisí owes its
existence to 17th-century
refugees from Mániot feuds
(see p194). Its main building
is Moní Agíou Panteleímonos,
where the reconstructed room
in which Ali Pasha was shot
can be visited, the bullet holes
still visible in the floor. Other
rooms contain a few of his
possessions, some costumes
and period prints.

Stalactites in the Pérama Caves

Environs

Greece's largest cave network,
the **Pérama Caves**, are near
the village of Pérama, 4 km
(2 miles) north of Ioánnina.
They were discovered in 1940
by a shepherd hiding from
the Germans, but only fully
explored years later. Now there
are regular guided tours taking
visitors along the 1,700 m
(5,600 ft) of passages, where
multicoloured lights pick out
the stalactites and stalagmites.

🗿 Pérama Caves

Pérama. **Tel** 26510 81521.
🕐 9am–7pm daily. 🎫

The theatre of Dodóni, one of the largest in Greece

Dodóni ⑥
Δωδώνη

Epirus. **Road map** B3. **Tel** 26510
82287. 🚌 🕐 8am–8pm daily (to
3pm Nov–Mar). ● main public hols.
🎫 free on Sun. ♿

Dating to at least 1,000 BC,
the Oracle of Zeus at Dodóni
is the oldest in Greece and was
second in status only to the
one at Delphi *(see pp228–9)*.
The site is located 22 km
(14 miles) southwest of
Ioánnina in a placid green
valley on the eastern slopes
of Mount Tómaros.

The oracle focused on a
sacred oak tree ringed with
tripods which held a number
of bronze cauldrons placed so
that they touched each other.
Prophecies were divined from
the sound these made, in
harmony with the rustling of
the oak leaves, when one
of the cauldrons was struck.
Petitioners would inscribe
their questions on lead
tablets for the
priestess to read
to Zeus; some
of these have
been found
on the site
and can be
seen in the
Archaeological
Museum in Ioán-
nina. The reputed
power of the oak
tree was such that
Jason, on his quest
for the Golden Fleece *(see
p220)*, travelled across from
the Pílio to acquire one of its
branches to attach to his ship,
the Argo. By the 3rd century
BC a colonnaded courtyard

**Justinian, the last Roman
Emperor to visit Dodóni**

was built around the tree for
protection; it contained a
small temple of which only
foundations remain. The tree
was uprooted in AD 393 on the
orders of the Roman Emperor
Theodosios (ruled 379–395)
in accordance with his policy
of stamping out pagan practices. He also believed that
buried treasure might be
found beneath the site.

The main feature of Dodóni
today is the theatre, which,
with its capacity for 17,000
spectators, is one of the largest
in Greece. Its walls rise to 21 m
(69 ft) and are supported by
solid towers where kestrels
now nest. Used by the ancient
Greeks for dramatic performances, the theatre was later
converted by the Romans into
an arena for animal fights; bulls
and big cats would have been
kept in the two triangular pens
on either side of the stage. The
whole structure of the theatre
was restored in the early 1960s
and is now used for
performances in
summer. Dodóni
also includes
the ruins of
a stadium,
acropolis and
Byzantine
basilica – all
reminders of
the time when
this valley was
the location of
a flourishing
market town.

Dodóni fell into ruin in the
6th century AD when the
Roman Emperor Justinian
decided to found the new
and more easily defendable
city of Ioánnina.

The tiered, amphitheatre-shaped town of Párga, seen across Párga Bay

Párga ❼
Πάργα

Epirus. **Road map** B3. 🚶 2,000.
🚌 ⛴ Tue.

Párga, the main beach resort of Epirus, is a busy holiday town whose charms are often overwhelmed by the number of summer visitors. The Venetian fortress dominating the west side of the harbour was built in the late 16th century on the site of a building destroyed in 1537 during a brief period of Turkish rule. The Ottomans later returned under the command of Ali Pasha (see p210), who bought the town from the British in 1819. After this, many of Párga's inhabitants left for Corfu, though it was regained by the Greeks in 1913.

There are two small beaches within walking distance of the town centre and two larger ones about 2 km (1 mile) away: Váltos, the biggest, is to the north and Lychnos to the southwest. Fish restaurants line Párga's waterfront, affording fine views across the harbour to a group of small islands.

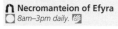

Greek Orthodox priests in Párga

Environs
37 km (23 miles) south of Párga is the **Necromanteion of Efyra** (Oracle of the Dead), the mythological gateway to Hades. Steps descend to the vaults where, in the 4th century BC, drugs and mechanisms may have heightened the sensation of entering the Underworld for visitors who sought advice from the dead.

🏛 **Necromanteion of Efyra**
⏰ 8am–3pm daily. 📷

Kassópi ❽
Κασσώπη

Zálongo, Epirus. **Road map** B3.
🚌 ⏰ daily.

The Kassopians were a tribe which lived in this region in the 4th century BC. The remains of their capital city stand on a hillside plateau overlooking the Ionian Sea, from where the island of Paxoí is plainly visible. Kassópi is reached by a pleasant walk through pine groves from the village of Kamarína. A site plan

illustrates the layout of the once-great city, now the home of birds and lizards.

Just above it is **Moní Zalóngou**, with its monument commemorating the women of Soúli who threw themselves from the cliffs in 1806 rather than be captured by Turkish-Albanian troops.

The remains of the city of Kassópi

Préveza ❾
Πρέβεζα

Epirus. **Road map** B3. 🚶 13,000.
✈ 🚌 ⛴ 🛈 Eleftheriou Venizélou (26820 60671). ⛴ daily (fish).

Often seen as a transit point, the charming town of Préveza repays a longer visit, particularly for the lively atmosphere among its waterfront cafés and tavernas. It is picturesquely situated on the northern shore of the narrow "Channel of Cleopatra", at the mouth of the Amvrakikós Gulf. It was here that the naval Battle of Actium was fought in 31 BC (see p34).

Two ruined forts, on either side of the straits, recall the town's Venetian occupation in 1499, though in 1798 it passed, via the French, into the hands of Ali Pasha *(see p210)*.

Environs
Seven km (4 miles) north of Préveza stand the ruins of **Nikópoli** ("Victory City"), built by the Roman Emperor Octavian to celebrate his victory at Actium. The city was founded on the site where the emperor's army was camped. Later sacked by the Goths, it was finally destroyed by the Bulgars in 1034. The remains are dominated by the city walls and the theatre. A museum displays artifacts from the site which is quite overgrown.

🏛 Nikópoli
Tel 26820 41336. ◯ *8:30am–3pm daily.* ● *main public hols.* ◙ *(museum only).*

Arta ⑩
Άρτα

Epirus. **Road map** B3. 🏠 *33,000.* 🚌 🏫 *Krystalli Sq (26810 78551).* ◯ *7am–3pm Mon–Fri.* 🍴 *Mon–Sat (veg).*

Though it is the second largest town in Epirus, after Ioánnina, Arta remains largely untouched by tourism. This traditional Greek market town has a lively, bazaar-like area, established by the Turks who occupied Arta from 1449 to 1881. The **fortress** dates from the 13th century when the city was the capital of the despotate of Epirus. Stretching from Thessaloníki to Corfu, this was an independent Byzantine state set up after the fall of Constantinople in 1204 *(see p37)*. It lasted until the start of the Turkish occupation.

Timber-framed houses in the Old Quarter of Tríkala

Some of the town's many 13th- and 14th-century Byzantine churches can be found in the streets near the fortress. The most striking is the **Panagía Parigorítissa**. Built between 1283 and 1296, it is a three-tier building topped with towers and domes. **Agía Theódora**, on Pýrrou, contains the marble tomb of the saintly wife of 13th-century Epirot ruler Michael II.

Approaching from the west, the main road into town crosses the river Arachthos by a 17th-century stone **bridge**. According to local folklore, the builder of the bridge, frustrated by each day's work being ruined by the river at night, was advised by a bird that the problem could be solved by putting his wife in the bridge's foundations. This he did, burying her alive, after which the bridge was successfully completed.

Metéora ⑪
See pp216–17.

Tríkala ⑫
Τρίκαλα

Thessaly. **Road map** C2. 🏠 *68,000.* 🚌 🏫 🍴 *Mon–Sat.*

Tríkala was the home of Asklepios, the god of healing, and today is the market centre for the very fertile plain of Thessaly. As such it is a thriving town with a number of remains from its Turkish past. One is the **market** near the main square, another the **Koursoúm Tzamí**, a graceful mosque built in 1550 on the south side of the River Lithaíos. Surrounding the **fortress** is the Old Quarter of Varósi, with a number of Byzantine churches *(see pp20–21)*. The fortress stands on the site of the ancient acropolis, which was built in the 4th century BC. It is situated in beautiful grounds overlooking the river.

Vale of Tempe ⑬
Κοιλάδα των Τεμπών

Thessaly. **Road map** C2. 🚌

As the E75 approaches Macedonia, it follows the river Pineíos through the Vale of Tempe – the fertile valley where Apollo was said to have purified himself after slaying the serpent Python. Close to the **Wolf's Jaws** or **Lykostómio** (the narrowest point of the gorge) is the **Spring of Daphne**, where a bridge leads to the chapel of **Agía Paraskeví**, carved out of the rock. The **Kástro Gónnon** at the northern end of the Vale was built by Perséas, leader of the Macedonians during the war with Rome *(see pp32–3)*, to control what has long been a vital route between Central and Northern Greece.

The arched packhorse bridge of Arta, leading into town from the west

Metéora ⓫
Μετέωρα

Icon of Our Lord, Varlaám

The natural sandstone towers of Metéora (or "suspended rocks") were first used as a religious retreat when, in AD 985, a hermit named Barnabas occupied a cave here. In the mid-14th century Neílos, the Prior of Stagaí convent, built a small church. Then in 1382 the monk Athanásios, from Mount Athos, founded the huge monastery of Megálo Metéoro on one of the many pinnacles. Twenty-three monasteries followed, though most had fallen into ruin by the 19th century. In the 1920s stairs were cut to make the remaining six monasteries more accessible, and today a religious revival has seen the return of monks and nuns.

Monastic cells

Outer walls

LOCATION OF MONASTERIES OF METEORA

Rousánou
Moní Rousánou, perched precariously on the very tip of a narrow spire of rock, is the most spectacularly located of all the monasteries. Its church of the Metamórfosis (1545) is renowned for its harrowing frescoes, painted in 1560 by the iconographers of the Cretan school.

VARLAAM
Founded in 1518, the monastery of Varlaám is named after the first hermit to live on this rock in 1350. The *katholikón* was built in 1542 and contains some frescoes by the Theban iconographer Frágkos Katelános.

Megálo Metéoro
Also known as the Great Meteoron, this was the first and, at 623 m (2,045 ft), highest monastery to be founded. By the entrance is a cave in which Athanásios first lived. His body is buried in the main church.

◁ Moní Rousánou on the left in the foreground, with Moní Varlaám towering behind

Katholikón
Dedicated to Agioi Pántes (All Saints), the church is adorned with frescoes, including one of Theofánis (right) and Nektários, its founders.

The refectory contains a small icon museum.

VISITORS' CHECKLIST

Thessaly. **Road map** B2.
Efthymiiou Vlahava 1 (24323 50274). **Megálo Metéoro** Apr–Oct: 9am–5pm Wed–Mon; Nov–Mar: 9am–4pm Thu–Mon. **Varlaám** Apr–Oct: 9am–4pm Sat–Thu; Nov–Mar: 9am–3pm Sat–Wed. **Agios Nikólaos** 9am–3:30pm Sat–Thu (Nov–Mar: 9am–1pm). **Rousánou** Apr–Oct: 9am–6pm daily; Nov–Mar: 9am–2pm Thu–Tue. **Agía Triáda** Apr–Oct: 9am–5pm Fri–Wed; Nov–Mar: 10am–3pm Fri–Tue. **Agios Stéfanos** Apr–Oct: 9am–1:30pm & 3:30–5:30pm Tue–Sun; Nov–Mar: 9:30am–1pm & 3–5pm Tue–Sun. all monasteries.

Ascent Tower
Goods and people were winched up by a windlass mechanism, made in 1536.

Net descending from tower

Entrance

THE BUILDING OF THE MONASTERIES
Though it is unknown how the first hermits reached the tops of these often vertical rock faces, it is likely that they hammered pegs into tiny gaps in the rock and hauled building materials to the summits. Another theory is that kites were flown over the tops, carrying strings attached to thicker ropes which were made into the first rope ladders.

Pílio 🕐
Πήλιο

Taxiárchis church fresco, Miliés

The mythological home of the forest-loving centaurs, the Pílio peninsula, with its woods of chestnut, oak and beech, is one of the most beautiful regions of the mainland. The mountain air is sweet with the scent of herbs which, in ancient times, were renowned for their healing powers. The area became populated in the 13th century by Greeks retreating from the Ottomans *(see pp38–9)*, under whose rule they were taxed onerously. Most villages were built close to mountain monasteries, though the thick stone walls and narrow windows of a typical Pílio house indicate how uncertain their freedom really was. After centuries of protecting their culture, this is now one of the few areas of Greece to have a strong local cuisine.

Makrinítsa
Cars are banned from the steep cobbled streets of this traditional village (see p220).

Agía Kyriakí
Overlooked by the isolated hilltop village of Tríkeri, this small fishing port lacks a beach and hotels but has a working boatyard and good, simple fish tavernas for those very few visitors who take the trouble to travel here.

Anakasiá, now little more than a suburb of Vólos, has a museum to the Greek painter Theófilos Chatzimichaïl.

Vólos is the capital of the region, straddling the only route into the peninsula. It has an excellent Archaeological Museum *(see p220).*

Palió T

THEOFILOS CHATZIMICHAIL

Born on Lésvos in 1873, Theófilos came to the Pílio in 1894 after reportedly killing a Turk in Smyrna. His favoured medium was the mural, though he also painted ceramics and the sides of fishing boats, *kafeneío* counters or horse carts when the mood struck him. He executed numerous mural commissions in the Pílio, notably at the Kontós mansion in Anakasiá. Though unhappily isolated, and mocked by the locals for his strange habits (he dressed in the costumes of his heroes, including Alexander the Great), he had a passion for all things Greek. After Lésvos's unification with Greece in 1912, he returned home destitute and ill. His fortunes changed after meeting his future patron Stratís Eleftheriádis who provided for the painter's needs until Theófilos's death in 1934.

Konstantinos Palaiológos **mural (1899) by Theófilos**

KEY

▬▬	Major road
▬▬	Minor road
═══	Non-asphalt road
- - -	Ferry route
🛈	Tourist information
⚡	Viewpoint

Vyzítsa

Mansions have been converted to guest-houses in this small village with its cobbled streets and large main square surrounded by old plane trees.

VISITORS' CHECKLIST

Thessaly. **Road map** D3. 🚗 🚌
🚢 *Vólos.* ℹ️ *opposite KTEL bus station, Lambraki & Sekéri sts, Vólos (24210 30940).* **Archaeological Museum**, Athanasáki 1, Vólos. **Tel** 24210 25285. ⬜ 8:30am–3pm Tue–Sun. ● *main pub hols.* 📷 ♿ **Folk Museum Miliés Tel** 24230 86602. ⬜ 10am–2pm, 6–9pm daily. **Theófilos Museum, Anakasiá Tel** 24210 47340. ⬜ 8am–2:30pm Mon–Fri. ● *main public hols.*

Agios Ioánnis

has one of the Pílio's most popular beaches.

Tsagkaráda is a delightful mountain village on wooded slopes. In its central square is the largest and oldest (1,000 years) plane tree in Greece.

Agios Ioánnis
Moúresi
Tsagkaráda
Mylopótamos
Kalamáki
Miliés
Neohóri
Afétes
Sikí
Potistiká
Argalastí
Katigiórgis
Plataniás
Skiáthos
Vólos

Miliés

This hill-village has a Folk Museum of local artifacts. Frescoes, such as this 18th-century Archangel Michael, adorn the church, the Taxiárchis.

Argalastí

This is the main town of the southern Pílio, attractively set on the edge of a plateau. Though it has a busy market, its few tavernas and cafés retain a peaceful atmosphere.

Plataniás

With its fine beach and boats travelling back to Vólos and to Skiáthos island, Plataniás is popular with Greek tourists. A number of fish tavernas provide excellent seafood.

Exploring the Pílio

Travelling by car, a circular tour of the northern villages can be made in a day following the road southeast from Vólos to Afétes, via Tsagkaráda. The hills in this region rise to 1,650 m (5,415 ft) at the summit of Mount Pílio, and in addition to dense woodlands, the area produces a large number of apples, pears, peaches and olives. While less dramatic, the southern Pílio is still hilly enough to ensure that many villages are at the end of single "dead end" roads, making travel here time consuming.

Restored traditional mansions on the hillside of Makrinítsa

Vólos

Vólos is one of Greece's fastest growing industrial centres and, since it was devastated by earthquakes in the 1950s, it is difficult to imagine its mythological past. Once the site of ancient Iolkós, the home of Jason, who went in search of the Golden Fleece, Vólos's history is illustrated by what can be found in the excellent **Archaeological Museum**. The museum contains an extensive collection of painted funerary stelae from the 3rd century BC, found at Dimitriás on the far side of the Gulf of Vólos. Collections of Neolithic pottery from the nearby sites of Sésklo and Dimíni can also be found and there is a room dedicated to the Ancient games held in Thessaly, many of which involved horses.

Northern Villages

From Vólos the road leads southeast, past Ano Lechónia, through the "Vólos Riviera", providing a circular route of the mountainous northern Pílio. On weekends during summer, a traditional Pílion train runs from Káto Lechónia to Miliés. From the popular inland resorts of **Miliés** and **Vyzítsa** (the latter preserved as a "traditional settlement" by the government), the road turns north past Tsagkaráda to **Agios Ioánnis**. This is the main resort of the east coast; the beaches of Papá Neró and Pláka are particularly fine and are both within easy walking distance. Some of the Pílio's best restaurants can be found in nearby **Moúresi**.

Returning towards Vólos, take the turning to **Makrinítsa** – a traditional mountain village, regarded as the most important destination for any traveller of the area. Founded in the 13th century by refugees from the first sacking of Constantinople (see p37), the village has beautiful churches, the most impressive being Agios Ioánnis, and the Moní Theotókou. Several traditional mansions also survive, some functioning as guest houses. Close to Agios Ioánnis, there is a café with an interior decorated with frescoes painted by the artist Theófilos (see p218).

Anakasiá is the last village before Vólos and home to the delightful Theófilos Museum.

JASON AND THE ARGONAUTS

According to legend, the Golden Fleece came from a winged ram sent by Hermes, the gods' messenger, to protect two children, Helle and Phrixus, from their evil stepmother. Though Helle drowned, Phrixus was reared in Kolchis, in present-day Georgia, where the ram was sacrificed and its fleece given to the king, Aeëtes. Years later, Jason, Phrixus's cousin, set sail from the kingdom of Iolkós (now Vólos) after his half-brother usurped the throne. Jason was in search of the Fleece, which made its wearer invincible. With a crew of 50, Jason came to Kolchis where King Aeëtes set several tasks before relinquishing the Fleece. After falling in love with the king's daughter, Medea, Jason achieved his tasks and the Argonauts carried the Fleece back to Iolkós in triumph.

Detail from *The Golden Fleece* (c.1905) by Herbert Draper (1864–1920)

Fisherman with his nets at the waterfront, Vólos

For hotels and restaurants in this region see pp270–73 and pp291–4

Sarcophagus detail outside the Thebes Archaeological Museum

Thebes 🟦
Θήβα

Stereá Elláda. **Road map** D4.
🏛 20,000. 🚉 🚌

Although it was briefly the most powerful city of Greece, in the 4th century BC, the Thebes of today is little more than a quiet provincial town. It played an important role in the power struggles of Classical Greece, until defeated by Philip II of Macedon. Thebes' original acropolis has been built over through the years, but excavations have unearthed Mycenaean walls as well as jewellery, pottery and important tablets of Linear B script which are now in the **Archaeological Museum**. One of the highlights of the museum is the collection of Mycenaean sarcophagi, similar to those found on Crete. The museum's courtyard and well-tended garden stand alongside a 13th-century Frankish tower, all that remains of a castle ruined in 1311 by the Catalans.

A bridge over the river bed, a short walk eastwards from the museum, marks the traditional site of the Fountain of Oedipus, where the legendary King Oedipus is said to have

THE LEGEND OF OEDIPUS

According to legend, Oedipus was the ill-fated son of Laius and Jocasta, the king and queen of Thebes. Even before his birth, the Delphic Oracle *(see p228)* had foretold that he would kill his father and become his mother's husband. To defy the prophecy, Laius abandoned Oedipus, though the child was rescued and reared by the king and queen of Corinth whom Oedipus believed to be his real parents. Years later, when he heard of the prophecy, Oedipus fled to Thebes, killing a man on his way, unaware that he was King Laius. On reaching Thebes, he found the city gates barred by the Sphinx which he vanquished by solving one of its riddles. The Thebans made him their king and he married the widowed Jocasta. When the truth about his past was revealed, Oedipus blinded himself and spent his final days as an outcast.

Oedipus and the Sphinx, from a 5th-century BC cup

washed blood from his hands after unwittingly killing his father on his way to the city.

🏛 **Archaeological Museum**
Plateía Threpsiádou 1.
Tel 22620 27913.
🕐 until 2014. 📷 ♿

Environs
Ten km (6 miles) north lie the ruins of **Gla**, once a Mycenaean stronghold *(see pp178–80)*. Its walls are 3 km (2 miles) long and up to 5 m (16 ft) high, surrounding a hill where the ruins of a palace and agora can be found.

Monastery of Osios Loúkas 🟦

See pp222–3.

Mount Parnassus 🟦
Όρος Παρνασσός

Stereá Elláda. **Road map** C3.
🚌 *Delfoí.* 🛈 *Vasiléon Pávlou & Freideríkis 44, Delfoi (22650 82900).*
🕐 *7:30am–2:30pm daily.*

Rising to a height of 2,457 m (8,061 ft), the limestone mass of Mount Parnassus dominates the eastern region of Stereá Elláda. The lower slopes are covered with Cephalonian fir, and beneath them, in summer, the wild-flower meadows burst into colour. Vultures and golden eagles are common, as are wolves which come down from the Píndos Mountains *(see p206)* in winter.

The village of **Aráchova** is the best base for exploring the area and is renowned for its wine, cheese and sheep-skin rugs. There are many mountain trails for summer hikes, though a detailed walking map is recommended. Reaching the top of Liákoura, the highest peak, involves a long hike and camping overnight on the mountain.

From Aráchova, the ski centre at **Fterólaka** is only 26 km (16 miles) away. Open from December to April, it provides a chair lift to 1,900 m (6,250 ft); from here a ski lift can be taken up to the ski slopes. In summer, Fterólaka functions as an excursion centre.

Fir-covered foothills beneath the ridge of Mount Parnassus

Monastery of Osios Loúkas ⑯
Μονή Οσίου Λουκά

Dedicated to a local hermit and healer, Holy Luke, Osios Loúkas monastery was architecturally one of medieval Greece's most important buildings. It was built by Emperor Romanós in c.1011 who extended an earlier church dating from AD 944. The octagonal style of the main church became a hallmark of late Byzantine church design *(see pp20–21)*, while the mosaics inside lifted Byzantine art into its final great period. During the time of the Ottoman Empire *(see pp38–9)*, Osios Loúkas witnessed a great deal of fighting, as the cannons in the courtyard testify. Here in 1821, Bishop Isaias declared his support for the Greek freedom fighters.

Madonna mosaic

The Theotókos, built in the early 11th century, is a smaller church dedicated to the Mother of God; its name means "god-bearing".

The north transept contains medallion-shaped mosaics of saints.

The monastic cells are small with arched roofs.

The exterior is a mixture of dressed Póros stone and red brick.

West portal

The narthex is the western entrance hall; it contains a number of mosaics of Christ's Passion.

The monastery seen from the west with the slopes of Mount Elikónas in the background

★ Washing of the Apostles' Feet
Based on a style dating to the 6th century, this 11th-century work is the finest of the narthex mosaics. Set on a gold background, it depicts Christ teaching his apostles humility.

For hotels and restaurants in this region see pp270–73 and pp291–4

STAR FEATURES

★ Washing of the Apostles' Feet

★ Crypt

VISITORS' CHECKLIST

8 km (5 miles) E of Dístomo.
Road map C4. **Tel** 22670 22797.
Site & Museum ☐ May–Sep:
8am–6pm daily; Oct–Apr: 8am–
5pm daily. 🕸 📷

Dome
The main dome is decorated with an imposing mural of Christ surrounded by saints and angels, painted in the 16th century to replace fallen mosaics.

The apse has a mosaic of the Virgin and Child pre-dating a devastating earthquake in 1659.

The katholikón, or main church, dates to 1011 and is built in the octagonal style.

★ **Crypt**
This 10th-century shrine, from the original site, contains the sarcophagus of Holy Luke, and such frescoes as this Descent from the Cross.

The southwest chapel has early 11th-century frescoes.

The refectory was used as a workshop as well as for meals; it now contains a museum of Byzantine sculpture.

HOLY LUKE

Born in Aegina in 906, Osios Loúkas ("Holy Luke") is known to have been a spiritual child who, in his early teens, left home to seek isolation in central Greece and developed a reputation as a healer. In around 940 he arrived at this spot on the western slopes of Mount Elikónas, with its glorious view over a peaceful valley of cornfields and groves of almond and olive trees. Here he settled with some disciples, adding the gift of prophecy to his healing powers. He died in 953, by which time the first monastic cells and the site's first small church had been constructed.

The waterfront houses of Galaxídi in the Gulf of Corinth

mound are the famous sulphur springs from which Thermopylae was given its name, which means the "Hot Gates".

The present landscape has changed considerably from the narrow gorge of old; the coastline to the north has been extended by the silt brought down by the River Spercheiós, pushing the sea back over 5 km (3 miles).

Lamía Museum
Kástro. **Tel** 22310 29992.
◯ 8:30am–3pm Tue–Sun.
⬤ main public hols. 🗟 ♿

Ancient Delphi ⑲

See pp228–31.

Gulf of Corinth ⑳
Κορινθιακός Κόλπος

Stereá Elláda. 🚌 *to Náfpaktos.*

The northern coast of the Gulf of Corinth contains several well-known resorts as well as many tiny coastal villages far removed from the usual tourist route. All are served by major roads which, like the resorts, offer fine views across the gulf to the mountains of the Peloponnese.

From Delphi the main road leads southwards through the largest olive grove in Greece, passing **Itéa**, a busy port. The church of Agios Nikólaos, 17 km (11 miles) west, stands on a hill surrounded by the old stone buildings of **Galaxídi**. The history of the town is told in the **Nautical Museum** while the 19th-century mansions at the waterfront are reminders of the great wealth brought by the town's shipbuilding industry. Though the industry cleared the region of trees, a reforestation scheme begun early in the 20th century has successfully restored the area to its former beauty. The next major town is **Náfpaktos**. Though perhaps less attractive than Galaxídi, it still possesses plenty of charm and character.

Lamía and Thermopylae ⑱
Λαμία καί Θερμοπύλαι

Stereá Elláda. **Road map** C3.
🏛 68,000. 🚌 ℹ️ *Leof. Kalivion 14, (22310 32289).* 🚢 *Sat.*

Set in the valley between two wooded hills, Lamía is typical of many medium-sized Greek towns; though it is little known, it has much to offer, with a lively Saturday market. A 14th-century Catalan **kástro**, built on the site of the town's ancient acropolis, provides excellent views over the roofs to the surrounding countryside.

Lamía is chiefly associated with the Lamian War (323–322 BC) when Athens tried to throw off Macedonian rule after the death of Alexander the Great *(see pp32–3)*. This is recalled at the **Lamía Museum**, which also has displays of architectural remains from Delphi *(see pp228–31)*.

A short drive east of Lamía, the Athens road crosses the **Pass of Thermopylae**. It was here, in 480 BC, that an army of some 7,000 soldiers, under the command of Leonidas I of Sparta, met an overwhelming force from Persia whose numbers Herodotus *(see p56)* cites as 2,641,610. Though Leonidas held the pass for a number of days, the Persians forced a path through and attacked the Greeks from the rear. Only two Greek soldiers survived the ordeal after which all of central Greece, including Athens, fell to the Persians. The Persian land forces were eventually defeated by Athens and her allies at the Battle of Plataiai in 479 BC *(see p29)*.

An impressive bronze statue of King Leonidas, cast in 1955, stands at the roadside opposite the burial mound of the soldiers who died here. Just to the left of the

**Statue of King
Leonidas at the Pass
of Thermopylae**

ΜΟΛΩΝ
ΛΑΒΕ

A Venetian fortress stands above the town, its ramparts running down as far as the beach, almost enclosing the harbour. The Venetian name for the town was Lepanto. In 1571, the famous naval Battle of Lepanto *(see p38)*, in which the Venetians, Spanish and Genoese defeated the Ottomans, was fought here. A popular story to emerge from the battle purports that the Spanish author Miguel de Cervantes (1547–1616) lost an arm in the conflict, though in fact only his left hand was maimed.

At **Antírrio** the coast comes closest to the Peloponnese, and from here a new suspension bridge and regular car ferry cross the stretch of water known as the "Little Dardanelles" to Río, on the southern shore. Beside the harbour stands the originally Frankish and Venetian Kástro Roúmelis. Another castle can be seen across the water on the Peloponnese.

🏛 Nautical Museum
Mouseíou 4, Galaxídi. *Tel* 22650 41558. ☐ 8:30am–4pm Mon–Fri, 10am–4pm Sat & Sun. ☐ *main public hols.* 🎫

Mesolóngi ㉑
Μεσολόγγι

Stereá Elláda. **Road map** B3.
🏘 *12,000.* ☷ ⛴ *Tue & Sat.*

Meaning "amid the lagoons", Mesolóngi is a town perfectly located for fishing, though the industry is now in decline. In 1821 the town became a centre of resistance to the Turks during the War of Independence *(see pp40–41)*, when a leader, Aléxandros Mavrokordátos, set up his headquarters here. In January 1824 Lord Byron *(see p149)* came to fight for the liberation of Greece, but died of a fever in April. His heart lies beneath his statue in the Garden of Heroes.

Nearby, the Gate of the Exodus is a tribute to those who fought the Turks in 1826. Nine thousand Greeks were killed in battle here and those that survived detonated their explosives as they were taken prisoner by the enemy. This self-sacrifice led to the Turks surrendering Mesolóngi in 1828 without firing a shot. A small museum charts the history of the town.

Statue of Lord Byron at Mesolóngi

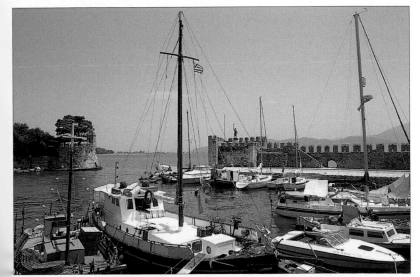
The fortified harbour of Náfpaktos in the Gulf of Corinth

Ancient Delphi ⓲
Δελφοί

According to legend, when Zeus released two eagles from opposite ends of the world their paths crossed in the sky above Delphi, establishing the site as the centre of the earth. Renowned as a dwelling place of Apollo, from the end of the 8th century BC individuals from all over the ancient world visited Delphi to consult the god on what course of action to take, in both public and private life. With the political rise of Delphi in the 6th century BC and the reorganization of the Pythian Games (see p230), the sanctuary entered a golden age which lasted until the Romans came in 191 BC. The oracle was abolished in AD 393 with the Christianization of the Byzantine Empire under Theodosius.

Siphnian Treasury caryatid

LOCATOR MAP

The Athenian Treasury was built after the Battle of Marathon (see p145) and reconstructed in 1906.

Vouleuterion (Delphic Council House)

To museum (see p231)

Siphnian Treasury

SACRED WAY

SACRED WAY

THE ORACLE OF DELPHI

The Delphic Oracle was the means through which worshippers could hear the words of the god Apollo, spoken through a priestess, or *Pythia*, over the age of 50. Questioners paid a levy called a *pelanos* and sacrificed an animal on the altar. The question was then put to the *Pythia* by a male priest. The *Pythia* would answer in a trance, perhaps induced by vapours from a crack in the ground over which she sat on a tripod. Her incantations were interpreted by the priest, though the answers were often ambiguous. King Croesus of Lydia (reigned 560–546 BC) came to ask if he should make war against Cyrus the Great of Persia and was told that if he crossed a river then he would destroy a great empire. In marching on Cyrus his troops crossed the River Halys and he did destroy an empire, though it turned out to be his own.

The main entrance was once a market place (agora) where religious objects could be bought.

The Rock of the Sibyl marks the place where, according to legend, Delphi's first prophetess pronounced her oracles.

★ **Sacred Way**
Leading to the Temple of Apollo, this path was lined with up to 3,000 statues and treasuries, built by city-states to house their people's offerings.

◁ **Dramatic view over the theatre at Delphi**

THE SANCTUARY OF APOLLO

Also known as the Sacred Precinct, this is at the heart of a complex that also included a stadium and a sacred spring *(see pp230–31)*. It is entered through an agora from which the Sacred Way winds through the ruins of memorials and treasuries.

VISITORS' CHECKLIST

Mount Parnassus, Stereá Elláda. **Road map** C4. *Tel* 22650 82312. 🚌 **Site & Museum** ⬜ 8:30am–7pm Tue–Sun (to 3pm Nov–Mar), 1:30–7:45pm Mon. ⬤ main public hols. 📷 ♿

To the stadium *(see p230)*

The theatre, built 2,500 years ago, seats 5,000 people. It rivals Epidaurus *(see pp184–5)* as one of the finest theatres in Greece.

★ Temple of Apollo

A temple has stood on this site since the 6th century BC, but the remains visible today date from the 4th century BC. Some reconstruction work has been done since French archaeologists uncovered the foundations in 1892, to give an impression of its original grandeur.

SACRED WAY

A column once supported a statue of Prusias, King of Bithynia.

RECONSTRUCTION OF DELPHI IN 200 BC

Vouleuterion

Theatre

Sacred Way

Athenian Treasury

Siphnian Treasury

Archaic Treasuries

Meeting Hall of the Knidians

Temple of Apollo

Stoa of Attalos

Altar of the Chians

Stoa of the Athenians

Sikyonian Treasury

Magistrates' Hall

Tripod of Plataiai

STAR SIGHTS

★ Temple of Apollo

★ Sacred Way

Exploring Delphi

The first excavations at Delphi began in 1892, uncovering a much larger area than is apparent now. Though it is most famous for the Sanctuary of Apollo, Delphi also had a sanctuary dedicated to the goddess Athena, whose temple, along with a structure known as the *tholos*, can be seen in a second enclosure to the south. North of the theatre is the stadium where the Pythian Games were held. These, after the Olympic Games *(see p173)*, were the most important sporting event in the Greek calendar, providing an opportunity for strengthening the ethnic bond of the Greek nation which was otherwise divided into predominantly rival city-states.

Caryatid from the Siphnian Treasury

�� **Marmaria Precinct**
Southeast of the Temple of Apollo, a path leads to the Marmaria Precinct, or "marble quarry", where the Sanctuary of Athena Pronaia can be found. At the sanctuary's entrance stand the ruins of a 4th-century BC temple dedicated to Athena. At the far end of the sanctuary are the remains of an earlier temple to the goddess, which was built around 510 BC. Between the two temples stands the Marmaria's most remarkable, and most photographed, monument: the circular *tholos*. The purpose of this structure is still unknown. The rotunda dates from the start of the 4th century BC, and was originally surrounded by 20 columns. Three of

The Stadium, viewed from the remains of the entrance archway

these columns were re-erected in 1938. They stand to provide some hint of the building's former beauty.

🛊 **Stadium**
This is one of the very best-preserved stadia in the country. Almost 200 m (655 ft) long and partly hewn out of the rocks above the main sanctuary, it held 7,000 spectators who gathered for the field and track events every four years during the Pythian Games. The games grew out of a musical festival, held in the theatre every eight years, to celebrate Apollo's mythical slaying of the serpent Python. Though poetry and musical recitals remained central to the occasion, from 582 BC athletic events in the stadium were added and the festival became known as the Pythian Games. All prizes in these tournaments were purely honorary; each winner was awarded the traditional laurel wreath and the right to have his statue in the sanctuary.

Made entirely of limestone from Mount Parnassus, the present structure dates from Roman times and most of the seating is still intact. The best-preserved seats are the backed benches on the north side, made for the presidents of the games and honoured guests.

🛊 **Castalian Spring**
Before entering the Sacred Precinct, it is believed that everyone visiting Delphi for religious purposes, including

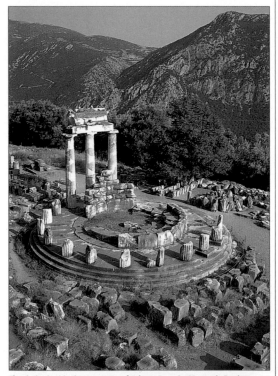

The tholos beside the Sanctuary of Athena Pronaia, Marmaria Precinct

For hotels and restaurants in this region see pp270–73 and pp291–4

athletes, was required to purify themselves in the clear but icy waters of the Castalian Spring – this process principally involved the washing of their hair. The Oracle *Pythia* *(see p228)* would also wash here before making her pronouncements. The visible remains of the fountain date either from the late Hellenistic or the early Roman period. A number of niches in the surrounding rock once held the votive offerings left for the nymph Castalia, to whom the spring was dedicated.

It is said that the British romantic poet Lord Byron *(see p149)* once plunged into the spring, inspired by the belief that the waters would enhance the poetic spirit.

The niches of the Castalian Spring

♠ Gymnasium

Water from the Castalian Spring ran down to this area to provide cold baths (until the Romans added hot baths in the 2nd century AD) for athletes training for the Pythian Games. The original cold baths, which can be seen in a square courtyard, are some 9 m (30 ft) in diameter. East of the baths lies the Palaestra, or training area, surrounded by the remains of what once were changing rooms and training quarters. As well as an outdoor running track, a covered track 180 m (590 ft) in length was used in bad weather. The gymnasium was built on many levels due to the sloping terrain and was also used for intellectual pursuits – Delphi's poets and philosophers taught here.

🔲 Delphi Museum

The museum at Delphi contains a collection of sculptures and architectural remains of an importance second only to those of the Athenian Acropolis *(see pp94–101)*.

There are 13 rooms of exhibits, all on the ground floor. In one of the rooms there is a scale model that reconstructs the Sanctuary of Apollo in a triumph of limestone whites, blue marble, gold and terracotta. The sanctuary is surrounded by friezes and statues and its size and former beauty is represented vividly.

Votive chapels, or "treasuries", lined the Sacred Way *(see p228)* and contained offerings of thanks, in the form of money or works of art, from towns grateful for good fortune following a favourable prophecy from the Oracle. The Theban Treasury, for example, was established after the victory of Thebes at the Battle of Leuktra in 371 BC. There are two rooms dedicated to the surviving sculpture from the Siphnian and Athenian treasuries, the wealth of the former illustrated by an outstanding frieze depicting the Greek heroes waging war on the giants. The colossal Naxian Sphinx was presented by the

wealthy citizens of Náxos in 560 BC; it stands 2.3 m (7.5 ft) high and once had its place atop a column reaching over 10 m (33 ft) in height.

The most famous of the museum's exhibits is a life-size bronze statue, the *Charioteer*. The statue was commissioned by a Sicilian tyrant named Polyzalos to commemorate a chariot victory in the Pythian Games in 478 BC. Another notable exhibit is the sculpture of *Three Dancing Girls* grouped around a column. The column is believed to have supported a tripod of the kind sat on by the *Pythia* as she went into her oracular trances. The girls are thought to be celebrating the feast of the god Dionysos *(see p52)* who also resided in the sanctuary. His presence was honoured in the winter months when Apollo was resting or away elsewhere. Don't miss the Omphalos, or "navel" stone. This is a Hellenistic or Roman copy of the stone that was believed to have marked the place above which Zeus's eagles met, establishing the sanctuary of Delphi as the centre of the earth *(see p228)*.

The bronze Charioteer

Detail from the frieze of the Siphnian Treasury on display in the Delphi Museum

NORTHERN GREECE

MACEDONIA · THRACE

*M*acedonia is Greece's largest prefecture and contains the country's second city, Thessaloníki. It is the homeland of Alexander the Great, and the heart of the ancient Hellenistic Empire. In contrast, Thrace has been largely influenced by Turkish culture but, like Macedonia, it is an area of comparatively unexplored natural beauty, with many mountain ranges and rivers.

The name Macedonia derives from the Makednoi, one of the tribes who first inhabited the region in the late 4th century BC. The legacy of the Macedonian Empire is evident in the many ancient sites, including Vergína, the location of King Philip II of Macedon's tomb; Pélla, the birthplace of Alexander; and Díon, Philip's city in the foothills of Mount Olympos. During the reign of the Roman Emperor Galerius in the 3rd century AD, many fine monuments were built, including the landmark arch in Thessaloníki. The Byzantine era also left an outstanding legacy of architecture, seen in the many churches throughout Northern Greece. Muslim influences remain strong,

Head of Serapis in the Thessaloníki Archaeological Museum

particularly in Thrace, where eastern-style bazaars and minarets can still be seen. Macedonia and Thrace have a cooler, damper climate than much of Greece and hence a flourishing flora. Bordering Central Greece is the country's highest mountain, Olympos, and in the northwest lie the beautiful Préspa Lakes. Local produce includes tobacco from Thrace, and wine from Náousa.

In contrast to the busy beaches on its western side, the Chalkidikí peninsula in Macedonia has the holy Mount Athos to the east. After a purported visit from the Virgin Mary, the Byzantine Emperor Monomáchos banished women and children from the site. This decree is still valid today.

Villagers at a taverna in the Néstos Valley

◁ Moní Grigoríou on the holy peninsula of Mount Athos

Exploring Northern Greece

Northern Greece offers varied pleasures. The bustle of modern Thessaloníki can be combined with a beach holiday in Chalkidikí, or with an exploration of some of the ancient Macedonian sites. Lovers of natural history will appreciate the National Park around the Préspa Lakes on the border with Albania, and the Dadiá Forest and Evros River Delta to the east near Turkey. Walkers will want to explore the paths of Mount Olympos. Kastoriá and Kavála, two relatively little-known Greek towns, both reward a lengthy visit as well as making excellent bases for travelling further afield. Kavála offers access to the fascinating but little-visited region of Thrace. This region's three main towns – Xánthi, Komotiní and Alexandroúpoli – all offer the attractive combination of Greek and Turkish influence. Alexandroúpoli is also ideal as a family holiday resort with its beaches and seafront cafés.

A typical stall at the fruit and vegetable market in Xánthi, selling local produce

Reedbeds by the Mikrí Préspa lake

SIGHTS AT A GLANCE

GETTING AROUND

Thessaloníki's airport serves both
international and domestic routes.
Airports at Kastoriá, Kozáni and
Alexandroúpoli are for domestic
flights only. Ferry connections link
Thessaloníki with the Sporades, and
Kavála and Alexandroúpoli with the
northern Aegean islands. Fast trains
travel south from Thessaloníki to
Athens, and east into Thrace. The
main E75 highway runs south to
Athens, while the E90 highway
joins Thessaloníki to Thrace.
Buses go from Thessaloníki to
Alexandroúpoli and Kastoriá.

LOCATOR MAP

Kastaniés

Orestiáda

Káto
Nevrokópi

Rodópi

Néstos

Didymóteicho

E85

Paranéstio

NÉSTOS
VALLEY 16

Echínos

Soufli

T H R A C E   *sápka*

Dadiá

Dráma

14

Stavroúpoli

XÁNTHI 17

Iasmos

19 **KOMOTINÍ**

22 **DADIÁ**
FOREST

12

Alistráti

E90 2

Limni
Vistonida

Sápes

Néstos

KAVÁLA 15

18

Xylagani

Istanbul

Eleftheroúpoli

AVDIRA

MARÓNEIA 20

Féres

E90 2

Keramotí

21 **ALEXANDROÚPOLI**

Thásos

Thracian
Sea

Enos

Pangaío

nfípoli

E90 2

0 kilometres		50
0 miles		20

eira

erissós

Ouranoúpoli

SEE ALSO

rvouroú

MOUNT
14 **ATHOS**

• *Where to Stay* pp273–5

SITHONIÁ

Athos
2033m

• *Where to Eat* pp294–5

Sárti

to Karrás

Kalamítsi

KEY

—	Dual-carriageway
= =	Road under construction
—	Major road
····	Minor road
—	Scenic route
·-·-	Main railway
—	International border
—	Regional border
△	Summit

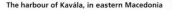

The harbour of Kavála, in eastern Macedonia

Beautiful landscape of the Préspa Lakes

Préspa Lakes ①
Εθνικός Δρυμός Πρεσπών

Macedonia. **Road map** B1. 🚌 to
Flórina. ℹ️ Agios Germanós (23850
51211).

This is the only national
park in Greece which is
made up largely of water.
It is one of the mainland's
most beautiful and unspoilt
places and was little visited

in the past because of its
rather inaccessible location.
The border with Albania runs
through the southwest corner
of the Megáli Préspa lake,
joining the border of the
Former Yugoslav Republic
of Macedonia. The Greek area
of the lake, together with the
smaller Mikrí Préspa lake and
surrounding countryside,
make up the 255 sq km
(100 sq miles) of national park,

established in 1974. The area
is so important for wildlife
that Mikrí Préspa and the
reedbeds that fringe it form
a park within a park, a core
of some 49 sq km (19 sq miles)
regarded as a complete
protection area. The boundary
of the core area is clearly
indicated by signs to prevent
accidental trespass.

Over 1,300 species of plant
can be found here, including
the endemic *Centaurea
prespana*, which has small
daisy-like flowers. There are
over 40 species of mammal,
such as bears, wolves, otters,
roe deer, wild boar and wild
cats. The area is also one of
the last remaining breeding
refuges in Europe for the
Dalmatian pelican, whose
numbers are down to less
than 1,000 pairs worldwide,
with about 150 of these
nesting in the Préspa Lakes.
Other birds more frequently

Wetland Wildlife

In contrast to the dry and stony terrain found
in much of Greece, the north has some
outstanding wetlands with a range of different
habitats. Reed-fringed lake margins hold large
colonies of breeding birds and amphibians,
while the open water is home to numerous
fish and aquatic insects. The marshes are rich
in flowers and full of songbirds; the manmade habitats such as saltpans and lagoons
offer sanctuary to nesting waders.

Lake Korónia *is easy to view from nearby
villages, most of which have their own
colonies of white storks. In spring,
terrapins and frogs gather in the shallow
margins of the lake.*

Kentish plovers nest on the
margins of wetlands, such
as the Préspa Lakes.

The Préspa Lakes *support
colonies of rare Dalmatian
pelicans. When nesting they
need the peace and quiet
this protected area provides.*

The Axiós Delta is home to
dragonflies and, on the
margins, a wealth of spring
flowers and bee orchids.

Whipsnakes are common in
northern Greece, particularly
around Lake Korónia.

Kastoriá

Macedonia

Thessaloníki

seen include herons, cormorants, egrets, storks, golden eagles and goosanders.

Scattered around the lakes are several small villages. One of these, on the shore of Megáli Préspa, is **Psarádes**, a picturesque village where fishermen provide a boat service on to the lake. From the boat you can

Psarádes village on the banks of Megáli Préspa

see hermitages, icons painted on the rocks by the shore, and two churches: the 15th-century **Panagía Eleoúsa** and the 13th-century **Metamórfosi**. To the east of Mikrí Préspa is **Mikrolímni**. The village has wet meadows to the north that are rich in birdlife. Southwest of Mikrolímni a path leads to the Ellinikí Etaireía Biological Station, used as a base by research scientists who want to stay in the area while studying.

In summer, the beaches of fine, pale sand that stretch alongside Megáli Préspa can be enjoyed along with a dip in the blue, but rather cold, waters of the lake.

Fresco from Metamórfosi church

Environs

Northeast of the park lies the village of **Agios Germanós**, which has an 11th-century Byzantine church and a number of traditional houses, built in the local architectural style. The village is also home to the **Préspa Information Centre** which has a permanent exhibition explaining the ecological importance of the Préspa National Park. Guides are available to show visitors around the park, but this must be arranged in advance.

Just out of the village, a road leads up to the summits of Kaló Neró, at 2,160 m (7,090 ft), and Mázi, at 2,060 m (6,760 ft), which give superb views across the lakes below.

Glossy ibises *have one of their last remaining European strongholds in the wetlands of northern Greece. Seen in good light, their feathers have a metallic sheen.*

Purple herons nest in the reed-beds of the Evros Delta.

Pórto Lágos's lagoons, pools and marshes are a haven for ruddy shelducks

The Evros Delta *lies close to the border with Turkey and access to many of the best areas can be difficult. Numerous water birds, including little egrets, nest and feed in easily viewed locations.*

Xánthi

avála

Thrace

Alexandroúpoli

KEY

▮	Préspa Lakes
▮	Axiós Delta
▮	Lake Korónia
▮	Néstos Delta
▯	Pórto Lágos
▮	Evros Delta
—	National boundary

The Néstos Delta *is one of the finest wet-lands in Greece. Many species of birds inhabit the extensive reedbanks and clumps of trees, in particular large breeding colonies of herons and egrets.*

0 kilometres   50

0 miles   50

Kastoriá ❷

Καστοριά

Macedonia. **Road map** B2.
🏠 *17,000.* ✈ *10 km (6 miles) S of
Kastoriá.* 🚌 🛈 *Plateía Olympiakí
Flóga (24670 29630).* ✎ *Wed.*

Kastoría is the Greek for
"place of beavers". These
animals used to live in Lake
Kastoriá (also known as Lake
Orestiáda) by which the town
stands, one of the loveliest
settings in Greece. Evidence
of a prehistoric settlement was
unearthed here in 1940. In
200 BC the Romans captured
the town, then known as
Keletron. The beavers first
brought the furriers here in
the 17th century and, despite
the fact that the animals were
extinct in the area by the 19th
century, trading continued.
By then the furriers were
also importing unwanted
fur scraps, including
mink castoffs, and mak-
ing desirable garments
out of them. The fur
trade exists today,
with the crafts-
men still making
the fur coats that
can be bought
in shops here,
in Thessaloníki
and Athens.

The town pros-
pered as a result
of the fur trade,
as its several
remaining 17th-
and 18th-century mansions
testify. Most of these are found
in the southeast quarter of the
town. The elegant Skoutári
and Nanzí mansions have
interior courtyards and three
floors. The ground floor in
each case is built of stone; the
upper two are made of wood.
They have fine timbered rooms
fitted with cupboards, hearths
and raised platforms. The lower
stone floor is used for storage,
while the living quarters are
in the wooden upper floor
which juts out over the street.

The town's **Folk Museum** is
housed in the Aïvazí mansion.
Built in the 15th century, it was
lived in until as recently as
1972. It now has an eloquent
display of the lifestyle of the
wealthy fur traders. There is
typically elaborate woodwork

The Skoutári mansion in Kastoriá,
built in the 18th century

in the salon on the upper
floor. The kitchens beneath
and the wine cellar have also
been restored.

Another notable feature
of the town are its many
Byzantine churches. Fifty-four
survive, and most are listed as
ancient monuments, including
the 11th-century **Panagía
Koumbelídiki**, situated
towards the south end
of Mitropóleos. The
church is named after
its unusually tall
dome (or *kubbe*, in
Turkish). Some
of the churches
are tiny and
hidden away in
Kastoriá's laby-
rinth of streets,
as they were
originally private
chapels. Many
are closed to
the public, with
some of their
icons removed,
most of which are now on
display in the **Byzantine
Museum**, which is also
sometimes referred to as the
Archaeological Museum. The

**Apse and cupola of
Panagía Koumbelídiki**

small collection has exquisite
pieces on display, including
some fine icons.

🏛 **Folk Museum**
Kapetán Lázou 10. **Tel** *24670
28603.* ☐ *10am–5pm Tue–Sat,
11am–5pm Sun.* ● *main public
hols.* ▨

🏛 **Byzantine Museum**
Plateía Dexamenís. **Tel** *24670
26781.* ☐ *8:30am–3pm Tue–Sun.*
● *main public hols.*

Siátista ❸

Σιάτιστα

Macedonia. **Road map** B2. 🏠 *5,000.*
🛈 *Plateía Tsistopoúlou (24650 21280).*

Siátista was founded in the
1430s, after the Turkish
conquest of Thessaloníki.
Like Kastoriá, the town
flourished as a result of the
fur trade despite the lack of
local fur. Sable and martin
remnants were brought in,
mainly from Russia, made up
into garments, and then traded
or sold in Western Europe.

The wealth that this created
in the 18th century went into
the building of many fine
mansion houses. The
Ottoman influence in their
decoration is strong. The
Nerantzopoúlou mansion is
one of several in the town
that can be visited. Keys
and directions to the other
mansions, including the
Manoúsi and **Poulkídou**,
can also be obtained here.

🏛 **Nerantzopoúlou Mansion**
Plateía Chorí. **Tel** *24650 22254.*
☐ *Tue–Sun.* ● *main public hols.*

View across Siátista, in the Mount Askion range, western Macedonia

The impressive peaks of the Mount Olympos range rising above the village of Litóchoro

Mount Olympos ❹
Όλυμπος

17 km (10 miles) W of Litóchoro, Macedonia. **Road map** C2. 🚌 Litóchoro. 🏠 Town Hall: Agios Nikoláou 17, Litóchoro (23523 50100).

The name Mount Olympos refers to the whole range of mountains, 20 km (12 miles) across. The highest peak in the range, at 2,917 m (9,571 ft), is Mýtikas. The whole area constitutes the Olympos National Park.

Over 1,700 plant species are found here, many of them endemic to the park. Chamois, boars and roe deer also live in this area.

Roman mosaic from Ancient Díon

The base for walkers is the village of **Litóchoro**, a lively place with several hotels and tavernas. Walking maps are available and a marked trail leads up into the national park. Mýtikas can be reached in a demanding walk of at least six hours. It is imperative to camp out overnight or stay in one of the two mountain refuges, rather than attempt to get up and down in a day.

Environs

About 10 km (6 miles) north of Litóchoro is the village of Díon, which has an excellent museum showing finds from **Ancient Díon**. This site is near the modern village and splendidly set between the

coast and the Olympian peaks, its very name deriving from Díos, or "of Zeus". To the Macedonians it was a holy city and in the 4th century BC some 15,000 people lived here. The flat plains were used as a military camp and rallying point by King Philip II of Macedon (see pp32–3). Although Díon was a military camp, rather than a civilian city, there was a temple to Zeus, a theatre and a stadium at the site. Later, the Romans built a city here. The ruins visible today date mainly from that era, and include fine mosaics from the 2nd century AD and well-preserved Roman baths. There is also a theatre and the remnants of a sanctuary dedicated to the

Egyptian goddess Isis. She was worshipped by the Romans as a foreign deity, along with many others that were similarly "adopted" into the pantheon. A second temple, dedicated to Zeus, has also been unearthed here.

The bright and modern **Díon Museum** in the village shows films of the excavations, and it is worth seeing before visiting the site. Also on display are toys, kitchen utensils and jewellery, all finds from the sanctuary of Isis. Together they give a vivid picture of life in Ancient Díon.

🏛 **Ancient Díon**
E of Díon. ☐ 8am–7pm daily (to 3pm in winter). ● main public hols. ⌨ www.ancientdion.org

🏛 **Díon Museum**
Díon. **Tel** 23510 53206. ☐ 8am–7pm Tue–Sun (8:30am–3pm in winter). ● main public hols. ⌨

THE HOME OF ZEUS

Zeus, chief and most powerful of the ancient Greek gods, lived on Mount Olympos along with the other immortals and was thought to be responsible for the destinies of men. He was also god of weather and thunderstorms. Many of the myths tell of Zeus's amorous liaisons and his numerous children, some of whom were gods or goddesses and some heroes (see pp52–3). He was worshipped at Olympia and at Dodóni in Epirus, site of the oldest oracle in Greece.

Vergína ❺
Βεργίνα

12 km (7 miles) SE of Véroia, Macedonia. **Road map** C2. 🚌 **Museum** *Tel*
23310 92347. ⭘ *Jun–Oct: noon–7pm
Mon, 8:30am–7pm Tue–Sun; Nov–May:
8:30am–3pm Tue–Sat (to 7pm Sun).*
🎫 *(tickets also valid for Royal Tombs).*

Outside the village of
Vergína, during excavations in
1977, archaeologist Professor
Manólis Andrónikos found an
entrance to a tomb. The
bones inside included a skull
with one eye socket
damaged, evidence that the
tomb belonged to King Philip
II of Macedon, who received
such a wound in the siege of
Methóni. The bones were
discovered in a stunning gold
funerary box, embellished
with the symbol of the Macedonian Sun. The discovery
confirmed that this area was
the site of Aigai, the first capital
of Macedon. The finds from
this tomb, as well as finds
from several other **Royal
Tombs** nearby, are now on
display in the museum here
and are considered the most
important in Greece since
Schliemann's discoveries at
Mycenae *(see pp178–80).*
A short walk further along
the road from Philip's tomb
are some earlier discoveries,

**Terracotta head of a young man,
from the Museum at Véroia**

known as the **Macedonian
Tombs**. The dark interior hides
splendid solid marble doors
and a beautiful marble throne.
The **Palace of Palatítsia**
stands beyond on a mound. It
is thought to have been first
occupied in about 1000 BC,
though the building itself
dates from the 3rd century BC.
Today only low foundations
remain, along with the ruins
of a theatre 100 m (330 ft)
below, thought to be the site
of Philip II's assassination.

🏛 **Royal Tombs, Macedonian
Tombs, Palace of Palatítsia**
Tel 23310 92394. ⭘ *Apr–Oct:
8am–7:30pm Tue–Sun, 1:30–7:30pm
Mon; Nov–Mar: 8:30am–3pm Tue–
Sun.* ⬤ *main public hols.* 🎫

THE MACEDONIAN ROYAL FAMILY

The gold burial casket found at Vergína is emblazoned with
the Macedonian Sun, the symbol of the king. Philip II was
from a long line of Macedonian kings that began in about
640 BC with Perdiccas I. Philip was the first ruler to unite
the whole of Greece as it existed at that time. Also incorrectly
known as the Macedonian Star, the Sun is often seen on
flags within the region. Much of Greece's pride in the symbol
lies in the fact that Alexander the Great used it throughout
his empire *(see pp32–3).* He was just 20 when his father was
assassinated at Aigai in 336
BC. He inherited his father's
already large empire and
also his ambition to
conquer the Persians.
In 334 BC Alexander
crossed the Dardanelles
with 40,000 men and
defeated the Persians in
three different battles,
advancing as far as the
Indus Valley before he
died at the age of 33.
With his death the Mace-
donian Empire divided.

**Burial casket featuring the
Macedonian Sun**

Véroia ❻
Βέροια

Macedonia. **Road map** C2.
🏛 *48,000.* 🚌 🚗 🏠 *Tue.*

The largest town in the
region, Véroia is interesting
mainly for its 50 or so
barnlike churches, which
have survived from the 17th
and 18th centuries.
The town's **Archaeological
Museum** has a good selection
of exhibits, discovered locally,
and the bazaar area bustles
on market days, as Véroia is
the centre of the local peach-
growing industry.

🏛 **Archaeological Museum**
Anoixéos 47. *Tel 23310 24972.*
⭘ *8am–3pm Tue–Sun.* ⬤ *main
public hols.* 🎫

**Chília Déndra park at Náousa,
near Lefkádia**

Lefkádia ❼
Λευκάδια

Macedonia. **Road map** C2.
Tel 23320 41121. 🚌 ⭘ *8:30am–
3pm Tue–Sun.* ⬤ *main public hols.*

The four Macedonian Tombs
of Lefkádia are set in a quiet
agricultural area. The caretaker is usually at one of the
two tombs that are sign-
posted. The first of these is
the **Tomb of the Judges**, or
Great Tomb. This, the largest
tomb, with a chamber 9 m
(30 ft) square and a frescoed
façade portraying Aiakos and
Rhadamanthys, the Judges of
Hades, has been restored.
Beyond is the **Anthemíon
Tomb**, or Tomb of the

Pebble mosaic of the Lion Hunt from the House of the Lion Hunt at Ancient Pélla

Flowers, with well-preserved flower paintings on the roof. The key to the **Tomb of Lyson and Kallikles** is sometimes available from the caretaker. The entrance is through a metal grate in the roof. The fourth tomb, called the **Tomb of Kinch** after its Danish discoverer, or the **Tomb of Niafsta** after its one-time occupant, is closed to visitors.

Environs
Renowned for the large park of Chília Déndra (1,000 trees), also known as Agios Nikólaos, **Náousa** is the home of the Boutári wine-making family. It is situated on the edge of the hills above the plain that extends east to Thessaloníki. Like Edessa, Náousa has waters flowing through it. Riverside tavernas in the park offer fresh trout as well as the good local wine.

Edessa ⓫
Έδεσσα

Macedonia. **Road map** C1. 🏠 16,000. 🚌 🚉 🅸 Parko Katarrákton (23810 20300). ◯ 10am–6pm daily. 🛥 Thu.

Edessa is the capital of the modern Pélla region and a popular summer resort. It is renowned for its waterfalls, which plunge down a ravine from the town to the valley floor below. The largest fall is the **Káranos**, at 24 m (79 ft), which has a cave behind it. The surrounding gardens and park are pleasant, with cafés and restaurants.

Ancient Pélla ⓬
Πέλλα

38 km (24 miles) NW of Thessaloníki, Macedonia. **Road map** C1.
🚌 *Tel* 23820 31160.
Site ◯ 8:30am–3pm daily.
Museum ◯ 8am–8pm Tue–Sun (to 3pm Nov–Mar), 1:30–8pm Mon. 🔴 main public hols. 🖼 🅴

This small site, which straddles the main road, was once the

Káranos waterfall at Edessa

flourishing capital of Macedon. The court was moved here from Aigai (near modern Vergína) in 410 BC by King Archelaos, who ruled from 413 to 399 BC. It is here that Alexander the Great was born in 356 BC, and later tutored by the philosopher Aristotle. Some sense of the existence of a city can be gained from a plan of the site, which shows where the main street and shops were located. King Archelaos's Palace is believed to have been north of the main site.

The site has some of the best-preserved and most beautiful pebble mosaics in Greece. The stones are uncut and have been carefully picked not only for their size, but also for their warm, subtle colouring. Dating from about 300 BC, the mosaics include vivid hunting scenes. One of the most famous is of Dionysos riding a panther. The mosaic is protected from the weather in the now-covered House of the Lion Hunt. This was built at the end of the 4th century BC and originally comprised 12 rooms around three open court-yards, the whole structure being 90 m (295 ft) long by 50 m (165 ft) wide.

Thessaloníki ⑩

Θεσσαλονίκη

Lion from the Archaeological Museum

Thessaloniki, also known as Salonica, is Greece's second city, founded by King Kassandros in 315 BC. The Romans made it capital of their province of Macedonia Prima in 146 BC, and in AD 395 it became part of the Byzantine Empire. In 1430 it was captured by the Turks who held it until 1912. Today Thessaloníki is a bustling cosmopolitan city. It has a flourishing cultural life and is a major religious centre, with an array of splendid churches (see p248), such as Agía Sofía and Agios Dimítrios, which is the largest church in Greece.

Cafés and fountains in the park near Plateía Chánth

Exploring Thessaloníki

Greece's second city is also a very busy port, which adds to the bustle and the wealth of this fascinating metropolis. Situated on the Thermaic Gulf, it has an attractive waterfront promenade, known as the *paralía*, and a pleasant leafy park. It also boasts a large number of beautiful Byzantine churches (see p248). In recent years Thessaloníki has developed its international exhibition facilities and become a major trade fair centre. The city has many museums, including the Archaeological Museum (see pp246–7).

The Great Fire of August in 1917 destroyed nearly half the buildings within the medieval walls, including the entire Jewish quarter. Some, however, survived, and many from the

Furniture shop in the back streets

original Ottoman bazaar have been restored. One such building is the **Bezesténi**, once a hall for valuables and now home to plush shops. The **Modiáno**, a covered meat and produce hall, is named after the Jewish family who once owned it. West of Modiáno are some of the best *ouzerí* bars, and **Plateía Aristotélous** is home to many posh cafés.

⋔ Arch of Galerius

Egnatía.

The principal architectural legacy of Roman rule is found at the eastern end of the long main street, Egnatía, which was itself a Roman construction, known as Via Egnatia. Here stands the Arch of Galerius, built in AD 303 by Galerius (then Caesar of the East, or deputy emperor) to celebrate his victory over the Persians in AD 297. Its carvings show scenes from the battle.

Section of carving from the Arch of Galerius

There was once a double arch here, with a palace to the south. Some of its remains can be seen in Plateía Navarínou.

⋔ White Tower and Paralía

On the waterfront. *Tel* 2310 267832.
☐ 8:30am–3pm Tue–Sun. 🖼
Probably Thessaloníki's most famous sight is the White Tower on the *paralía*. Built in 1430, the Turks added three such towers to the 8-km (5-mile) city walls. Today it houses rotating exhibitions on several floors of small circular rooms. The original stone steps climb up to a roof with lovely views of the *paralía*.

⋔ Rotónda

Filíppou.
Standing north of the Arch of Galerius is the Rotónda. It is thought that this impressive building was constructed as a mausoleum for Galerius, emperor of the eastern Roman Empire AD 305– 311. Today it is closed, but it has been used in the past both as a church – it is also known as Agios Geórgios – and as a mosque. The minaret nearby is now the only one in Thessaloníki.

📷 Museum of Byzantine Culture

Leofórou Stratoú 2. *Tel* 2310 306400.
☐ Apr–Oct: 8am–8pm Tue–Sun, 1:30–8pm Mon; Nov–Mar: 8:30am– 3pm Tue–Sun, 10:30am–5pm Mon.
🔘 main public hols. 🖼 🛗
Situated behind the Archaeological Museum (see pp246–7), this small, modern museum was opened in 1995. On display are Byzantine icons that date from the 15th to the 19th centuries, and fine jewellery. All of the items are beautifully displayed and and there are plans to expand the collection.

White Tower on the seafront

was under Turkish rule. Photographs, newspapers, weapons, documents and personal items tell the story well. Vivid tableaux depict the struggle and its effect on ordinary people. In one, a Turk with a rifle bursts violently into a schoolroom while a Greek freedom fighter hides under the floorboards. This was the celebrated Pávlos Melás, who fought to free Macedonia from the Turks. Also on display in the museum are his gun and dagger.

🔯 Museum of the Macedonian Struggle

Proxénou Koromilá 23. **Tel** 2310 229778. ☐ 10am–2pm Mon–Sat. ⬤ main public hols.

This is situated in a late 19th-century mansion which originally housed the Greek Consulate when Thessaloníki

🔯 Folklife and Ethnological Museum

Vasilíssis Olgas 68. **Tel** 2310 830591. ☐ 9am–3pm Fri–Tue, 9am–9pm Wed. 🖼

This museum is a 20-minute walk from the Archaeological Museum. There are displays

VISITORS' CHECKLIST

Macedonia. **Road map** C2. 🏠 1,000,000. ✈ 25 km (15 miles) SE of Thessaloníki. 🚢 off Koundouriótou. 🚉 Monastiríou. 🚌 78 (local bus), Monastiríou (Intercity buses). 🛈 Tsimistí 136 (2310 221100); Airport (2310 985000); Passenger Ferry Terminal (2310 500310). 🎭 Cultural Festival: Oct.

of folk costumes, and detailed small models showing rural activities such as ploughing, winnowing, threshing, and children playing. The gruelling life of the nomadic Sarakatsan shepherds is well documented, and a vivid display shows the incredible events at the annual fire-walking ceremony in Lagkadás, a village 20 km (12 miles) northeast of Thessaloníki. The museum also hosts several temporary exhibitions throughout the year and has an extensive archive of fascinating period photography showing the reality of life during the early 20th century.

THESSALONIKI TOWN CENTRE

Railway Station 800m (900 yards)

Osios David, Agios Dimitrios

PLATEIA DHIKASTIRION

FILIPPOU

LEONIDA IASONIDOU

ARMENOPOULOU

ARIANOU

Agios Nikólaos Orfanós

Bezesténi

Panayia Halkéon

SOLOMOU

VENIZELOU

EGNATIA

Panayía Ahiropíitos

① Rotónda

AMYNIS

Jewish Museum

ERMOU

Modiáno

PLATEIA ATHONOS

KOMNINON

Agía Sofía ③

Arch of Galerius ②

PLATEIA AGIAS SOFIAS

P. P. YERMANOU

SVOLOU

GOUNARI

PLATEIA SINDRIVANIOU

PLATEIA ELEFTHERIAS

Port 200m (220 yards)

ARISTOTELOUS

MITROPOLEOS

AGIAS SOFIAS

TSIMISKI

IKTINOU

④ Plateía Aristotélous

⑤ Cathedral

Museum of Macedonian Struggle

PROXENOU KOROMILA

PLATEIA NAVARINOU

DIMITROU

IPODROMIOU

FILIKIS ETERIAS

ETHNIKIS

ANGELAKI

PAVLOU MELA

NIKIS

PLATEIA CHANTH

YERMANOU

White Tower ⑥ and Paralía

NIKIS

Théatro Kípou

Archeological Museum ⑦

STRATOU

PLATEIA LEFKOU PYRGOU

Vassilikó Théatro

Museum of ⑧ Byzantine Culture

| 0 metres | 400 |
| 0 yards | 400 |

Key to Symbols see back flap

Folklife and Ethnological Museum
Airport
25 km (18 miles) ✈

Thessaloníki Archaeological Museum
Αρχαιολογικό Μουσείο Θεσσαλονίκης

This modern museum, opened in 1963, contains a host of treasures. It concentrates on the finds made within the city and at the many sites in Macedonia. The displays progress chronologically through the ages, giving a clear picture of the area's history. The inner rooms surrounding the courtyard house a number of fabulous gold items from ancient Macedon, including the treasures discovered during excavations at Macedonian cemeteries. The annexe basement contains a small exhibition on the prehistory of Thessaloníki.

Faïence Vase
Found in a 2nd-century BC grave in Thessaloníki, this ornate vase is from Ptolemaic Egypt and is the only such faïence vase in Greece.

Field House
Garden Grave

★ Floor Mosaics from a Thessaloníki House
These detailed mosaics depicting marine-world mythology are Roman. This mosaic shows a nereid (sea nymph) and a dolphin.

GALLERY GUIDE
An outer circle of rooms surrounds a block of inner rooms housing a collection of Macedonian gold. The outer rooms contain treasures from the first centuries of Thessaloníki and the kingdom of Macedon. The basement of the annexe holds a display of prehistoric antiquities and temporary exhibitions.

Main entrance

Outdoor courtyard with Roman floor mosaic

Marble Sarcophagus
This 2nd- or 3rd-century Roman sarcophagus is decorated with a vivid relief depicting an Amazon battle. The Amazons, a mythical warrior tribe of women, were a favourite subject for artists (see p55).

Statue of Harpokrates
The marble statue of Harpokrates, the son of Isis and Osiris, was found in Thessaloníki at the site of a sanctuary devoted to Serapis and other Egyptian gods. It has been dated to the end of the 2nd century.

VISITORS' CHECKLIST

Manóli Andrónikou & Leof
Stratoú. *Tel* 2310 830538.
3. ☐ Apr–Oct: 8am–8pm
Tue–Sun, 1:30–8pm Mon; Nov–
Mar: 8:30am–3pm Tue–Sun,
10:30am–5pm Mon. ● public
hols. 🌐 🔲 www.amth.gr

★ Gold Bracelet from Europos
This gold bracelet is one of the highlights of the collection of Macedonian gold. It dates from the 3rd century BC and is accompanied in the exhibition by other gold finds of the 6th century BC to the 2nd century BC.

KEY TO FLOORPLAN

☐	Prehistoric collection
☐	The Gold of Macedon
☐	Macedonia: 7th century BC to late antiquity
☐	Thessaloníki: Metropolis of Macedonia
☐	Manólis Andrónikos room
☐	Towards the birth of cities
■	Temporary exhibitions
☐	Macedonia: Fragments to pixels
☐	Non-exhibition space

Lower Floor

Atrium

STAR EXHIBITS

★ Gold Bracelet from Europos

★ Floor Mosaics from a Thessaloníki House

★ Dervéni Krater

★ Dervéni Krater
Dating from c.300 BC, this bronze wine-mixing vase stands 80 cm (31 in) high. The detailed figures of maenads are exquisite; Dionysos and Ariadne are shown on the front. The volutes at the top are decorated with the head of Herakles.

Exploring Thessaloníki's Churches

Thessaloníki has the richest collection of Byzantine churches in Greece. Of the hundreds of 5th-century basilicas that once stood across the country, only two remain. Both of these, Agios Dimítrios and Acheiropoítos, are in Thessaloníki. The 8th-century Agía Sofía is a very significant Byzantine building, both for its mosaics and its role in influencing future architectural development. Three different 14th-century churches – Agios Nikólaos Orfanós, Agioi Apóstoloi and Agía Aikateríni – give an insight into what was a period of architectural innovation.

Agía Sofía church

The mosaic of Ezekiel's vision in Osios Davíd

🏛 Agios Dimítrios

Agíou Dimitríou. ◻ 6am–9:30pm daily. 🔲 **Crypt** ◻ 10:30am–8pm Sun, 12:30–7pm Mon, 8am–8pm Tue–Sat.

This, the largest church in Greece, was entirely rebuilt after the fire of 1917, which destroyed the 7th- and 13th-century fabric of the basilica. The oldest, 3rd-century AD portion is the crypt. Originally a Roman bath, this, according to legend, is the site of the imprisonment, torture and murder in 305 AD of the city's patron saint Dimítrios – a Roman soldier converted to Christianity and martyred on the orders of Emperor Galerius. Six small 5th–7th-century mosaics are found both on the piers flanking the altar and high up on the west side of the church. These mosaics rank among the finest in Greece and include depictions of Dimítrios with young children, or in the company of the church's builders.

🏛 Osios Davíd

Kástro. ◻ daily.
This delightful small chapel was founded some time in the late 5th century. Behind the altar is an original vivid mosaic of the *Vision of Ezekiel*, rare in that it depicts Christ without a beard. In marvellous condition, it owes its freshness to having been concealed beneath plaster and only discovered in 1921. There are also some frescoes from the 12th century, including a fine *Baptism* and *Nativity*. Although the church is usually locked, there is a caretaker who greets visitors and will unbolt the doors.

🏛 Agía Sofía

Plateía Agías Sofías. ◻ 8:30am–2pm, 5:30–8pm daily.
The church of Agía Sofía is dedicated to the Holy Wisdom (Sofiá) of God, just like the mosque of the same name in Istanbul. It was built in the mid-8th century. In 1585 it became a mosque, but was reconsecrated as a church in 1912. It contains many mosaics and frescoes dating back to the 9th and 10th centuries, including a fine *Ascension* scene in the 30-m (100-ft) high dome. The entrance formerly had a portico, which was obliterated during an Italian air raid in 1941. The imposing nature of the building is emphasized by its location in a partially sunken garden.

🏛 Agios Nikólaos Orfanós

Kástro. ◻ 8am–2:45pm Tue–Sun; key available from warden at Irodhotou 17, opposite the church. 🔲
Situated in a garden plot amongst the lanes of the ancient Kástra district, or upper town, this small, triple-apsed 14th-century church began life as a dependency of the larger Moni Vlatádon, further up the hill. Today, Agios Nikólaos Orfanós retains the richest and best-preserved collection of late Byzantine frescoes in the city. Distributed over the central cella and both aisles, they show rare scenes from the Passion, including Christ mounting the Cross, and Pilate seated in judgment.

Agios Dimítrios, the largest church in Greece

The stretch of sandy beach at Kallithéa on Kassándra

west coast, **Sáni** has excellent beaches and a luxury resort complex. There are quiet bays around the village of **Possídi**, on a promontory halfway down the west coast. On the east coast, **Néa Fókaia** still functions as a fishing village in spite of the steady invasion of tourism, whereas **Kallithéa**, to the south, is the largest resort on Kassándra.

Northern Chalkidikí ⓫
Βόρεια Χαλκιδική

Macedonia. **Road map** D2.
🚌 to Polýgyros.

The north of Chalkidikí is a quiet and delightful hilly region, often overlooked by those whose main interests are the beaches to the south. A glimpse of the hidden interior is given when visiting the **Petrálona Caves**, situated on the edge of Mount Katsíka, 55 km (34 miles) southeast of Thessaloníki. It was in these red-rock caverns in 1960, the year after the caves were discovered by local villagers, that a skull was found. It was believed to be that of a young woman, aged about 25 when she died. A complete skeleton was subsequently discovered, and these are the oldest bones yet to be found in Greece, dating back at least 250,000 years, and possibly even 700,000. Amid the stalactites and stalagmites, reconstructions of the cave dwellers have been arranged in the caves, along with the bones, teeth and tools that were also found here.

In the northeast of the area is the small village of **Stágeira**, the birthplace of Aristotle (384–322 BC). On a hilltop, just outside the village, is a huge white marble statue of the philosopher, and there are sweeping views over the surrounding countryside.

🏛 Petrálona Caves
Mount Katsíka, 55 km (34 miles) SE of Thessaloníki. **Tel** 23730 71671.
🕐 9am–4pm daily. ⚫ main public hols. 📷

Kassándra ⓬
Κασσάνδρα

Southern Chalkidikí, Macedonia. **Road map** D2.
🚌 to Kassándreia.

Much of this area's population was killed in the War of Independence in 1821, and the numbers never really recovered. Little was left on the promontory of Kassándra other than a few fishing villages. However, over the last 30 years, many resorts have sprung up. **Néa Poteídaia** marks the start of Kassándra proper and straddles the narrow neck of the peninsula, with a good sandy beach, a marina and an attractive town square. On the

Statue of Aristotle, Stágeira

Sithonía ⓭
Σιθωνία

Southern Chalkidikí, Macedonia.
Road map D2. 🚌 to Agios Nikólaos.

While the peninsula of Sithonía is only marginally larger than Kassándra, it has fewer resorts and a thickly wooded interior. The peninsula begins at **Metamórfosi** which has a sandy beach shaded by pine trees. **Vourvouroú** is one of the first villages you come to on the north side. A collection of villas spreads along the coast, with a few hotels and a selection of eating places.

To the south of this area is a long undeveloped stretch of coast, with several unspoilt beaches, until you reach the large resort of **Sárti**. At the tip of Sithonía is **Kalamítsi**, little more than a sandy beach and a few bars, while **Pórto Koufó** at the end of the west coast is still a pleasant fishing village set on a bay amid wooded hills. The **Pórto Karrás** resort, halfway down the west coast, was set up by the Karrás wine family. It has three hotels, a marina, a shopping centre, watersports, horseriding, a golf course and tennis.

Boats docked at Pórto Koufó on Sithonía

Mount Athos ⑭

`Αγιον'Ορος

Mount Athos monk

To the Greeks, this is the Holy Mountain, which at 2,030 m (6,660 ft) is the highest point of Chalkidikí's most easterly peninsula. Unique in Greece, Athos is an autonomous republic ruled by the 1,700 monks who live in its 20 monasteries. Only adult males may visit the peninsula, but it is possible to see many of the monasteries from a boat trip along the coast. Together, they include some fine examples of Byzantine architecture and provide an insight into monastic life.

THE MONASTERIES OF ATHOS

– – – Ferry route

Ouranoúpoli
The main town on Athos is where boat trips around the peninsula start.

Zográfou was founded in AD 971, but the present buildings are 18th- and 19th-century.

To Ouranoúpoli ←

MOUNT ATHOS FROM THE WEST

This illustration shows the view seen when travelling by boat along the west of Athos. The most northerly monastery on this coast is Zográfou and the most southerly is Agíou Pávlou. The eastern monasteries are covered on p254.

Xiropotámou was founded in the 10th century, but the present buildings date from the 18th century.

Kastamonítou was founded in the 11th century by a hermit from Asia Minor.

Xenofóntos was founded in the late 10th century. A second chapel was built in 1837, using some 14th-century mosaic panels.

0 kilometres 15
0 miles 10

Docheiaríou
This 10th-century monastery houses a fragment of the True Cross and an icon of the Virgin with healing powers.

Agíou Panteleímonos
Also known as Rosikón (of the Russians), this 11th-century monastery's imposing walls hide many colourful onion-domed churches, evidence of the Russian Orthodox influence on Athos.

◁ **The monastery of Agíou Panteleímonos, Mount Athos**

Agíou Pávlou
This monastery houses 90 monks, many from Zákynthos and Kefalloniá, and has some 13,000 books and manuscripts in its library.

Símonos Pétras was named after Saint Simon who founded the monastery in the 14th century AD after seeing a strange light burning on this remote ridge one Christmas night.

Agíou Dionysíou is perched 80 m (260 ft) above the sea. Its walls conceal the 16th-century church of Agios Ioánnis Pródromos.

Mount Athos

Néa Skíti belongs to Agíou Pávlou.

Dáfni is Athos's port and has a population of 16. A bus goes from here to the capital, Karyés, 15 minutes away.

Grigoríou
Founded in the 14th century, this monastery was totally rebuilt after a disastrous fire in 1761 which destroyed all but a few holy relics. About 40 monks live here today.

VISITING MOUNT ATHOS

Only 14 non-Orthodox men per day are allowed to visit Mount Athos, with a stay of 4 nights. To apply, send a fax request with your preferred start date to visit, together with a copy of your passport, to the Ministery of Macedonia and Thrace at +2310 270092. Apply well in advance. Once confirmed, you must book the monasteries you wish to visit; the Ministery has the monastery telephone numbers. On the day of your visit, be at the Ouranópolis Pilgrims' Bureau by 8:30am to collect your *Diamenterion* (official permit); bring your confirmation and passport. Boats leave daily at 9:45am for the monasteries. For more information, contact the Pilgrims Bureau, 109 Egnatia Street, 54622 Thessaloníki, Greece (tel: +2310 833733).

Vatopedíou refectory

Exploring Mount Athos

Not all of the 20 monasteries on Athos can be seen from the popular boat trips from Ouranoúpoli, although some boats do go round the whole peninsula. A few are hidden in the mountains and others cling to the eastern coast of the peninsula. In addition to the Greek Orthodox monasteries on Mount Athos, there is one Russian (Agíou Panteleímonos), one Bulgarian (Zográfou) and one Serbian (Chelandaríou). Remote hermitages and monastic villages in the hills of the peninsula are preferred by some monks, as a quieter alternative to the relatively busy monastery life.

The East Coast Monasteries

The first monastery to be founded on Athos was the **Megístis Lávras** (Great Lavra). It is situated at the southeastern end of the peninsula, on a rocky outcrop *(see pp36–7)*. It was founded in AD 963 by Athanásios the Athonite, and is the only one of the monasteries never to have suffered from fire. It also has the largest font of all the monasteries, which is outside, shaded by a cypress tree said to have been planted over 1,000 years ago by Athanásios himself.

Halfway along the eastern coast stand the monasteries of Ivíron and Stavronikíta. **Moní Ivíron** was founded in the late 10th century by a monk from Iberia (modern Georgia), hence its name. Its church was built in the early 11th century and restored in 1513. The monastery's main courtyard contains another 16 chapels, one housing a miraculous icon of the Virgin Mary. **Stavronikíta**, to the north, stands on top of a rocky headland. It was first mentioned in a document dated AD 1012.

Moní Vatopedíou, one of the largest monasteries on Athos, is sited on a small promontory at the northern end of the east coast. It was founded in the latter half of the 10th century, and a notable feature is its *katholikón*, or main church, also built in the 10th century. It contains icons dating from the 14th century, though they have been retouched over the years. A wealthy monastery, it is among the best preserved on Mount Athos.

Painting in Megístis Lávras

ORTHODOX LIFE ON MOUNT ATHOS

Monks growing their own fruit and vegetables

Under the Byzantine time system operating on Athos, midnight is at dawn, and morning services begin about an hour before – around 3 or 4am, Greek time. A monk walks around striking a small wooden *símandro* (a carved plank) with a mallet to wake the other monks and call them to prayer. The monks eat two meals a day, consisting mostly of food they grow themselves. There are 159 fasting days in the year when only one meal is allowed which must contain no fish, eggs, cheese, milk or even oil. Meals are eaten after the morning and evening services, and the time in between is spent working, resting and praying.

The Megístis Lávras monastery, with its red *katholikón* in the centre

For hotels and restaurants in this region see pp273–5 and pp294–5

Kavála ⑮
Καβάλα

Macedonia. **Road map** D1.
🏘 *56,000.* ✈ *35 km (22 miles) SE of Kavála.* 🚢 🚌 🚢 *daily.*

Kavála's history goes back to its foundation in the 6th century BC by settlers from Thásos and Erétria. It became part of the Roman Empire in 168 BC, and is where St Paul first set foot on European soil in AD 50 or 51 on his way to Philippi. The biggest impact, however, was the Turkish occupation from 1371 to 1912. It was the Turks who built the 16th-century aqueduct here. Mehmet Ali (1769–1849), the Pasha of Egypt, was born in Kavála. His **birthplace**, a well-preserved house set in gardens, is marked by a bronze statue of Ali on horseback. The house is closed to the public but a bar in the grounds is open during the summer.

Kavála is a busy city, with an industrial port that also has a ferry service to the northeast Aegean islands. Life centres

Sculpture by Polýgnotos Vágis

around the harbour below the castle, which is floodlit at night. At its eastern end there is a busy fish, fruit and vegetable market. To the west is the **Archaeological Museum**, which has finds from Avdíra *(see p256)*, including a dolphin mosaic and a painted sarcophagus. The Municipal Museum on Kapnergatis Square (closed for ongoing refurbishment) has works by local artists, in particular the sculptor Polýgnotos Vágis (1894–1965).

The **Tobacco Museum** features a unique range of artifacts and documents relating to the cultivation and production of tobacco, from the agricultural process to the commercialization of tobacco products.

🏛 **Mehmet Ali's Birthplace**
Theodórou Poulídou 63. ⏲ *gardens only – evenings in summer.*

The town and harbour of Kavála

🏛 **Archaeological Museum**
Erythroú Stavroú 17. **Tel** *2510 222335.* ⏲ *8:30am–8pm Tue–Sun (to 3pm Nov–Mar), 1:30–8pm Mon.* ● *main public hols.* 🦽 🛗

🏛 **Tobacco Museum**
K. Paleologou 4. ⏲ *9am–2pm Mon–Fri.* **www**.tobaccomuseum.gr

Néstos Valley ⑯
Κοιλάδα του Νέστου

Macedonia/Thrace border.
Road map D1. 🚆 🚌 *Xánthi (liable to be cancelled Nov–Apr).*

The Néstos river rises high in the Rodópi mountains in Bulgaria and its meandering course down to the Aegean near the island of Thásos marks the boundary between Macedonia and Thrace. On its way it threads through remote and inaccessible gorges, fed by other rivers and streams, until it passes under the scenic mountain road which links Xánthi in Thrace with the town of Dráma in Macedonia. This road, sometimes closed by snowdrifts in winter, makes for a spectacular scenic drive through the wooded gorge, past the valley's heavy beech forests and scattering of small villages. **Stavroúpoli**, the largest of these villages, has a good café in its village square.

Xánthi ⑰
Ξάνθη

Thrace. **Road map** E1. 🏘 *25,000.* 🚆 🚌 🚢 *Sat.*

Founded in the 11th century, it was not until the 1800s that Xánthi flourished with the development of the tobacco industry. Displays on tobacco are included in the **Folk Museum**, housed in two old mansions. The museum's collection includes embroidery, jewellery and costumes. Xánthi's main square has cafés and fountains, and east of the square is the bazaar. This is overflowing on Saturdays when people of all nationalities and religions visit the busiest market in the area.

🏛 **Folk Museum**
Antiká 7. **Tel** *25410 25421.* ⏲ *9am–2:30pm Tue–Sun.* 🦽

The lush landscape of the Néstos Valley

The monastery of Agios Nikólaos on the banks of Lake Vistonída

Avdira ⑱
`Άβδηρα

6 km (4 miles) S of modern Avdira, Thrace. **Road map** E1. 🏛
Tel 25410 51988. ◯ *8am–2pm daily.* ⬤ *main public hols.*

The ancient city of Avdira was founded in the mid-7th century BC by refugees from Klazomenae in Asia Minor. The site is quite dispersed and overgrown. Most of what can be seen today dates from the Roman period. Some Archaic and Classical ruins are also evident, including the acropolis. The remains of its walls stand on a small headland, and ancient graves have been discovered just outside the walls. Part of the original city wall can also be seen.

Environs
Along the road from Avdira to Maróneia is **Lake Vistonída**, a haven for wildlife. At one end is Pórto Lágos (*see pp236–7*), an old harbour with the white monastery of Agios Nikólaos.

Komotiní ⑲
Κομοτηνή

Thrace. **Road map** E1.
🏘 38,000. 🚉 🚌 🚍 *Tue.*

Only 25 km (16 miles) from the Bulgarian border to the north, and less than 100 km (62 miles) from Turkey to the east, Komotiní is a fascinating mix of Greek and Turkish influence. First founded in the late 4th century AD, it was taken by the Turks in 1363,

and remained part of the Ottoman Empire until 1920. Over 500 years of Turkish rule have left their mark on the town, especially since the area's Muslims were excluded from the population exchange following the Greek defeat in Asia Minor in 1922. There is a thriving market with fish, cattle and tobacco for sale, along with a good selection of fresh produce grown in fertile land. The many old wooden shops sell everything from bric-a-brac to genuine, valuable antiques.

A feel of the town's recent past is given in the well-cared-for **Museum of Folk Life and History**. Its few rooms,

The domed roof and tall minaret of a Turkish mosque, Komotiní

in an 18th-century mansion, are crammed with costumes, local copperware and domestic items. There is also a particularly good collection of embroidery, including examples of a type known as Tsevrés, used in Thracian wedding ceremonies. The town's **Archaeological Museum** displays the best of the finds from the sites at ancient Avdira and Maróneia, including gold jewellery found in 4th-century BC graves at Avdira. A 4th-century BC clay mask of Dionysos is on display, found at the god's sanctuary at Maróneia. The museum also has an extensive coin collection, painted sarcophagi, votive reliefs and maps.

Finial from a gravestone, Archaeological Museum, Komotiní

🏛 **Museum of Folk Life and History**
Agíou Georgíou. *Tel* 25310 25975.
◯ 10am–1pm daily. ⬤ main public hols. 🎦 ♿ limited.

🏛 **Archaeological Museum**
Symeonídi 4. *Tel* 25310 22411.
◯ 8:30am–3pm daily. ⬤ main public hols.

Maróneia ⑳
Μαρώνεια

5 km (3 miles) SE of modern Maróneia, Thrace. **Road map** E1.
🚌 *to modern Maróneia.* ◯ *daily.*
⬤ *main public hols.* 🎦 ♿

The road to ancient Maróneia leads through tobacco and cotton fields, past woodland and small rural communities.

A signpost to the harbour of Agios Charálampos shows the way down a track to the remains of the site, which is in a scenic position overlooking the sea. The city flourished from the 8th century BC until AD 1400. Olive groves now cover the area, which sits between Mount Ismaros and the sea, but a small theatre has been discovered and renovated. Further down the track are the remnants of a sanctuary, thought to have been dedicated to Dionysos, whose son, Maron, is credited with founding Maróneia.

Beyond the city of ancient Maróneia is the developing harbour of **Agios Charálampos**, surrounded by red cliffs, topped by a large hotel, a taverna and a scattering of houses.

Environs
Medieval **Maróneia** is a tiny but attractive place, mainly a farming community but with some larger mansions that provide evidence of a more prosperous past.

Alexandroúpoli ㉑
Αλεξανδρούπολη

Thrace. **Road map** E1. 🏠 36,000.
✕ 🚌 🚗 🚃 🚌 Tue.

Alexandroúpoli lacks the cultural mix and history of other large Thracian towns. It was only built up in 1878, under the Turkish name of Dedeagaç (meaning "Tree of the Holy Man"), derived from a group of hermits who first settled here in the

The landmark lighthouse in Alexandroúpoli

15th century. Prior to that, it was simply an unremarkable fishing village. Alexandroúpoli was renamed in 1919 after the Greek king at the time, Aléxandros.

Today the town is a thriving holiday resort with a port, its own domestic airport, and train connections east to Istanbul, north into Bulgaria and west to Thessaloníki.

In the evening the promenade by the long stretch of beach is thronged with people, both visitors and locals. The lighthouse, built in 1800, is situated along the seafront. It is the town's most famous feature and is lit up at night.

Inland from the promenade is a warren of narrow streets with junk shops, grocers, cobblers, goldsmiths and fish

restaurants. The best eating places are around tiny Plateía Polytechneíou. North from the square, beyond the main road, is the modern cathedral of Agios Nikólaos, notable for the **Ecclesiastical Art Museum** contained in its grounds. This fine collection of icons and other religious items is unfortunately seldom open, but those with a particular interest in seeing it may ask for access at the cathedral.

🏛 **Ecclesiastical Art Museum**
Palaiológou. **Tel** 25510 82282.
⬤ Tue–Sat. ⬤ main public hols.

Dadiá Forest ㉒
Δάσος Δαδιάς

27km (17 miles) N of Féres, Thrace.
Road map F1. 🚗 🚌 Féres.
ℹ 1 km (0.5 miles) N of Dadiá village (25540 32209).

North of the small town of Féres in the Evros valley is the lovely Dadiá pine forest. Covering a series of hills known as the Evros Mountains, it is considered to be one of the best places in Europe for observing rare birds. Of special interest is the presence of birds of prey, an indication of the remote location of the forest. There are 39 known species of birds of prey in Europe, 26 of which live and nest in this region.

Rare black vulture

There is an information centre in the heart of the forest, and observation huts have been placed near feeding stations, built to help preserve the rarer species that nest here. This is one of the black vulture's last refuges in eastern Europe. The forest is home to a huge number of protected and endangered species, including imperial eagles, golden eagles, griffon vultures, sparrowhawks and peregrines. Early morning is the best time to watch the different birds as they fly on the first thermals of the day.

Old mansion in modern Maróneia

TRAVELLERS' NEEDS

WHERE TO STAY

Accommodation in Greece is best described as functional in most cases, though a new generation of boutique hotels is slowly emerging. However, it is nearly always abundant in a country so heavily dependent on the tourist industry and, as a consequence, is good value compared with most European destinations. Despite inroads of commercialization in the busier resorts, hospitality off

Doorman at the Grande Bretagne hotel, Athens

the beaten track can still be warm and heartfelt. Various types of accommodation are described over the next four pages. Information is included for the network of campsites and the more limited facilities for hostelling and alpine refuge stays. The listings section *(see pp264–75)* includes over 150 places to stay, ranging from informal *domátia* (rooms) to luxurious hotels and accommodation in restored buildings.

Malvásia Hotel *(see p269)* at Monemvasía, restored by the EOT during the 1970s

HOTELS

Most Greek hotels are of standard Mediterranean concrete architecture, though in coastal resorts height limits restrict towering structures. Many surviving hotels date from the 1967–74 Junta era, when massive investment in "modern" tourism was encouraged. A very few Neo-Classical, or older, hotels remain, now benefiting from government preservation orders. Hotels built since the 1980s are generally designed with more imagination and sensitivity to the environment. The more expensive hotels will have a correspondingly higher level of service, offered by trained personnel.

CHAIN HOTELS

Greece, with its tradition of family business ownership, has not taken to the idea of chain hotels. However, the largest chain, **Grecotel**, comprises 27 luxury and 4-star resort hotels, many of which offer facilities such as health centres and spas, both in the capital and across the mainland. Other smaller chains, such as **Chandrís** and **Diváni**, offer accommodation in Athens, Thessaloníki, Corfu and Chios, and Diváni also has hotels in central Greece. **Club Mediterranée** and **Aldemar Hotels** are two other well-known chains.

RESTORED SETTLEMENTS AND BUILDINGS

During the 1970s, the EOT (Greek Tourist Office) began sponsoring the restoration of derelict buildings in vernacular style. The completed units usually offer value for money and an exceptionally atmospheric environment, though preservation considerations often mean that bathrooms are shared. Such properties are found at Areópoli and Vátheia in the Máni, at Makrinítsa on the Pílio, at Megálo Pápigko in Epirus, and at Monemvasía. Some,

such as the complex at Megálo Pápigko, have been privatized, with variable effects on efficiency.

Private entrepreneurs have seized the initiative in such renovation projects, installing small and medium-sized hotels in centuries-old buildings. Particularly successful ventures can be found at Stemnítsa, Galaxídi, Náfplio, and in several villages of the Zagória region and the Pílio.

DOMATIA

A large proportion of Greek accommodation is in *domátia*, or rented rooms. In the past, these often used to be in the home of the managing family, but nowadays they are far more likely to be within a separate, modern, purpose-built structure. They tend to be good value compared with hotels of a similar standard. Increasingly they have en suite bathrooms, are well appointed with neutral pine furniture, and often have a kitchen for the use of guests. There is usually no communal area,

Front exterior of the King Othon Hotel, Náfplio *(see p269)*

◁ Seafront café at Koróni in the Peloponnese

The luxurious spa at Diváni Apollon Palace & Spa, Vouliagmeni *(see p268)*

however, and hot water is provided either by an electric immersion heater or by a solar heating device.

GRADING

The EOT grade Greece's hotels and *domátia*. Hotel categories range from 1-star up to 5-star and are graded according to the location and amount of facilities available. *Domátia* range from 1-star to 3-star. There is supposed to be a direct correlation between amenities and the classification, but there are many local deviations – usually the result of a dispute with local authorities.

A sign for rooms to rent

One-star hotels, with the most basic facilities and narrow profit margins, are almost extinct. Two-star still survive, and these should have at least some en suite rooms. In a 3-star hotel, all rooms must have en suite baths, and the hotel must have some sort of common area, if only a small combination bar and breakfast area where a basic continental breakfast can be served.

Four-star hotels have extra amenities such as a full-service restaurant, a more substantial breakfast, and at least one sports facility, such as a pool or tennis court. Five-star hotels are usually at seafront locations, and offer all conceivable diversions, as well as aids for the business traveller, such as conference

halls and telecommunications facilities. Deluxe category hotels are effectively self-contained resort complexes. One-star *domátia,* with baths down the hall and "jail-like" decor, are on the way out, now supplanted by modern 2-star blocks that guarantee bathrooms en suite and often have the benefit of a shared kitchen for the use of visitors. Three-star *domátia* are nearly synonymous with apartments. The furnishings are superior and there is generally landscaping outside the building. A well-equipped kitchen is fitted into each unit.

PRICES

The price of hotel rooms and *domátia* should correspond to their official category, though this depends on the season and their location. In Athens, for €50 or under, it is possible to find a 1-star *domátio* for two without en suite bathroom, or a 1/2-star hotel; €75 should cover a 2-star double *domátio,* while 3-star *domátia* and 3-star hotels charge €100. Four-star hotels ask €100 to €150 per double room; 5-star hotels typically cost €150 to €300. Deluxe resorts are exempt from the EOT price

control scheme and can run in excess of €300 per night.

All of these rate approximations are for high season, including VAT and taxes; prices can drop by almost 50 per cent in early spring or late autumn. Hotel rates include breakfast. Stays of less than three nights can carry a surcharge in high season. In mainland skiing resorts there is often a vast difference in weekend and mid-week rates.

OPENING SEASONS

Mainland hotels stay open year-round, except those at seafront resorts, which operate only from May to October. Hotels in skiing areas, conversely, may open only during the winter period.

BOOKING

The most common and cost-effective way of booking accommodation is through a package holiday agency. If you contact a hotel direct, do so by fax so that the transaction is recorded in writing. You may need to provide a credit card number or send travellers' cheques to the value of the first night's stay. It is also possible to book a hotel via the internet. A useful address to try is www.united-hellas.com.

Conservatory at Grande Bretagne hotel, Athens *(see p267)*

Monastery on Mount Athos *(see p252)*, Northern Greece

YOUTH HOSTELS

The Greek mainland has three IYHF (International Youth Hostel Federation) recognized youth hostels *(xenón neótitos)*. They are all found in Athens. For more information, contact the **IYHA** (International Youth Hostel Association) in England, or the **YHA** (Youth Hostel Association) in Greece. In addition, there are a handful of unofficial hostels, which can provide a standard of accommodation that is just as good, if not better.

Greek hostels are not nearly as regimented as their northern European equivalents. Even without an IYHF card you can usually stay if a vacancy is available. However, if there are two of you, a less expensive *domátio* is better value.

ALPINE REFUGES

Mountains of the Greek mainland are dotted with over 40 alpine refuges *(katafýgia)*. Very few are continuously staffed – two on Mount Olympos *(see p241)* and one on Mount Gamíla, in the Píndos range, being notable exceptions – so you must contact the relevant branch of the **EOS** (Greek Alpine Club) to rent keys. This is expensive and not worthwhile unless you muster a large group. The **EOOA** and **SEO** *(see p263)* may also provide information on refuges. Some of the mountain huts make wonderful base camps, fully equipped with kitchens, bed linen, and well-designed common areas; others are little more than shacks originally built for shepherds or fire-control personnel. Another complication is that, as many were built at a time when approaches to the mountain ranges were quite different, today they are often located well away from the preferred hiking routes.

RURAL TOURISM

Conceived during the 1980s to give women in the Greek provinces a measure of financial independence, rural tourism allows foreigners to stay on a bed-and-breakfast basis in a village house, but also provides the opportunity to participate, if desired, in the daily life of a farming community. Information on agrotourism can be obtained from www.agro-tour.net, from the Hellenic Agrotourism Federation or from the Greek National Tourist Organisation website *(see p307)*.

MONASTERIES

The less-visited monasteries and convents in Greece operate *xenónes* or hostels, intended primarily for Greek Orthodox pilgrims on weekend visits. Pilgrims will always have priority, but it is often possible to find a vacancy at short notice.

Accommodation is of the spartan-dormitory variety, with a frugal evening meal and morning coffee also provided; it is customary to leave a donation in the *katholikón* (main church).

The monasteries on Mount Athos are the most accustomed to non-Orthodox visitors, though these are open to men only. Visits – especially in high season – need to be carefully planned, as the procedure for reserving space and obtaining an entry permit to this semi-autonomous monastic republic is suitably Byzantine *(see p253)*.

CAMPING

The Greek mainland has nearly 150 campsites that are officially recognized. Most of them are in attractive seafront settings, and usually cater to caravanners as well. The last few still owned by the EOT, or by the local municipality, are being sold off; most are

Mountain refuge, Kóziakas mountain, Tríkala

privately run. All but the most primitive sites have hot showers heated by solar power, shady landscaping and a snack bar or café. Power hookups are generally available for an extra fee

The most luxurious campsites are miniature holiday villages, with swimming pool, tennis courts, laundry rooms, banking and postal facilities, and bungalows for the tentless. Established sites usually have the advantage of mature shady trees.

The ground is often sun-baked and very hard, so short pegs that can be banged in with a mallet are best. For a regularly updated booklet on campsites and their amenities, contact the **Panhellenic Camping Association**.

DISABLED TRAVELLERS

The guide *Holidays and Travel Abroad*, published by **Disability Rights UK** *(see p307)*, provides details on wheelchair access to the more established hotels in Greece. Contact **Tourism for All** *(see p307)* for an information sheet with hotels and useful contact numbers in Greece.

The hotel listings in this guide *(see pp264–75)* indicate which establishments have suitable facilities, such as lifts and ramps, for the disabled.

Greek information sources for disabled travellers tend to be rudimentary; the EOT only publishes a question-naire, which can be sent to specific accommodation establishments to assess their suitability.

FURTHER INFORMATION

An invaluable booklet is published yearly by the **Hellenic Chamber of Hotels**. It is called *Guide to Hotels*, and a current copy can be obtained from their office. The booklet covers all officially registered hotels, indicating prices, facilities and their operating season. The guide does not, however, offer information on *domátia* or villas. The EOT also periodically

Camping in one of the valleys of the Pindos mountain range

publishes an informative leaflet entitled *Rural Tourism*. Two other hotel manuals, which are both issued by private organizations, are the *Greek Travel Pages* (GTP) and the *Tourist Guide of Greece*. They are not as complete or authoritative as the EOT guides, but are published more frequently. The GTP is monthly, offering only skeletal information unless the hotel concerned has purchased advertising space; this is also true of the quarterly publication *Tourist Guide of Greece*.

Swimming pool at Karavostasi Beach hotel *(see p271)*

DIRECTORY

CHAIN HOTELS

Aldemar Hotels
Kifisias 262, 14562 Kifisia.
Tel 210 628 8400. www.
aldemarhotels.com

Chandrís Hotels
Syngroú 377, 17564 Paleó
Fáliron, Athens.
Tel 210 948 4730.
www.chandris.gr

Club Méditerranée
Vouliagmenis 576A,
16451 Athens.
Tel 210 994 7300.
www.clubmed.com

Diváni Hotels
Vas. Alexándrou 2, 16121
Athens. *Tel 210 720 7000*.
www.divanis.com

Grecotel
Kifissias 64b,
Maroúsi, 15125 Athens.
Tel 210 728 0300.
www.grecotel.gr

HOSTELS

IYHA (UK)
Tel 01707 324 170.
www.hihostels.com

YHA (Greece)
Student & Traveller's Inn,
Kydathinaion 16,
Plaka, Athens.
Tel 210 324 4808.
www.studenttravellers
inn.com

ALPINE REFUGES

EOOA (Ellinikí Omospondía Oreivasías kai Anarrixisis)
(Hellenic Federation of Mountaineering & Climbing)
Milióni 5,
10673 Athens.
Tel 210 364 5904.
www.eooa.gr

EOS (Ellinikós Orei-vatikós Sýndesmos)

(Greek Alpine Club)
Lékka 23–25, 10562
Athens.
Tel 210 321 2355.
www.eosathinon.gr

SEO (Sýllogos Ellínon Oreivatón)
(Association of Greek Climbers)
Plateía Aristotélous 5,
Thessaloníki.
Tel 2310 224710.
www.seoreivaton.gr

CAMPING

Panhellenic Camping Association
Stadíou 24,
10564 Athens.
Tel 210 362 1560.
www.panhellenic-camping-union.gr

DISABLED TRAVELLERS

Disability Rights UK
Tel 020 7250 3222.
www.radar.org.uk

Tourism for All
Tel 0303 303 0146.
www.tourismforall.
org.uk

FURTHER INFORMATION

Greek Travel Pages
Tel 210 324 7511.
www.gtp.gr

Hellenic Chamber of Hotels
Tel 213 216 9900.
www.grhotels.gr

Tourist Guide of Greece
Tel 210 864 1688.
www.tggr.com

Choosing a Hotel

The hotels in this guide have been selected across a wide price range for their good value, exceptional location, comfort or style. All rooms have private bath unless otherwise indicated. The chart lists hotels by region, starting with Athens. For Athens map references, *see* pp128–35; for other map references see inside back cover.

PRICE CATEGORIES
The following price ranges are for a standard double room with tax per night during the high season. Breakfast is not included, unless specified.

€ under €50
€€ €50–€90
€€€ €90–€130
€€€€ €130–€200
€€€€€ over €200

ATHENS

EXARCHEIA Orion-Dryades €
Anexartisias 5, corner Emmanouil Mpenáki, 114 73 **Tel** *21038 27362* **Fax** *21038 05193* **Rooms** *38*   **Map** *3 A2*

These co-managed adjacent hotels, opposite the Lófos Stréfis park, are a mecca for young travellers seeking medium-term accommodation. The cheaper Orion (no en suite rooms) has a rooftop communal lounge with fantastic views; the Dryades has wood-panelled rooms, while both hotels have self-catering kitchens. **http://orion-dryades.com**

EXARCHEIA Best Western Museum Hotel €€
Mpoumpoulínas 16, 106 82 **Tel** *21038 05611* **Fax** *21038 00507* **Rooms** *90*   **Map** *3 A1*

This hotel takes its name from the National Archaeological Museum at the front, and is popular with academic visitors. The rooms are up to the standards of the Best Western chain without being especially distinctive. There are also triples and quads for families. **www.bestwestern.gr**

EXARCHEIA Exarchion €€
Themistokléous 55, 106 83 **Tel** *21038 00731* **Fax** *21038 03296* **Rooms** *58*   **Map** *2 F3*

The dated rooms of this 1960s high-rise, with their linoleum floors and dark furniture, are ready for a facelift, but they do have fridges, air conditioning and TVs; given the price and the location in the heart of the district's nightlife scene, you can't complain. The mezzanine breakfast room is cheerful enough. **www.exarchion.com**

ILISIA Airotel Alexandros €€
Timoléontos Vássou 8, 115 21 **Tel** *21064 30464* **Fax** *21064 41084* **Rooms** *93*   **Map** *4 F3*

The bland façade gives nothing away, but once inside, the Airotel proves welcoming, with a lively bar-brasserie and designer furniture in the lobby. Rooms may be a little on the small side, but those without a balcony are a bit larger, as are the 19 suites. **www.airotel.gr**

ILISIA Hilton €€€€
Vassilis Sofías 46, 115 28 **Tel** *21072 81000* **Fax** *21072 81111* **Rooms** *306*   **Map** *4 D5*

For years the only five-star hotel in the city centre, the Hilton's pre-Olympics overhaul has again vaulted it into the top rank, with the rooms retaining their large balconies. The hotel's three restaurants and huge outdoor pool (open to the public for a fee) are still major meeting points. **www.hiltonathens.gr**

KOLONAKI Periscope €€€€
Charitos 22, 106 75 **Tel** *21072 97200* **Fax** *21072 97206* **Rooms** *22*   **Map** *3 B5*

Just a 5-minute walk from Kolonaki Square, this smart design hotel opened in 2005. All rooms have wooden floors and minimalist furniture in blacks, greys and whites. The luxury penthouse suite occupies the roof terrace and has an open-air Jacuzzi with stunning city views. Facilities include a gym, restaurant and cocktail bar. **www.periscope.gr**

KOLONAKI St George Lycabettus €€€€
Kleoménous 2, 106 75 **Tel** *21074 16000* **Fax** *21072 90439* **Rooms** *157*   **Map** *3 B4*

Situated just off Platía Dexamenís halfway up Lykavittós Hill, the St George offers a rooftop pool, two well-regarded restaurants, and a bar that's a popular local hangout. The rooms are a mix of retro and modern minimalist; try to get a south-facing one with a view over the city. **www.sglycabettus.gr**

KOUKAKI Marble House €
Alley off Anastasíou Zínni 35, 117 41 **Tel** *21092 28294* **Fax** *21092 26461* **Rooms** *16*   **Map** *5 C4*

The helpful Nikoloulias family's pension has an enviable location on a quiet cul-de-sac. The simple but tidy rooms upstairs, most with bath and balcony, are complete with pine furniture and white tiles. There are two slightly larger ground floor studios. Vastly popular in season, so book well in advance. **www.marblehouse.gr**

KOUKAKI Art Gallery €€
Erechtheíou 5, 117 42 **Tel** *21092 38376* **Fax** *21092 33025* **Rooms** *21*   **Map** *6 D4*

This family-run pension-hotel, named for the artwork on the common–area walls, has received a make over, which means refreshed furnishings and upgraded bathrooms for the parquet-floored rooms. There are two family suites and a pleasant breakfast bar (with an Acropolis-view terrace). **www.artgalleryhotel.gr**

Key to Symbols *see back cover flap*

MAKRYGIANNI Acropolis View

Wemster 10, 117 42 **Tel** *21092 17303* **Fax** *21092 30705* **Rooms** *32* **Map 5 C3**

Many rooms at this small hotel, located on a quiet street near the Acropolis, live up to the hotel's name, as does the popular roof garden. The white rooms are on the small side, but have been redecorated with black furniture and marble baths. Wi-Fi access and unusually low rates in Jun–Aug. **www.acropolisview.gr**

MAKRYGIANNI Diváni Palace Acropolis

Parthenónos 19–25, 117 42 **Tel** *21092 80100* **Fax** *21092 14993* **Rooms** *250* **Map 6 D3**

This popular business and conference hotel has vast common facilities, though the underground restaurant is gloomily lit. Equally subterranean are exhibited sections of the Themistoklean Long Walls, discovered when the hotel was built. Rooms are a good size; there's also a small pool area and summer rooftop garden. **www.divanis.gr**

MAKRYGIANNI Hera

Falirou 9, 117 42 **Tel** *21092 36682* **Fax** *21092 38269* **Rooms** *38* **Map 6 E3**

Refurbished as a boutique hotel, the Hera's rooms are on the small side but lack for nothing; it's worth paying extra for fifth floor suites with bigger balconies. Further delights are the dome-lit atrium breakfast room and the year-round rooftop bar-restaurant with great views of the Acropolis. **www.herahotel.gr**

MAKRYGIANNI Herodion

Rovértou Gkálli 4, 117 42 **Tel** *21092 36832* **Fax** *21092 11650* **Rooms** *90* **Map 6 D3**

The Herodion has lovely common areas: the café-restaurant with patio seating shaded by wild pistachios, and the roof garden with two Jacuzzi tubs and the Acropolis a stone's throw away. Functional but fair-sized rooms, some with disabled-friendly baths and Acropolis views, have coco-fibre mattresses. **www.herodion.gr**

MAKRYGIANNI Philippos

Mitsaíon 3, 117 42 **Tel** *21092 23611* **Fax** *21092 23615* **Rooms** *50* **Map 6 D3**

The Philippos, sister hotel of the Herodion around the corner, is probably better for families as there are many quad rooms; otherwise you've the same efficient service, the same stunning common areas, and a similar clientele avoiding the standard identikit mid-range hotels. As with the Herodion, book online for best prices. **www.philipposhotel.gr**

MONASTIRAKI Carolina

Kolokotróni 55, 105 60 **Tel** *21032 43551* **Fax** *21032 43550* **Rooms** *34* **Map 2 E5**

This budget hotel, occupying an interwar building in the heart of the bazaar, had a pre-Olympics refit which bumped prices up slightly in exchange for a better standard in the tile-floored rooms with their cheerful blue furniture. No frills in the common areas, other than a bar. **www.hotelcarolina.gr**

MONASTIRAKI Cecil

Athinás 39, 105 54 **Tel** *21032 17079* **Fax** *21032 17079* **Rooms** *40* **Map 2 D5**

One of the oldest buildings in central Athens, dating from the 1850s, has been restored as a good-value character hotel with soundproofed, tastefully decorated, en suite rooms. Breakfast (charged separately) is abundant, featuring homemade jams, plus there's a roof terrace. **www.cecilhotel.gr**

NEOS KOSMOS Athenaeum Intercontinental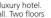

Leofóros Andréa Syngroú 89–93, 117 45 **Tel** *21092 06000* **Fax** *21092 06500* **Rooms** *603* **Map 5 B5**

Original artworks decorate both the sumptuous common areas and individual rooms at Athens' largest luxury hotel. Standard units are like suites elsewhere, with separate sitting area, though bathrooms are surprisingly small. Two floors of suites have their own lounge and breakfast area. Look for seasonal rates or Internet deals. **www.ichotelsgroup.com**

NEOS KOSMOS Athenian Callirhoe

Kallirόis 32, corner Petmezá, 117 43 **Tel** *21092 15353* **Fax** *21092 15342* **Rooms** *84* **Map 6 E4**

Athens' first boutique hotel offers three grades of designer decorated rooms (including non-smoking), with Internet acccess and double glazing. An Oriental theme bar, a small gym and a branch of the superb Corfiot-Italian restaurant Etrusco (on the roof with Acropolis views in summer) complete the profile. **www.tac.gr**

NEOS KOSMOS Ledra Marriott

Leofóros Andréa Syngroú 115, 117 45 **Tel** *21093 00000* **Fax** *21093 58603* **Rooms** *314* **Map 5 B5**

Like most other top hotels in town, the Ledra Marriott had a much-needed complete overhaul before the Olympics; most standard rooms have a balcony, and there's a gym and spa. The restaurants, particularly the Polynesian-themed Kona Kai, are worth a visit. **www.marriott.com**

OMONOIA Art Athens Hotel

Márnis 27, 104 32 **Tel** *21052 40501* **Fax** *21052 43384* **Rooms** *30* **Map 2 D2**

Boutique hotels are now ten a penny in Athens, but this one – occupying a converted Neo-Classical mansion – is one of the best. Light cream tones characterize the wood-floored rooms, accented by colourful original artwork. Everything is hi-tech, from lighting to voice mail to individual thermostats. Service is excellent. **www.arthotelathens.gr**

OMONOIA Delphi Art Hotel

Agíou Konstantínou 27, 104 37 **Tel** *21052 44004* **Fax** *21052 39564* **Rooms** *40* **Map 2 D3**

Formerly a six-storey 1930s apartment block next to the National Theatre, this has been converted into a stylish hotel with all mod cons (including Internet access), without sacrificing original features such as bay windows and French doors opening onto balconies with wrought-iron railings. Common areas include three bar-cafés. **www.delphiarthotel.com**

OMONOIA The Alassia €€€

Sokrátous 50, 104 31 **Tel** *21052 74000* **Fax** *21052 74029* **Rooms** *82*   **Map** *2 D3*

A designer hotel, deploying lots of polished metal, futuristic furniture, recessed lighting and marble surfaces in the common areas, and understated, soundproofed (if slightly small) guest rooms with Internet access. The location doesn't get much more central, but this is the least interesting corner of Omónoia. **www.thealassia.com.gr**

PEDION ÁREOS Radisson Park €€

Leofóros Alexándras 10, 106 82 **Tel** *21088 94500* **Fax** *21082 38420* **Rooms** *152*   **Map** *3 A1*

The refurbishment of this classic business hotel focused on the large, comfortable if not cutting-edge rooms, the best of which face the Pédion Áreos park across the boulevard. There's a conference centre and small roof pool, but the main draw is the rooftop restaurant and bar. **www.athensparkhotel.gr**

PLAKA Acropolis House €€

Kódrou 6–8, 105 58 **Tel** *21032 22344* **Fax** *21032 44143* **Rooms** *19*   **Map** *6 E1*

Athens' first mansion turned pension-hotel, Acropolis House offers a mix of en suite and basic rooms, most with high ceilings (some with murals). The academic and student clientele swap books and use the communal fridge. The Neo-Classical building's listed status prevents a much-needed facelift from occurring. **www.acropolishouse.gr**

PLAKA Kimon €€

Apóllonos 27, 105 57 **Tel** *21033 14658* **Fax** *21032 14203* **Rooms** *14*   **Map** *6 E1*

Much the cheapest hotel in this part of Pláka, the Kimon – if you overlook a total lack of communal amenities – is a good option. The rooms are all en suite, painted cheerfully and come complete with mock-antique furniture (such as iron bedsteads), as well as TV and telephones. **www.kimonhotelathens.com**

PLAKA Phaedra €€

Chairefontos 16, corner of Adrianoú, 105 58 **Tel** *21032 38461* **Fax** *21032 27795* **Rooms** *21*   **Map** *6 E2*

Located at the intersection of two pedestrian lanes, the Phaedra had a thorough makeover before the Olympics and offers the best budget value in the area. Although not all tiled-floor rooms are en suite, each has an allocated bathroom and TV, while some have balconies. Pleasant ground floor breakfast room.

PLAKA Student and Travellers Inn €€

Kydathinaion 16, 105 58 **Tel** *21032 44808* **Fax** *21032 10065* **Rooms** *30*   **Map** *6 E2*

On a pretty pedestrian street in the heart of Pláka, this friendly, upscale hostel offers shared and individual accommodation in single, double, triple and quadruple rooms, some with en suite bathrooms. There's an internal courtyard for relaxing, plus Internet access. **www.studenttravellersinn.com**

PLAKA Central €€€

Apóllonos 21, 105 57 **Tel** *21032 34357* **Fax** *21032 25244* **Rooms** *84*   **Map** *6 E1*

Italian designer furniture, marble-clad bathrooms and wooden flooring set the tone for this revamped hotel, with warm-toned soft furnishings in the comfortable, soundproofed rooms, some of which interconnect. There are four conference rooms, and a rooftop bar with a small spa and view of the Acropolis. **www.centralhotel.gr**

PLAKA Hermes €€€

Apóllonos 19, 105 57 **Tel** *21032 35514* **Fax** *21032 11800* **Rooms** *45*   **Map** *6 E1*

Part of a small group of four co-owned hotels, the Hermes has a very pleasant ground floor lounge-bar-café as well as the inevitable roof terrace. The rooms – some with balconies – vary in size, but all have polished wood floors, large, well-equipped bathrooms and designer touches. **www.hermeshotel.gr**

PLAKA Plaka €€€

Kapnikaréa 7, corner of Mitropóleos, 105 56 **Tel** *21032 22706* **Fax** *21032 11800* **Rooms** *67*   **Map** *6 D1*

A sister hotel to the Hermes, the Plaka anticipated by some years the Olympic Games renovation frenzy, and has worn well. From the leather sofas in the lobby to the striking colour schemes in the wood-floored rooms, the place is sleek and tasteful. Many nearby hotels boast roof gardens; the Plaka's is one of the best. **www.plakahotel.gr**

PLAKA Electra Palace €€€€€

Navárchou Nikodimou 18–20, 105 57 **Tel** *21033 70000* **Fax** *21032 41875* **Rooms** *131*   **Map** *6 E1*

This deluxe hotel in Pláka attracts attention with its Neo-Classical façade. The interior lives up to this promise, with plush rooms, antique and mock-antique decor, a wellness centre, plus plans for a rooftop pool. Rooms facing the garden are quieter. It's worth paying extra for a suite. **www.electrahotels.gr**

PSYRRI Arion €€

Agíou Dimitríou 18, 105 54 **Tel** *21032 40415* **Fax** *21032 40419* **Rooms** *51*   **Map** *2 D5*

The Arion is yet another member of the Stathopoulos chain that also runs the Plaka and Hermes. It has a rather bland exterior without balconies, and slightly forbidding common areas, though the rooms have attractively glassed-in bathrooms. There is also a rooftop bar with Acropolis views. **www.arionhotel.gr**

PSYRRI Fresh €€

Sofokléous 26 & Kleisthénous, 105 52 **Tel** *21052 48511* **Fax** *21052 48517* **Rooms** *133*   **Map** *2 D4*

The closest design hotel to the town centre, Fresh combines minimalist chic with shockingly vibrant colours, right down to the balcony partitions. Rooms are small but cleverly designed – you can control the blinds from your bed to reveal views of the interior rock gardens. Stylish rooftop pool and bar. Wi-Fi access. **www.freshhotel.gr**

PSYRRI O&B Athens Boutique Hotel
*Leokoriou 7, 105 54 **Tel** 21033 12950 **Fax** 21033 12942 **Rooms** 22*   *Map 1 C5*

This small, exclusive design hotel lies close to Thiseío metro station. Wood, leather and glass predominate, with splashes of orange. All the rooms have en suite marble bathrooms and Internet access. The O&B Athens All Day Bar Restaurant offers great dishes of Mediterranean cuisine. **www.oandbhotel.com**

STATHMOS LARISSIS Oscar
*Filadélfias 25, 104 39 **Tel** 21088 34215 **Fax** 21082 16368 **Rooms** 124*   *Map 1 C1*

The Oscar's main advantage is its position opposite the main Athens train station – ideal for late-night arrivals or early-morning departures to/from the airport or the north mainland. The common facilities, including a rooftop pool, are more than you would expect for this price, though rooms are a little dull. **www.oscar.gr**

SYNTAGMA Athens Cypria
*Diomeias 5, 105 63 **Tel** 21032 38034 **Fax** 21032 48792 **Rooms** 115*   *Map 6 E1*

The exterior of this hotel just off pedestrianized Ermoú is deceptively bland. Inside, earth-toned rooms with small balconies are matched by the colour scheme and stone dressing in the lobby. A disadvantage is the complete lack of common areas, other than a small café-bar with tables on the pavement. **www.athenscypria.com**

SYNTAGMA Metropolis
*Mitropóleos 46, 105 63 **Tel** 21032 17871 **Fax** 21032 17469 **Rooms** 22*   *Map 6 D1*

This small, five-storey hotel enjoys views over its namesake, the Mitrópoli (Cathedral), and on to the Acropolis from the upper rooms. Rooms are basic, with vinyl floors and balconies, though the staff are friendly and the price is reasonable. There are no common areas, and breakfast is not provided. **www.hotelmetropolis.gr**

SYNTAGMA King George Palace
*Vassiléos Georgíou 3, Plateía Syntágmatos, 105 64 **Tel** 21032 22210 **Fax** 21032 50504 **Rooms** 102   Map 6 F1*

The 1936-founded King George is more intimate and personal than other luxury hotels in the immediate vicinity, but boasts similar antique Belle Epoque decor, a small pool in the fitness centre, and a rooftop restaurant. Rooms are a good size, all unique, with handmade furniture in Second Empire style, and all mod cons. **www.classicalhotels.com**

SYNTAGMA Grande Bretagne
*Vassiléos Georgíou 1, Plateía Syntágmatos, 105 64 **Tel** 21033 30000 **Fax** 21032 28034 **Rooms** 321   Map 6 F1*

Originally built in 1842 for King Otto, the Grande Bretagne has always been Athens' most exclusive hotel. Its restaurants and bars stand out in their own right: Alexander's Bar has an 18th-century tapestry of Alexander the Great, and the brasserie and rooftop restaurant are justifiably busy. **www.grandebretagne.gr**

THISEIO Phidias
*Apostólou Pávlou 39, 118 51 **Tel** 21034 59511 **Fax** 21034 59082 **Rooms** 15*   *Map 5 B1*

This small, quiet hotel had a light touch-up for the Olympics but prices haven't quite caught up yet. The lobby and breakfast area are 1970s relics, the rooms small but perfectly adequate, with refurbished showers and flooring. The front eight rooms have views towards the Acropolis that most mid-town de luxe outfits envy. **www.phidias.gr**

AROUND ATHENS

KIFISIA Pentelikon
*Diligiánni 66, 145 62 **Tel** 21062 30650 **Fax** 21080 19223 **Rooms** 44*   *Road Map D4*

Built in 1929, but Belle Epoque rather than Art Deco in style, the rambling Pentelikon, set in extensive landscaped gardens, is Athens' most elegant suburban hotel. There are extensive conference and banqueting facilities, including the Michelin-starred Vardis restaurant (closed Aug). Each spacious room is individually decorated. **www.pentelikon.gr**

KIFISIA Semiramis
*Charíláou Trikoúpi 48, 145 62 **Tel** 21062 84400 **Fax** 21062 84499 **Rooms** 52*   *Road Map D4*

As cutting-edge as its near neighbours in Kefalári district are retro, this design hotel isn't for everyone. The colour scheme runs to chartreuse, dark lavender and hot pink, while the contemporary furniture is intended to be looked at as much as sat on. The rooms sport every hi-tech gadget imaginable. **www.yeshotels.com**

PIRAEUS Mistral
*Alexándrou Papanastasíou 105, 185 33 **Tel** 21041 17150 **Fax** 21041 22096 **Rooms** 80*   *Road Map D4*

This mid-range hotel overlooks Mikrolímano from a good site in Kastélla district. Rooms are low-key, with sea views; the common areas are light and airy and there is a rooftop pool. An ideal place for an overnight before an early-morning ferry (though a taxi should be arranged as it's too far to walk to the port). **www.mistral.gr**

RAFINA Avra
*Arafinídon Álon 3, 190 09 **Tel** 22940 22780 **Fax** 22940 23320 **Rooms** 96*   *Road Map D4*

This renovated hotel is well placed on the shore for a pre-ferry overnight stay. Not all of the beige and tan rooms actually overlook the sea, however, and the Avra has set its sights firmly on the conference and business trade. **www.hotelavra.gr**

SOUNIO Grand Resort Lagonissi

🛏 🏊 🚶 🗐 🅿 ⚐ €€€€€

Lagoníssi, 40th klm Athens-Soúnio, 190 10 **Tel** *22910 76000* **Fax** *22910 24534* **Rooms** *346* **Road Map** *D4*

Set on a landscaped, foot-shaped peninsula 7 km (4.3 miles) before Soúnio, this ultra-luxurious self-contained resort has several beaches and restaurants, a vast spa and its own helipad. There are four levels of rooms, bungalows and very expensive villas, the latter with their own pool and gym. Open Apr–Oct. **www.grandresort.gr**

VOULIAGMENI The Margi

🛏 🏊 🗐 🅿 €€€€

Litoús 11, 166 71 **Tel** *21089 29000* **Fax** *21089 29143* **Rooms** *90* **Road Map** *D4*

This boutique hotel has antiques and Persian rugs in the common areas, wood floors and tawny ochre decor in the rooms (some with hot tubs, but all with music systems and broadband), and a good buffet breakfast. There is an Oriental theme bar-café (with low divans) beside the outdoor pool. The beach is close by. **www.themargi.gr**

VOULIAGMENI Arion Resort & Spa, Astir Palace

🛏 🏊 🚶 🗐 🅿 ⚐ €€€€€

Apóllonos 40, 166 71 **Tel** *21089 02000* **Fax** *21089 62582* **Rooms** *570* **Road Map** *D4*

Superbly sited on a private pine-clad peninsula 25 km (15.5 miles) from central Athens, this all-inclusive resort comprises three separate units (in ascending order of cost and modernity: Aprhodite, Nafskika, Arion). Private beaches, marinas, and every activity from jet-skiing to paragliding to yoga. Popular for international conferences. **www.astir-palace.com**

VOULIAGMENI Diváni Apollon Palace & Spa

🛏 🏊 🚶 🗐 🅿 ⚐ €€€€€

Agíou Nikoláou 10, corner of Ilíou, 166 71 **Tel** *21089 11100* **Fax** *21096 58010* **Rooms** *286* **Road Map** *D4*

An ideal solution for a seaside holiday still within Greater Athens city limits, this all-inclusive resort dominates Kavoúri beach from a garden setting. Excellent sports facilities – including tennis courts and two outdoor sea water pools, two restaurants (Mythos is on the beach) and of course the thalassotherapy spa. **www.divanis.gr**

THE PELOPONNESE

AREOPOLI Xenonas Londas

🛏 €€

Off Plateía Taxiarchón, 230 62 **Tel** *27330 51360* **Fax** *27330 51012* **Rooms** *4* **Road Map** *C5*

This tower-mansion has been sympathetically converted into a small, sophisticated inn by Iakovos, painter and chef, and Han Jakob. The colourful textiles and wall tones are in the best of taste. Local honey and Iakovos's marmalade are served at breakfast (included in the price). **www.londas.com**

CORINTH Hotel Ephira

🗐 €€

Ethnikís Antistaseos 52, 201 00 **Tel** *27410 22434* **Fax** *27410 24514* **Rooms** *45* **Road Map** *C4*

Occupying a 1970s building in the centre of New Corinth, the Ephira offers clean and comfortable accommodation. An adequate buffet breakfast is served on a mezzanine level and there is a café with a small garden, but the hotel does not have a restaurant. Helpful and friendly staff. **www.elphirahotel.gr**

DIAKOFTO Chris-Paul

🛏 🏊 🗐 🅿 ⚐ €€

Next to railway station, 250 03 **Tel** *26910 41715* **Fax** *26910 42128* **Rooms** *24* **Road Map** *C4*

Named after the owners' children and situated a few minutes' walk from the railway station, this hotel is ideal for the Vouraikos Gorge cog-railway trip. Rooms are well-maintained, with balconies overlooking the small pool or surrounding orchard; bathrooms are well-equipped. Bar for light meals. Open Apr–Oct. **www.chrispaul-hotel.gr**

DIMITSANA Amanites

🗒 🅿 €€€

In the village, 220 07 **Tel** *27950 31090* **Fax** *27950 31091* **Rooms** *7* **Road Map** *C4*

Conveniently situated in the centre of the mountain village of Dimitsana, this cosy, family-run hotel is housed in a modern building decorated in a traditional style. It offers a fully equipped office for business travellers and free Wi-Fi. There is also a family room with board games. Breakfast is included. **www.amanites.gr**

FOINIKOUNTA Porto Finissia

🗒 🗐 €€

Near the waterfront, 240 06 **Tel** *27230 71358* **Fax** *27230 71458* **Rooms** *27* **Road Map** *C5*

Just a stone's throw from the beach of Foinikounta, the Porto Finissia offers comfort and convenience. Rooms have a fridge, as well as balconies with pretty ironwork railings and useful fold-out sun-canopies; most have relaxing sea views towards the island of Schíza. There is a large breakfast room and bar. Open May–Oct. **www.portofinissia.gr**

GYTHEIO Githio

🚶 🗐 €€

Vassiléos Pávlou 33, 232 00 **Tel** *27330 23452* **Fax** *27330 23523* **Rooms** *6* **Road Map** *C5*

This fine Neo-Classical building from 1864 was formerly a gentleman's club; it's now a stylishly refurbished hotel above an ice cream parlour, overlooking the seafront and harbour. Elegant, high-ceilinged rooms sleep two or three; two four-bed apartments have kitchen facilities. Breakfast is served in an area carved out of the natural rock. **www.gythionhotel.gr**

KALAMATA Akti Taygetos Resort

🛏 🏊 🗐 🅿 ⚐ €€€

Mikrí Mantineía, south of Kalamáta, 241 00 **Tel** *27210 42000* **Fax** *27210 64501* **Rooms** *74* **Road Map** *C5*

A well-designed low-rise complex with sweeping sea views and extensive gardens threaded by stone paths and studded with palms around a large pool. Predominantly white rooms are furnished tastefully with iron beds and marble-top tables. There's a small swimming cove just below the grounds. **www.aktitaygetos.gr**

Key to Price Guide *see p264* **Key to Symbols** *see back cover flap*

KALAVRYTA Filoxenia

Ethnikís Andistáseos 10, 250 01 **Tel** *26920 22493* **Fax** *26920 23009* **Rooms** *28* **Road Map** *C4*

With a distinct alpine ambience, wood panel decor and efficient service, the Filoxenia caters for skiers in winter and tourists and pilgrims in summer. Rooms are well-equipped: facilities include Internet connection, hydromassage and central heating. Balconies have mountain views. Prices rise from Dec to Apr. **www.hotelfiloxenia.gr**

KALOGRIA Kalógria Beach

North end of beach, 270 52 **Tel** *26930 31380* **Fax** *26930 31381* **Rooms** *96* **Road Map** *B4*

Sports-oriented hotel, particularly popular with French tourists, offering tennis, volleyball and mini-golf, in addition to a wide range of water sports at the Blue Flag-awarded beach; rock-climbing pitches are nearby. After dark, the nightclub kicks in. Three main buildings, plus bungalows, set in spacious gardens. **www.peloponnestravel.gr**

KARDAMYLI Cardamili Beach

Northern end of Ritsla beach, 240 22 **Tel** *27210 73180* **Fax** *27210 73184* **Rooms** *34* **Road Map** *C5*

Situated in a large orchard on the beachfront, and a short distance from the village, the hotel has rooms in the main building and a number of garden bungalows; some of the latter have kitchen facilities. All rooms have a fridge and views of the sea or mountains. A taverna and swimming pool on site. Open Apr–Oct. **www.kardamilibeach.info**

KORONI Zaga Mylos

On the ridge overlooking the town, 240 04 **Tel** *27250 22385* **Fax** *27250 29028* **Rooms** *32* **Road Map** *C5*

Ten minutes' walk from the castle and from lovely Zánga Beach – after which it is named – this modern hotel has a cloth-sailed windmill decoratively incorporated into its whitewashed facade. Comfortable rooms are equipped with a fridge and have sea-view balconies. Breakfast is included. Open Apr–Oct. **www.zagamiloshotel.gr**

MESSINIA The Romanos Resort

Navarino Dunes, Costa Navarino, 240 00 **Tel** *27320 95000* **Fax** *27320 95500* **Rooms** *444* **Road Map** *B5*

Surrounded by a verdant hillside landscape with sweeping views of the sea, this luxurious resort offers family rooms and large suites. Amenities include a pool, golf course and organized activities for children, which allows parents to relax or indulge in their own favourite sports. **www.romanoscostanavarino.com**

METHONI Castello

Odós Miaoúli, 240 06 **Tel** *27230 31300* **Fax** *27230 31300* **Rooms** *13* **Road Map** *C5*

A small hotel, almost opposite the entrance to Methoni's huge fortress and a few minutes' stroll from the beach. The rooms have balconies and lovely views of the castle, sea or the town, as does the roof bar. Breakfast is available in the attractive garden. Both the garden and building overflow with potted plants. Open May–Oct. **www.castello.gr**

MONEMVASIA Belessis

Harbour district, 230 70 **Tel** *27320 61217* **Rooms** *20* **Road Map** *C5*

Belessis is a traditional, family-run guesthouse offering guests a choice of two, three or four bedroom apartments. All apartments have their own kitchen and balcony, making it an ideal option for families. The biggest attraction, besides the pretty buildings, is its location just 50 m from the beach. **www.belessishouse.com**

MONEMVASIA Malvásia

Inside the Kástro, 230 70 **Tel** *27320 61160* **Rooms** *34* **Road Map** *C5*

Named after the malmsey wine historically grown in the area and spread over three sites in the old city, Malvásia offers sympathetically restored rooms, each different, with traditional furnishings and antique furniture, some with wooden floors, fireplaces and kitchenette facilities. Most rooms have terraces or sea views. **www.malvasia-hotel.gr**

MYKINES Belle Helene

Tsoúnta 15, 212 00 **Tel** *27510 76225* **Fax** *27510 76179* **Rooms** *5* **Road Map** *C4*

This historical building (built in 1862) is where Heinrich Schliemann stayed for some of his excavations in the 1870s – his bed is still in use. Later visitors included Agatha Christie and Virginia Woolf. The ambience is still almost Victorian and bathrooms are not en suite, but the restaurant and hospitality are excellent. **bellhel@utenet.gr**

NAFPLIO Byron

Plátonos 2, 211 00 **Tel** *27520 22351* **Fax** *27520 26338* **Rooms** *18* **Road Map** *C4*

An elegant hotel with antique furniture, in a tastefully restored mansion above Ágios Spyrídon church. Rooms are modestly decorated in a simple but charming style, with wooden floors and rugs. Some rooms have a view or balcony. Breakfast can be taken on the patio. Internet facilities are available. **www.byronhotel.gr**

NAFPLIO King Othon 1 & 2

Farmakopoúlou 4/Spiliádou 5, 211 00 **Tel** *27520 27585* **Fax** *27520 27595* **Rooms** *21* **Road Map** *C4*

This restored mansion, originally the Ionian Bank and retaining its spectacular curving wooden staircase, is near the old town centre. Rooms vary, some having balconies, but bathrooms are small. Breakfast is served in a flower-filled courtyard. Othon 2, nearby, has slightly larger rooms and suites. **www.kingothon.gr**

NAFPLIO Grande Bretagne

Plateia Filellínon, 211 00 **Tel** *27520 96200* **Fax** *27520 96209* **Rooms** *20* **Road Map** *C4*

This three-storey Neo-Classical building on the seafront has been transformed into an elegant hotel. All rooms feature dark hardwood furniture, high ceilings and marble-trimmed bathrooms; a few lucky ones have balconies. The restaurant here serves international cuisine. Breakfast is included. **www.grandebretagne.com.gr**

NEOS MYSTRAS Byzantion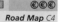

Village centre, 231 00 **Tel** *27310 83309* **Fax** *27310 20019* **Rooms** *22*   **Road Map** *C5*

Ideally situated for exploration of the nearby Mystras site or walking in the foothills of Taygetos, the Byzantion offers quiet, spacious rooms with castle views and a pleasant pool-garden. The hotel has a bar and café (breakfast is included), and tavernas are a few minutes stroll away. Popular with groups, so book early. **www.byzantionhotel.gr**

OLYMPIA Pelops

Varelás 2, 270 65 **Tel** *26240 22543* **Fax** *26240 22213* **Rooms** *18*   **Road Map** *B4*

Stylishly refurbished by friendly Greek-Australian owners Theodore and Susanna, the well-equipped rooms all have balconies, and wireless Internet access is available. The hotel is within easy walking distance of the archaeological sites. Cooking and art courses are offered. Breakfast is included. **www.hotelpelops.gr**

PATRA Art Primarolia

Óthonos and Amalías 30, 262 21 **Tel** *2610 624900* **Fax** *2610 623559* **Rooms** *15*   **Road Map** *C4*

Ensconced in a converted 1930s distillery, the 15 suites of this hotel have plenty of subdued soft furnishings and art on the walls. There's more contemporary Greek art displayed in the atrium, plus a sauna and bar downstairs. There are often substantial discounts off the steep rack rates. **www.arthotel.gr/primarolia**

PORTO HELI Aks Porto Heli

Shoreline, 210 61 **Tel** *27540 98000* **Fax** *27540 51549* **Rooms** *214*   **Road Map** *D4*

A complete seaside holiday village, popular with Athenians and tourists alike, the Aks Porto Heli is set in lovely mature gardens. All conceivable diversions are offered, including sailing, water-skiing, mini-golf, tennis and a scuba centre. The rooms are large though the suites are definitely worth the extra. Breakfast is included. **www.akshotels.com**

POULITHRA Akrogiali

Shore road, 223 00 **Tel** *27570 29106* **Fax** *27570 29108* **Rooms** *11*   **Road Map** *C4*

Family-run, stone-clad hotel in a large garden at the edge of the village, well-positioned for fabulous sunrises over the sea, just a few metres away. Spacious, comfortable rooms and apartments, the latter with a fridge and well-equipped kitchen; all have mosquito nets, and sea- or mountain-view balconies. **www.hotel-acrogiali.gr**

SPARTI Sparta Inn

Thermopylon 105–109, 231 00 **Tel** *27310 21021* **Fax** *27310 24855* **Rooms** *145*   **Road Map** *C5*

Away from Spárti's noisiest main street, but within walking distance of both the centre and main archaeological site, this large hotel provides unexciting decor but comfortable rooms with fridges and large bathrooms. Wireless Internet facilities are available. **www.spartainn.gr**

STAVRI GEROLIMENAS Tsitsiris Castle

Tsitsiris Castle, 23 071 **Tel** *27330 56297* **Fax** *27830 56296* **Rooms** *20*   **Road Map** *C5*

This two century-old complex of stone buildings and towers offers a remote, comfortable base for exploration of the Mani on foot or by car. Rooms overlook the attractive gardens; traditional furnishings and decor are in harmony with the architecture. At its heart is a cosy, vaulted breakfast room. Open Apr–Oct. **www.tsitsiriscastle.gr**

STEMNITSA Country Club Trikolonion

Arcadia, 220 24 **Tel** *27950 29500* **Fax** *27950 81512* **Rooms** *18*   **Road Map** *C4*

Sumptuous establishment with opulent yet intimate public areas reminiscent of a gentleman's club, decorated with Greek engravings and lithographs. Bedrooms are themed in olive-green, gold or blue; the four suites feature a hearth and hydromassage shower. Internet access. Gym, sauna, Jacuzzi and massage. Breakfast included. **www.countryclub.gr**

ZACHLOROU Romantzo

Next to railway station, 250 01 **Tel** *26920 22758* **Fax** *26920 22758* **Rooms** *8*   **Road Map** *C4*

Aptly named for its romantic setting, this basic but lovely rustic wooden hotel overlooks a tiny rural rail halt on the Kalavryta cog-railway. Rooms are small but have private bathrooms and balconies. The restaurant serves hearty food at a handful of tables under streamside trees. A good base for walkers.

CENTRAL AND WESTERN GREECE

ÁGIOS IOANNIS Sofokles

Seafront, north end, 370 12 **Tel** *24260 31230* **Fax** *24260 31021* **Rooms** *20*   **Road Map** *C3*

This professionally run hotel tries a bit harder than the competition at this beach resort. There is a century-old stone-walled ground floor lounge, oblique or direct sea views from most rooms, a tasteful breakfast terrace and an attractive pool. Open May–Oct. **www.sofokleshotel.com**

ARACHOVA Xenonas Generali

Down stair-path, below clocktower, 320 04 **Tel** *22670 31529* **Fax** *22670 32287* **Rooms** *10*   **Road Map** *C3*

This inn offers the best standard in town. The named rather than numbered rooms are each different, though most have fireplaces and views south to the Pleistós gorge. The decor is sweet yet a little outdated, but the welcome is warm and the breakfasts are unusual. Indoor pool, spa, Turkish bath and sauna. **www.generalis.gr**

Key to Price Guide *see p264* **Key to Symbols** *see back cover flap*

ARGALASTI Agamemnon

Village centre, 370 06 **Tel** *24230 54557* **Fax** *24230 55867* **Rooms** *11* **Road Map** *D3*

This historic village-centre mansion – where the poet Kostas Varnalis stayed while posted as a teacher here in the early 1900s – has been restored in impeccable taste as a small hotel. Antiques adorn the common areas and the bar-restaurant. The guest rooms have stone or wood floors and some have fireplaces. **www.agamemnon.gr**

DAMOUHARI Damouchari

Hamlet centre, on Pílio Peninsula, 370 12 **Tel/Fax** *24260 49840* **Rooms** *14* **Road Map** *C3*

This mock village of stone-built studio cottages is arrayed under a small pool near the highest point of the sloping site. Antiques and wood trim enliven the units, while *objet-trouvé* decor dominates the Kleopatra Miramare bar. Block-booked much of the year by tour companies, but there's a waterside annexe of five state-of-the-art rooms. **www.damouchari.gr**

DELFOI Orfeas

Ifigenías Syngroú 35, 330 54 **Tel** *22650 82077* **Fax** *22650 82079* **Rooms** *22* **Road Map** *C3*

Guest rooms at this quietly located hotel are spacious and well maintained, and the top floor (with superb views) has been refurbished. There's a lift – unusual in such a small hotel – and better-than-average parking on the street outside, plus a pleasant area where breakfast (which is included) is served.

DELFOI Pan

Pávlou and Fredheríkis 53, 330 54 **Tel** *22650 82294* **Fax** *22650 83244* **Rooms** *20* **Road Map** *C3*

Most rooms here have fine views of the gulf. The best rooms sleep four and are in the attic. Immediately across the street is a slightly pricier annexe, with larger rooms and bathrooms, including bathtubs, but without the views of the older building. **www.panartemis.gr**

DELFOI Sun View

Apóllonos 84, 330 54 **Tel** *22650 82349* **Fax** *22650 82815* **Rooms** *7* **Road Map** *C3*

At the far western end of the main commercial street, this pension offers fair-sized rooms in pastel colours with original wall art, though rear-facing units are a bit dark. There's a pleasant, four-table breakfast area on the ground floor, and good on-street parking adjacent. Breakfast is included.

GALAXIDI Galaxa

Hirólakkas bay, west hillside, 330 52 **Tel** *22650 41620* **Fax** *22650 42053* **Rooms** *10* **Road Map** *C3*

Management style at this superbly sited hotel might best be described as casual, but this has its advantages; your host is frequently drinking and eating with guests in the popular garden-bar, where breakfast (included in the price) is served. Most of the rooms have some sort of sea view, all share blue-and-white decor and miniature bathrooms.

GALAXIDI Ganimede

Níkou Gourgoúri 20, 330 52 **Tel** *22650 41328* **Fax** *22650 42160* **Rooms** *7* **Road Map** *C3*

Since 2005 the Ganimede has been under the energetic management of Chrissoula Papalexi, whose family have overhauled this much-loved 1960s inn. There are six doubles in the former captain's mansion and a family suite with loft and fireplace across the courtyard garden, where copious breakfasts are served. **www.ganimede.gr**

IGOUMENITSA (REGION) Karavostasi Beach

Pérdika, 461 00 **Tel** *26650 91104* **Fax** *26650 91568* **Rooms** *47* **Road Map** *B3*

The setting of this resort hotel – among lush gardens 140 m (460 ft) behind the best beach on the Epirot coast – is its biggest selling point. Some of the simply furnished, marble-clad rooms spread over four wings have sea views, while the landscaped pool-bar area makes an attractive breakfast venue. Open Easter–Oct. **www.hotel-karavostasi.gr**

IOANNINA Kastro

Androníkou Paleológou 57, 452 21 **Tel** *26510 22866* **Fax** *26510 22780* **Rooms** *7* **Road Map** *B2*

This early 20th-century house inside Ioánnina's Kástro has been tastefully restored as an inn. Its rooms are mostly equipped with double iron beds. Cooler downstairs units (fans but no air con) near the breakfast room are slightly cheaper, though upstairs rooms with wooden ceilings are preferable. Limited street parking just outside. **www.hotelkastro.gr**

IOANNINA Politeia

Anexartisías 109, 454 44 **Tel** *26510 22235* **Fax** *26510 30090* **Rooms** *11* **Road Map** *B2*

Built on the site of an old tradesmen's hall, this hotel is an oasis of calm in the bazaar area. It retains some period details, such as stone walls and its original arrangement around a courtyard. Choose between standard studios at the back or upstairs apartments that can sleep four. Breakfast is included. **www.etip.gr**

KALAMPAKA Alsos House

Kanári 5, 422 00 **Tel** *24320 24097* **Fax** *24320 79191* **Rooms** *9* **Road Map** *B2*

This small inn at the heart of Kalampáka's oldest quarter offers a mix of doubles, triples and a 4-bed family suite, all with balconies and sharing a well-equipped communal kitchen. The multilingual proprietor is a mine of information on the surrounding area. **www.alsoshouse.gr**

KALAMPAKA Odyssion

Patriárchou Dimitriou 30, 422 00 **Tel** *24320 22320* **Fax** *24320 75307* **Rooms** *22* **Road Map** *B2*

Set back from the road and thus quieter than the norm for this town, this hotel offers good sized rooms with a mix of tile and parquet floors. There's a cheerful breakfast salon; plans for a pool and rear garden are pending permission from the archaeological authorities as the Odyssion backs right onto the rock formations. **www.hotelodysseon.gr**

KARPENISSI (REGION) Amadryades

Voutyro, village centre, 361 00 **Tel** *22370 80921* **Rooms** *6*   **Road Map** *C3*

This complex of two restored stone buildings comprises five wood- or tile-floored standard rooms plus one suite, all with working fireplaces and a shared balcony. Common facilities include a huge, sunny lawn with chaise longues, and a reasonably priced café where breakfast can be taken. Open all year. **www.amadryades.gr**

KARPENISSI (REGION) Hellas Country Club

Néo Mikró Horió, village centre, 360 75 **Tel** *22370 41570* **Fax** *22370 41577* **Rooms** *29*   **Road Map** *C3*

This is the Karpenisiotis Valley's upmarket option; an established venue for adventure activities (especially rafting and canyoning) and skiing. The best rooms have balconies facing the garden and Mt Kaliakoúdha. Facilities include a gym, restaurant, conference/events hall and café. Five luxury suites. Breakfast is included. **www.hellascountry.gr**

KARYTSA Dohos

At the edge of the village, 400 07 **Tel** *24950 92001* **Fax** *24950 92002* **Rooms** *9*   **Road Map** *C2*

Perched partway up the forested slope of Mt Kíssavos, with views extending from Mt Ólympos to the Sithonía peninsula, Dohos occupies one of the most spectacular sites in Greece. Huge wood-floored rooms have fireplaces and balconies facing the Thermaïc Gulf. Antique-filled common areas include a sauna-*hammam*. Breakfast is included. **www.dohos.gr**

KASTRAKI Doupiani House

West of Kastráki-Metéora access road, 422 00 **Tel** *24320 77555* **Fax** *24320 24078* **Rooms** *11*   **Road Map** *B2*

The most peacefully set pension in Kastráki also has great views of the Metéora formations from most of the simple rooms. The proprietors serve breakfast in the fine hotel garden and can direct walkers to local hikes. Demand is such that an annexe is under construction. **www.doupianihouse.com**

KONITSA Grand Hotel Dentro

Town access road from main road, 441 00 **Tel** *26550 29365* **Fax** *26550 29366* **Rooms** *18*   **Road Map** *B2*

While perhaps not grand, this hotel offers the best calibre of lodging for miles around. Standard doubles, some with balconies and views over the Aóös river plain, have good bathrooms. The four attic suites (two suitable for families) have fireplaces and hydromassage units. Take meals here or at To Dentro taverna up the road. **www.grandhoteldentro.gr**

MAKRYNITSA Pandora

On the slope below the central lane, 370 11 **Tel** *24280 99404* **Fax** *24280 90113* **Rooms** *17*   **Road Map** *C3*

This three-storey stately mansion may not, with its 1859 vintage, be the oldest in the village, but it has plenty of charm in its interior staircase and fireplaces with porcelain hoods. Rooms are spacious, though bathrooms are small, owing to preservation considerations. Breakfast is included, and there are good views of the gulf. **www.pandoramansion.gr**

MEGALO PAPIGKO Xenonas Kalliopi

On lane leading from church belfry, 440 04 **Tel** *26530 41081* **Fax** *26530 41081* **Rooms** *7*   **Road Map** *B2*

About the best-value budget accommodation in Megálo Pápigko, the Kalliopi offers en suite, soberly furnished upstairs rooms, most with fireplaces and good views. An added bonus are the filling home-made meals available at the popular courtyard taverna downstairs. Breakfast is included. Open year-round. **www.kalliopi-papigo.com**

MEGALO PAPIGKO Xenonas Papaevangelou

Near the very top of the village, 440 04 **Tel** *26530 41135* **Fax** *26530 41988* **Rooms** *14*   **Road Map** *B2*

A bit hard to find, but worth the effort, this inn built in Zagorian style has large, unique, brightly lit rooms, many with views of Mt Gamíla. The best unit is a self-catering studio amid well-tended gardens. Inviting common areas include a combination breakfast salon and bar, where local snacks are served. **www.hotelpapaevangelou.gr**

METSOVO Kassaros

On road leading south from main square, 442 00 **Tel** *26560 41800* **Fax** *26560 41262* **Rooms** *24*   **Road Map** *B2*

All rooms at this hotel have views across the ravine to Anílio village, though the attic units are the most spacious. There is typical Metsovan folk-kitsch decor in the common areas. The management organizes summer or winter outdoor activities in the nearby mountains, providing all the necessary equipment. Breakfast is included. **www.kassaros.gr**

MIKRO PAPIGKO Xenonas Dias

Village centre, 440 04 **Tel** *26530 41257* **Fax** *26530 41892* **Rooms** *12*   **Road Map** *B2*

A trekker-friendly inn, distributed over two separate buildings (the older structure has more character). Rooms are simple but wood-floored, en suite and cheerful. The two buildings span a sometimes lively restaurant which also serves as the village bar and *kafeneío*. Open all year, with seasonal courtyard seating. **www.diaspapigo.gr**

MOURESSI The Old Silk Store

Village centre, opposite the bakery, 370 12 **Tel** *24260 49086* **Fax** *24260 49565* **Rooms** *5*   **Road Map** *C3*

This 19th-century mansion, lightly restored by Cornish proprietress Jill, features a lush garden with hydrangeas, distant sea views, a barbeque area and high-ceilinged rooms. There's also a self-contained, pricier studio cottage (formerly the village barbershop). Breakfasts include excellent bread and preserves. Closed Feb. **www.pelionet.gr/oldsilkstore**

NAFPAKTOS Akti

Northwest end of Grímpovo beach, 303 00 **Tel** *26340 28464* **Fax** *26340 24171* **Rooms** *46*   **Road Map** *C3*

The Sakellaris brothers thoroughly updated this hotel in 2005, enlarging and modernizing its rooms – about half of which have gulf views. Rooftop suites (sleeping two to three) are palatial and worth the extra cost. An airy, cheerful breakfast salon gives a good start to the day. **www.akti.gr**

Key to Price Guide *see p264* **Key to Symbols** *see back cover flap*

PARGA Lichnos Beach

Just south of town, 480 60 **Tel** *26840 31257* **Fax** *26840 31157* **Rooms** *89*   **Road Map** *B3*

This self-contained resort makes a good-value choice for families. A mix of standard rooms and bungalows set in lush grounds are numerous enough that tours don't completely monopolize it. Tennis court, pool, and a private beach with watersport facilities compensate for somewhat dated rooms. Breakfast is included. **www.lichnosbeach.gr**

PARGA Magda's Apartments
€€
North end of town, off road to Agiá village, 480 60 **Tel** *26840 31228* **Fax** *26840 31690* **Rooms** *36*   **Road Map** *B3*

This complex offers either older studios or superior apartments let by the week, in a hillside garden environment with mountain and partial sea views. There's a terrace pool, small spa, good breakfasts and live musical evenings. Hospitable hosts. Book well in advance. Open Easter–late-Oct. **www.magdas-apartments.parga.com**

PORTARIA Kritsa
€€
Main village square, 370 11 **Tel** *24280 99121* **Fax** *24280 90008* **Rooms** *8*   **Road Map** *C3*

A previously undistinguished interwar building has been transformed into some of the best-value accommodation on Pílio. There are two suites and four *plateía*-facing rooms with balconies; more attention has been paid to the room decor than the small bathrooms. Breakfast is included, and there is a very good restaurant. **www.hotel-kritsa.gr**

TRIKALA Panellinion
€€
Plateía Ríga Feraíou, 421 00 **Tel** *24310 73545* **Fax** *24310 27350* **Rooms** *22*   **Road Map** *C2*

This elegant 1914 building has hosted leading Greek politicians and artists of the era, and less happily served as the local Italian and German HQ during World War II. Individual rooms, some with balconies and small tubs in the bathrooms, are parquet-floored. There's a mezzanine bar and decent restaurant. Breakfast is included. **www.hotelpanellinion.com**

TRIKALA (REGION) Pyrgos Mantania
 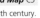 **€€**
Tría Potamiá district, near Kalirrói village, 422 00 **Tel** *24310 87351* **Fax** *24310 87743* **Rooms** *29*   **Road Map** *B2*

This stone-clad complex was only built in 2002, but you wouldn't know it, so convincing are the architectural details. Rooms vary from large doubles on the first floor to even bigger top-floor family suites with fireplaces. An attractive bar-restaurant specializes in wild trout and other locally sourced products. Breakfast is included. **www.mantania.gr**

TSEPELOVO Gouris
€
Easterly quarter of village, up cobbled lanes, 440 10 **Tel** *26530 81214* **Rooms** *8*   **Road Map** *B2*

One of the friendlier hotels in Zagóri, run by Anthoula Gouri, widow of local tourism pioneer Alexis Gouris. She can usually be found at the traditional Kafeníou Gouri on the *plateía* (where breakfast is served). Rooms are simple but en suite. Consider half-board, as independent restaurants in Tsepélovo are unremarkable. **www.epirus.com/hotelgouris**

VYZITSA Archontiko Karagiannopoulou
€€€
North of the through road, 370 10 **Tel** *24230 86717* **Fax** *24230 86878* **Rooms** *6*   **Road Map** *C3*

The best maintained of Vyzítsa's half-dozen mansion-inns, this four-storey structure was built in the late 18th century. The interior features wooden staircases, carved ceiling rosettes, stained-glass panels in the windows and extensive lounges on the second floor. Breakfast (included in the price) is served in the courtyard. **www.karagiannopoulou.com**

ZAGORA Archontiko Gayanni
 €€
Near the village centre, 370 01 **Tel** *24260 23391* **Fax** *24260 22091* **Rooms** *9*   **Road Map** *C3*

This gorgeous three-storey mansion dating from 1770 has Aegean views, a beautiful garden, ample parking, a genial host and copious breakfasts in a separate building that was once the family bakery. The en suite rooms have been meticulously but not overly restored, with tasteful decor and antiques in the hallways. Open all year. **www.villagayannis.gr**

NORTHERN GREECE

AMMOULIANI ISLET, ATHOS Gripos
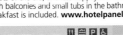 **€**
Between Ágios Geórgios and Megáli Ámmos beaches, 630 75 **Tel** *23770 51049* **Rooms** *14*   **Road Map** *D2*

Ammoulianí is Macedonia's only inhabited island, apart from Thássos. This inn, set between two of its best beaches, has terracotta-tiled rooms with copper antiques, beamed ceilings and broad balconies overlooking the garden where peacocks and pheasants can be heard and a popular, good-value *ouzeri* operates.

ARNAIA Oikia Alexandrou
 €€
Plateía Patriárchou Vartholomaíou tou Prótou, 630 74 **Tel/Fax** *23720 23210* **Rooms** *10*   **Road Map** *D2*

This Macedonian-style mansion dating from 1812 has been lovingly restored by two architects, descendants of the original builders. The rooms (including one suite) are upstairs, most with working fireplaces and all with antique furnishings. Breakfast is served in the excellent restaurant, which is also open to non-guests. **www.oikia-alexandrou.gr**

CHALKIDIKI Akrotiri
 €€
Marmara, 630 80 **Tel/Fax** *23750 721 91* **Rooms** *17*   **Road Map** *D2*

Situated right on the coast, this family-run establishment offers clean, well-maintained rooms, most of which have balconies with views of the sea. There is no restaurant, but each room features a kitchenette for guest use. The small village square is a five-minute walk away. **www.akrotirimarmaras.gr**

DADIA Dadiaselo
Dadiá village, 684 00 **Tel** *25540 32333* **Fax** *25540 32345* **Rooms** *6* **Road Map** *F1*

To partake in raptor-sighting at the Dadiá Forest Reserve – one of Greece's most important habitats for birds of prey – you really have to stay the night locally. The spacious en suite rooms at this hotel are ideal. They are equipped with kitchenettes, and there are also tavernas and cafés in the village. **www.dadiaselo.gr**

EDESSA Varosi
Archiepiskópou Meletíou 45–47, 582 00 **Tel** *23810 21865* **Fax** *23810 28872* **Rooms** *8* **Road Map** *C1*

Named after the *varósi* or old quarter in which it's located, this family-run inn stands out for its warmth of welcome and copious breakfasts. The rooms have open fireplaces and period decor. Reservations are usually mandatory – book ahead to avoid disappointment. Breakfast is included. **www.varosi.gr**

FANARI Fanari
East edge of village, behind the beach, 670 63 **Tel** *25350 31300* **Fax** *25350 31388* **Rooms** *32* **Road Map** *E1*

Hotels in nearby Xánthi tend to be noisy and overpriced, so the fishing-port and resort of Fanári provide a more attractive option. The Fanari hotel is white, modern and quietly sited; all rooms have a sea view. Breakfast is included, and there is a restaurant that is open in the summer. Fish tavernas are nearby. **www.fanari-hotel.gr**

KASTORIA Archontiko tou Vergoula
Aidítras 14, 521 00 **Tel** *24670 23415* **Rooms** *12* **Road Map** *B2*

This mansion in the Doultsó hillside quarter, dating from 1857, has been meticulously and tastefully restored as one of Kastoriá's premier boutique hotels. Rooms with unimpeded lake views are pricier. There's a salon where the complimentary breakfast is served and a wine bar that is only open at weekends. **www.vergoulas.gr**

KASTORIA Hotel Kastoria du Lac
Nikis 122, Nordkveste, 521 00 **Tel/Fax** *24670 29453* **Rooms** *37* **Road Map** *B2*

Built on the shore of Lake Kastoriá, this hotel is located a short walk from Kastoriá town centre. Guests enjoy spacious en suite rooms, most of which have a view of the lake, and a buffet breakfast. Other amenities include free Wi-Fi and car rental facilities. The hotel also organizes sightseeing trips around the local area. **www.hotel-kastoria.gr**

KAVALA Esperia
Erythroú Stavroú 44, 654 03 **Tel** *2510 229621* **Fax** *2510 220621* **Rooms** *105* **Road Map** *D1*

This hotel is housed in a 1970s-era building opposite the archaeological museum. It offers decent facilities, including a breakfast terrace, good soundproofing (the side or rear rooms will be quietest) and a small conference centre. Breakfast is included. **www.esperiakavala.gr**

KAVALA Imaret
Poulídou 30–32, 651 10 **Tel** *2510 620151* **Fax** *2510 620156* **Rooms** *26* **Road Map** *D1*

This Ottoman-era *imaret* or hostel for theological students has been stunningly refurbished as a five-star hotel with no detail overlooked. The former students' cells have music systems and original fireplaces; there's also a working *hammam*, wellness treatments and a trickling fountain in the central courtyard. **www.imaret.gr**

KERKINI Oikoperiigitis
Village centre, 620 55 **Tel** *23270 41450* **Fax** *23270 41476* **Rooms** *18* **Road Map** *D1*

Lake Kerkíni, just 500 m (1,640 ft) from this inn, has become one of Greece's premier bird-watching venues. Oikoperiigitis organizes boating on the lake and excursions on nearby Mt Belés. The wood- and stone-built inn has rooms and apartments spread over two buildings. Snacks and drinks served in the lounge/library. Open all year. **www.oikoperiigitis.gr**

LITOCHORO Villa Drosos
Archeláou 20, Ágios Geórgios district, 602 00 **Tel** *23520 84561* **Fax** *23520 84563* **Rooms** *13* **Road Map** *C2*

The Villa Drosos may not have the unimpeded mountain views of the central-square hotels, but it does offer excellent standards in its small but balconied rooms, the best of which overlook the swimming pool and a small wood. The breakfast room has a fireplace, and the restaurant serves good grills. Open all year. **www.villadrosos.gr**

MARONEIA Roxani Country House
Edge of village, 694 00 **Tel** *25330 21501* **Fax** *25330 21500* **Rooms** *26* **Road Map** *E1*

Rooms at this purpose-built hotel are large, if simply furnished, with all amenities and good views. Breakfasts, served outdoors in good weather, are copious, and the enthusiastic owner arranges every conceivable local activity for guests, from archery to sea-kayaking to mountain biking. Open all year. **www.ecoexplorer.gr**

NEOS MARMARAS Kelyfos
North of turning for Porto Karras complex, 630 81 **Tel** *23750 72833* **Fax** *23750 72247* **Rooms** *40* **Road Map** *D2*

On a hilltop near Néos Marmarás with sweeping sea views, this pleasant complex of buildings scattered among pines and palms comprises a mix of standard rooms, suites and studios, all spacious and tastefully appointed. Studios and suites have fireplaces and self-catering areas. The restaurant is excellent. **www.kelyfos.gr**

NYMFEO La Moara
Hilltop beyond Nymfeo village, 530 78 **Tel** *23860 31377* **Fax** *23860 31131* **Rooms** *8* **Road Map** *E1*

Opened by the wine-producing Boutari family in 1993 as one of Greece's first boutique hotels, La Moara offers rooms with wooden floors and state-of-the-art bathrooms. The cellar has over 100 varieties of foreign and domestic wines. There are two lounges as well as a garden. Breakfast is included. Closed Mon pm–Wed am; Jul. **www.lamoara.gr**

Key to Price Guide *see p264* **Key to Symbols** *see back cover flap*

PRESPA LAKES Agios Achilleios
Agios Achílleios islet, Mikrí Préspa lake, 530 77 **Tel** *23850 46601* **Fax** *23850 46601* **Rooms** *10* **Road Map** *B1*

Car-free Agios Achílleios island, ringed by reeds, is joined to the mainland by a metal pedestrian bridge, though in winter you can walk across the ice sheet to the island. The stone-clad inn comprises nine standard rooms and one attic suite, plus a ground-floor restaurant featuring local specialities.

PRESPA LAKES To Petrino
Near top of Agios Germanós village, 530 77 **Tel** *23850 51344* **Fax** *23850 51854* **Rooms** *9* **Road Map** *B1*

The largest village in the Préspa basin, Agios Germanós offers late Byzantine churches and views of the larger lake, as well as this stone-built, wood-floored inn converted from a private dwelling, with heat provided in part by wood-burning stoves.

SYMVOLI Faraggi Hotel
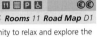
Km 17 National Road Dráma–Thessaloníki, 620 47 **Tel** *23240 81667* **Fax** *23240 81405* **Rooms** *11* **Road Map** *D1*

Located on the banks of the Aggitis river, this charming hotel offers visitors the opportunity to relax and explore the beautiful countryside in the area. A number of walking paths start right by the hotel's entrance. All rooms have a view, and there is also a fine restaurant. **www.hotelfaraggi.gr**

THESSALONIKI Nepheli
Komninon 1, Panorama, 552 36 **Tel** *2310 342002* **Fax** *2310 342080* **Rooms** *70* **Road Map** *C2*

The Nepheli offers spacious rooms with large balconies and all the amenities you would expect from a four-star hotel. Extras include a health club and extensive conference facilities. The rooftop restaurant offers fine dining and panoramic city views; a complimentary buffet breakfast is included in the price. **www.nepheli.gr**

THESSALONIKI Orestias Kastorias
Agnóstou Stratiótou 14, corner Olymbou, 546 31 **Tel** *2310 276517* **Fax** *2310 276572* **Rooms** *37* **Road Map** *C2*

An unbeatable location – a quiet corner a few paces from Agios Dimítrios basilica – and keen pricing are this hotel's main selling points. Most rooms, which lack balconies but are fairly spacious, have been converted to en suite status. There are no common areas to speak of, but complimentary coffee is always available. **www.okhotel.gr**

THESSALONIKI Le Palace

Tsimiskí 12, 546 24 **Tel** *2310 257400* **Fax** *2310 256589* **Rooms** *53* **Road Map** *C2*

The city's first boutique hotel is located in a 1926 Art Deco building. The large, double-glazed rooms have contemporary bathrooms, while the common areas preserve some interwar touches. There's a mezzanine lounge and restaurant, which serves an outstanding buffet breakfast (included in the price), and a café. **www.lepalace.gr**

THESSALONIKI Tourist

Mitropóleos 21, 546 24 **Tel** *2310 270501* **Fax** *2310 226865* **Rooms** *37* **Road Map** *C2*

One of the few surviving interwar buildings in this area, the Tourist features parquet-floored lounges, a period lift and irregularly shaped rooms with en suite bathrooms. It's been featured in many publications on the city and has a staunchly loyal word-of-mouth clientele, so reservations are mandatory. Breakfast is included. **www.touristhotel.gr**

THESSALONIKI Bristol
Oplopoioú 2, corner Katoúni, 546 25 **Tel** *2310 506500* **Fax** *2310 515177* **Rooms** *20* **Road Map** *C2*

Situated near the Ladádika nightlife district, the Bristol is housed in a converted 19th-century building. A complimentary breakfast is served in the central atrium, while there's a bistro-bar on-site as well as the respected Deipnosofistis restaurant. Rooms have varied colour schemes, wood floors and antique furnishings. **www.bristol.gr**

THESSALONIKI Panorama

Analípseos 26, Panorama, 552 36 **Tel** *2310 344871* **Fax** *2310 344872* **Rooms** *50* **Road Map** *C2*

If you have a car, this hotel in the southeastern hillside suburb of Panórama is an excellent choice, as parking in the city centre is nearly impossible. This 1970s structure has been renovated and room furnishings updated. Despite the name, only third-floor rooms have a view over the city and Thermaic Gulf. Breakfast is included. **www.hotelpanorama.gr**

THESSALONIKI Electra Palace

Plateía Artistotélous 9, 546 24 **Tel** *2310 294000* **Fax** *2310 294001* **Rooms** *138* **Road Map** *C2*

This landmark semicircular building's common areas are palatially fitted with walnut and marble trim and chandeliers, while the wood-trimmed rooms – with every conceivable gadget – have ochre and red decor. Amenities include a rooftop pool, fitness centre, English-themed bar and two restaurants. Breakfast is included. **www.electrahotels.gr**

THESSALONIKI Macedonia Palace
Megálou Alexándrou 2, 546 40 **Tel** *2310 897197* **Fax** *2310 897211* **Rooms** *283* **Road Map** *C2*

A seafront hotel (though half the rooms face inland), the Macedonia Palace is a favourite haunt of businessmen and VIPs. Accordingly, there are plenty of conference facilities and two celebrated restaurants (the Porphyra has sweeping views). There's also a gym, sauna and outdoor ground-level pool. Breakfast is included. **www.classicalhotels.com**

VERGINA Vergina
Main through road, Vergína Imatheías, 590 31 **Tel** *23310 92510* **Fax** *23310 92511* **Rooms** *10* **Road Map** *C2*

Modern Vergína village offers a quieter alternative to staying in Véria, the nearest town 16 km (10 miles) northwest, and allows an early-morning visit to the Royal Tombs before crowds appear. This block of simple but well-kept rented rooms, most with balconies, stands just a few steps from the tomb complex. A good breakfast is included in the price.

WHERE TO EAT

To eat out in Greece is to experience the democratic tradition at work. Rich and poor, young and old, all enjoy their favourite local restaurant, taverna or café. Greeks consider the best places to be where the food is fresh, plentiful and well-cooked, not necessarily where the setting or the cuisine is the fanciest. Visitors too have come to appreciate the simplicity and health of the traditional Greek kitchen – olive

A local cheese from Métsovo

oil, yoghurt, vegetables, a little meat and some wine, always shared with friends. The traditional three-hour lunch and siesta – still the daily rhythm of the countryside – is now only a fading memory for most city Greeks, who have adapted to a more Western European routine. But the combination of traditional cooking and outside influences has produced a vast range of eating places in Greece, with somewhere to suit almost everyone.

Casual dining in a central Athens restaurant

TYPES OF RESTAURANT

Often difficult to find in more developed tourist resorts, the *estiatórion*, or traditional Greek restaurant, is one of Europe's most enjoyable places to eat. Friendly, noisy and sometimes in lovely surroundings, *estiatória* are reliable purveyors of local recipes and wines, particularly if they have been owned by the same family for decades. Foreigners unfamiliar with Greek dishes may be invited into the kitchen to choose their fare. In Greece, the entire family dines together and takes plenty of time over the meal, especially at weekends.

Estiatória range from the very expensive in Athens, Thessaloníki and wealthier

suburbs to the incredibly inexpensive *mageirió* or *koutoúki*, popular with students and workers. Here there is little choice in either wines or dishes, all of which will be *mageireftá* (ready-cooked). The food, however, is home made and tasty and the barrel wine is at the very least drinkable, often good, and sometimes comes from the owner's home village.

Some restaurants may specialize in a particular type of cuisine. In Thessaloníki, for example, and in the suburbs of Athens, where Asia Minor refugees settled after 1923, you may find food to be spicier than the Greek norm, with lots of red peppers and such dishes as *giaourtlú* (kebabs drenched in yoghurt and served on pitta bread) or lamb-brain salad.

The menu in a traditional restaurant tends to be short, comprising at most a dozen

A sign for a taverna in Párga

mezédes (starters or snacks), perhaps eight main dishes, four or five cooked vegetable dishes or salads, plus a dessert of fresh or cooked fruit, and a selection of local and national wines.

Many hotels have restaurants open to non-residents. Smaller country hotels occasionally have excellent kitchens, and serve good local wines, so check on any that are close to where you are staying.

In the last few years a new breed of young Greek chefs has emerged in *kultúra* restaurants, developing a style of cooking that encompasses Greece's magnificent raw materials, flavours and colours. These dishes are served with the exciting new Greek wines.

Athenian restaurant interior fusing classic and contemporary styles

Waiter outside a restaurant in Pláka, Athens

TAVERNAS

One of the great pleasures for the traveller in Greece is the tradition of the taverna, a place to eat and drink, even if you simply snack on *mezédes* (Greeks rarely drink without eating). Traditional tavernas are open from mid-evening and stay open late; occasionally they are open for lunch as well. Menus are short and seasonal – perhaps six or eight *mezédes* and four main courses comprising casseroles and dishes cooked *tis óras* (to order), along with the usual accompaniments of vegetables, salads, fruit and wine.

Like traditional restaurants, some tavernas specialize in the foods and wines of the owner's home region, some in a particular cooking style and others in certain foods.

A *psarotavérna* is the place to find good fish dishes but, because fish is expensive, these tavernas often resemble restaurants and are patronized mainly by wealthy Greeks and tourists. In small fishing villages it is quite different and you may find the rickety tables of a *psarotavérna* literally on the beach. Close to the lapping waves the owner may serve fish that he himself caught that morning.

For delicious grills try a *psistariá,* a taverna that specializes in spit-roasts and char-grilling *(sta kárvouna)*. In countryside *psistariés* lamb, kid, pork, chicken, game,

offal, lambs' heads and even testicles are char-grilled, and whole lamb is roasted on the spit. At the harbourside, fish and shellfish are grilled and served with fresh lemon juice and olive oil. Country, family-run tavernas and cafés will invariably provide simple meals, such as omelettes and salads throughout the day, but many of these places close quite early in the evening. After your meal in the taverna, follow the Greeks and enjoy a visit to the local *zacharoplasteío (see p278)* for sweets and pastries.

CAFES AND BARS

Cafés, known as *kafeneía,* are the pulse of Greek life, and even the tiniest hamlet has a place to drink coffee or wine. Equally important is the function it performs as the centre of communication – mail is collected here, telephone calls made, and newspapers read, dissected and discussed. *Kafeneía* serve Greek coffee, sometimes *frappé* (instant coffee served cold, in a tall glass), soft drinks, beer, ouzo and wine. Most also serve some kind of snack to order. All open early and remain open until late at night.

As the social hub of their communities, country *kafeneía,* as well as many in the city, open seven days a week.

A *galaktopoleío,* or "milk shop", has a seating area where you can enjoy fine yoghurt and honey; those around Plateía Omonoías in Athens remain open for most of the night.

A *kapileío* (wine shop with a café-bar attached) is the place to try local wines from the cask, and you may find a few bottled wines as well. The owner is invariably from a wine village or family and will often cook some simple regional specialities to accompany the wine.

In a *mezedopoleío,* or *mezés* shop, the owner will not only serve the local wine and the *mezédes* that go with it, but also ouzo and the infamous spirit, raki, both distilled from the remnants of the grape harvest. Their accompanying *mezédes* are less salty than those served with wine.

No holiday in Greece is complete without a visit to an *ouzerí.* Some of the best of these are to be found in Thessaloníki and in Athens' central arcades. You can order a dozen or more little plates of savoury meats, fish and vegetables and try the many varieties of ouzo that are served in small jugs. A jug or glass of water accompanies the ouzo to wash it down. These are traditionally inexpensive, noisy and fun places to eat and drink.

Bottle of ouzo

Outdoor tables on the patio at the Kritsá Hotel restaurant *(see p293)*

Enjoying outdoor dining in Pláka, Athens

FAST FOOD AND SNACKS

Visitors can be forgiven for thinking Greeks never stop eating, for there seem to be snack bars on every street and vendors selling sweets, nuts, rolls, and seasonal corn and chestnuts at every turn.

Although American-style fast-food outlets dominate city streets, it is easy to avoid them by trying the traditional Greek eateries. The extremely cheap *souvlatzídiko* offers chunks of meat, fish or vegetables roasted on a skewer and served with bread, while an *ovelistírio* serves *gýros* – meat from a revolving spit in a pitta bread pocket. The food is sold *sto chéri* (in the hand).

Many bakeries serve savoury pies and a variety of tasty bread rolls, and in busy city neighbourhoods you can always find a *kafeneío* serving substantial snacks and salads. Street vendors sell *kouloúria* (rolls), small pies, corn on the cob, roast chestnuts, nut brittle and candies. Snacks are often local specialities: tiny open pizza-like pies in Thessaloníki; pies of wild greens or cheese in Métsovo; and small flavourful sausages in Ioánnina.

If you have a sweet tooth you will love the *zacharoplasteío* (literally, "shop of the sugar sculptor"). The baker there makes traditional sweet breads, tiny sweet pastries and a whole variety of fragrant honey cakes.

BREAKFAST

For Greeks, this is the least important meal of the day. In traditional homes and cafés a small cup of Greek coffee accompanies *paximádia* (slices of rusk-like bread), *koulourákia* (firm, sesame-covered or slightly sweet rolls in rings or S-shapes) or pound cakes with home-made jam. Elsewhere, and in many city *kafeneía*, this has been replaced by a large cup of brewed coffee and French-style croissants or delicious brioche-style rolls, also called *kouloúria*. In the summer, some *kafeneía* will still serve fresh figs, thick yoghurt, pungent honey and slightly sweet currant bread.

RESERVATIONS

The more expensive the restaurant, the more advisable it is to make a reservation, and it is always worth doing so at the weekend. In country areas, and in the suburbs, it is the practice to visit the restaurant or taverna earlier in the day, or the day before, and check on the dishes to be served. The proprietor will take your order and reserve any special dish that you request.

Serving *gýros* on an Athens street

WINE

Restaurateurs in Greece are only now learning to look after bottled wines. If the wine list contains the better bottles, such as Ktíma

Merkoúri, Seméli or Strofiliá, the proprietor probably knows how to look after the wine and it will be safe to order a more expensive bottle. For a good-value bottle, there are the nationally known Cambás or Boutári wines.

Traditional restaurants and tavernas may only stock carafe wine, which is served straight from the barrel and is always inexpensive. Carafe wines are often of the region and, among Greek wines, the rosé in particular is noted for having an unusual but pleasing flavour.

HOW TO PAY

Greece is still largely a cash society. If you need to pay by credit card, check first that the restaurant takes credit cards, and if so, that they take the card you intend to use – many proprietors accept some but not others. *Kafeneía* almost never take credit cards, and café-bars rarely, but many will be happy to take travellers' cheques. In rural areas, country tavernas, restaurants and *kafeneía* will only accept cash.

The listings in this guide indicate whether or not credit cards are accepted at each establishment.

SERVICE AND TIPPING

Greeks take plenty of time when they eat out and expect a high level of attention. This means a great deal of running around on the part

Patrons outside a kebab restaurant in Athens

Interior patio of Ouzerí Aristotélous in Thessaloníki *(see p295)*

of the waiter, but in return they receive generous tips – as much as 20 per cent if the service is good, though more often a tip is 10–15 per cent. Prices in traditional establishments do include service, but the waiters still expect a tip so always have coins ready to hand.

Western-style restaurants and tourist tavernas sometimes add a service charge to the bill; their prices can be much higher because of trimmings, such as telephones and air conditioning.

Bread ring seller, Athens

DRESS CODE

The Greeks dress quite formally when dining out. Visitors should wear whatever is comfortable, but skimpy tops and shorts and active sportswear are not acceptable, except near the beach, although it is unlikely that tourist establishments would turn custom away. Some of the most expensive city restaurants, especially those attached to hotels, request formal dress; the listings indicate which places fall into this category.

In summer, if you intend dining outside, take a jacket or sweater for the evening.

CHILDREN

Greek children become restaurant and taverna habitués at a very early age – it is an essential part of their education. Consequently, children are welcome everywhere in Greece except in

the bars. In formal restaurants children are expected to be well behaved, but in summer, when Greeks enjoy eating outside, it is perfectly acceptable for children to play and enjoy themselves too. Facilities such as highchairs are unknown except in the most considerate hotel dining rooms, but more casual restaurants and tavernas are fine for dining with children of any age.

SMOKING

Smoking is commonplace in Greece and until recently establishments maintaining a no-smoking policy have been difficult to find. However, new EU regulations make it obligatory for all restaurants to have no-smoking areas. In practice, of course, change is slow but for at least half the year you can always dine outdoors.

Drying octopus at a restaurant in Geroliménas, on the Máni peninsula *(see p199)*

WHEELCHAIR ACCESS

In country areas, where room is plentiful, there are few problems for wheelchair users. In city restaurants, however, it is a different matter, and access is often restricted. The streets themselves have uneven pavements and many restaurants have narrow doorways and possibly steps. Restaurants that do have wheelchair access are indicated in the listings pages of this guide. Also, the organizations that are listed on page 307 provide information for disabled travellers in Greece.

VEGETARIAN FOOD

Greek cuisine provides plenty of choice for vegetarians. Greeks enjoy such a variety of dishes for each course that it is easy to order just vegetable dishes for first and main courses in traditional restaurants, tavernas or *kafeneía*. Vegetable dishes are substantial, inexpensive, imaginatively prepared and satisfying.

Vegans may have more of a problem, for there are few places in Greece catering for special diets. However, as Greek cooking relies little on dairy products, it is possible to follow a vegan diet almost anywhere in Greece.

PICNICS

The best time to picnic in Greece is in spring, when the countryside is at its most beautiful and the weather is not too hot. The traditional seasonal foods, such as Lenten olive oil bread, sweet Easter bread, pies filled with wild greens, fresh cheese and new retsina wine, all make perfect fare for picnics. Summer is the ideal time for eating on the beach. The best foods for summer snacks are peaches and figs, yoghurt and cheese, and tomatoes, various breads and olives.

The Flavours of Greece

The ancient Greeks regarded cooking as both a science and an art – even a topic for philosophy. In out-of-the-way places on the mainland and on the more far-flung islands, you will still find dishes, ingredients and culinary styles untouched by time. Elsewhere, Greek cookery has been much influenced by the Ottoman Empire, with its spiced meat dishes, and filled pastries and vegetables. In the recent past, Greek cuisine was often thought of as peasant food. Today, it is that very simplicity, and its reliance on seasonal, local produce, that makes Greek food so popular with visitors.

Oregano and thyme

Island fisherman returning to harbour with the day's catch

varied as the terrain: fish from the sea and, from the mountains, sheep, goat and game. From the hills come several varieties of cheese, olives and honey.

CENTRAL AND NORTHERN GREECE

Mainland Greece, with its long and chequered history, is a place where regional food boundaries are blurred and a variety of cooking traditions coexist. The meat and fruit dishes of Thessaloníki show a Jewish influence; the spices, sausages and oven cooking of Ioánnina stem from Ottoman times; while a love of sheep's cheese, pies and offal came to Métsovo and the Epirus mountains with the Vlach shepherds. The spicy food of the North is the legacy of the 1922 Greek immigrants from Asia Minor, while the Balkan influence is obvious in the use of pickles, walnuts and yogurt.

ATHENS AND THE PELOPONNESE

The capital is essentially a city of immigrants from the countryside, the islands and the shores of the eastern Mediterranean. That diversity is reflected in its markets and its cuisine. Street food is a quintessential part of Athens life. In the Peloponnese ingredients are as

Mussels   Octopus   Sardines   Sea bass   Crayfish
Prawns   Red mullet
                                            Clams

Selection of seafood from the clear waters of Greece

REGIONAL DISHES AND SPECIALITIES

Sweets such as nougat, *pastéli* (honey-sesame candy), *loukoumádes* (yeast doughnuts in syrup) and *chalvás* (halva, or sweetmeats) have been a part of Greek street life since the days of Aristotle. They are sold in small shops or stalls. *Píttes*, or pies, are a speciality of the western Epirus region. Fillings range from game or offal to cheese and vegetables, often combined with rice or pasta. Reflecting Middle-Eastern influences, *soutzoukákia*, a speciality of northern Thrace and Macedonia, are meat patties flavoured with coriander, pepper and cumin. *Choirinó kritikó*, the classic dish of inland Crete villages, is thick pork cutlets baked until tender, while *sýka me tyrí* is a summer *mezés*, dessert or snack, of fresh figs with *mizythra* cheese, made from whey.

Olives

Fakés *is a sour Peloponnese soup of green lentils, lemon juice or wine vinegar, tomatoes, herbs and olive oil.*

Produce on sale in a typical Greek market

THE ISLANDS

Each group of islands has a distinct culinary identity reflecting its geographical location and history. Many Ionian dishes are pasta based, a legacy of the era of Venetian occupation. Those of the Cyclades are intensely flavoured. The cooks of the Dodecanese and Northeast Aegean benefit from the rich harvest of the surrounding sea. Crete is unique in its long Turkish occupation and taste for highly spiced dishes, and Cretan cooking has a number of recipes specific to the island. The use of pork, a legacy of antiquity, is more popular here than anywhere else in Greece. Some lovely kitchen utensils and unusual ingredients from Minoan times have been excavated by archaeologists on Crete.

FISH AND SEAFOOD

The warm and sheltered waters of the Aegean are the migratory path for tuna and swordfish, and a feeding ground for tasty anchovies and sardines. Coves and caves around the hundreds of rocky islands shelter

Bread being baked in an outdoor communal oven

highly prized red mullet, dentex and parrot fish, while the long shoreline is home to shellfish and crustaceans. Fish are usually served with their heads on: to Greeks this is the tastiest part, and it helps to identify the variety.

OTHER PRODUCE

Greece is home to the largest variety of olives in the world. They are cured by methods used for thousands of years. The best quality olive oil, extra-virgin, is made by pressing just-ripe olives only. Greece produces sheep's, cow's and goat's cheeses, usually named by taste and texture, not place of origin.

WHAT TO DRINK

Wine has been part of Greek cultural life from the earliest times. Major wine-producing areas include Attica, Macedonia and the Peloponnese. Mavrodaphne is a fortified dessert wine from Pátra. Traditional Greek specialities include *tsípouro*, distilled from the residue of crushed grapes; retsina, a wine flavoured with pine resin *(see p147)*; and the strong, aniseed-flavoured spirit ouzo. Coffee in Greece is traditionally made from very finely ground beans boiled up with water in a long-handled *mpríki* (coffee pot) and drunk from a tiny cup. It is served in cafés rather than tavernas.

Spetzofáï, *from central Greece, is sautéed slices of spicy country sausage with herbs and vegetables.*

Barboúnia, *or red mullet, has been the most esteemed fish in Greece since antiquity. It is usually simply fried.*

Loukoumádes *are a snack of small deep-fried doughnuts soaked in honey-syrup and sprinkled with cinnamon.*

The Classic Greek Menu

The traditional first course is a selection of *mezédes*, or snacks; these can also be eaten in *ouzerís*, or bars, throughout the day. Meat or fish dishes follow next, usually served with a salad. The wine list tends to be simple, and coffee and cakes are generally consumed after the meal in a nearby pastry shop. In rural areas traditional dishes can be chosen straight from the kitchen. Bread is considered by Greeks to be the staff of life and is served at every meal. Village bakers vary the bread each day with flavourings of currants, herbs, wild greens or cheese. The many Orthodox festivals are celebrated with special breads.

Greek pitta breads

Souvlákia *are small chunks of pork, flavoured with lemon, herbs and olive oil, grilled on skewers.*

Choriátiki saláta, *Greek salad, combines tomatoes, cucumber, onions, herbs, capers and feta cheese.*

ΜΕΖΕΣ
Mezés

Olives — Ελιές
Eliés

Salted mullet roe dip — Ταραμοσαλάτα
Taramosaláta

Yogurt and cucumber dip — Τζατζίκι
Tzatzíki

Σουβλάκια
Souvlákia

Chickpea (garbanzo) purée — Ρεβυθοσαλάτα
Revythosaláta

Aubergine (eggplant) purée — Μελιτζανοσαλάτα
Melitzanosaláta

Ντολμάδες
Ntolmádes

Vine leaves stuffed with rice — Μελιτζάνες ιμάμ μπαϊλντί
Melitzánes imám baïldí

Χωριάτικη σαλάτα
Choriátiki saláta

Stuffed baked aubergines (eggplant) —

ΨΑΡΙΑ
Psária

Πλακί
Plakí

Fish are at their best around the coast and on the islands — Σχάρας
Scháras

Τηγανιτά καλαμάρια
Tiganitá kalamária

Fried squid —

Psária plakí *is a whole fish baked in an open dish with vegetables in a tomato and olive oil sauce.*

Scháras *means "from the grill". It can be applied to meat or fish, or even vegetables. Here, grilled swordfish has been marinated in lemon juice, olive oil and herbs before being swiftly char-grilled.*

MEZEDES

Mezédes are eaten as a first course or as a snack with wine or other drinks. *Taramosaláta* is a purée of salted mullet roe and bread-crumbs or potato. Traditionally a dish for Lent, it is now on every taverna menu. *Melitzanosaláta* and *revythosaláta* are both purées. *Melitzanosaláta* is grilled aubergines (eggplant) and herbs; *revythosaláta* is chickpeas (garbanzos), coriander and garlic. *Melitzánes imám baïldí* are aubergines filled with a purée of onions, tomatoes and herbs. *Ntolmádes* are vine leaves stuffed with currants, pine nuts and rice.

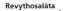

Revythosaláta

Ntolmádes

Taramosaláta

Melitzánes imám baïldí

Typical selection of mezédes

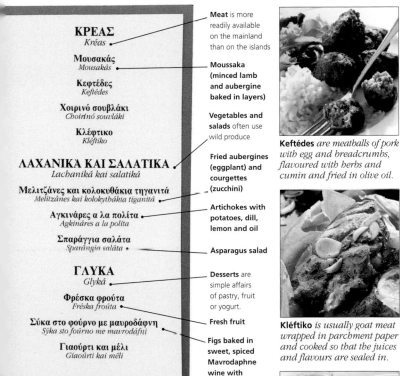

ΚΡΕΑΣ
Kréas

Μουσακάς
Mousakás

Κεφτέδες
Keftédes

Χοιρινό σουβλάκι
Choirinó souvláki

Κλέφτικο
Kléftiko

ΛΑΧΑΝΙΚΑ ΚΑΙ ΣΑΛΑΤΙΚΑ
Lachaniká kai salatiká

Μελιτζάνες και κολοκυθάκια τηγανιτά
Melitzánes kai kolokythákia tiganitá

Αγκινάρες α λα πολίτα
Agkináres a la políta

Σπαράγγια σαλάτα
Sparángia saláta

ΓΛΥΚΑ
Glyká

Φρέσκα φρούτα
Fréska froúta

Σύκα στο φούρνο με μαυροδάφνη
Sýka sto foúrno me mavrodáfni

Γιαούρτι και μέλι
Giaoúrti kai méli

Meat is more readily available on the mainland than on the islands

Moussaka (minced lamb and aubergine baked in layers)

Vegetables and salads often use wild produce

Fried aubergines (eggplant) and courgettes (zucchini)

Artichokes with potatoes, dill, lemon and oil

Asparagus salad

Desserts are simple affairs of pastry, fruit or yogurt.

Fresh fruit

Figs baked in sweet, spiced Mavrodaphne wine with orange-flower water

Keftédes *are meatballs of pork with egg and breadcrumbs, flavoured with herbs and cumin and fried in olive oil.*

Kléftiko *is usually goat meat wrapped in parchment paper and cooked so that the juices and flavours are sealed in.*

Sweet pastries *filled with nuts and honey, syrup-drenched cakes, pies, doughnuts and glyká (candied fruits) are mainly eaten in cafés. The most famous of all are bakla-vas, with layers of filo pastry and nuts, and kataïfi, known to tourists as "shredded wheat".*

Giaoúrti kai méli *(yogurt with honey) is served in speciality "milk shops", to be eaten there or taken home.*

Choosing a Restaurant

The restaurants in this guide have been selected across a wide range of price categories for their good value, traditional food and interesting location. This chart lists the restaurants by area, starting with Athens. Unless otherwise stated, the restaurants listed here are open for lunch and dinner daily.

PRICE CATEGORIES
The following price ranges are for a three-course meal for one, including a half bottle of house wine (or equivalent), tax and service.

€ under €15
€€ €15–€25
€€€ €25–€35
€€€€ €35–€45
€€€€€ over €45

ATHENS

AMPELOKIPOI Balthazar
€€€

Tsoha 27, 115 21 **Tel** 21064 41215   **Map** 4 E2

This contemporary bar and restaurant boasts a beautiful, palm-filled garden illuminated by coloured lanterns. The Mediterranean cuisine includes creative dishes such as chicken couscous with orange sauce and there is a good selection of home-made desserts. In the evenings, the resident DJ creates a vibrant club atmosphere. Book ahead. Closed Sun.

AMPELOKIPOI Vlassis
€€€€

Pastér 8, off Plateía Mavíli, 115 21 **Tel** 21064 63060   **Map** 4 F3

Occupying a two-storey interwar house, Vlassis sticks to its tested formula of abundant, rich, retro cooking. Order mezédes like cabbage ntolmádes from the diskos, and then place your order for suckling pig or grilled thrápsalo (giant squid). The place fills by mid-evening, so book ahead. Closed Sun dinner; Aug.

ANO PETRALONA Chrysa
€€€

Dimofóntos 81, 118 52 **Tel** 21034 12515   **Map** 5 3A

This tastefully decorated taverna is a trendy exception to the numerous traditional eateries in the area. The fare is a modern take on Greek cuisine, for example salmon, chicken and duck dishes in simple sauces, and the welcoming proprietress usually waits on you herself. Open for dinner. Closed Sun; Aug.

EXARCHEIA I Lefka
€€

Mavromicháli 121, 114 72 **Tel** 21036 14038   **Map** 3 B2

Last of this district's old-style tavernas, I Lefka has winter seating indoors under the retsina barrels and a summer courtyard with scuffed tables. Try the mavromátika (black-eyed peas), beef stew, koukiá (broad beans) or the baked quince dessert. Closed in the summer.

EXARCHEIA Mparmpa Giannis
€€

Emmanouil Mpenáki 94, 106 81 **Tel** 21038 24138   **Map** 2 F3

A favourite that hasn't changed much in decades, this place dishes up consistently good mageireftá and a handful of grills. On any given day there might be giouvarláki (rice and meat balls in avgolémono), stewed okra or baked pérka fish. The tables in pedestrianized Derveníon fill first in summer. Closed Sun dinner; Aug.

EXARCHEIA Pinaleon
€€

Mavromicháli 152, 114 72 **Tel** 21064 40945   **Map** 3 B2

This well-loved winter taverna, named after the highest mountain on Chíos (from where the owner hails), has a cult following for its rich mezédes, meaty mains and own-made wine. It's noisy, with closely packed tables and rempétiki music in the background. Book ahead. Closed Jun–Sep.

EXARCHEIA Rozalia
€€

Valtetsiou 59, 106 81 **Tel** 21033 02933   **Map** 2 F2

Rozalia has become more commercialized since its garden was enclosed for all-year use, but the food – a mix of mageireftá, a few grills and mezédes – is still worthwhile. Typical winter platters include spanakórizo (spinach rice), tiganiá (pork-chunk fry-up), cabbage ntolmádes and rabbit stew. As usual, the mezédes are offered on a diskos.

EXARCHEIA Salero
€€

Valtetsiou 51, 106 81 **Tel** 21038 13358   **Map** 2 F3

Come to Salero's brightly coloured space (where the red and yellow of the Spanish flag dominate) for unique specialities from the Iberian peninsula. Among the highlights on the menu are breaded shrimps with sweet and sour sauce and almonds. There is also a wide selection of tapas and wines, and a relaxed, convivial atmosphere.

EXARCHEIA Fasoli
€€€

Emmanouil Mpenáki 45, 106 81 **Tel** 21033 00010   **Map** 2 F3

Fasoli is excellent value at mid-range prices, and has stylish decor featuring suspended lighting. The food is Greek with creative twists, such as lentil salad, biftéki roulade and light pasta dishes. Read the chalkboard for daily specials and desserts. Closed Sun.

Key to Symbols see back cover flap

EXARCHEIA Giantes
Valtetsíou 44, 106 81 **Tel** *21033 01369*   **Map** *2 F3*

The modern Greek menu at Exárcheia's most upscale eatery changes by the season, according to the organically produced ingredients sourced. You might be served wild greens, monkfish, lamb and sun-dried tomatoes or *tas kebab* stew. In summer dine in the tiled courtyard; in winter in the warm-toned interior.

GAZI Mamacas
Persefónis 39, 104 35 **Tel** *21034 64984*   **Map** *1 A5*

The original new-wave taverna that kick-started the gentrification of Gázi, Mamacas is still steaming along after its 1998 opening. The fare is wholesome, updated Greek like Cretan *dákos* salad (rusks, tomato, cheese, oregano) and cuttlefish with greens. The decor is trendy and the clientele equally so. After midnight DJ sounds predominate.

GAZI Sardelles
Persefónis 15, 104 35 **Tel** *21034 78050*

Located in a neighbourhood not generally known for inexpensive restaurants, Sardelles has carved out a niche purveying the humbler varieties of seafood like *sardélles* (sardines). The prices may be cheap but the decor is modern enough.

GAZI Varoulko
Pireós 80, 104 35 **Tel** *21052 28400*   **Map** *1 C4*

Michelin-starred chef Lefteris Lazarou has diversified from the innovative fish dishes at the original Piraeus branch of Varoulko to create unlikely recipes such as goat risotto and cold tropical-fruit soup for dessert. Booking ahead is recommended despite the vast, multilevel and somewhat clinical space. Closed lunch; Sun.

ILISIA Galaxy Restaurant
Hilton, Vassilísis Sofías 46, 115 28 **Tel** *21072 81407*   **Map** *4 D5*

Located at the Hilton Athens hotel *(see p264)*, the Galaxy Restaurant has a spectacular roof-top setting with incredible views of the Acropolis. The menu is full of mouth-watering Mediterranean and Japanese dishes such as fresh-grilled fish cooked on charcoal barbecues. On long summer evenings relax with a martini. Open May–Oct; evenings only.

KOLONAKI Il Postino
Grivaíon 3, alley off Skoufá, 106 73 **Tel** *21036 41414*   **Map** *3 A4*

Cosy, genuine *osteria* with old-photo decor and equally retro music on the sound system. The unpretentious, home-made cooking, supervised by an Italian chef with an illustrious track record in Athens, comprises of pasta dishes, rabbit stew and starters like marinated anchovies. Open from lunch until the small hours. Closed Sun.

KOLONAKI Kavatza
Spefsipou 30, 106 75 **Tel** *21072 41862*   **Map** *3 B5*

This minimalist, tastefully decorated restaurant offers a wide range of traditional Greek cuisine. Start your meal with an appetizer of marinated anchovies, then move on to home-made dishes such as moussaka, roasted lamb or pork with potato mash, and wash them down with Greek beer or wine. Open Mon–Sat (daily Oct–Apr).

KOLONAKI Prytaneion
Milioni 7–9, 106 73 **Tel** *21036 43353*   **Map** *3 A5*

Laid out over three floors, this restaurant offers a good choice of Mediterranean cuisine. Enjoy a coffee or a light snack; more substantial options include a variety of pasta dishes, fresh seafood, grilled meats and organic salads. The walls are decorated with works by well-known Greek artists.

KOLONAKI Ouzadiko
Kameádou 25–29, 106 76 **Tel** *21072 95484*   **Map** *3 5C*

This *ouzeri* claims to offer more varieties of *ouzo* and *tsípouro* to wash down *lakérda* (white-fleshed marinated bonito), *hortópitta* and *revythokeftédes* (chickpea croquettes) than anywhere else in town. Always crowded and convivial, it's a popular hangout for politicians and journalists. Closed Sun dinner; Mon; Aug.

KOLONAKI To Kioupi
Plateia Kolonakíou 4, 106 73 **Tel** *21036 14033*   **Map** *3 A5*

A classic basement *magereío* that had a light refit around the millennium. G*ída vrastí* (stewed goat), *gouronópoulo* (suckling pig), baked fish, *angináres ala políta* (artichokes with carrots, potatoes and dill), *chórta* and beans, plus palatable wines feature on the menu. Closed Sun; Aug and summer evenings.

KOLONAKI Kiku
Dimokrítou 12, 106 73 **Tel** *21036 47033*   **Map** *3 A5*

An award-winning Japanese eatery, Kiku blends a contemporary minimalist interior with sushi (served at a separate bar), sashimi and tempura. There are also some less common options on offer including *udon* noodles and *yaki soba*. Closed lunch; Sun.

KOLONAKI Orizontes Lykavittou
Lykavittós Hill, 106 75 **Tel** *21072 27065*   **Map** *3 B4*

The views are sky-high and so are the prices (for dishes like sea bass with tagliatelle) at this spot near the summit of the hill, accessible only by the funicular or a long hike up through the pines. Seating is either in a conservatory or on a terrace.

KOUKAKI Edodi   €€€€€
Veïkou 80, 117 42 **Tel** *21092 13013*   **Map** 5 C4

The winner of several national awards, this intimate, eight-table restaurant on the upper floor of a Neo-Classical house is tucked away in a quiet part of town. Creations such as duck in cherry sauce or smoked-goose *carpaccio* feature on the menu. Save room for the creative desserts. Good wine list. Closed lunch; Sun and summer.

MAKRYGIANNI Manimani   目   €€€
Falírou 10, 117 42 **Tel** *21092 18180*   **Map** 6 D3

Discreetly occupying the top storey of a 1930s house, this outfit takes its name from the Máni peninsula, but the food is in fact pan-Greek-mainland: meat, salads, *mezédes*, rare cheeses and a few desserts. Willing staff, a decent wine list and a dearth of nearby eateries mean mandatory bookings. Open Tue–Sat dinner, Sun lunch; closed Mon.

METAXOURGEIO Alexander the Great   🔳目   €€
Megalou Alexandrou 3–7, 104 37 **Tel** *21052 27990*   **Map** 1 C3

Renowned for its Greek hospitality, this restaurant offers diners wonderfully authentic cuisine at an affordable price. Specials include *spetsofáï* (sausages with tomatoes and green peppers) and cabbage rolls stuffed with herby beef and béchamel sauce. Be sure to take advantage of the garden in summer.

MONASTIRAKI Thanassis   🔳🔳目   €€
Mitropóleos 69, 105 55 **Tel** *21032 44705*   **Map** 6 D1

Perennial candidate for best purveyor of *souvlákia* and *yíros* in town, Thanassis is always packed with Athenians queuing for a take-away or waiting for a table (you can't book ahead). It's frenetic and there's pressure to give up your seat quickly, but for a quick bite you can't beat it. The side dish of peppers is delicious.

MONASTIRAKI Café Avissynia   🔳🎵   €€€
Kynéttou 7, off Plateía Avissynías, 105 55 **Tel** *21032 17047*   **Map** 5 C1

Tables indoors and out are always packed at weekend lunchtimes and Friday evenings when entertainment is provided by an accordionist and singer. The food – Macedonian staples, mussel *pilaf*, baked feta – is rich and the clientele verging on the bohemian. Closed Sun dinner, Mon; summer.

MONASTIRAKI To Kouti   🔳🔳   €€€€
Adrianou 23, 105 55 **Tel** *21032 13229*   **Map** 5 C1

On a pedestrian street skirting the ancient Agora and offering fine Acropolis views, this long-standing eatery attracts a young, arty crowd. The menu features colourful salads, pasta and inspired meat and fish dishes. A great spot for lunch while sightseeing.

OMONOIA Obi   🔳🔳   €
Plateía Agíon Theodóron 4 & Skouleníou 2, 105 59 **Tel** *21032 10512*   **Map** 2 E5

An informal café-restaurant in a Neo-Classical building close to Plateía Klafthmonos, just off the busy thoroughfare of Stadíou. Local business people come here for a light lunch of reasonably priced, regional Greek specialities. Closed Sun.

OMONOIA Restó   🔳🔳目   €€
Akadimías 84, 106 78 **Tel** *21038 10026*   **Map** 2 E3

Restó is all about organic, healthy eating. The meals here are freshly prepared using locally grown produce that is entirely free from pesticides. A wide choice of salads is available as well as sandwiches and soups. Those with a larger appetite can opt for one of the Greek-Mediterranean hot dishes on offer. Closed Sun.

OMONOIA Athinaïkon   🔳目   €€€
Themistokléous 2, 106 78 **Tel** *21038 38485*   **Map** 2 E3

This busy *ouzerí* was established in 1932 but moved here in the early 1990s. It is renowned for its good service, marble tables and fresh seafood *mezédes* like mussels *saganáki*, paella and fried *gávros* (anchovies), though meat platters also appear on the menu. Decorated in wood trim, old photos and black-and-white-tiled floors. Closed Sun; Aug.

OMONOIA Olive Garden   目   €€€
Panepistimíou 52 (Titania Hotel), 106 78 **Tel** *21038 38511*   **Map** 2 E3

Olive Garden is set on an elegant roof top at the heart of Athens. The focus of the menu is contemporary Mediterranean cuisine which is complemented by the attentive service. The restaurant attracts both locals and hotel guests with its wonderful views. A less atmospheric branch with similar fare is on Mitropóleos, just off Sýntagma.

OMONOIA Bacaro   ♿🔳目   €€€€
Sofokléous 1 and Aristeídou, 105 59 **Tel** *21032 11882*   **Map** 2 E4

This smart bar-restaurant is located inside a peaceful courtyard adorned with potted olive trees. The menu features creative Mediterranean cuisine and the complex also includes an art gallery and a delicatessen stocking quality Greek products. Closed Sun dinner.

OMONOIA Ideal   目   €€€€
Panepistimíou 46, 106 78 **Tel** *21033 03000*   **Map** 2 E3

A city centre institution since 1922, serving international cuisine (*schnitzel* and chops) along with more exciting, and more Hellenic dishes of the day such as milk-fed veal with aubergine (eggplant) and stuffed courgettes (zucchini). Locals love both the consistent food quality and the Art Nouveau interior. Closed Sun.

Key to Price Guide *see p284* **Key to Symbols** *see back cover flap*

PANGRATI O Vyrinis
Archimidous 11 & Arátou, 116 36 **Tel** *21070 12153* €€€
Map *7 B3*

A much-loved neighbourhood taverna, now being managed by the grandsons of the founder. They've spruced up the interior, but left alone the ornamental wine barrels and the good-value fare, which includes salads, *mezédes* and creative main dishes. Popular garden in summer. Closed Sun dinner; Mon; Aug.

PANGRATI The Sushi Bar
Plateía Varnáva 4, corner Stílponos, 116 36 **Tel** *21075 24354* €€€€
Map *7 B4*

Part of a small Athens-based chain, this outlet has a wooden-floored and high-ceilinged dining area with a few tables, though they're equally geared up for take-away orders. All the sushi standards are on offer, alongside a few tempura snacks as well. Open dinner; Sat–Sun lunch.

PANGRATI Spondi
Pyrronos 5, 116 38 **Tel** *21075 64021* €€€€€
Map *7 B4*

Under the command of a French chef, Michelin-starred Spondi is among the best special-occasion Athens eateries. Housed in a Neo-Classical building with a stone courtyard, it offers rich cuisine that combines Continental and Pacific influences, such as herb- or truffle-flavoured duck, followed by decadent desserts. Closed lunch.

PEDION AREOS St'Astra
Leofóros Alexándras 10, 106 82 **Tel** *21088 94500* €€€€
Map *2 F1*

This designer-furnished restaurant on the top floor of the Park Hotel enjoys enviable views of the Acropolis and Lykavitós Hill through its ample windows. The cuisine is slightly overpriced but includes such delights as duck with ginger and redcurrant sauce and terrine of *foie gras*. Closed lunch; Sun & Mon.

PLAKA Klimataria
Klepsydras 5, 105 55 **Tel** *21032 11215* €€
Map *6 D2*

Within walking distance of the Acropolis, Klimataria is in a prime location. The style is typical of a Greek taverna and has retained the same decor since the 1960s. Klimataria serves up all of the old favourites including *moussaka*, *tzatziki* and slow-cooked meat dishes and breads from its own bread oven. Live music at weekends.

PLAKA O Damigos (Ta Bakalarákia)
Kydathinaion 41, 105 58 **Tel** *21032 25084* €€
Map *6 E2*

The last surviving basement joint in the area, O Damigos has decor that seemingly hasn't changed since the place was founded in 1865. The barrels here actually contain good *retsina*, and the cod with garlic sauce *(bakalarákia)* is the big attraction. Closed lunch; Mon; summer.

PLAKA O Kouklis (Scholarchio)
Tripódon 14, 105 57 **Tel** *21032 47605* €€
Map *6 E2*

Founded in 1935, this *ouzeri-mezedopoleio* with its ever-popular terrace has managed to maintain low prices without sacrificing quality. The waiter brings 18 different platters – including flaming sausages – to choose from on the *dískos* (giant tray); wash it all down with the house wine or a carafe of *ouzo*.

PLAKA O Platanos
Diogénous 4, 105 57 **Tel** *21032 20666* €€
Map *6 D1*

Taking its name from the *plátanos* (plane) tree outside, this 1932-founded taverna showcases meat-based stews and *laderá* (cooked vegetable dishes) in its repertoire. Their exceptionally good barrelled *retsina* has been profiled in Niko Manesi's *The Greek Wine Guide*. Closed Sun.

PLAKA Psarras (Palaia Taverna tou Psarra)
Erechthéos 16, corner Erotokritou, 105 57 **Tel** *21032 18733* €€€
Map *6 D2*

In business since 1898, this classic taverna operates out of two restored old premises across from each other on a landscaped square. The standard but well-presented Greek starters are usually more accomplished than the mains (which always include fish). Celebrity patronage over the years means prices are on the up.

PSYRRI Kouzina
Sarri 44, 105 54 **Tel** *21032 15534* €€
Map *1 C5*

This bar-restaurant occupies a cosy, stone and wood, double-height interior space during winter, with tables moving up to the roof terrace in summer. The menu features creative Mediterranean cuisine and there's also an adjoining open-air cinema from Jun–Sep. Closed Mon.

PSYRRI Taverna tou Psyrri
Aischylou 12, 105 52 **Tel** *21032 14923* €€€
Map *1 C5–C6*

The first to open its doors and still one of the most popular tavernas in Pysrrí, Tou Psyrrí has two levels of noisy indoor seating and features all the traditional favourites in big portions. The chalkboard menu (in Greek only) is strong on fish. Show up early to get a seat as bookings are not accepted.

PSYRRI To Zeidoron
Ag. Anargiron 17, 105 54 **Tel** *21032 15368* €€€
Map *1 C5*

Psyrrí has firmly established itself as Athens' favourite nighttime playground and To Zeidoron is a fine place to kick off the evening. Diners feast on modern taverna fare in an old stone building with a light and airy upper-level glass extension. There are also several highly coveted tables outside on the street.

PSYRRI Hytra

Navárchou Apostóli 7, 105 52 **Tel** *21033 16767*

Map *1 C5*

The nouvelle Greek cuisine at this Michelin-starred eatery matches the minimalist decor. Mains like *synagrída* fish with spinach and *mavromátika* (black-eyed peas) are followed by artisanal desserts such as yogurt and coffee mousse. There's also a set 15-platter *mezédes* menu. Closed lunch; Sun and Jun–Sep.

THISEIO Stavlos

Iraklidón 10, 118 51 **Tel** *21034 52502*

Map *5 B1*

Housed in what were royal stables during the 19th century, Stavlos was one of the first cafés to colonize the area in the late 1990s. There is a stone- and wood-trimmed bar, club, gallery and upscale restaurant. The fare is Greek with Italian influences.

THISEIO Filistron

Apostólou Pávlou 23, 118 51 **Tel** *21034 67554*

Map *5 B1*

Filistron is not really a full-on taverna but more of a light-snack café/bar with *mezédes* platters, a good-quality, full Greek wine list, *tsípouro* (the north-mainland distilled spirit), *ouzo*, coffees and novelty drinks like *vinsanto* from Santorini. The big draw is the summer roof terrace with striking views of the Acropolis. Closed Mon.

THISEIO To Steki tou Ilia

Thessaloníkis 7 & Eptachálkou 5, 118 51 **Tel** *21034 22407*

Map *1 A5*

Both premises put tables out in the street in summer and serve little other than the *païdákia* (lamb chops) for which they are famous (though there are also salads and a few dips). Open for dinner (and lunch on weekends); closed Mon (winter) and part of Aug.

THISEIO Pil Poul

Apostólou Pávlou 51 and corner Poulopoúlou, 118 51 **Tel** *21034 23665*

Map *5 B1*

Diners sit in tastefully decorated rooms in this former Neo-Classical mansion, with roof-terrace seating in summer. The menu offers French and Mediterranean-tinged creative cooking like beef fillet with truffles or grouper baked in champagne sauce, served by uniformed waiters. Open dinner; closed Mon.

AROUND ATHENS

KESSARIANI Trata O Stelios

Plateía Anagennísseos 7–9, 161 21 **Tel** *21072 91533*

Road Map *D4*

One of the best of a handful of seafood restaurants around this central square, Trata combines the virtues of fresh ingredients with efficient service, especially at crowded Sunday lunches. There's fish soup as well as the usual grilled and fried seafood. Closed Aug.

KIFISIA Souvlakia Kifissias

Othonos 99, 145 61 **Tel** *21080 11093*

Road Map *D4*

Souvlákia and *gyros* (spit-roast pork served in wraps) are the speciality at this informal eatery. Other menu choices range from hearty salads, garlic pie and marinated lamb ribs to more unusual options such as spit-roasted ostrich. Eat in or take away.

KIFISIA Berdema

Vasilíssis Amalías 20, 145 61 **Tel** *21080 13853*

Road Map *D4*

Sister restaurant to Berdema in Kolonáki, this branch is located in the upmarket district of Kifisia. This cosy restaurant with a warm atmosphere serves traditional specialities from Northeast Greece as well as oriental dishes. The food here is unbeatable, especially signature dishes such as the spit-roasted meat with hot tomato sauce. Closed Sun dinner.

PIRAEUS Achinos

Aktí Themistokléous 51, 185 34 **Tel** *21045 26944*

Road Map *D4*

This split-level restaurant built against a seaside cliff is a *mezedopolío* strong on seafood, offering good value in a somewhat touristy area near the Naval Museum. If you order scaly fish you'll exceed the stated price category but you can fill up perfectly well on less expensive vegetarian and seafood platters. Closed Mon.

PIRAEUS Vasilenas

Aitolikoú 72, 185 45 **Tel** *21046 12457*

Road Map *D4*

A well-loved haunt in a less glamorous part of Piraeus, Vasilenas has undergone a comprehensive refurbishment. Set menus are rarely good value in Greece but this one – consisting of 16 courses – is. It features meat choices in addition to the fish and seafood repertoire. Open dinner; closed Sun, part of Aug.

PIRAEUS Jimmy and the Fish

Aktí Koumoundoúrou 46, Mikrolímano, 185 33 **Tel** *21041 24417*

Road Map *D4*

Among various waterside establishments at Mikrolímano, Jimmy and the Fish with its Hellenic blue and white decor has the best position, some of the best service and seafood, in a see-and-be-seen environment. Fish, salads, grilled octopus and steamed mussels all feature on the menu. Book ahead at weekends.

PIRAEUS Kollias €€€€€

Syngrou 303 and Dimosthenous, 175 64 **Tel** *21046 29620*   **Road Map** *D4*

It's worth the trek to this out of the way seafood specialist hidden behind an apartment block. Owner-chef Tassos Kollias sources shellfish and other seafood delicacies like sea urchins, oysters and barracuda from across the country for *mezédes* to accompany more usual scaly fish. Closed Sun dinner; two weeks Aug.

PORTO RAFTI Psaropoula-Bibikos 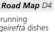 €€€

Leofóros Avlakíou 118, 190 09 **Tel** *22990 71292*   **Road Map** *D4*

Ideally placed in this family beach resort for a tasty lunch after touring the ruins at Brauron, the long-running Psaropoula-Bibikos restaurant offers seafood *mezédes* followed by grilled fish or meat plus a few *mageireftá* dishes of the day.

RAFINA Ioakeim €€€

Harbourfront, 190 09 **Tel** *22940 23421*   **Road Map** *D4*

One of the best – and priciest – of several seafood tavernas around Rafína's scenic harbour, Ioakeim has been around since the 1950s. Try the grilled or fried fish garnished with leaf salads or *krítamo* (rock samphire), and the various bean-based *mezédes*. Popular with locals. Closed Tue.

RAFINA Kavouria tou Asimaki €€€

Harbourfront, 190 09 **Tel** *22940 24551*   **Road Map** *D4*

Kavouria tou Asimaki is the first restaurant you come to as you descend to the harbour from Rafina main square. Not to be bypassed, it is considered by many to be the town's finest. The kitchen serves a cornucopia of fish and seafood, but there are also some good Greek meat specialities on the menu. Splendid views of the port and sea beyond.

SOUNIO Syrtaki €€€

2km (1 mile) north of Poseidon Temple, 195 50 **Tel** *22920 39125*   **Road Map** *D4*

One of the closest non-touristy tavernas to the ancient site, this has a traditional menu featuring various *pittes* (turnovers) as *mezédes* and spit-roasted meat and grilled fish for mains. The shaded terrace has sweeping views of the sea.

VARKIZA Island 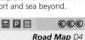 €€€€

Km 27 on Athens–Soúnio road, 166 72 **Tel** *21096 53563*   **Road Map** *D4*

Island is a combination bar/restaurant/club on a clifftop, which attracts a glamorous clientele. The cuisine is modern Mediterranean, along with a tapas bar; booking is vital at weekends (seatings from 9pm on). The club, with dance floor, only gets going after midnight. Open dinner May–Oct.

THE PELOPONNESE

ANCIENT CORINTH Archontikó 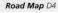 €€

Paralía Lecheoú, 200 06 **Tel** *27410 27968*   **Road Map** *C4*

Overlooking the coastal road, about 3.5 km (2 miles) west of town, near the Lechaion archaeological site, this taverna offers well-prepared meat dishes and *mezédes*. Specialities include *kokkinistó Archontiko*, a wine-based meat stew with mushrooms, and cockerel *kokkinistó* with pasta. Popular with locals, so book ahead. Open lunch (Sun only).

GIALOVA, NEAR PYLOS Chelonaki €€

Waterfront, 240 01 **Tel** *27230 23080*   **Road Map** *B5*

The seafront 'Little Turtle' looks out over the serene waters of the Navaríno Bay, which is particularly beautiful at sunset. Home-made food, fresh fish, and a friendly, laid-back atmosphere make it popular with unhurried locals and tourists alike. Occasional live music. Rooms are also available.

GYTHEIO Poulikakos €€

Central plateía, 232 00 **Tel** *27330 22792*   **Road Map** *C5*

Situated right on the beach, this family-run restaurant is a favourite with both locals and visitors in the know. Specialities include grilled catch of the day and colourful salads, all prepared with the freshest ingredients and the best olive oil produced in the area.

GYTHEIO Saga 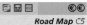 €€

Odós Tzanetáki, opposite Marathonísi, 232 00 **Tel** *27330 21358*   **Road Map** *C5*

From ground-floor premises under the eponymous French-Greek-owned pension, this restaurant spreads tables across the narrow pavement and along the sea wall opposite. Excellent for fresh fish, with a wide choice in the chiller cabinet – including several types of sea bream – plus fish soup, shrimp *saganáki* with cheese, and charcoal-grilled octopus.

ILIAS Irene €

Krestena, Ilias **Tel** *26250 24833*   **Road Map** *C4*

Irene restaurant prides itself on producing delicious, Greek home-made dishes. Locally sourced ingredients are used such as seasonal vegetables and oil from the Peloponnese. Wash it all down with some local wine and take in the fine Greek hospitality as well as the great views.

KALAMATA Kríni
Evangelistrías 40, 241 00 **Tel** *27210 24474*
Road Map *C5*

Set in the up and coming Marina neighbourhood, Krini is a cosy taverna open most of the year providing a good selection of fish and seafood, as well as more traditional meat grills and *mageireftá*. Good wine, service and hospitality. Closed Sun lunch.

KORONI Kagkelários
Harbourfront, 240 04 **Tel** *27250 22648*
Road Map *C5*

Situated by the water's edge in the small harbour of Koroni, this very popular fish taverna and *ouzeri* has fresh seafood delivered directly from the owner's small boat each evening. Specialities include small fish, lobster with pasta, and sea-urchin salad, but its signature dish is plain octopus, cooked to perfection.

KOSMAS Maleatis Apollion
Central plateía, 210 52 **Tel** *27570 31494*
Road Map *C5*

The mountain village of Kósmas, just below a pass through the Párnon range, makes an ideal lunch stop when travelling between Geráki and Náfplio. Of several tavernas on the leafy and beautifully paved square, Maleatis Apollion offers good mountain food such as bean soup and local lamb and goat. Wonderfully cool in summer.

KYPARISSI Tíris
Mitrópoli district, north side of bay, 230 52 **Tel** *27320 55260*
Road Map *C5*

A delightful family-run taverna, where several relatives help out in the kitchen from noon until late. The speciality is excellent seafood and fish, but there are also meat grills and a *mageireftá* dish of the day. Friendly service and superb value.

LYGOURIO Leonídas
Village centre, 210 52 **Tel** *27530 22115*
Road Map *C4*

Leonídas offers hearty Greek dishes (grills, stews and *mageireftá*) in a rustic taverna and garden. Immensely popular with both the audience and performers at the Epidaurus theatre 4 km (2.5 miles) away. The walls are decorated with photos of famous patrons – actors, presidents and prime ministers. Book ahead. Open Jun–Sep.

METHONI Klimatariá
Odós Miaoúli, 240 06 **Tel** *27230 31544*
Road Map *B5*

This family-run establishment is famed for its beautifully prepared and extensive range of *mezédes* and *mageireftá*, featuring both traditional dishes with a twist and exotic dishes, with plenty for vegetarians. There's a small, romantic, flower-filled courtyard with vine-covered pergolas. Excellent wine.

MONEMVASIA Matoúla
Inside the Kástro, 230 70 **Tel** *27320 61660*
Road Map *C5*

Opened in 1950, Matoúla is traditional inside, with old photos of Monemvasiá, however most diners gravitate towards the walled garden, which is partly shaded by trees and overlooks the sea and red-tiled roofs of Kástro. Try simple dishes such as local macaroni, *pastítsio* and fresh fish.

MONEMVASIA Skorpiós
South coast road, Géfyra district, 230 70 **Tel** *27320 62090*
Road Map *C5*

South of the bridge linking the mainland with the rock of Monemvasiá is Skorpios, with seating outside and unimpeded views towards the rock. Good *mezédes* like *tzatzíki* and *tyrokafterí* (spicy cheese dip) and simple small fish like marinated *gávros* and *atheriná* are served. Good wine.

NAFPLIO Ómorfo Tavernáki
Vassilísis Ólgas 16, 211 00 **Tel** *27520 25944*
Road Map *C4*

This taverna on one of old Náfplio's narrower lanes is famous for its *kolokotroneïko* (pork in a wine sauce), *bekrí mezé* (pork morsels in red sauce), and *spetzofái* (sausage and pepper stew), plus grills and seafood. Cheerful decor, reliable quality and speedy service, with seating inside and on the lane.

NAFPLIO Ta Fanária
Staïkopoúlou 13, corner Soútsou, 211 00 **Tel** *27520 27141*
Road Map *C4*

This long-running restaurant offers outdoor seating under climbing vines; indoor seating is limited and for winter only. Ta Fanária is best for lunch when *mageireftá* such as *moussakás* and *soutzoukákia* emerge fresh from the oven. There's good *retsina* from Mégara to wash it all down.

PATRA Mýthos
Trión Navárhon 181, corner Ríga Feraíou, 262 22 **Tel** *26103 29984*
Road Map *C4*

Pedestrianized Trión Navárhon, linking the fishing port with Áyios Andréas basilica, is home to numerous tavernas. One of the best and oldest is Mýthos, with imaginative lighting and antiques. The proprietress serves up *pittes* (turn-overs), salads and pasta dishes. There's a separately managed beer bar on the top floor. Open dinner. Closed Aug.

PLAKA LEONIDIOU Bekárou (Michael & Margaret)
Harbourfront, 223 00 **Tel** *27570 22379*
Road Map *C5*

Run by the Bekárou clan since 1830, this taverna is named after the current owners. It is an atmospheric, historic seafront taverna in the picturesque centre of the port. Fresh fish is on offer (though squid may be frozen). Try the sweet-tasting local *tsakoniki* aubergines.

PYLOS Gregory's

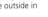

Kalamatas 2, 240 01 **Tel** *27230 22621*   **Road Map** *B5*

An unassuming, old-fashioned taverna on the main square of Pylos, serving traditional Greek *mageireftá* – including goat and *kokkinistó* (meat stewed with wine) – plus local pasta, grilled meat and grilled fish. At the back is a pleasant garden, open to diners in the summer.

RIO Naut-Oiko

Poseidonas 12, 265 00 **Tel** *26109 95992*   **Road Map** *C4*

With tables on the beach, this restaurant enjoys an unbeatable location. The menu offers a selection of traditional Greek dishes prepared with an imaginative twist, ideal for those with adventurous taste buds. Naut-Oiko is a popular venue in Rio, so booking well in advance is recommended, especially at weekends.

SPARTI Elysé

Konstantínou Palaiológou 113, 231 00 **Tel** *27310 29896*   **Road Map** *C5*

This elegant restaurant with pastel-pink decor offers a good range of traditional Greek casseroles and grills, made from sheep, goat and game, and seasoned well. There are also delicious vegetable and fish dishes. Dine outside in the summer.

VYTINA Ta Kókkina Pitharia

Town centre, 220 10 **Tel** *27950 22540*   **Road Map** *C4*

Situated near the centre of town, this taverna has a cosy, stone-walled interior with an impressive fireplace. A wide range of local specialities include rabbit, hare or venison *stifádo*, roast wild boar in a claypot, *kioulmbási* (lamb with garlic and *graviera* cheese) and *argeítiko* (goat cooked in the oven for 14 hours). Vegetarians will find plenty to eat, too.

CENTRAL AND WESTERN GREECE

AGIOS IOANNIS (PILIO) Poseidónas

On shore road, 370 12 **Tel** *24260 31222*   **Road Map** *D3*

A rarity in a resort such as Agios Ioánnis, Poseidónas is a year-round fish taverna, the oldest one here, with a guaranteed source of fresh seafood. Fish is plainly prepared and reasonably priced. The speciality is *kakaviá* (fish soup), which should be ordered in advance.

ARACHOVA Panagióta

Top of village, 320 04 **Tel** *22670 32735*   **Road Map** *C3*

This taverna up near Agios Geórgios church is a good place to sample local specialities in a white-tablecloth environment, away from the commercialization of the main road. Dishes include chicken soup, stewed lamb, and cheese-based recipes. Closed Mon–Wed Jul–Aug.

DELPHOI Vakchos

Apollonos 31, Fokida, 330 54 **Tel** *22650 83186*   **Road Map** *C3*

Located on the upper street in Delphoí town centre, this charming, family-run taverna serves traditional Greek food and a good selection of wines and spirits. The terrace is open all year round and boasts splendid views over the hills and the Gulf of Corinth beyond.

DIAVA (KALAMPAKA ENVIRONS) Neromylos

Pigí Goúra, top end of Diáva village, 422 00 **Tel** *24320 25224*   **Road Map** *B2*

This village taverna in a former watermill some 4 km (2.4 miles) southwest of Kalampáka is a favourite with local families. The summer terrace seating is attractive. Besides trout, high calibre ingredients include their own meat and *galotyri* as well as vegetarian *mezédes*. Open dinner, Sun lunch; closed Mon in low season.

ELATI Sta Rizá

Village centre, 420 32 **Tel** *26530 71550*   **Road Map** *B2*

Sta Rizá has a reputation for good local cuisine, with such dishes as *zygoúri* (lamb stew) and *lachanópita* (green vegetable turnover) coming to the fore. Weather permitting, there's table seating out on the terrace with full views of the Gamíla summit-ridge. Closed Wed & Thu Oct–Jun.

GALAXIDI Albatross

Inland, on the road between the two churches, 330 52 **Tel** *22650 42233*   **Road Map** *C3*

The cheapest and one of the best tavernas in Galaxidi offers good *mageireftá* from a brief daily menu. This might include octopus, spinach/cheese pie, rabbit stew, pale *taramasaláta* and the house speciality *samári* (pancetta in savoury sauce). Limited quantities are cooked and reservations are not taken, so get there early.

GAVROS (KARPENISSI REGION) To Spíti tou Psará

On through road, 360 75 **Tel** *22370 41202*   **Road Map** *C3*

"The Fisherman's House" might seem an odd name for this taverna at the bottom of the valley between Megálo Hório and Mikró Horió, but it receives top marks for its grilled trout, as well as *píttes*, dips, vegetable starters and local wine. Summer seating on the rear terrace overlooks the riverside trees.

IOANNINA Fýsa Roúfa

Avéroff 55, 452 21 **Tel** *26510 26262*   **Road Map** *B2*

Slightly elevated prices for *mageireftá* such as baked fish, suckling pig and *spetzofáï* are amply justified by the calibre of the cooking, quick service and large portions. Unusually, there's also plenty of desserts at this busy venue. Cosy loft seating for winter and decorated with old photos from Parga, the proprietor's birthplace. Open 24 hours a day.

IOANNINA To Agnanti

Pamvotides 2, Molos, 452 21 **Tel** *26510 22010*   **Road Map** *B2*

In the centre of town, with a large terrace overlooking Lake Pamvotis and the Isle of Ali Pasha, this sophisticated restaurant serves regional specialities, such as smoked trout and *arnáki limonato* (lamb in lemon sauce), made from locally-sourced ingredients. This is a popular venue for wedding receptions.

KALAMPAKA Archontariki

Town Centre, 422 00 **Tel** *24320 22449*   **Road Map** *B2*

Located opposite the post office in the centre of Kalampáka, this eatery has a spacious dining room with floor-to-ceiling windows, and a front terrace. The typical Greek taverna fare includes *choriátiki saláta* (Greek salad), *gemistá* (tomatoes and peppers stuffed with rice) and *kokkinisto* (beef cooked in a thick red sauce).

KASTRAKI Parádeisos

Main through road, below village centre, 422 00 **Tel** *24320 22723*   **Road Map** *B2*

Most of Kastráki's dozen or so places to eat are *psistariés* (grillhouses); the best is probably Parádeisos, with fine views from its terrace. Here you can feast on *kebab* (loose chunks, not wrapped in pitta), red-bean salad, red peppers and a beer.

KATIGIORGIS Flísvos

On the beach, 370 06 **Tel** *24230 71071*   **Road Map** *D3*

Both *mageireftá* and famously fresh fish are served at tables on the sand, with only slightly bumped-up prices considering the number of excursion boats that call here from Skiáthos. Dishes might be garnished with *ftéri* (fried fern) and *tsitsíravla* (marinated terebinth shoots). Closed Nov–Mar.

KIPOI Stou Miháli

South edge of village, on through road, 440 10 **Tel** *26530 71630*   **Road Map** *B2*

The only full-service taverna for quite some distance around is fortunately excellent, with an emphasis on traditional Zagorian *píttes*, game like wild boar and venison, broad beans with greens and more conventional stews, all washed down with a purplish wine. Seating outdoors in summer, otherwise indoors near a fireplace.

KONITSA To Déndro

At sharp bend in town access road from main highway, 441 00 **Tel** *26550 23982*   **Road Map** *B2*

To Déndro takes its name from the enormous plane tree out the front, nurtured by the burbling fountain. The restaurant is strong on baked goat *(gástra)* or lamb, proprietor Yiannis's famous *féta psiti* (baked cheese spiked with hot green chillies) and good wine from Zítsa.

KONITSA Bourazani

54 km from Ioannina towards Konitsa **Tel** *26550 61283*   **Road Map** *B2*

Bourazani is located just a stone's throw away from the environmental park in Konitsa. A wide variety of dishes are available, all made using fresh, organic produce. The dishes based around deer or rabbit come highly recommended. Open all year round.

KORONISIA Myrtariá (Paténtas)

Shore road, south flank of village, 471 00 **Tel** *26810 24021*   **Road Map** *B3*

On the shore of the Amvrakikós Gulf 25 km (15.5 miles) southwest of Arta, sleepy Koronisía, an island joined to the mainland by a long causeway, is a favourite destination of seafood enthusiasts. Myrtariá is the most consistently open and reliable taverna, with fair prices for impeccably prepared sole, mullet and the famous gulf-raised prawns.

LAMIA Enaristotelous

Aristotélous 3, up steps from Plateía Laoú, 351 00 **Tel** *22310 31502*   **Road Map** *C3*

Housed in a building which dates back to 1891, with a stunning interior for winter seating and an alluring summer courtyard, this restaurant serves up rich Middle-Eastern and Macedonian recipes. Many dishes are cheese- or fish-based. Wash mains down with Límnos wine and enjoy the complimentary dessert crêpes.

MILIES To Salkimi

Central plateía, 37 010 **Tel** *24230 86010*   **Road Map** *D3*

Open all year round, this popular taverna housed in an impressive wooden structure is renowned all over the Pílio peninsula. In addition to its excellent selection of wines, To Salkimi offers a variety of *pitas* (pies) and local dishes prepared with aubergines, mushrooms and cheese.

MILINA (PILIO) Sákis

South end of waterfront, 370 06 **Tel** *24230 66078*   **Road Map** *D3*

Sákis is a consistently good, traditional eatery with reasonable prices. You can assemble a tasty meal of seafood, plus two or three *mezédes* and wine and still have change from a 20-euro note. Try *gávros* (anchovy) or *soupiés* (cuttlefish).

Key to Price Guide *see p284* **Key to Symbols** *see back cover flap*

MONASTIRAKI Iliópoulos
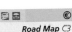

11 km (7 miles) east of Nafpaktos; east end of village, on gulf shore, 330 56 **Tel** *26340 52111*   **Road Map** *C3*

This, the most celebrated of a handful of tavernas in an attractive gulf-side village, has a superb selection of fish, plus a few shellfish appetizers and home-made *pittes*. For a pre- or post-prandial swim, there's a pebble beach just below the outdoor seating terrace. Closed Sun (winter).

NAFPAKTOS Ev-Oinos

Stenopazaro, 303 00 **Tel** *26340 28266*   **Road Map** *C3*

Situated in the Old Town, this *ouzerí* can satisfy even the most demanding taste buds with its selection of traditional Greek dishes, many of them featuring a combination of cheese and seasonal vegetables. Among the highlights are the dishes prepared with halloumi, a Cypriot cheese. In summer, Ev-Oinos opens after 6pm.

NEO MIKRO HORIO (KARPENISSI REGION) To Horiátiko

Central plateía, 360 75 **Tel** *22370 41257*   **Road Map** *C3*

To Horiátiko is a popular, reliable eatery for grilled meat that draws customers from miles around. Other dishes include *fasolákia* (French beans), sausages, *tzatzíki* and various turnovers. The staff cope well with the crowds, and it is popular for weddings and parties. Closed Mon.

PARGA Golfo Beach

Behind Gólfo cove, 480 60 **Tel** *26840 32336*   **Road Map** *B3*

Kyria Evangelia is the heart and soul of one of the oldest tavernas in town, with a cult following for her sustaining, home-made *mageireftá*, encompassing all the usual stews, *ntolmádes* and dips. Golfo Beach is open from breakfast (for those staying in the rooms upstairs) until 11pm. Open May–Oct.

PARGA Kastro 1380

Town centre, 480 60 **Tel** *26840 32164*

Located at the top of the hill, at the entrance to the castle, this romantic dining spot boasts superb town and sea views. The extensive menu is made up of Greek classics and other European cuisine, and the meat and seafood dishes are excellent. The restaurant is only open for dinner but the adjoining bar serves drinks and snacks during the day.

PARGA ENVIRONS: SARAKINIKO BAY Tou Chrístou

Sarakiniko cove, 5 km (3 miles) below Agiá village, 480 60 **Tel** *26840 35207 or 69779 82207*   **Road Map** *B3*

Only a few select vegetable dishes are cooked daily at this beach taverna, but quality is high and seafood (except for squid and octopus) is served fresh. Excellent micro-winery products are added bonuses, as is the garden with a swimming pool to keep children entertained. It's advisable to book and pre-order in peak season. Open May–Oct.

PILIOU Agnati

Tsagkarada Piliou **Tel** *24260 49210*   **Road Map** *B3*

Overlooking the village square, this traditional Greek taverna offers dishes such as roasted pork shank with quinces or rooster in a tomato sauce with pasta, complemented by a wide selection of Greek and Spanish wines. This restaurant is very popular so advance booking is recommended, especially in the summer. Closed May.

PILIOU Dipnosofistis

Tsagkarada Piliou **Tel** *24260 49825*   **Road Map** *B3*

Coffee bar/restaurant Dipnosofistis opened in 1992 in one of the greatest areas of Piliou, Tsagkarada. Its founders were inspired by the mythical mountain and the harmony of the colours and the landscape. All dishes are traditional Greek in style and home-made.

PORTARIA Kritsá

Central plateía, 370 11 **Tel** *24280 90006*   **Road Map** *C3*

On the ground floor of the eponymous hotel, this restaurant provides similarly high standards, with large portions, professional service, an elegant environment including table linens and specialities such as parsley-purée dip, Skópelos olive biscuits and a hearty rendition of *spetzofáï*, accompanied by excellent local wine.

PREVEZA Skaloma

Lygia Harbour, 481 00 **Tel** *26820 56240*   **Road Map** *B3*

Affording lovely views over the fishing harbour, Skaloma serves generous portions of reasonably priced seafood. Choices include fresh squid, sardines and mussels, and the house wine is excellent. There is a neatly kept garden for outdoor dining and occasional live music.

TRIKALA Mezedokamómata

Ypsilántou 16–18, 421 00 **Tel** *24310 76741*   **Road Map** *C2*

Opened in 1997, Mezedokamómata was the first of many small tavernas and *tsipourádika* (the local variant of an *ouzerí*) to colonize and gentrify the old tradesmen's quarter of Manávika. It's still going strong, though the food – standard fried *ouzerí* fare – can be heavy. There's a vast, bare-brick interior for the cooler months.

TRIKALA Palaiá Istoriá

Ypsilántou 3, Manávika district, 421 00 **Tel** *24310 77627*   **Road Map** *C2*

One of the best and more consistently open of the *ouzeri* in this warren of lanes, Palaiá Istoriá displays a light touch and fair prices in dishes such as sardines, grilled portobello mushrooms and hot peppers. The interior decor features photos honouring Trikala's favourite son, *rempétika* great Vassilis Tsitsanis.

TSOUMERKA Panorama
Central plateía, Agnata 471 00 **Tel** *26850 31000*   **Road Map** *B3*

A family-run restaurant, Panorama prepares home-made local dishes, including a wide variety of *pitas* (pies) and grilled meats. Outdoor seating during the summer months affords great views of the mountains. However, remember that evenings can be chilly up here, so bring a cardigan. Open daily Jul–Sep; weekends and holidays in winter.

ZAGORA (PILIO) Pétros Lándis
Plateía Agíou Georgíou, 370 01 **Tel** *24260 23666*   **Road Map** *C3*

Just off the cobbled path leading up from the square, this long-running taverna claims to be open all day every day. Portions of goat in lemon sauce, sausage, grilled meats, *chórta* and various *píttes* may be on the small side, but views over the church and its belfry to the Sporádes islands provide ample compensation. Open all year.

NORTHERN GREECE

ALEXANDROUPOLI To Nisiótiko
G. Zarífi 1, 681 00 **Tel** *25510 20990*   **Road Map** *E1*

It is worth heading 400 m (quarter of a mile) west of the ferry dock and train station area, with their overpriced tavernas, to this seafood specialist with its nautical decor. Besides the usual grilled, fried and raw scaly fish and shellfish, they serve a dill-flavoured seafood risotto. Open all year.

KASTORIA Krontíri
Orestiádos 13, Doultsó district, 521 00 **Tel** *24670 28358*   **Road Map** *B2*

This *mezedopoleío* would be popular just for its lakeside setting, with tables at the shoreline (as well as indoors during winter). But what draws crowds is its impeccable cuisine based largely on local recipies – such as pickled-cabbage *ntolamádes*, pork and cheese in a clay pot, or veal with plums.

KAVALA Elia
Batis beach, 653 02 **Tel** *25102 43181*   **Road Map** *D1*

Located on Batis beach, 4 km (2 miles) west of Kavála city centre, Elia is a charming eatery serving modern Greek fare. Dishes, including meat and seafood options and colourful salads, are served at whitewashed tables overlooking the sea. Relax and enjoy the view with a glass of wine or *tsípouro*.

KAVALA Pános Zafíra
Plateía Karaóli ke Dimitríou 20, 653 02 **Tel** *25102 27978*   **Road Map** *D1*

Tavernas on this harbourside have a reputation for being touristy and overpriced, but Pános Zafíra provides fresh fish and a wide range of casserole dishes – *pastítsio* (macaroni pie), aubergine (eggplant) recipes, stews – to discerning locals and those waiting for an afternoon or late-night ferry.

KOMOTINI To Petrino
Serron 25, 691 00 **Tel** *25310 73650*   **Road Map** *E1*

Housed in a former municipal building dating from 1908, To Petrino has a traditionally decorated dining room where a wide range of Greek specialities are served. The fresh fish and seafood dishes, in particular, are worth trying, accompanied by a perfectly dressed salad. Open 10am–2pm.

LITOCHORO Gastrodromío en Olympo
Agiou Nikolau, 602 00 **Tel** *23520 21300*   **Road Map** *C2*

Most tavernas in Litóchoro, used to a stream of visitors heading quickly through town en route to the mountain, don't make a special effort; Gastrodromeo does, with good renditions of suckling pig and rabbit stew, plus a decent wine list – at a price.

PRESPA REGION, PSARADES VILLAGE Syntrofía
Village centre, 530 77 **Tel** *23850 46107*   **Road Map** *B1*

Syntrofía offers home-made dishes such as *fasoláda* (bean soup) made from the famous Préspa beans, fried fish of a species found only in the lake here, and the proprietor's own wine. If you're especially taken with the place, there are simple rooms to rent upstairs.

THESSALONIKI I Myrovólos Smýrni
Komninón 32, 546 24 **Tel** *23102 74170*   **Road Map** *C2*

The most popular of several *ouzerís* near the west entrance of the Modiáno (covered market), I Myrovólos Smýrni serves market stallholders and manual labourers early on, office workers for lunch, and students and young people at night. Try the cheese-stuffed squid, Smyrniot meatballs or scallops, washed down with *tsípouro* or wine.

THESSALONIKI Ta Koumparákia
Egnatía 140, 546 22 **Tel** *23102 71905*   **Road Map** *C2*

Hiding inconspicuously in a pedestrian zone behind the Byzantine church of the Transfiguration, this little *ouzeri* offers an array of Macedonian-style cuisine, including some spicy dishes and *tursí* (pickled vegetables), as well as the more usual salads, grills and meat dishes. Closed Sun dinner; Mon.

Key to Price Guide *see p284* **Key to Symbols** *see back cover flap*

THESSALONIKI Tiffany's

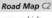

€

Iktínou 3, 546 22 **Tel** *23102 74081 or 23102 74022*

Road Map *C2*

Long-running meat specialist with a loyal local clientele drawn by the consistent quality of its classic menu, which includes such favourites as T-bone steak, veal with okra and aubergine (eggplant) *bourekákia* (turnovers). There are outdoor tables in the pedestrian lane here.

THESSALONIKI Tsaroúchas

€

Olýmbou 78, 546 46 **Tel** *23102 71621*

Road Map *C2*

This is one of the oldest and best of the city's *patsatzídika* (restaurants specializing in tripe-and-trotter soup – the classic Greek hangover cure). There are other choices for the squeamish, as well as Anatolian sweets such as *kazandibí* (upside-down baked pudding). Closed mid-Jul–mid-Aug.

THESSALONIKI Aristotélous

€€

Aristotélous 8, 546 23 **Tel** *23102 33195*

Road Map *C2*

This is a classic, long-running *ouzerí* with two arcaded salons separated by a summer courtyard dotted with marble-top tables. The fare is strong on seafood such as *mydopílafo* (rice with mussels), stuffed cuttlefish, and *galéos skordaliá* (small shark with garlic sauce). Closed mid-Jul–mid-Aug.

THESSALONIKI Kamares

€€

Plateía Agíou Georgíou 11 **Tel** *23102 19686*

Road Map *C2*

Located close to the Roman-Byzantine *Rotónda*, this neighbourhood favourite offers salads, attractively priced seafood and a few meat grills, accompanied by white wine from Limnos. In summer Kamares has seating beside the little park. Booking recommended.

THESSALONIKI Kitchen Bar

€€

B' Port Depot, 546 27 **Tel** *23105 02241*

Road Map *C2*

Sitting on the jetty of the town's harbour, this eatery occupies a restored warehouse with views of Thessaloniki's famous White Tower. Expect Mediterranean cuisine, with an emphasis on barbecued meat and fish dishes. The open-plan kitchen means you can watch the chefs at work.

THESSALONIKI Louloudádika

€€

Komninón 20, 546 24 **Tel** *23102 25624*

Road Map *C2*

The name comes from this *ouzerí*'s location in the flower market, opposite the former Jewish women's baths. The decor is smart, with cheerfully painted walls and proper tablecloths and the fare is strong on seafood, includes cuttlefish, fresh scaly fish and humbler items such as bean soup and barrelled wine. Closed Sun dinner.

THESSALONIKI To Yedí

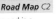

€€

Paparéska 13, Áno Póli **Tel** *23102 46495*

Road Map *C2*

At the top of the old town, just below the Yedi Kule citadel, this popular *ouzerí* has a variable menu offering mainland dishes such as cabbage *ntolmádes*, Piliot *spetzofáï* and clay-pot casseroles. House *ouzo*, *tsípouro* or *retsína* is the norm, though there is also bottled wine. Spontaneous music sessions on *bouzoúki* and *baglamás*.

THESSALONIKI Vrotós

€€

Metropolítou Gennadíou 6, off Plateía Áthonos, 546 30 **Tel** *23102 23958*

Road Map *C2*

Around the millennium Plateía Áthonos became the focus of a restaurant/*ouzerí* boom. Vrotós is one of the best and most popular, with something for everyone: vegetable dishes with or without cheese, meat, seafood, and a good wine list. Narrow indoor premises; reservations recommended in the cooler months. Closed Sun.

THESSALONIKI Yiannis Fish Tavern

€€

Kountouriotí 25, Néa Kríni suburb **Tel** *23104 45758*

Road Map *C2*

Originally opened by the head of the family Yiannis, this family-run taverna is now run by his two sons and is a firm favourite with the locals. It specializes in fish and always has a wide range of fresh fish dishes to choose from. Open all year.

THESSALONIKI Ta Nisiá

€€€

Proxénou Koromilá 13, 546 23 **Tel** *23210 22447*

Road Map *C2*

Open since 1981, this upscale restaurant purveys a balanced mix of scaly fish, shellfish and meat recipes. Typical platters include *kakaviá* (fish soup), stewed octopus, roast pork in wine sauce and creative desserts. The wine list is unusually comprehensive. Pleasant interior, with island colours and decor. Closed Sun; Aug.

THESSALONIKI Zythos Dore

€€€

Tsirogiánni 7, by White Tower, 546 21 **Tel** *23102 79010*

Road Map *C2*

More or less opposite the White Tower, Zythos Dore combines retro decor – marble tables, floor tiles, ceiling fans – with contemporary Greek and Continental recipes. There are lots of choices for vegetarians (vegetable soup, lentil/bean salad) as well as plenty of meat and game dishes and a wide range of bottled and barrel beer. Book ahead at weekends.

XANTHI Ta Fanarakia

€

Georgíou Stávrou 14, 671 00 **Tel** *25410 73606*

Road Map *E1*

The student population of the local University of Thrace guarantees a wide choice of *ouzerís* in the old quarter, especially along this pedestrianized street. The menu is written in school copybooks and the stock trade is Turkish-influenced meat platters as well as *pansétta* (pork spare ribs). Occasional improvised music nights in winter.

SHOPPING IN GREECE

Shopping in Greece can be entertaining, particularly when you buy directly from the producer. There is a wide range of shops and boutiques, as well as corner stores and department stores. Markets provide a colourful shopping experience, whether you are looking for olives, sugary sweets or traditional handicrafts. In smaller villages, embroiderers, lace makers and potters can often be seen at work. Leather goods, carpets, rugs and jewellery are also widely available, as are religious icons. Most other goods in Greece have been imported and carry a heavy mark-up. For information on shopping in Athens see pages 114–17.

VAT AND TAX-FREE SHOPPING

Almost always included in the price, FPA *(Fóros Prostithe-ménis Axías)* – the equivalent of VAT – is about 23 per cent in Greece.

Visitors from outside the EU who stay less than three months may claim this money back on purchases over €120. A "Tax-Free Cheque" form must be completed in the shop, a copy of which is then given to the customs authorities on departure. You may be asked to show your receipt or goods as proof of purchase.

Tax-free shop symbol

OPENING HOURS

Allowing for plenty of exceptions, shops and boutiques are generally open on Monday, Wednesday and Saturday from 9am to 2:30pm, and on Tuesday, Thursday and Friday from 9am to 1:30pm and 5 to 9pm. Department stores remain open Monday to Friday from 9am to 9pm and Saturday from 9am to 6pm. Supermarkets, found in all but the smallest communities, are often family-run and open long hours, typically Monday to Saturday from 8 or 9am to 8 or 9pm. Sunday shopping is possible in most tourist resorts and also in some of the suburban shopping malls in Athens. The corner *períptero* (street kiosk), found in nearly every town, is open from around 7am to 11pm or midnight, selling everything from aspirins to ice cream, as well as bus tickets and phonecards.

MARKETS

Most towns in Greece have their weekly street market *(laïkí agorá)*, a colourful selection of fresh fruit and vegetables, herbs, fish, meat and poultry – often juxtaposed with shoes and underwear, fabrics, household items and sundry electronic equipment. In the larger cities, the street markets are in a different area each day, usually opening early and packing up by about 2pm, in time for the siesta. Prices are generally cheaper than in the supermarkets, and a certain amount of bargaining is also acceptable, at least for non-perishables. This guide gives market days in the information under each town entry.

In Athens, there is a famous Sunday-morning flea market that is held around Plateía Monastirakíou and its radiating streets, which should not be missed if you are in the city *(see p87)*.

"Brettos" distillery and liquor store, in Athens

FOOD AND DRINK

Culinary delights to look out for in Greece include honey – the best varieties coming from the mountain villages – a wide selection of cured olives, high quality olive oil, and fresh and dried herbs and spices. A great selection of nuts is also available, including pistachios, hazelnuts and sunflower seeds.

The famous Greek feta cheese is widely available, and delicious in a salad or with rustic bread. The sweet breads and biscuits of the *zacharoplasteío* (cake and pastry shop) are another must. Sweetened with honey and syrup, Greek pastries are mouthwateringly good.

Greece is also renowned for several alcoholic drinks, including *oúzo* (an aniseed-flavoured spirit), *retsína* (a resinated wine), brandy, the firewater *tsípouro* and *rakí* (a type of distilled wine).

Souvenir shop window in Párga, central Greece

What to Buy in Greece

Traditional handicrafts, though not particularly cheap, do offer the most genuinely Greek souvenirs. Handicrafts cover a range of items from finely wrought gold reproductions of ancient pendants to rustic pots, wooden spoons and handmade sandals. Some of the country's best ceramics can be found in the markets and shops of Athens' northern suburb, Maroúsi. Brightly coloured embroidery and wall-hangings are produced in many villages throughout Greece, where they are often seen hanging out for

Rugs for sale at Aráchova

sale, along with thick *flokáti* rugs, which are handwoven from sheep or goat's wool. These are made mainly in the Píndos Mountains and can also be found at Aráchova, near Delphi *(see p221)*. In the small, rural communities, crafts are often cottage industries, earning the family a large chunk of its annual income. Here, there is room to engage in some bartering over the price. The *Shopping in Athens* section, on pages 114–17, indicates places within the capital where traditional crafts may be bought.

Gold jewellery *is sold in larger towns or cities. Modern designs are found in jewellers such as Lalaounis, and reproductions of ancient designs in museum gift shops.*

Icons *are generally sold in shops and monasteries. They range from very small portraits to substantial pictures. Some of the most beautiful, and expensive, use only age-old traditional techniques and materials.*

Ornate utensils, *such as these wooden spoons, are found in traditional craft shops. As here, they are often hand-carved into the shapes of figures and produced from the rich-textured wood of the native olive tree.*

Kombolói, *or worry beads, are a traditional sight in Greece; the beads are counted as a way to relax. They are sold in souvenir shops and jewellers.*

Kitchenware *is found in most markets and in specialist shops. This copper coffee pot (mpríki) is used for making Greek coffee.*

Leather goods *are sold throughout Greece. The bags, backpacks and sandals make useful and good-value souvenirs.*

Ornamental ceramics *come in many shapes and finishes. Traditional earthenware, often simple, functional and unglazed, is frequently for sale by the roads on the outskirts of Athens and the larger towns.*

SPECIALIST HOLIDAYS AND OUTDOOR ACTIVITIES

Many organized tours and courses cater for the special interests of visitors to Greece. You can follow in the footsteps of the apostle Paul or take a train ride through history; you can visit ancient archaeological sites with a learned academic as your guide, sample Greek wine, improve your

White-water rafting

writing skills, draw wild flowers or paint the Greek landscape. Sailing and windsurfing holidays are available, as are walking tours and botanical and birdwatching expeditions. There are also plenty of opportunities to watch sporting events. Many organized holidays include food and accommodation in the price.

A scenic railway journey through the Greek countryside

ARCHAEOLOGICAL TOURS

For those interested in Greece's ancient past, a tour to some of the famous archaeological sites can make a fascinating and memorable holiday. You can choose from an array of destinations and itineraries, all guided by qualified archaeologists. As well as visiting ancient ruins, many tours also take in Venetian fortresses, Byzantine churches and frescoes, museums and monasteries

An archaeological guided tour

en route to the archaeological sites. **Andante Travels** runs specialist tours guided by archaeologists, while **Ramblers Holidays**, **ACE Study Tours**, **Travelsphere** and **Martin Randall** all organize tours of Classical sites.

WRITING AND PAINTING

With its vivid landscape and renowned quality of light, Greece is an inspirational destination for artistic endeavour. Courses in creative writing or drawing and painting are available at all levels and are conducted by professional tutors, well established in their craft. **Greeka.com** offers a range of painting and drawing courses, as well as creative writing workshops.

WINE TASTING

The quality of Greek wine has increased enormously in recent years, with some vineyards winning international medals, a prospect that was unlikely a decade ago. A variety of tours of vineyards

around Athens are arranged by the wine tour specialists **Arblaster and Clarke**.

RAILWAY HOLIDAYS

The rail network in Greece is not extensive, nor is it used much by visitors, who tend to prefer the country's excellent bus system. It does, however, have one of the greatest railway journeys in Europe, on the narrow-gauge track to the mountain town of Kalávryta *(see p168)* from Diakoftó. A trip on this railway can be arranged as part of a larger Greek tour through **Great Rail Journeys** in the UK. **Ffestiniog Travel** also arranges tailor-made rail trips around Greece, going east as far as Alexandroúpoli *(see p257)*.

Beautiful spring wildflowers

NATURE TOURS

Much of the Greek countryside is rich in birdlife and noted for its spring flowers. The shorelines are also good for wildlife. Specialist tour operators, such as **Limosa Holidays**, **The Travelling Naturalist**, **Naturetrek** or **Sunbird**, offer package

A horse-riding holiday along the azure coast

holidays that guide visitors through the ornithology and botany of Northern Greece and the Peloponnese. The **Hellenic Ornithological Society** can also be contacted for advice on birdwatching in Greece.

WALKING AND CYCLING

Greece is a paradise for walkers, particularly in the spring when the countryside is at its greenest and the wild flowers are in bloom. The best locations are in the mountain ranges of the Taÿgetos in the Peloponnese *(see p195)* and the Píndos range in central Greece *(see p206)*, where **Sherpa Expeditions** has both guided and self-guided tours. **Trekking Hellas** arranges walking holidays in these regions as well as tours to the remote mountain areas of Agrafa and Stereá, offering a harsh landscape to explore at the southern end of the Píndos range. **Exodus** offers a similar service in these and other regions, using its own hiking leaders and tour guides.

Greek Options includes walking holidays in the Máni, based in the resort of Stoúpa *(see p195)* and organized by a local travel agent. The Máni also features in the **Inntravel** programme of walking holidays, as does the Pílio peninsula *(see pp218–20)*.

Travelsphere offers a week's trekking in Chalkidikí *(see p249)*, while walking and cycling trips in and around Athens, using a local company, can be booked through **Hidden Greece**. **Bikegreece** offers coast to coast cycling tours that are suitable for

all abilities and can also arrange tailor-made holidays for families.

Downhill skiing on Mount Parnassus

RIDING

The Pílio peninsula *(see pp218-20)*, home to the legendary Centaurs – half-man and half-horse – is an ideal place for a riding holiday. **Ride World Wide** offers two different riding itineraries. One follows a coastal route, while the other takes you into the lushly wooded hills of this unspoiled corner of Greece.

SKIING

There are several ski centres throughout the mainland, including some within easy reach of Athens – the closest being Mount Parnassus, near Delphi *(see p221)*. Depending on snow conditions, the season runs from the start of January to the end of April.

Costs are low compared with other European resorts, though facilities are quite basic. However, the Greek mountain resorts certainly provide an interesting alternative to the all-too-familiar names elsewhere in southern Europe.

For more information on skiing in Greece, contact the **Hellenic Skiing Federation**, or pick up a copy of the EOT's booklet entitled *Mountain Refuges and Ski Centres*; it is free from tourist offices and describes all the major ski centres.

WATERSPORTS

All along Greece's coastline, facilities for watersports are numerous. Visitors will find everything from windsurfing and water-skiing to jet-skiing and parasailing in the larger resorts, and many of the shops and beach huts that rent equipment also offer instruction. Kayaking, white-water rafting and canoeing holidays are organized by **Trekking Hellas**. Canoeing and rafting trips on the Gulf of Corinth near Pátra can also be booked through **Hidden Greece**.

Windsurfing in the Peloponnese

SNORKELLING AND SCUBA DIVING

The amazingly clear waters of the Mediterranean reveal a world of submarine life and archaeological remains. Snorkelling can be enjoyed almost anywhere along the coast, though scuba diving is restricted due to many submerged ancient artifacts. Greece is highly protective of its antiquities, and it is forbidden to remove them, or even to photograph them. The law is quite strict, so make sure you go with a reputable company.

A list of places where oxygen equipment may be used is available from the Greek National Tourism Organization (GNTO) *(see p307)*. The Athens-based **Aegean Dive Centre** organizes diving trips along the Attica coast, and tuition is available for those with no previous diving experience.

Scuba diver exploring the submarine life

SAILING HOLIDAYS

Sailing holidays can be booked through charter companies either in Greece or abroad. The season runs from April to late October, and itineraries range from a few days to several weeks.

Charters fall into four main categories. Bareboat charter,

A sailboat under power along the Corinth Canal in the Peloponnese *(see p167)*

without a skipper or crew, is available to anyone with sailing experience (most companies require at least two crew members to have a basic skipper's licence). Crewed charters range from the services of a paid skipper, assistant or cook to fully crewed yachts with every imaginable luxury. Chartering a yacht as part of a flotilla – typically in a group of six to 12 yachts – provides the opportunity for independent sailing with the support of a lead boat contactable by radio. **Sunsail** and **Thomas Cook** offer this kind of holiday, as well as holidays that mix cruiser sailing with shore-based dinghy sailing and windsurfing. Contact the **Hellenic Sailing Federation** for more information.

CRUISES AND BOAT TRIPS

Running from April to October, cruise options range from the luxury of a large liner or handsome tall sailing ship to inexpensive mini-cruises and boat trips. The former can be booked through the big operators such as **Swan Hellenic**, **Sunvil** or **Voyages of Discovery**, while the tall ships belong to **Star Clippers**. Mini-cruises and boat trips can be organized locally and are best booked through **Ghiolman Yachts** or at a travel

agent on the spot. For a listing of cruise companies sailing to Greece, visit the Passenger Shipping Association website (www.discover-cruises.co.uk).

A luxury cruise ship

SPAS

The Greek mainland is not as well served with spas as some of the islands, such as Crete and Santoríni, but several of the resort hotels on Chalkidikí *(see p249)* do have excellent facilities. Many tour operators feature them, including **Seasons** in the UK.

UNUSUAL ACTIVITIES

Not everyone wants to do a bungee-jump into the Corinth Canal, but for those who do, it can be arranged. The tour operator **Hidden Greece** specializes in finding places off the beaten track and also offers unusual activities. In addition to the bungee-jump they can book you two actor-guides in character as citizens from 460 BC to take you on a tour around Athens.

DIRECTORY

ARCHAEOLOGICAL TOURS

ACE Study Tours
Babraham, Cambridge,
CB22 3AP, UK.
Tel 01223 841 055.
www.acestudytours.co.uk

Andante Travels
The Old Barn, Old Road,
Alderbury, Salisbury,
SP5 3AR, UK.
Tel 01722 713800.
www.andantetravels.
co.uk

Martin Randall
Voysey House,
Barley Mow Passage,
London W4 4GF, UK.
Tel 020 8742 3355.
www.martinrandall.com

Ramblers Holidays
Lemsford Mill, Lemsford
Village, Welwyn Garden
City, Herts, AL8 7TR, UK.
Tel 01707 331133.
www.ramblersholidays.
co.uk

Travelsphere
Compass House,
Rockingham Road, Market
Harborough, Leicestershire,
LE16 7QD, UK.
Tel 0844 567 9966.
www.travelsphere.co.uk

WRITING AND PAINTING

Greeka.com
Makrigianni 26A, 18537
Piraeus. *Tel* 210 4526
900. www.greeka.com

WINE TASTING

Arblaster and Clarke Wine Tours
Cedar Court, 5 College
Street, Petersfield, Hamp-
shire, GU31 4AE, UK.
Tel 01730 263111.
www.winetours.co.uk

RAILWAY HOLIDAYS

Ffestiniog Travel
First Floor, Unit 6,
Snowdonia Business Park,
Penrhyndeudraeth,
Gwynedd, LL48 6LD, UK.
Tel 01766 772 030.
www.festtravel.co.uk

Great Rail Journeys
Saviour House,
9 St Saviourgate,
York, YO1 8NL, UK.
Tel 01904 521936.
www.greatrail.com

NATURE TOURS

Hellenic Ornith-ological Society
Vasileos Irakleiou 24,
10682 Athens.
Tel 210 822 7937.
www.ornithologiki.gr

Limosa Holidays
West End Farmhouse,
Chapel Field, Stalham,
Norfolk, NR12 9EJ, UK.
www.limosaholidays.
co.uk

Naturetrek
Cheriton Mill,
Cheriton, Alresford,
Hants, SO24 0NG, UK.
Tel 01962 733051.
www.naturetrek.co.uk

Sunbird
26B Market Sq, Potton,
Bedfordshire, SG19 1DF,
UK. *Tel* 01767 262522.
www.sunbirdtours.co.uk

The Travelling Naturalist
PO Box 3141, Dorchester,
Dorset, DT1 2XD, UK.
Tel 01305 267994.
www.naturalist.co.uk

WALKING AND CYCLING

Bikegreece
Karaiskáki 13,
10554 Athens.
Tel 210 453 5567.
www.bikegreece.com

Exodus
Grange Mills, Weir Road,
London, SW12 ONE, UK.
Tel 020 8675 5550.
www.exodus.co.uk

Greek Options
26 High Street, Tring,
Herts, HP23 5AH, UK.
Tel 0844 800 4787.
www.greekoptions.co.uk

Hidden Greece
10 Upper Square, Old
Isleworth, TW7 7BJ, UK.
Tel 020 8758 4707.
www.hiddengreece.co.uk

Inntravel
Whitwell Grange, York,
YO60 7JU, UK.
Tel 01653 617 001.
www.inntravel.co.uk

Sherpa Expeditions
131a Heston Road,
Hounslow, Middlesex,
TW5 0RF, UK.
Tel 020 8577 2717.
www.sherpa-walking-
holidays.co.uk

Travelsphere
See Archaeological Tours.

Trekking Hellas
Saripolou 10, 10682
Athens. *Tel* 210 331
0323. www.trekking.gr

RIDING

Ride World Wide
Staddon Farm,
North Tawton, Devon,
EX20 2BX, UK.
Tel 01837 82544.
www.rideworldwide.
co.uk

SKIING

Hellenic Skiing Federation
Karagiórgi Servías 7,
10563 Athens
Tel 210 323 0182.
www.eox.gr

WATERSPORTS

Hidden Greece
See Walking and Cycling.

Trekking Hellas
See Walking and Cycling.

SCUBA AND SNORKELLING

Aegean Dive Centre
Zamanou 53 & Pandoras
Glyfáda, 16674 Athens.
Tel 210 894 5409.
www.adc.gr

SAILING HOLIDAYS

Hellenic Sailing Federation
Naftathlitiki Marina,
78550 Kallithea.
Tel 210 940 4825.
www.eio.gr

Sunsail
TUI Travel House, Crawley
Business Quarter, Fleming
Way, Crawley, West
Sussex RH10 9QL, UK.
Tel 0141 586 800.
www.sunsail.eu

Thomas Cook
The Thomas Cook
Headquarters, London
WC2E 7EN, UK.
Tel 0844 895 0045.
www.thomascook.com

CRUISES AND BOAT TRIPS

Ghiolman Yachts
8 Propileon St, Acropolis,
Athens. *Tel* 210 325
5000.

Star Clippers
Olympus House, 2
Olympus Close, Ipswich,
Suffolk, IP1 5LN, UK.
Tel 0845 200 6145.
www.starclippers.co.uk

Sunvil
Upper Square,
Old Isleworth, Middlesex,
TW7 7BJ, UK.
Tel 020 8568 4499.
www.sunvil.co.uk

Swan Hellenic Cruises
Lynnem House, 1 Victoria
Way, Burgess Hill, West
Sussex, RH15 9NF, UK.
Tel 0844 488 1046.
www.swanhellenic.com

Voyages of Discovery
Lynnem House,
1 Victoria Way,
Burgess Hill, West Sussex,
RH15 9NF.
Tel 0844 822 0802.
www.voyagesof
discovery.co.uk

SPAS

Seasons
Lakeside, St David's Park,
Nr Chester, CH5 3YE, UK.
Tel 01244 202002.
www.seasons.co.uk

UNUSUAL ACTIVITIES

Hidden Greece
See Walking and Cycling.

SURVIVAL GUIDE

PRACTICAL INFORMATION

Greece's appeal is both cultural and hedonistic. The country's physical beauty, hot climate and warm seas, together with the easy-going outlook of its people, are all conducive to a relaxing holiday. It does pay, however, to know something about the nuts and bolts of Greek life – when to visit, what to bring, how to get around and what to do if things

The GNTO's Greek tourism emblem

go wrong – to avoid unnecessary frustrations. Greece is no longer the cheap holiday destination it once was, though public transport, vehicle hire, eating out and hotel accommodation are still fairly inexpensive compared to most west European countries. The many tourist offices *(see p307)* offer information on all the practical aspects of your stay.

Boats sailing near the Greek coast in high summer

WHEN TO GO

High season – July and August – is the hottest *(see p49)* and most expensive time to visit Greece; it is also very crowded on the coast. December to March are the coldest and wettest months, with many hotels and restaurants closed for the winter.

Skiing in Greece is possible from January to April, with around 20 mainland resorts to choose from *(see p299)*.

Spring (late Apr–May) is one of the loveliest times to visit – the weather is sunny but not debilitatingly hot, there are relatively few tourists about, and the countryside is ablaze with brightly coloured wild flowers *(see pp22–3)*.

VISAS AND PASSPORTS

Visitors from EU countries need a valid passport or ID card to enter Greece and do not need a visa. Some non-EU citizens such as those from the US, Canada, Australia and New Zealand, do not need a visa, but do need a valid

passport for a stay of up to 90 days (there is no maximum stay for EU visitors). For longer stays, a resident's permit must be obtained from the **Aliens' Bureau** in Athens or the local police. Visitors should check visa requirements with a Greek embassy before travelling.

Any non-EU citizen planning to work or study in Greece should contact their local Greek consulate about visas and work permits.

CUSTOMS INFORMATION

EU residents can import alcohol, perfumes and tobacco without limits so long as they are for personal use. Visitors entering Greece from non-EU countries should check the following website for details of quantities that they can import free of charge: http://greece.visahq.com/customs.

Note also that the unauthorized export of antiquities and archaeological artifacts from Greece is a serious offence, with strong penalties ranging from hefty fines to prison sentences.

Any prescription drugs that are brought into the country should be accompanied by a copy of the prescription *(see pp308–9)*.

TOURIST INFORMATION

Tourist information is available in many towns and villages in the form of government-run EOT offices (*Ellinikós Organismós Tourismoú*, also often referred to as **Greek National Tourism Organization, GNTO**), municipal tourist offices, the local tourist police *(see p308)* or travel agencies. Many of these offices operate only in summer. The GNTO publishes an array of tourist literature and brochures, but be aware that not all of this information is always up to date or reliable.

The addresses and phone numbers of the GNTO and municipal tourist offices are listed throughout this guide. A list of major Greek festivals and cultural events is given on pages 44–8, but it is also worth asking your nearest tourist office about what's happening locally.

Getting information at a City of Athens infopoint

◁ The attractive harbour of Paralía Ástros, south of Náfplio

EAM 1630336   ΕΥΡΩ **7** ΕΥRΟ
    ΕΝΤRΑΝCΕ ΤΙCΚΕΤ

Ticket for the National Archaeological Museum

ADMISSION PRICES

Most state-run museums and archaeological sites charge an entrance fee of €3–€12. However, visitors aged 18 or under from EU countries are entitled to free admission, as are EU travellers carrying an International Student Identity Card (ISIC) (see p306). Reductions of around 25 per cent are granted to EU citizens aged 65 and over (use your passport as proof of age), and reductions of 50 per cent to non-EU students armed with an ISIC card.

Though most museums and sites are closed on public holidays (see p48), the ones that do stay open are free of charge. Admission to all state-run museums and archaeological sites is free on Sundays between November and April.

OPENING HOURS

Opening hours tend to be vague in Greece, varying from day to day, season to season and place to place. In addition to this, the financial crisis that the country has been experiencing since 2010 is having significant impact on many attractions, causing staff budget cuts and reduced opening hours. Although the opening times in this book have been checked at the time of going to print, they are likely to keep changing. It is advisable to use the times in this book as a rough guideline only and to check with local information centres before visiting a sight.

Most attractions usually close on Mondays and main public holidays. Small and private museums may be closed on local festival days in addition to main public holidays.

Monasteries and convents are open during daylight hours but will close for a few hours in the afternoon.

Most shops and offices are also closed on public holidays and local festival days, with the exception of some shops in tourist resorts. The dates of major local festivals are included in the Visitors' Checklists in each main town entry in this guide.

SOCIAL CUSTOMS AND ETIQUETTE

For a carefree holiday in Greece, it is best to adopt the local philosophy: *sigá, sigá* ("slowly, slowly"). Within this principle is the ritual of the afternoon siesta, a practice that should be taken seriously, particularly during the hottest months, when it is almost a physiological necessity.

Like anywhere else, common courtesy and respect are appreciated in Greece, so try speaking a few words of the language, even if your vocabulary covers only the basics (see pp348–52).

Though formal attire is rarely needed, modest clothing (trousers for men and skirts for women) is de rigueur for churches and monasteries. Topless sunbathing is generally tolerated, but nude bathing is officially restricted only to a few designated beaches.

In restaurants, the service charge is always included in the bill, but tips are still appreciated – the custom is to leave around 10 per cent if you were satisfied with the service. Public toilet attendants should also be tipped. Taxi drivers do not expect tips, but they are not averse to them either; likewise, hotel porters and chambermaids.

In 2010, Greece introduced a law officially banning smoking in enclosed public spaces, including in restaurants, bars and cafés. An estimated forty per cent of Greeks smoke, and many ignore this law. Restaurant and café owners prefer to turn a blind eye to this, for fear of losing custom. Many bar staff smoke too. All the same, visitors should avoid smoking in enclosed public spaces; smoking in outdoor areas such as café terraces is permitted.

Note that Greek police will not tolerate rowdy or indecent behaviour, especially when fuelled by excessive alcohol consumption; Greek courts impose heavy fines or even prison sentences on people who behave indecently.

RELIGION

About 97 per cent of the population is Greek Orthodox. The symbols and rituals of the religion are deeply rooted in Greek culture, and they are visible everywhere. Saints' days are celebrated throughout Greece (see p48), sometimes on a local scale and sometimes across the entire country.

Greek Orthodox monasteries and churches, many dating back centuries, are among the country's top cultural attractions. Visitors to these sacred places should dress respectably (shoulders and legs covered for both men and women) and refrain from taking photographs (this is officially forbidden, though rules do vary).

A Greek priest

Regarding religious minorities, the largest group are the Muslims of Thrace, which constitute only about 1.2 per cent of the country's total population. Many immigrants from Muslim countries such as Bangladesh, Pakistan, Afghanistan and Somalia, as well as Albania, now live in Athens. In addition, there is a sizeable community of Roman Catholics, including ethnic Greeks and immigrants from Poland and the Philippines, who are catered for by the Roman Catholic Archdiocese of Athens.

Sign for disabled parking

TRAVELLERS WITH SPECIAL NEEDS

There are few facilities for the disabled in Greece, so careful advance planning is essential; sights that have wheelchair access will have a wheelchair symbol at the start of their entry in this guide. Organizations such as **Disability Rights UK** and **Tourism for All** are invaluable sources of information. Agencies such as **Accessible Travel and Leisure** and **Responsible Travel** arrange holidays specifically for disabled travellers.

Note that disabled visitors (with a person assisting them) are entitled to free entry to state-run museums and archaeological sites.

TRAVELLING WITH CHILDREN

Children are much loved by the Greeks and welcomed just about everywhere, including restaurants, where waiters will be happy to suggest special dishes for them. Baby-sitting facilities are provided by some hotels on request, but always check before booking. Some coastal resorts also have special amenities such as playgrounds, children's pools and even Kids' Clubs with organized activities.

Those aged 18 or under from EU countries enjoy free admission to state-run museums and archaeological sites, as do children aged 5 and under from non-EU countries. Concessions of up to 50 per cent are offered on most forms of public transport for children aged 10 and under (in some cases, 8 and under).

Swimming in the sea is generally safe for kids, but keep a close eye on them, as lifeguards are rare in Greece. Choose sandy beaches in sheltered bays with shallow water. Be aware of the hazards of overexposure to the sun and dehydration (see p309).

STUDENT AND YOUTH TRAVELLERS

Concessions are offered on train, metro and bus travel in Greece to students below the age of 25 with a valid **International Student Identity Card (ISIC)**. They may also need to show their passport. There are plenty of deals to be had getting to Greece, especially during low season. Agencies for student and youth travel include **STA Travel**. Before setting off, it is worth joining **Hostelling International** to enjoy discounts in Greek hostels. Most state-run museums and archaeological sites are free to EU students with a valid ISIC card; non-EU students with an ISIC card are usually entitled to a 50 per cent reduction.

An International Student Identity Card

There are no youth concessions available, but occasional discounts are possible with an International Youth Travel Card (IYTC), which can be obtained from any STA office by travellers under the age of 26.

WOMEN TRAVELLERS

Greece is by and large a very safe country, and local communities are generally welcoming. Foreign women travelling alone are usually treated with respect, especially if they are dressed modestly. Although local men openly display their interest in women, making it clear that you are not interested in them is usually enough to curtail any flirtation. Like elsewhere, hitchhiking alone in Greece carries potential risks and is not advisable.

TIME

Greece is 2 hours ahead of Britain, 1 hour ahead of countries on Central European Time (such as France and Italy), 7 hours ahead of New York, 10 hours ahead of Los Angeles and 8 hours behind Sydney.

Greece puts the clock forward to summertime, and back again to wintertime, on the same days as other EU countries, in order to avoid any confusion when travelling around Europe.

ELECTRICITY

Greece, like other European countries, runs on 220 volts/ 50 Hz AC. Plugs have two round pins (those for appliances that need to be earthed have three). The adaptors needed for British electrical appliances and the transformers for North American equipment are difficult to find in Greece, so bring one with you.

CONVERSION CHART

Greece uses the metric system, with two small exceptions: sea distances are expressed in nautical miles and land is measured in *strémmata*, the equivalent of about 0.1 ha (0.25 acre).

Kids enjoying the shallow waters at a sandy beach

Imperial to Metric
1 inch = 2.54 centimetres
1 foot = 30 centimetres
1 mile = 1.6 kilometres
1 ounce = 28 grams
1 pound = 454 grams
1 pint = 0.6 litres
1 gallon = 4.6 litres

Metric to Imperial
1 millimetre = 0.04 inches
1 centimetre = 0.4 inches
1 metre = 3 feet 3 inches
1 kilometre = 0.64 miles
1 gram = 0.04 ounces
1 kilogram = 2.2 pounds
1 litre = 1.8 pints

RESPONSIBLE TOURISM

Greece is lagging behind most EU countries in environmental awareness – recycling is scarcely practised, illegal dumping in rural areas is the norm, and waste management is a major problem.

However, there is much interest in renewable energy sources. Greece has great potential for developing solar energy – many families already have solar panels for heating water (they can sell the surplus to the National Grid), and there have been talks about producing solar power on a far larger scale. Wind energy is already used to some extent on the islands, but here too there is potential for further exploitation.

Agrotourism (working farms that offer accommodation and meals to visitors) is well established on the island of Crete and is being developed on the mainland too. Contact the **Hellenic Agrotourism Federation** or **Guest Inn** for a list of agrotourism establishments.

Visitors can support local communities by shopping for local produce at the Central Market in Athens *(see p117)* and Modiáno Market in Thessaloníki *(see p244)*, as well as the open-air street markets held weekly in various neighbourhoods of Athens. In some areas, you can buy local specialities directly from the producers – for example, formaella cheese in Araxova (near Delphi) and metsovone cheese in Metsovo – and visit vineyards for wine tastings and direct purchases.

Ethical tour operators include the UK-based **Responsible Travel** and the Athens-based **Trekking Hellas**; both run adventure sports packages including activities such as hiking, mountain biking, sea kayaking and rafting. The Athens-based **Ecotourism Greece** is a useful source of ideas for rural destinations, activities and small family-run hotels.

DIRECTORY

VISAS AND PASSPORTS

Aliens' Bureau
Petrou Ralli 24,
Tavros, Athens.
Tel 210 340 5828.

EMBASSIES

Australia
Level 6, Thon Building,
Kifissias & Alexandrias
Avenue, Ambelokipi,
11523 Athens.
Tel 210 870 4000.

Canada
Gennadíou 4,
11521 Athens.
Tel 210 727 3400.

Ireland
Vassiléos Konstantínou 7,
10674 Athens.
Tel 210 723 2771.

New Zealand (Consulate)
Kifissias 76, Ambelokipi,
11526 Athens.
Tel 210 692 4136.

United Kingdom
Ploutárchou 1,
10675 Athens.
Tel 210 727 2600.

United States
Vasilíssis Sofías 91,
10160 Athens.
Tel 210 721 2951.

TOURIST INFORMATION OFFICES

Greek National Tourism Organization (GNTO)
Head office:
Tsoha 7, 11521 Athens.
Tel 210 870 7000.
www.visitgreece.gr
Information centre:
Dionysiou Areopagitou
18–20, 11742 Athens.
Tel 210 331 0529.

GNTO Australia and New Zealand
Underwood House,
Suite 307, 37–49 Pitt St,
Sydney, NSW 2000.
Tel (2) 9241 1663.

GNTO United Kingdom and Ireland
4 Conduit St,
London W1S 2DJ.
Tel 020 7495 9300.

GNTO USA
305 E 47th Street, New
York, New York 10017.
Tel (1212) 421-5777.

TRAVELLERS WITH SPECIAL NEEDS

Accessible Travel and Leisure
Tel 01452 729 739.
www.accessibletravel.co.uk

Disability Rights UK
Tel 020 7250 3222.
www.radar.org.uk

Responsible Travel
Tel 01273 600 030.
www.responsibletravel.com

Tourism for All
Tel 0303 303 0146.
www.tourismforall.org.uk

STUDENT TRAVELLERS

Hostelling International
2nd Floor, Gate House,
Fretherne Road,
Welwyn Garden City,
Herts AL8 6RD.
Tel 01707 324 170.
www.hihostels.com

International Student Identity Card (ISIC)
www.isic.org

STA Travel
52 Grosvenor Gardens,
London SW1W 0AG.
Tel 0871 230 0040.
www.statravel.co.uk

RESPONSIBLE TOURISM

Ecotourism Greece
Tel 211 108 9998.
www.ecotourism-greece.com

Guest Inn
Tel 210 960 7100.
www.guestinn.com

Hellenic Agrotourism Federation (SEAGE)
Tel 693 650 0670.
www.agroxenia.net

Responsible Travel
Tel 01273 600 030.
www.responsibletravel.com

Trekking Hellas
Tel 210 331 0323.
www.trekking.gr

Personal Health and Security

Strikes and protest marches have always been regular features of Greek life. However, the rise in unemployment and in the cost of living caused by the ongoing economic crisis have led to higher levels of public unrest. Despite this, Greece remains a safe country to visit, although it is best to avoid protest marches and demonstrations, which can turn violent – especially in Athens, and most notably on Sýntagma Square, in front of the Greek Parliament. Crime is rare outside Athens, where the biggest danger is the road – Greece has one of the highest accident rates in Europe. Considerable caution is recommended, for both drivers and pedestrians.

Fire service emblem

POLICE

Regular Greek police officers wear blue uniforms and keep a relatively low profile. However, there are several special units, the most conspicuous being the riot police (MAT), who wear a khaki military-type uniform and a helmet with a visor. The MAT are usually only seen at unruly demonstrations.

In addition, there are the tourist police, who combine normal police duties with dispensing advice to tourists. Tourist police wear a cap with a white band, a white belt and white gloves, as well as a badge saying "Tourist Police" on their shirt. Should you suffer a theft, lose your passport or have cause to complain about restaurants, shops, taxi drivers or tour guides, your case should first be made to them. Every tourist police officer speaks several languages and each office claims to have at least one English speaker, so they can also act as interpreters if the case needs to involve the local police.

WHAT TO BE AWARE OF

Most crime-related problems centre on Athens. Crime levels outside large cities are low. Visitors are advised to avoid public demonstrations, in particular those in Athens' Sýntagma Square, which have become increasingly violent due to widespread public discontent. There has also been a rise in street muggings, especially around Omónoia Square, which is a gathering point for drug addicts, the homeless and other communities on the margins of society. Burglaries have also become more common than they once were.

Visitors should take sensible precautions such as keeping an eye on their bags in public, especially in crowded places, and keeping important documents and valuables in the hotel safe. If you do have anything stolen, contact the police or tourist police.

IN AN EMERGENCY

In case of emergencies, the appropriate services to call are listed in the directory on the opposite page. For accidents and other medical emergencies, a 24-hour ambulance service operates within Athens. Outside the capital, in rural towns and on the islands, it is unlikely that ambulances will be on 24-hour call. If necessary, patients can be transferred from local ESY (Greek National Health Service) hospitals or surgeries to a main ESY hospital in Athens by ambulance or helicopter.

A complete list of ESY hospitals, private hospitals and clinics is available from the tourist police.

HOSPITALS AND PHARMACIES

Emergency medical care in Greece is free for all EU citizens in possession of a European Health Insurance Card (EHIC), available from main post offices. For minor health problems, go to an IKA (Social Security Institute) polyclinic. All the main hospitals are in Athens, so if you have more serious issues, you will probably need to be taken to the capital. Also in Athens, **SOS Doctors** is a service that carries out emergency home visits for a fee. Public hospitals are often understaffed, and it is not unusual for relatives to help feed and provide basic nursing care for patients. Note that corruption is rife within the Greek healthcare system, and it is considered perfectly normal to offer doctors under-the-table payments for priority treatment.

Greek pharmacists are highly qualified and can not only advise on minor

Greek police officers wearing typical blue uniforms

Ambulance

Police car

ailments, but also dispense medication not usually available over the counter back home. Their premises, *farmakeía*, are identified by a green cross on a white background. Pharmacies are open from 8:30am to 2pm Monday to Friday, and they are usually closed in the afternoon and at weekends. However, in larger towns, a rota system is usually in place to maintain a daily service from morning to night. Details of on-duty pharmacies are posted in pharmacy windows.

Be sure to bring an adequate supply of any medication you may need while away, as well as a copy of the prescription with the generic name of the drug – this is useful not only in case you run out, but also for the purposes of customs when you enter the country.

Several international pharmaceutical companies have stopped selling to Greece due to delayed payments, so some drugs are now in short supply. Also be aware that codeine, a painkiller commonly found in headache tablets, is illegal in Greece.

MINOR HAZARDS

The most obvious thing to avoid is overexposure to the sun, particularly for the fair-skinned: always wear a hat and good-quality sunglasses, as well as a high-factor suntan lotion. Heat stroke is a real

Pharmacy sign

hazard for which medical attention should be sought immediately; heat exhaustion and dehydration are also serious. Be sure to drink plenty of water, even if you don't feel thirsty; if in any doubt, invest in a packet of electrolyte tablets (a mixture of potassium salts and glucose) to replace lost minerals. These are available at any pharmacy.

Tap water in Greece is generally safe to drink, but in remote communities it is a good precaution to check with the locals. Bottled spring water, for sale in shops and kiosks, is reasonably priced and often has the advantage of being chilled.

When swimming in the sea, hazards to be aware of are weaver fish, jellyfish and sea urchins. The latter are not uncommon and are extremely unpleasant if trodden on. If you do tread on one, the spine will need to be extracted using olive oil and a sterilized needle. Jellyfish stings can be relieved by applying vinegar, baking soda or various remedies sold at Greek pharmacies to the affected area. The sand-dwelling weaver fish has a powerful sting, its poison causing extreme pain. The immediate treatment is to immerse the affected area in very hot water to dilute the venom's strength.

No inoculations are required for visitors to Greece, though tetanus and typhoid boosters may be recommended by your doctor.

TRAVEL AND HEALTH INSURANCE

EU citizens should carry a European Health Insurance Card (EHIC) to receive free emergency medical care. Private medical insurance is needed for all other types of treatment. Visitors are strongly advised to take out comprehensive travel insurance – available from travel agents, banks and insurance brokers – covering both private medical treatment and loss or theft of personal possessions. Be sure to read the small print – not all policies, for instance, will cover you for activities of a "dangerous" nature, such as motorcycling and trekking; not all policies will pay for doctors' or hospital fees direct, and only some will cover you for ambulances and emergency flights home. Paying for your flight with a credit card such as VISA or American Express will provide limited travel insurance, including reimbursement of your air fare if the agent happens to go bankrupt.

DIRECTORY

COUNTRYWIDE EMERGENCY NUMBERS

Ambulance
Tel 166.

Coastguard patrol
Tel 108.

Emergencies
Tel 112.
www.sos112.info

Fire
Tel 199.

Police
Tel 100.

Road assistance
Tel 10400.

Tourist Police
Tel 171.

ATHENS EMERGENCY NUMBERS

Pharmacies
Tel 14944 (information on 24-hour pharmacies).

Poison treatment centre
Tel 210 779 3777.

SOS Doctors
Tel 1016.
www.sosiatroi.gr

Banking and Currency

Greece adopted the euro in 2002. Hit by the economic crisis of 2010, the country procured massive loans, but it soon emerged that it might be unable to repay them and therefore be forced to declare bankruptcy. In 2011, Greece's future within the Eurozone began to look uncertain. The impact of this situation on visitors remains to be seen. At the time of going to press, the economy had been stabilized thanks to yet more loans. Prices have risen, but the government may introduce tax exemptions in the tourism sector to encourage holiday-makers. If Greece did leave the Eurozone and readopt the drachma, foreign exchange rates would make the country a more competitive destination.

Visitors changing money at a foreign exchange bureau

BANKS AND BUREAUX DE CHANGE

Towns throughout Greece, as well as tourist resorts, have the usual banking facilities, including 24-hour cash machines (ATMs). Alternatively, you can change foreign currency and travellers' cheques into euros at a bureau de change. Some travel agents, hotels, tourist offices and car-hire agencies are also willing to do this. Always take your passport with you when cashing travellers' cheques, and check exchange rates and commission charges beforehand, since these vary greatly.

The main banks in the country are Ethniki Trapeza tis Ellados (National Bank of Greece), Alpha Bank, ATE Bank, Pireaus Bank, Emporiki Bank and Eurobank. Banks are open 8am–2pm Monday to Thursday and 8am–1:30pm on Friday. They are closed on public holidays *(see p48)* and may also be closed on any local festival days.

ATMS

Easily found in all Greek towns and resorts, ATMs can be used to withdraw cash using internationally recognized credit and debit cards. There has been a rise in ATM crime the world over, so exercise caution when using one, and always shield your PIN from passers-by.

CREDIT AND DEBIT CARDS

VISA, **MasterCard**, **American Express** and **Diners Club** are the most widely accepted credit cards in Greece. A credit card is the most convenient way to pay for air tickets, international ferry journeys, car hire, some hotels and large purchases. However, some small tavernas, shops and hotels do not take credit cards, so be sure to have cash with you when visiting these establishments.

A credit card can be used for drawing local currency at a cash machine. A 1.5 per cent processing charge is usually levied for VISA at banks and ATMs, but this does not apply to other cards. Cirrus and Plus debit card systems operate in Greece. Cash can be obtained using Cirrus at National Bank of Greece ATMs, and Plus at Commercial Bank ATMs. Be sure to tell your bank that you are travelling to Greece, so that your card is not blocked while you are away.

Travellers' cheques are the safest way to carry large sums of money. They are refundable if lost or stolen, though the process can be time-consuming. American Express and VISA are the best-known brands of travellers' cheques in Greece.

DIRECTORY

LOST CREDIT CARDS

American Express
Tel 00 44 1273 696 933
(call collect).

Diners Club
Tel 00 44 1252 513 500
(call collect).

MasterCard
Tel 001 636 722 7111
(call collect).

VISA
Tel 00 800 11638 0304 (toll-free).

LOST TRAVELLERS' CHEQUES

American Express
Tel 00 800 44 127569 (toll-free).

VISA
Tel 00 800 44 131410 (toll-free).

Queueing at an ATM

THE EURO

The euro (€) is the common currency of the European Union. It went into general circulation on 1 January 2002, initially for 12 participating countries, including Greece. The Greek drachma was phased out in March 2002. EU members using the euro as sole official currency are known as the Eurozone. Several EU members have opted out of joining this common currency. Euro notes are identical throughout the Eurozone countries, each one including designs of fictional architectural structures and monuments. The coins have one side identical (the value side), and one side with an image unique to each country. Both notes and coins are exchangeable in each of the Eurozone countries.

Bank Notes

Euro bank notes have seven denominations. The €5 note (grey in colour) is the smallest, followed by the €10 note (pink), €20 note (blue), €50 note (orange), €100 note (green), €200 note (yellow) and €500 note (purple). All notes show the stars of the European Union.

€5

€10

€20

€50

€100

€200

€500

€2

€1

50 cents

20 cents

10 cents

Coins

The euro has eight coin denominations: €2 and €1; 50 cents, 20 cents, 10 cents, 5 cents, 2 cents and 1 cent. The €2 and €1 coins are both silver and gold in colour. The 50-, 20- and 10-cent coins are gold. The 5-, 2- and 1-cent coins are bronze.

5 cents

2 cents

1 cent

Communications and Media

Post office logo

The Greek national telephone company is OTE (Organismós Tilepikoinonión Elládos). Telecommunications in Greece are good, and there are direct lines to all major countries; these are often better than local lines. Mobile phones are widespread and telecom companies compete for customers. There are Internet cafés in all main towns and resorts. Greek post is reasonably reliable and efficient, especially from the larger towns and resorts. The Greeks are avid newspaper readers, and in addition to a vast array of Greek publications, there are a few good English-language papers and magazines. Foreign newspapers are also available.

INTERNATIONAL TELEPHONE CALLS

Public telephones have become increasingly rare on the streets of Greece as more and more people now have mobile (cell) phones.

Making long-distance calls from a hotel can be very expensive. The best deals on long-distance calls are to be found at privately run call centres, which have sprung up in all the larger cities (often close to the train or bus station) to serve Greece's immigrant communities. Each call centre displays specific rates, as well as information about peak and cheap times, which vary depending on the country you are phoning.

MOBILE PHONES

The main mobile phone network providers are **Cosmote**, **Vodafone Greece** and **WIND Hellas**. To reduce the cost of calls while in Greece, it might be a good idea to purchase a Greek SIM card from one of these companies; however, this will work only if your phone is unlocked. Alternatively, you could use your network's roaming facility, but this can be expensive. All Greek mobile phone numbers begin with the digit "6".

INTERNET

There are many Internet cafés in all the main towns and resorts in Greece and their prices are very reasonable.

Two of the best ones in Athens are **Deligrece Café** and **Bits and Bytes**.

Some public spaces in Athens offer free Wi-Fi, notably around Sýntagma Square, Kotzia Square and Thiseío metro station. An increasing number of hotels also offer free Wi-Fi to their residents.

A sign advertising the services of an Internet café

POSTAL SERVICES

The Greek postal service is run by **ELTA**. Greek post offices *(tachydromeía)* are generally open 7:30am–2pm Monday to Friday, with some main branches, especially in larger towns or cities, staying open as late as 8pm and occasionally for a few hours at weekends. All post offices are closed on public holidays *(see p48)*.

Post boxes are usually bright yellow; some have two slots, marked *esoterikó* (domestic) and *exoterikó*

USEFUL DIALLING CODES

- Directory enquiries for calls within Greece: 11888
- International operator and directory assistance: 139
- For reverse-charge call instructions, call the international operator
- For international calls from Greece, dial 00, followed by the country code (see the list below), the local area code (minus the initial 0) and then the number.
  Australia 61
  Ireland 353
  New Zealand 64
  UK 44
  USA & Canada 1
- To call Greece from abroad, dial the international access code (see list below), followed by 30 (country code for Greece), the area code and then the number.
  Australia: 0011
  Ireland, New Zealand & UK: 00
  USA & Canada: 011

(overseas). Bright-red post boxes are reserved for express mail, both domestic and overseas. Express is a little more expensive, but it cuts delivery time by a few days. Airmail letters take three to six days to most European countries, and anywhere from five days to a week or more to North America, Australia and New Zealand.

Stamps *(grammatósima)* can be bought at post offices and occasionally from vending machines inside post offices.

The poste restante system – whereby mail can be sent to, and picked up from, a post office – is widely used in Greece, especially in more remote regions. Mail should be clearly marked "Poste Restante", with the recipient's surname underlined so that it gets filed in the right place. Proof of identity is needed when collecting the post, which is kept for a maximum of 30 days before being returned to the sender.

A standard Greek bright-yellow post box

If you are sending a parcel to a non-EU country, do not seal it before heading to the post office – its contents will need to be inspected by security before it is sent.

The main post offices in central Athens – on Sýntagma Square and at Aiólou 100 (just off Omónoia Square) – are indicated on the Street Finder maps *(see pp122–35)*.

International courier services such as **ACS** and **DHL**, both of which have offices in Athens and other major cities, offer the best solution for express deliveries.

NEWSPAPERS AND MAGAZINES

The trusty corner *períptera* (kiosks), bookshops in larger towns and tourist shops in the resorts often sell day-old foreign newspapers and magazines, though the mark-up is substantial. *Athens News* is an English-language weekly paper published in Athens on Fridays. It's a good source of information on local entertainment, festivals and other cultural goings-on, and

it also provides decent coverage of domestic and international news. Also in English, *Athens In Your Pocket* is a useful bi-monthly guide available at newspaper kiosks in the capital; it has listings and details of restaurants, bars and museums. *Odyssey*, a glossy English-language bi-monthly magazine about all things Greek, appeals mainly to the Greek diaspora.

The most popular Greek-language newspapers are *Kathimeriní*, *Eleftherotypía* and *Ta Néa*. The weekly Greek-language *Athinorama (see p118)* details cultural events in Athens.

TELEVISION AND RADIO

There are three state-run and several private TV channels, plus a host of cable and satellite stations from across Europe. The state-owned TV and radio broadcasting corporation is **ERT**. Most Greek stations cater to popular taste, with a mix of dubbed foreign soap operas, game shows, sport and films. Foreign-language films tend to be subtitled rather than dubbed. Satellite stations CNN and Euronews have international news in English around the clock. Guides detailing the coming week's television programmes are published in all the English-language papers.

With three state-owned radio channels and a plethora of local stations, the airwaves are positively jammed in Greece, and reception is not always dependable. Many stations are devoted exclusively to Greek music, either traditional or contemporary. There are also classical music stations, such as ERA-TRITO (95.6 FM), one of the three state channels, and modern music stations such as Rock FM (96.9 FM). For the daily news in English, you can pick up

the BBC World Service (90.2 FM in the Greater Athens area; frequency varies in other parts of Greece). The BBC can also be received over the Internet. Athens International Radio (AIR; 104.4 FM) broadcasts news bulletins, current affairs discussions and local information in English, German, French and a dozen more languages.

DIRECTORY

MOBILE PHONES

Cosmote
Tel 13838. www.cosmote.gr

Vodafone Greece
Tel 13830. www.vodafone.gr

WIND Hellas
Tel 13800. www.wind.com.gr

INTERNET

Bits and Bytes
Akadimias 78, Athens.
Tel 210 381 3830.

Deligrece Café
Akadimias 87, 10678 Athens.
Tel 210 330 1895.

POSTAL SERVICES

ACS
Tel 210 819 0000.
www.acscourier.gr

DHL
Tel 210 989 0000.
www.dhl.gr

ELTA
www.elta.gr

NEWSPAPERS AND MAGAZINES

Athens In Your Pocket
www.inyourpocket.com

Athens News
www.athensnews.gr

Athinorama
www.athinorama.gr (Greek only)

Kathimeriní
www.ekathimerini.com

Odyssey
www.odyssey.gr

TELEVISION AND RADIO

ERT
www.ert.gr

A typical street kiosk, selling a wide variety of newspapers and magazines

TRAVEL INFORMATION

Reliably hot, sunny weather makes Greece a popular destination for holiday-makers, particularly from northern Europe. From mid-May to early October, there are countless flights to Greece. For those with more time, it is also possible to reach the country by car, rail and coach. Travelling on the mainland is easy enough. An extensive bus network reaches even the tiniest communities, with frequent services on all major routes. Greece's rail network is skeletal by comparison, and aside from the inter-city expresses, service is much slower.

Logo of
Athens airport

Travelling by car offers the most flexibility, allowing visitors to reach places that are not accessible by public transport. However, road conditions are variable, and in remoter parts can be rough and dangerous (see p320). Some of the larger cities and popular tourist destinations can also be reached by plane from Athens and Thessaloníki. Note that strikes (a regular occurrence in Greece) can cause disruption to public transport both to and within the country, and that demonstrations in the capital often see the roads of central Athens closed to all traffic.

GREEN TRAVEL

To limit smog and traffic congestion in central Athens, driving restrictions apply – cars with registration numbers ending in an even number may drive in the city centre only on even dates of the month; cars with registrations ending in an odd number may drive in the city centre only on odd-numbered dates of the month (see p326).

The city buses run on natural gas, while trolley-buses are powered by electricity, making them both environmentally friendly.

Cycling in Athens is only for the brave. Local drivers have little respect for bicycles, and cycle lanes are non-existent. However, more people have started to use bicycles in the capital, and cyclists are now allowed to ride in the bus lanes.

For long-distance travel, Greeks have always preferred buses to trains. This has been even more true since 2011, when the already limited rail network suffered further cuts as a result of the economic crisis (see p318). The only fast and reliable railway line is the one linking Athens to Thessaloníki.

In rural areas (notably the Peloponnese), cycling and hiking holidays are ever more popular; visitors relish the glorious unspoilt landscapes.

ARRIVING BY AIR

The main airlines operating direct scheduled flights from London to Athens are **Aegean Airlines** and **British Airways**. In addition, several budget airlines – including **easyJet** (from London Gatwick, Manchester and Edinburgh to Athens; and from London

Gatwick to Thessaloníki) and **Ryanair** (from London Stansted to Thessaloníki and Pátra) – also connect the UK to the Greek mainland. The Irish airline **Aer Lingus** runs scheduled flights from Dublin to Athens, while all the major European carriers such as **Air France** and **Alitalia** also operate scheduled flights.

There are about 15 international airports around Greece that can be reached directly from Europe; however, most of these are located on the islands. On the mainland, Athens and Thessaloníki handle most scheduled flights. The other mainland international airports such as Préveza, Kalamáta, Kavála and Vólos – can be reached directly mainly by charter flights.

All scheduled long-haul flights to Greece land in Athens although many are not direct and will require changing at a connecting European city. There are direct flights to Athens from New York with **Delta** and from Philadelphia with **US Airways**, while **Air Canada** and **Air Transat** fly from Montreal and Toronto. **Air China** flies directly from Beijing to Athens. Although there are no direct flights to Athens from Australia or New Zealand, there are more than five flight routes daily from that part of the world that involve changing to a connecting flight at hubs in the Middle East.

Athens Elefthérios Venizélos International Airport

Light and spacious interior of Athens airport

CHARTER FLIGHTS AND PACKAGE DEALS

Charter flights to Greece are nearly all from within Europe, and mostly operate between the months of May and October. They are usually the cheapest option during peak season (Jul–Aug), when air fares rise steeply, though discounted scheduled flights are worth considering in low season, when there are few charters available.

Tickets are sold through airline websites and, to a lesser extent, by travel agencies either as part of an all-inclusive package holiday or as a flight-only deal. Companies operating charter flights to Thessaloníki from the UK throughout the summer are **Thomson Airways** (from East Midlands, London Gatwick, Luton and Manchester) and **Fly Thomas Cook** (from London Gatwick and Manchester).

Some real bargains can be found by buying tickets through price comparison websites such as **Kayak**, **Momondo**, **Skyscanner** and **Zugu**.

ATHENS AIRPORT

Greece's largest and most prestigious infrastructure development project for the millennium, **Elefthérios Venizélos – Athens International Airport** opened to air traffic in 2001. Located at Spata, 27 km (17 miles) southeast of the city centre, the airport handles the majority of Greece's international and domestic flights, as well as all of Athens' passenger and cargo flights. It has two runways, designed for simultaneous, round-the-clock operation, and a Main Terminal Building for all arrivals and departures. Arrivals are located on the ground floor (Level 0) and departures on the first floor (Level 1). Passengers are advised to check in as early as possible and to contact their airline in advance to find out the recommended time to arrive at the airport for their flight.

Service facilities include a shopping mall, restaurants and cafés in the Main Terminal Building and a five-star Sofitel hotel in the airport complex. Car-rental firms, banks, bureaux de change and travel agencies are all located in the arrivals area. There is also a small museum displaying archaeological findings from digs carried out in the airport area.

TRANSPORT FROM ATHENS AIRPORT

Metro line 3 (blue line) links the airport to Sýntagma and Monastiráki in the city centre from 6:33am until 11:33pm every 30 minutes, while the Proastiakos suburban rail service runs from 5:26am until 9.44pm from the airport to Ano Liosia just north of Athens (every 20 minutes) and to Kiato (every hour). From these it is possible to connect to the rest of the suburban or intercity rail network. Tickets for both metro and suburban rail journeys from the airport to the city centre cost €8 (single) and €14 (return).

Visitors who prefer to use road transport (for those arriving or departing between 11:30pm and 5:30am this is the only option), can take a bus, a taxi or a hired car. The X95 bus runs from the airport to Sýntagma Square, in the city centre, every 10–15 minutes (journey time: about 70 minutes). Bus X96 runs to Piraeus port every 20–25 minutes (journey time: about 90 minutes). Bus X93 runs to Kifisos and Liosion intercity bus stations in Athens every 25–30 minutes (journey time: about 65 minutes). Bus X97 runs to Dáfni metro station every 45–60 minutes (journey time: about 70 minutes). All four buses run 24 hours a day, and a single ticket costs €5. A taxi ride to the centre of Athens costs €35 by day and €50 by night (fixed prices). A six-lane toll motorway links the airport to the Athens ring road. Several car hire companies are also based at the airport (see p320).

Bus outside Athens Elefthérios Venizélos International Airport

THESSALONÍKI AND OTHER INTERNATIONAL AIRPORTS

Makedonia-Thessaloníki Airport is located 15 km (9 miles) southeast of Thessaloníki, in the north of the country. It handles a number of international scheduled flights, but only from the rest of Europe.

The number 78 bus, which runs 24 hours a day, links Thessaloníki airport to the city's central train station, a journey of about 45 minutes, costing €0.90. A taxi covering the same route takes about 20 minutes depending on traffic, but is considerably more expensive (€15–€20).

Greece's other mainland international airports (such as Kalamáta, Kavála and Préveza) are served by charter flights only, mostly from the United Kingdom, Germany, the Netherlands and Scandinavia, during the summer season (May through September).

DOMESTIC AND CONNECTING FLIGHTS

Greece's domestic airline network is fairly extensive. The majority of internal flights are operated by two Greek airlines: **Olympic Air** and **Aegean Airlines**; however, there are also a number of small private companies, including **Astra Airlines**, that provide flight connections between Thessaloníki and the rest of the country.

FLIGHT CONNECTIONS WITHIN GREECE

KEY
- International airport
- Domestic airport
- Air route

ISLAND	DISTANCE	FLYING TIME	ISLAND	DISTANCE	FLYING TIME
Corfu	381 km (237 miles)	40 minutes	Crete (Chaniá)	318 km (198 miles)	45 minutes
Rhodes	426 km (265 miles)	45 minutes	Santoríni	228 km (142 miles)	40 minutes
Skýros	128 km (80 miles)	40 minutes	Kos	324 km (201 miles)	45 minutes
Skiáthos	135 km (84 miles)	30 minutes	Mykonos	153 km (95 miles)	30 minutes
Límnos	252 km (157 miles)	45 minutes	Páros	157 km (98 miles)	35 minutes

Olympic Air planes on an airport runway

As well as having the largest number of international flights in Greece, Athens has the most connecting air services to other parts of the country. Both international and domestic flights use the city's Elefthérios Venizélos airport *(see p315)*.

Olympic Air operates direct flights from Athens to four mainland destinations (Thessaloníki, Ioánnina, Alexandroúpoli and Kavála); in addition it runs services to more than two dozen island airports. A number of inter-island services operate during the summer months, and about a dozen of these fly all year round.

Aegean Airlines operates direct flights from Athens' Elefthérios Venizélos to two mainland towns (Thessaloníki in the north and Kalamáta in the south) and to around a dozen islands.

FARES

Fares for domestic flights are often at least double the equivalent of a bus journey or deck-class ferry trip. Tickets and timetables for Olympic Air and Aegean Airlines flights are available from the respective websites, as well as from most major travel agencies. Bear in mind that flights tend to sell out quickly during the busy summer months – reservations are essential.

AIRPORT TAXES

A small airport departure tax (€8.51) is charged on domestic flights of between 62 and 466 air miles. For "international" flights (that is, those exceeding 466 air miles), the tax rises to €12.15. This tax applies only to flights departing from Athens International Airport. In a bid to strengthen the country's tourism industry, this tax was waived from all other Greek airports in 2011.

DIRECTORY

ARRIVING BY AIR

Aegean Airlines
Viltanióti 31,
14564 Athens.
Tel 210 626 1700.
www.aegeanair.com

Aer Lingus
www.aerlingus.com

Air Canada
www.aircanada.ca

Air China
214 Singrou Avenue,
17672 Athens.
Tel 210 722 0830.
www.airchina.com

Air France
7 Megalou Alexandrou
& Karaiskaki,
16452 Athens.
Tel 210 998 0222.
www.airfrance.com

Air Transat
www.airtransat.com

Alitalia
80 Poseidonos Avenue,
17455 Alimos.
Tel 210 998 8888.
www.alitalia.com

British Airways
Building Strovolos,
PO CY2001,
Nicosia,
Cyprus.
Tel 801 115 6000.
www.british-airways.com

Delta
Tel 210 998 0444.
www.delta.com

easyJet
Tel 210 353 0300.
www.easyjet.com

Ryanair
www.ryanair.com

US Airways
Tel 210 353 0365.
www.usairways.com

CHARTER FLIGHTS AND PACKAGE DEALS

Fly Thomas Cook
www.flythomascook.com

Thomson Airways
http://flights.thomson.
co.uk

FLIGHT COMPARISON WEBSITES

Kayak
www.kayak.co.uk

Momondo
www.momondo.com

Skyscanner
www.skyscanner.net

Zugu
www.zugu.co.uk

ATHENS AIRPORT

Elefthérios Venizélos – Athens International Airport
5th km Spata-Loutsa Ave,
19019 Spata.
Tel 210 353 0000.
www.aia.gr

THESSALONIKI AIRPORT

Makedonia – Thessaloníki Airport
PO Box 22605,
55103 Kalamaria,
Thessaloníki.
Tel 2310 985 000.
www.thessaloniki-airport.com

DOMESTIC FLIGHTS

Aegean Airlines
See Arriving by Air.

Astra Airlines
12 km Thessaloníki
Moudania Road/
Airport Area, GR 57001
PO Box 608 04,
Thermi Thessaloníki.
Tel 2310 489 390.
www.astra-airlines.gr

Olympic Air
1st km Varis Koropiou
& Ifaistou,
19400 Koropi.
Tel 210 355 0500.
www.olympicair.com

Travelling by Train

Greek railways' OSE logo

Greece's rail network is limited to the mainland and was always fairly skeletal by European standards. However, in 2011, as part of the restructuring of the debt-ridden Greek railways, train services were cut even further and some routes completely suspended. Except for the intercity express train linking Athens to Thessaloníki (a trip of about 5 hours), services tend to be extremely slow. On the plus side, non-express tickets are not expensive (cheaper than coach fares), and some lines allow you to experience Greece's rugged and beautiful countryside. An overnight sleeper service is available on the Athens–Thessaloníki route.

First- and second-class carriages of a non-express train

ARRIVING BY TRAIN

Travelling to Greece by train is expensive and difficult due to the reduction in rail services into and within the country since 2011, though there is an extensive bus network *(see p322)*. However, travelling to Greece by train may be a good option if you wish to make stopovers en route. From London to Athens, the main route takes around three days. The journey is through France, Switzerland and Italy, then by overnight ferry from an Italian port such as Ancona or Bari to the Greek port of Pátra, followed by a bus to Athens.

While some international train services may run into Greece, as of 2011, due to Greece's ailing economy, all Greek train services to and from the country have been suspended until further notice. These include routes into neighbouring Bulgaria and Turkey, though there is a TrainOSE bus service from Thessaloníki to Sofia in Bulgaria.

TRAVELLING AROUND GREECE BY TRAIN

Greece's railway infrastructure is owned by **OSE** (Organismós Sidirodrómon Elládos), and train services are run by **TrainOSE**. Athens forms the principal hub of the system. A northbound line from Laríssis station connects Athens to Thessaloníki, with branch lines to Vólos, and to Kardítsa, Tríkala and Kalampáka.

From Thessaloníki, there is a line travelling west to Edessa (going through Véroia)

and another travelling east to Alexandroúpoli (passing through Xánthi and Komotiní).

Destinations on the Peloponnese are no longer served by train, with the exception of Corinth. Trains depart from Laríssis station on the **Proastiakos** network, stopping at Corinth shortly before terminating at Kiato. Passengers heading for Pátra then have to change to a TrainOSE bus service to reach their final destination. There are plans to build a new standard-gauge line from Kiato to Pátra, but no dates have been set for this project. Proastiakos also runs a service from Athens' airport to Kiato via Nerantziotissa *(see p315)*.

There is a picturesque heritage route, the rack-and-pinion line between Diakoftó and Kalávryta on the Peloponnese *(see p168)*; this is not connected to the rest of the national rail network.

TRAIN TICKETS

Train tickets can be bought at any OSE office or railway station, as well as through the TrainOSE website.

There are two basic types of ticket: first and second class. Tickets for intercity express trains on the Athens–Thessaloníki line are more expensive, but worth it for the time they save.

When booking through the TrainOSE website there is a 10 per cent reduction on ticket prices, a 15 per cent reduction if you buy tickets at least two days before the beginning of your journey and a 20 per cent reduction

Laríssis station, the main railway station in Athens

Train station ticket window

on all return journeys. With the Intercity 6+1 ticket you get six intercity train tickets plus an extra ticket for free.

Travellers aged over 65 are entitled to a 25–50 per cent reduction on tickets. Children up to age 4 travel free; those aged 4–12 get a 50 per cent reduction, while teenagers and students below the age of 25 receive a 25% discount with an International Student Identity Card.

Rail passes issued by **InterRail** (a global pass for European residents that covers 30 countries) and **Eurail** (a global pass for non-European residents that covers 23 countries) are both honoured in Greece, though supplements are charged on some lines. The passes also allow reductions on some ferries between Italy and Greece. InterRail pass holders travel free of charge with Superfast *(see p323)* from Ancona to Pátra, while Eurail pass holders can travel free with both Superfast and Minoan *(see p323)* on the same route. There may be a small surcharge in high season (Jun–Sep) and a port tax.

A modern commuter train run by Proastiakos, linking Athens with Corinth

RAILWAY STATIONS IN ATHENS AND THESSALONIKI

Athens has one main terminal, **Laríssis Station**, which is located a 15-minute walk northwest of Omónoia Square and is served by metro Line 2 (red line). There are baggage storage facilities inside the station.

Thessaloníki Station is located a 15-minute walk west of the city centre. There are plans to build a one-line metro system in Thessaloníki (running from the east to the west of the city), with a stop at the train station, but there is no date for the start of this project.

DIRECTORY

TRAVELLING AROUND GREECE BY TRAIN

OSE
Sína 6, Athens.
Tel 1110.
Aristotélous 18,
Thessaloníki.
Tel 2310 598 120.
Tel 14511 (customer service).

Proastiakos
www.trainose.gr/proorismoi/
proastiakos-athinon

TrainOSE
www.trainose.gr (Greek only)

TRAIN TICKETS

Eurail
www.raileurope.co.uk

InterRail
Rail Europe Travel Centre,
193 Piccadilly,
London W1J 9EU.
Tel 08448 484 064.
www.interrailnet.com

RAILWAY STATIONS IN ATHENS AND THESSALONÍKI

Laríssis Station
Deligiánni,
10439 Athens.
Tel 210 823 7741.

Thessaloníki Station
Monastiriou 28,
54629 Thessaloníki.
Tel 2310 517 517.

GREEK RAIL NETWORK

Sidirókastro
Sérres
Xánthi
Kilkís
Dráma
Komotiní
Edessa
Alexandroúpoli
Thessaloníki
Véroia
Katerini
Litóchoro
Kalampáka
Lárisa
Tríkala
Kardítsa
Vólos
Stilída
Lamía
Leivadiá
Chalkída
Thebes
ATHENS
Kiato
Corinth

KEY

— Principal rail routes

0 kilometres   200

0 miles   100

Travelling by Road

Road sign to port

Travelling by car allows you to explore at your own pace. Greece's express highways (motorways) are the A1 (north–south from Thessaloníki to Athens, passing Lárisa en route); the A2 (east–west from Evros to Igoumenítsa, passing Thessaloníki en route); the A8 (east–west from Athens to Pátra, passing Corinth en route); and the A7 (under construction; north–south from Corinth to Kalamáta, passing Tripoli en route). Some stretches of these motorways are being upgraded, and roadworks may cause delays. However, the roads are designed to be fast, and tolls are charged for their use. The maps in this guide categorize the roads into four groups, from motorways in blue to non-asphalt roads in yellow *(see back flap)*.

You have priority

You have right of way

Do not use car horn

Wild animals crossing

Hairpin bend ahead

Roundabout ahead

ARRIVING BY CAR

The most direct overland routes to Greece are through the countries that made up the former Yugoslavia. Anybody considering this should be aware that road quality is poor through some parts of this route. Instead, many visitors choosing to drive from the UK to Greece head for Italy, then catch an overnight ferry from Ancona port to Pátra.

For a small fee, the **AA** and **RAC** will compile individual itineraries for motorists. They can also supply up-to-date information on route closures and potential hotspots. It is also worth asking their advice on insurance needs and on any special driving regulations for those countries en route.

In order to drive in Greece, you will need to have a full, valid national driving licence and insurance cover (at least third party is compulsory). **ELPA** (the Automobile and Touring Club of Greece) offers useful information on driving in Greece.

RULES OF THE ROAD

Driving is on the right in Greece. Road signs conform to European norms and are usually in both Greek and Roman scripts. However, on rural back roads, the names of villages are sometimes signposted in Greek only.

The speed limit for cars on national highways is 120 km/h (75 mph), on country roads it is 110 km/h (68 mph) and in towns 50 km/h (30 mph). For motorbikes, the speed limit on national highways is 90 km/h (55 mph), while on country roads it is 70 km/h (45 mph).

The use of seatbelts in cars is required by law, and children under the age of 10 are not allowed to sit in the front seat. Using a mobile phone (without hands-free) while driving is prohibited, although many Greeks ignore this law. Parking and speeding tickets must be paid at the local police station or at your car-hire agency.

TOLLS

Tolls are payable on all Greek motorways and on the Attiki Odos (the Athens ring road). There are also tolls to be paid when passing over the spectacular Rion-Antirio bridge (close to Pátra), and through the Artemission tunnel (on the Corinth–Tripoli motorway) and the Aktion undersea tunnel (close to Préveza). On major public holidays, be prepared for long tailbacks (and a lot of irate drivers) at busy toll booths on the motorways.

CAR HIRE

There are scores of car-hire agencies in every major city and resort, all offering a full range of cars and four-wheel-drive vehicles. International companies such as **Budget**, **Avis**, **Hertz**, **National** and **Europcar** (which have offices at Athens airport, as well as in the city centre) tend to be slightly more expensive than their local counterparts, though the latter are generally just as reliable.

The car-hire agency should have an agreement with an emergency recovery company, such as **Express Service** or **InterAmerican**, in the event of a vehicle breakdown. Also, be sure to check the insurance policy cover: third party is required by law, but personal accident insurance is also strongly recommended. A valid driving licence that has been held for at least one year is necessary, and there is a minimum age requirement, ranging from 21 to 25 years.

An emergency recovery vehicle

Rack of bicycles for hire at a coastal resort

MOTORBIKE, MOPED AND BICYCLE HIRE

Motorbikes and mopeds are readily available for hire in all the tourist resorts. Mopeds are ideal for short distances on fairly flat terrain, but for travel in more remote or mountainous areas a motorbike is essential.

Always make sure that the vehicle you hire is in good condition before you set out, and that you have adequate insurance cover; also check whether your own travel insurance covers you for motorbike accidents (many do not). Speeding in Greece is penalized by fines, drink-driving laws are strict, and helmets are compulsory.

Though less widely available, bicycles can be hired in some tourist resorts. The hot weather and tough terrain make cycling extremely hard work, though. On the positive side, bikes can be transported for free on most Greek ferries, and for a small fee on trains.

PETROL

Petrol stations are plentiful in urban centres, but few and far between in rural areas – always set out with a full tank to be on the safe side. Fuel is sold by the litre, and the price is comparable to most other European countries. There are usually either three or four grades available: super (95 octane), unleaded, super

Dual-language road sign, found on most routes

unleaded and diesel, which is confusingly called *petrélaio*.

Filling stations set their own working hours in Greece. They are generally open from around 7am or 8am to between 7pm and 9pm daily, and are closed on Sundays in many areas. Some stations in the larger towns are open 24 hours a day.

TAXIS

Taxis provide a reasonably priced way of making short trips around Greece. All taxis are metered, but for longer journeys a price can usually be negotiated per day or per trip. Also, drivers are generally amenable to dropping you off somewhere and returning to pick you up a few hours later.

In Athens taxis are plentiful and can simply be hailed on the street. In smaller towns it is best to find a taxi rank, which is likely to be either in the centre or by the bus or train station. Most rural villages have at least one taxi, and the best place to arrange for one is at the local *kafeneío* (café).

Although taxis are metered, it is worth getting a rough idea of the price before setting out. Round up to the nearest euro as a tip; luggage will incur an additional charge. In Greece, taxis are often shared with other passengers, each paying for their part of the journey.

HITCHHIKING

Greece is a relatively safe place for hitchhiking but, like anywhere else, there are potential risks. Women especially are advised against hitching alone. If you do hitchhike, finding a lift is usually easier in the less populated rural areas than on busy roads heading out from major towns and cities. Note that it is illegal to hitchhike on motorways.

MAPS

Visitors who intend to do much motoring around the country are advised not to give too much reliance to the maps issued by local travel agents and car-hire agencies, since these are rarely detailed enough. Instead, they should invest in the regional Orama Editions maps (available in Greece), or bring with them the Geo-Center regional road maps (1:300,000 range) or the single-sheet Freytag & Berndt maps (1:650,000).

DIRECTORY

ARRIVING BY CAR

AA
Tel 0800 072 3279 (UK).
www.theaa.com

ELPA
Mesogeíon 395,
15343 Agía Paraskeví.
Tel 210 606 8800.
Tel 10400 (road assistance).
www.elpa.gr

RAC
Tel 0800 015 6000 (UK).
www.rac.co.uk

CAR HIRE (ATHENS OFFICES)

Avis
Tel 210 687 9600.
www.avis.gr

Budget
Tel 210 898 1444.
www.budget-athens.gr

Europcar
Tel 210 921 1444.
www.europcar-greece.gr

Express Service
Tel 1154.
www.expressservice.gr

Hertz
Tel 210 626 4000.
www.hertz.gr

InterAmerican
Tel 1158.
www.interamerican.gr

National
Tel 210 349 3428.
www.nationalcar.gr

Travelling by Coach and Bus

Time permitting, bus travel is a good way of experiencing the country. Greece's bus system is operated by KTEL (Koinó Tameío Eispráxeon Leoforeíon), a syndicate of dozens of regional private companies. The network is comprehensive in that it provides every community with services of some sort: in rural villages this may be once a day; in remoter places, once or twice a week. Services between the larger centres are frequent and efficient.

International coaches also connect Greece with some of its neighbouring countries; these services are used mainly by immigrants who work in Greece.

Domestic coach, run by KTEL

ARRIVING BY COACH

Coach journeys from London to Athens take many days, involve several changes, and are not as cheap as a bargain air fare. Coaches are, however, cheaper than taking the train.

Top Deck is an adventure tour operator used mainly by young travellers. Some of their longer coach tours include Greece but do not necessarily depart from the UK – their 18-day European Horizons tour, for example, starts from Rome, Italy, and finishes in London, covering 10 countries in total and including three days' flotilla sailing in Greece.

TRAVELLING BY COACH

The Greek coach system is operated by a network of regional private companies under the umbrella of **KTEL**. It is extensive, with services to even the remotest destinations and frequent express coaches on all the major routes. Large cities usually have more than one terminal, each serving a different set of destinations.

Ticket sales are computerized for all major routes, with reserved seating on modern,

air-conditioned coaches. Buy your ticket in advance, as seats often sell out on popular routes and Greek coaches tend to leave a few minutes early.

In country villages, the local *kafeneío* (café) often serves as the coach station. You can usually buy your ticket from the owner; if not, it is possible to buy a ticket upon boarding.

COACH TOURS

In the resort areas, travel agents offer a wide range of excursions on air-conditioned coaches accompanied by qualified guides. These trips include visits to major archaeological and historical sites, other towns and seaside resorts and special events. Note that coach tours are best booked a day in advance.

In Athens, **Key Tours** and **Fantasy Travel** offer a range of mainland excursions, including one- and two-day coach tours to places like Mycenae, Delphi, Epidaurus or Meteóra.

COACH SERVICES FROM ATHENS & THESSALONÍKI

From Athens there are frequent coach services to all the larger mainland towns, apart from those in Thrace, which are served by coaches departing from **KTEL Thessaloníki**. Athens' **Terminal A** is situated 4 km (2 miles) northeast of the city centre. The terminal

serves Epirus, Macedonia, the Peloponnese and the Ionian islands of Corfu, Kefalloniá, Lefkáda and Zákynthos (ferry crossings are included in the price of the ticket). It takes 6 hours to reach Thessaloníki, and 2 hours 30 minutes to the port of Pátra.

Terminal B is situated north of Agios Nikólaos metro station, but is most easily reached by taxi. It serves most destinations in central Greece, such as Delphi (3 hours) and Vólos (6 hours).

Coaches to destinations around Attica (Soúnio, Lávrio, Rafína and Marathónas) leave from the Mavrommataíon coach terminal, on the corner of Leofóros Alexándras and 28 Oktovríou (Patisíon).

DIRECTORY

ARRIVING BY COACH

Top Deck
Level 1, 107 Power Road, Chiswick, London W4 5PY.
Tel 020 8987 3300.
www.topdecktours.co.uk

TRAVELLING BY COACH

KTEL
Tel 14505.
www.ktel.org

COACH TOURS

Fantasy Travel
19 Filellinon, 10557 Athens.
Tel 210 331 0530.
www.fantasy.gr

Key Tours
4 Kalirrois, 11743 Athens.
Tel 210 923 3166.
www.keytours.gr

COACH SERVICES FROM ATHENS & THESSALONÍKI

KTEL Thessaloníki
Giannitson 244, Thessaloníki.
Tel 2310 500 111.
www.ktel-thes.gr

Terminal A
Kifisoú 100, Athens.
Tel 210 512 4910.

Terminal B
Liosíon 260, Athens.
Tel 210 831 7096.

Travelling by Sea

Greek catamaran

The sea has always played an important role in the life and history of Greece. Today, the sea is a major source of revenue for the country, with millions of tourists descending each year for beach holidays on the Mediterranean and the Aegean, and thousands coming here for yacht-charter sailing holidays too. The Greek mainland and islands are linked by a vast network of ferries, catamarans and hydrofoils that serves the local population all year round, as well as tourists through the summer.

ARRIVING BY SEA

There are ferry crossings from the Italian ports of Ancona, Bari, Brindisi and Venice to Igoumenítsa in Epirus and Pátra in the Peloponnese. **Minoan** and **Superfast** are the main Greek companies covering these routes. In summer, reservations are advisable, especially if you have a car or want a cabin.

GREEK FERRY SERVICE

Athens' port, **Piraeus**, is the largest passenger port in Europe and one of the busiest in the world. From here, there are frequent ferry services (run by several private companies) to the islands of the Argo-Saronic, the Cyclades, the Dodecanese, the Northeast Aegean and Crete. Northeast of Athens, the smaller port of Rafína sees ferry departures for Evvia, plus some islands in the Cyclades.

Hellenic Seaways runs high-speed catamarans and hydrofoils, plus several ferries, from Piraeus to many islands in the Aegean Sea. The high-speed services cost about twice as much as the ferries, but the journey times are often twice as fast. However, catamarans and hydrofoils are more likely to be cancelled in the event of adverse weather.

Tickets can be purchased online or from travel agents in Athens. Advanced bookings are recommended for ferries in high season (especially if you have a car), and they are essential for high-speed catamarans and hydrofoils. Out of season, services (and prices) are reduced.

DIRECTORY

ARRIVING BY SEA

Minoan
25th August Street 17,
712 02 Heraklion, Crete.
Tel 2810 399 800.
www.minoan.gr

Superfast
Syngrou Avenue 123–125
& Torva 3, 11745 Athens.
Tel 210 891 9500.
www.superfast.com

GREEK FERRY SERVICE

Hellenic Seaways
Astiggos 6, Karaiskaki Square,
185 31 Piraeus.
Tel 210 419 9000.
www.hellenicseaways.gr

Piraeus Port Authority
Tel 210 406 0900
*(for emergencies outside
working hours).*
Tel 14541 *(for ferry timetables).*
www.olp.gr

CRUISES

Most cruise ships sailing the Mediterranean stop at Piraeus to give passengers a day in Athens. The port has 11 modern berths for cruise ships and can accommodate even the largest vessels.

PIRAEUS PORT MAP

This shows where you are likely to find ferries to various destinations.

Piraeus Port Authority:
Tel 210 455 0000.
**Coastal Services
Timetables**
Tel 14541.

KEY TO DEPARTURE POINTS

- Argo-Saronic Islands
- Northeast Aegean Islands
- Dodecanese
- Cyclades
- Crete
- International ferries
- Hydrofoils and catamarans

Key to symbols *see back flap*

Getting Around Athens

Trolleybus stop sign

The sights of Athens' city centre are closely packed, and almost everything of interest can be reached on foot. Walking is the best way of sightseeing in the city, especially in view of the traffic congestion, which can make both public and private transport slow and inefficient. The bus and trolleybus network provides the majority of public transport in the capital for Athenians and visitors alike; the three-line metro system offers a good alternative to the roads for some journeys. Taxis are another option and, with the lowest tariffs of any EU capital, they are worth considering even for longer journeys.

One of the fleet of yellow, blue and white buses

BUS SERVICES

Athens is served by an extensive bus network. Buses are white, yellow and blue. The network covers over 300 routes, connecting various districts to each other and to the city centre. All buses are ecologically friendly and run on natural gas. Bus journeys are inexpensive but can be slow and uncomfortably crowded, particularly in the city centre and during rush hours; the worst times are from 7am to 8:30am, from 2pm to 3:30pm and from 7:30pm to 9pm.

Note that to reach Piraeus port, metro Line 1 (green line) is infinitely faster and more convenient than the bus. Timetables and route maps (only in Greek) are available from **OASA**, the Athens Urban Transport Organization.

Tickets must be purchased in advance from a metro station or a *períptero* (street kiosk). Tickets can be bought individually or in a book of ten. The same ticket can be used on any bus, trolleybus, metro or tram, but must be validated in a ticket machine upon boarding. There is a penalty fine for not stamping your ticket, and tourists who are unfamiliar with this may be caught out by inspectors who board buses to carry out random checks. Tickets are valid for one ride only, regardless of the distance.

TROLLEYBUSES

Athens has a good network of trolleybuses, which are yellow and purple in colour and run on electricity. There are more than 20 routes that criss-cross the city centre and connect many of the main sights. Routes 7 and 8 are useful to reach the National Archaeological Museum from Sýntagma Square, while route 1 links Laríssis railway station with Omónoia Square and Sýntagma Square.

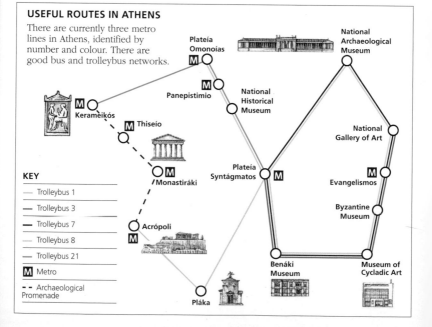

USEFUL ROUTES IN ATHENS

There are currently three metro lines in Athens, identified by number and colour. There are good bus and trolleybus networks.

Plateía Omonoías

National Archaeological Museum

Panepistímio

National Historical Museum

Kerameikós

Thiseío

National Gallery of Art

Plateía Syntágmatos

Evangelismos

Monastiráki

Byzantine Museum

Acrópoli

Benáki Museum

Museum of Cycladic Art

Pláka

KEY

— Trolleybus 1
— Trolleybus 3
— Trolleybus 7
— Trolleybus 8
— Trolleybus 21
Ⓜ Metro
- - Archaeological Promenade

An Athens trolleybus

Tickets can be bought at ticket machines at metro stations and at most street kiosks and must be validated upon boarding the trolleybus.

TRAMS

Athens' tram system, a project inaugurated for the 2004 Olympics, connects the city centre and the coast. There are just three lines, confusingly numbered 3, 4 and 5. Line 3 runs along the coast between Néo Fáliro and Voúla; Line 4 runs from Sýntagma Square to Néo Fáliro; and Line 5 runs from Sýntagma Square to Voúla. The trams operate 5:30am–1am daily (until 2:30am on Fridays and Saturdays).

Tickets can be bought at ticket machines at tram stops and must be validated at a machine at the tram stop before entering the tram.

METRO

The metro is fast and reliable. It was a key element in the restructuring of urban public transport for the 2004 Olympics, leading to the reduction in the number of private cars, as well as buses, in the city centre.

The metro has three lines: Line 1 (green line) runs from Kifissiá in the north to the port of Piraeus in the south, with central stops at Thiseío, Monastiráki, Omónoia and Victória. Most of the line is overland and only runs underground between Attikí and Monastiráki stations. The green line is used mainly by commuters who live in the northern suburbs, but it also offers visitors the fastest way of reaching Piraeus.

Line 2 (red line) and Line 3 (blue line) form part of a huge expansion of the system, most of which was completed in time for the 2004 Olympic Games. These two lines, which intersect at Sýntagma, were built 20 m (66 ft) underground in order to avoid interfering with material of archaeological interest. Both Sýntagma and Acrópoli stations feature impressive displays of archaeological finds uncovered during construction work.

Line 2 (red line) runs from Agios Antónios in northwest Athens to Agios Dimitrios in the southeast. Line 3 (blue line) runs from Egaleo to Doukissis Plakentias in the northeast, with some trains continuing on to Eleftheríos Venizélos airport. There are plans to extend Line 2 northwest to Peristeri and Anthoupoli, and southeast to Ilioupoli, Alimos, Argyroupoli and Elliniko, and to extend Line 3 west to Agia Marina. There are no fixed dates for their completion.

One ticket allows travel on any of the three lines and is valid for 90 minutes in one direction. You cannot exit a station and then go back to continue your journey with the same ticket. Tickets must be validated before boarding the train – use the machines at the entrances to all platforms. Trains run every five minutes, 5am–midnight on

Evangelismos metro sign

Line 1, and 5:30am–midnight on Lines 2 and 3. At weekends trains run from 5am to 2am.

WALKING

The centre of Athens is very compact, and most major sights and museums are within a 25-minute walk of Sýntagma Square, which is regarded as the city's centre.

Since the 2004 opening of the Archaeological Promenade, Athens has become infinitely more pleasant to navigate on foot. A broad car-free walkway running 4 km (2.5 miles), the promenade skirts the foot of the Acropolis to link the city's main ancient sites, as well as four metro stations. The streets of Dionissiou Areopagitou and Apostolou Pavlou run between Acrópoli metro station and Thiseío metro station (passing the Acropolis and the New Acropolis Museum); Adrianou street runs from Thiseío metro station to Monastiráki station (passing the Ancient Agora); and Ermou runs from Thiseío metro station to Kerameikós metro station (passing the Kerameikós archaeological site).

By day, Athens is still one of the safest European cities in which to walk around. However, it pays to be vigilant at night.

Archaeological remains on display at Sýntagma metro station

A yellow taxi on a street in Athens

TAXIS

Swarms of yellow taxis can be seen cruising the streets of Athens at most times of the day or night. However, trying to persuade one to stop can be a difficult task, especially between 2pm and 3pm, when taxi drivers usually change shifts. Then, they will only pick you up if you happen to be going in a direction that is convenient for them.

To hail a taxi, stand on the edge of the pavement and shout out your destination to any cab that slows down. If a cab's "taxi" sign is lit up, then it is definitely for hire (though often a taxi is also for hire when the sign is not lit). It is common practice in Athens for drivers to pick up extra passengers along the way, so it is worth flagging the occupied cabs too. If you are not the first passenger on board, make

No parking on odd-numbered months (Jan, Mar, etc)

No parking on even-numbered months (Feb, Apr, etc)

a note of the meter reading immediately; there is no fare sharing, so you should be charged for your portion of the journey only.

Despite a rise in prices, Athenian taxis are still very cheap by European standards – depending on traffic, you should not have to pay more than about €5 to travel to any destination within the downtown area, and between €6 and €9 from the centre to Piraeus. Higher tariffs come into effect between midnight and 5am and for journeys that exceed certain distances from the city centre. Fares to the airport, which is out of town at Spata, are now fixed at €35 in the daytime and €50 at night (midnight–5am).

There are also small surcharges for extra pieces of luggage weighing more than 10 kg (22 lbs), and for journeys from the ferry or railway terminals. Taxi fares are increased during holiday periods, such as Christmas and Easter.

For an extra charge (€3.50–€6), you can make a phone call to a radio taxi company and arrange for a car to pick you up at an appointed place and time. Radio taxis are plentiful in the Athens area. Telephone numbers of a few companies are listed in the Directory box.

DRIVING

Driving in Athens can be a nerve-racking experience and best avoided, especially if you are not accustomed to Greek road habits. Many streets in the centre are pedestrianized, and there are

also plenty of one-way streets, so you need to plan your route carefully.

Finding a parking space can be very difficult too. Despite appearances to the contrary, parking in front of a no-parking sign or on a single yellow line is illegal. There are pay-and-display machines for legal on-street parking, as well as underground car parks, though these usually fill up quickly.

In an attempt to reduce dangerously high air pollution levels, there is an "odd-even" driving system in force. Cars that have an odd number at the end of their licence plates can enter the central grid, also called the *daktýlios*, only on dates with an odd number, and cars with an even number at the end of their plates are allowed into it only on dates with an even number. To avoid being unable to access the *daktýlios*, some people have two cars – with odd and even plates. The "odd–even" rule does not apply to foreign cars; however, if possible, avoid taking your car into the city centre.

Sign for a pedestrianized area

DIRECTORY

PUBLIC TRANSPORT

Metro
Tel 210 519 4012.
www.amel.gr

OASA (buses/trolleybuses)
Metsovou 15. *Tel 185.*
www.oasa.gr

Trams
Tel 210 997 8000.
www.tramsa.gr

TAXIS

Athina 1
Tel 210 921 7942
(central Athens).

Ermis
Tel 210 411 5200 (Piraeus).

Hellas
Tel 210 645 7000
(central Athens).
Tel 210 801 4000
(north Athens).

ATHENS TRANSPORT LINKS

The hub of Athens' public transport is the area around Sýntagma Square and Omónoia Square. From this central area, the metro and various buses can be taken to Elefthérios Venizélos International Airport, the port at Piraeus and Athens' Laríssis train station. In addition, three tram lines connect the city centre with the Attic coast.

Bus X95 runs between the airport (*see p315*) and Sýntagma Square, and bus X96 links the airport to Piraeus (*see p323*). The airport is also served by

Line 3 (blue line) of the metro, from Sýntagma and Monastiráki. Metro Line 1 (green line, from Omónoia and Monastiráki) extends to Piraeus; the journey from the city centre to the port takes about half an hour. Trolleybus route 1 goes past Sýntagma metro station and Laríssis train and metro stations. Laríssis train station is also served by metro Line 2 (red line), from both Sýntagma and Omónoia.

Tram line 3 runs along the coast from Néo Fáliro to the seaside suburb of Voúla; tram line 4 runs from Sýntagma Square in the city centre to Néo Fáliro; and tram line 5

runs from Voúla to Sýntagma Square. These lines are especially useful if you are staying in a hotel along the coast, or if you wish to have a day on the beach.

Though more expensive than public transport, the most convenient way of getting to and from any of these destinations is by taxi. The journey times vary greatly, but if traffic is free-flowing, the journey from the city centre to the airport takes about 40 minutes; the journey from the city centre to Piraeus takes around 30 minutes; and the journey from Piraeus to the airport takes about 60 minutes.

ATHENS TRANSPORT LINKS

KEY

- Central Athens
- Metro line 1
- Metro line 2
- Metro line 3
- Metro line under construction
- Tram line
- Suburban railway
- Coach station
- Ferry port
- Dual-carriageway
- Major road
- Minor road

General Index

Acknowledgments

Dorling Kindersley would like to thank the following people whose contributions and assistance have made the preparation of this book possible.

Main Contributors

Marc Dubin is an American expatriate who divides his time between London and Sámos. Since 1978 he has travelled in every province of Greece. He has written or contributed to many guides to Greece

Mike Gerrard is a travel writer and broadcaster who has written several guides to various parts of Greece, which he has been visiting annually since 1964.

Andy Harris is a travel and food journalist based in Athens. He is the author of *A Taste of the Aegean*.

Tanya Tsikas is a Canadian writer and travel guide editor. Married to a Greek, she has spent time in Crete and currently lives in Oxford.

DEPUTY EDITORIAL DIRECTOR Douglas Amrine

DEPUTY ART DIRECTOR Gillian Allan

MANAGING EDITOR Georgina Matthews

MANAGING ART EDITOR Annette Jacobs

Additional Illustrations

Richard Bonson, Louise Boulton, Gary Cross, Kevin Goold, Roger Hutchins, Claire Littlejohn.

Design and Editorial Assistance

Emma Anacootee, Hilary Bird, Julie Bond, Elspeth Collier, Michelle Crane, Catherine Day, Mariana Evmolpidou, Jim Evoy, Emer FitzGerald, Jane Foster, Michael Fullalove, Emily Green, Lydia Halliday, Emily Hatchwell, Leanne Hogbin, Kim Inglis, Despoina Kanakoglou, Lorien Kite, Esther Labi, Maite Lantaron, Felicity Laughton, Delphine Lawrance, Nicola Malone, Alison McGill, Andreas Michael, Rebecca Milner, Ella Milroy, Lisa Minsky, Robert Mitchell, Adam Moore, Jennifer Mussett, Tamsin Pender, Marianne Petrou, Rada Radojicic, Jake Reimann, Ellen Root, Simon Ryder, Collette Sadler, Sands Publishing Solutions, Rita Selvaggio, Ellie Smith, Susana Smith, Claire Stewart, Claire Tennant-Scull, Amanda Tomeh, Helen Townsend, Dora Whitaker, Maria Zygourakis.

Dorling Kindersley would also like to thank the following for their assistance: The Greek Wine Bureau, Odysea.

Additional Research

Anna Antoniou, Garifalia Boussiopoulou, Anastasia Caramanis, Michele Crawford, Magda Dimouti, Shirley Durant, Jane Foster, Panos Gotsi, Zoi Groummouti, Peter Millett, Eva Petrou, Ellen Root, Tasos Schizas, Linda Theodora, Garifalia Tsiola, Veronica Wood.

Additional Photography

Stephen Bere, Mariana Evmolpidou, John Heseltine, Ian O'Leary, Steven Ling, Tony Souter, Clive Streeter, Jerry Young.

Artwork Reference

Ideal Photo S.A., The Image Bank, Tony Stone Worldwide.

Photography Permissions

Dorling Kindersley would like to thank the following for their assistance and kind permission to photograph at their establishments:

Ali Pasha Museum, Ioannina; City of Athens Museum; Museum of Greek Folk Art, Athens; V Kyriazopoulos Ceramic Collection; Kavala Modern Art Gallery; National Gallery of Art, Athens; National War Museum, Athens; Nicholas P Goulandris Foundation Museum of Cycladic and Ancient Art, Athens; Theatrical Museum, Athens; University of Athens Museum; Polygnotos Vagis Museum, Thassos. Also all other cathedrals, churches, museums, hotels, restaurants, shops, galleries, and sights too numerous to thank individually.

Picture Credits

a = above; b = below; c = centre; f = far; l = left; r = right; t = top.

Works of art have been reproduced with the permission of the following copyright holders: Vorres Museum *Water Nymph* (1995) Apostolos Petridis 150t.

The publisher would like to thank the following individuals, companies and picture libraries for permission to reproduce their photographs:

ALAMY IMAGES: Art Directors & TRIP/Bob Turner 315br; blphoto 46bl; CW Images/ Chris Warren 298bl; David Crousby 306tl; Danita Delimont 312cb; FAN Travelstock/Katja Kreder 278tl; GreekSportStock 299c; Andrew Holt 298cl; Peter Horree 10br, 11cl, 281tl; Kostas Pikoulas 308tl; Peter Titmuss 309cla; Werner Otto 298crb; Picpics 299br; picturescolourlibrary.com 11br; Robert Harding Picture Library Ltd/ Robert Harding World Imagery 281c, Terry Harris Just Greece Photo Library 47bl; AISA ARCHIVO ICONGRAFICO, Barcelona: Museo Archeologique Bari 57tr; Museo Archeologique Florence 54tl; AKG, London: 173t, 259; Antiquario Palatino 53bl; *Bilder aus dem Altherthume*, Heinrich Leutemann 228c; British Museum 95br; Edward Dodwell 87cr; Erich Lessing Akademie der Bildenden Künste, Vienna 54c; Musée du Louvre 53tl; National Archaeological Museum, Athens 26–7(d), 27t; Staatliche Kunstsammlungen, Albertinum, Dresden 31crb; Liebighaus, Frankfurt/Main 33c; Museum Narodowe, Warsaw 145b; Staatliche

Antikensammlungen und Glyptotek, München 4, 52b; Mykonos Museum 55t; ALLSPORT: Mike Hewitt 120t; ANCIENT ART AND ARCHITECTURE: 29cl, 30t, 34t, 34ca, 35cl, 37t, 56cb, 56b(d), 246cb, 254c; ANTIKENMUSEUM BASEL UND SAMMLUNG LUDWIG: 60–1, 185br(d); APERION: John Hios 184c; Kamarias Tsigamos 118c; APOLLO EDITIONS: 185t; ARGYROPOULOS PHOTO PRESS: 45t, 45ca, 47t, 47cb, 48cb; CENTRE FOR ASIA MINOR STUDIES: Museum of Greek Popular Musical Instruments Fivos Anoyianakis Collection 104t; ATHENS INTERNATIONAL AIRPORT: 314tc, 314bl, 315tl.

BEAU BRUMMEL RESTAURANT: 276br; BENAKI MUSEUM: 25b, 36ca, 39t, 39c, 41ca, 65br, 78–9 all; PAUL BERNARD: 33t; BIBLIOTHEQUE NATIONAL, Paris: Caoursin folio 175 38–9(d); BODLEIAN LIBRARY, Oxford: MS Canon Misc 378, 170v, 34cb; BRIDGEMAN ART LIBRARY, London: Birmingham City Museums and Art Galleries *Pheidias Completing the Parthenon Frieze,* Sir Lawrence Alma-Tadema 58t; Bradford Art Galleries and Museums *The Golden Fleece* (c.1904), Herbert James Draper 220br; British Museum, London *Cup, Tondo, with Scene of Huntsmen Returning Home* 29cr, *Black-necked Amphora, Depicting Boxers and Wrestlers* (c.550–525 BC) Nidosthenes 173cra; Fitzwilliam Museum, University of Cambridge *Figurine of Demosthenes,* Enoch Wood of Burslem (c.1790) (lead glazed earthenware) 57tl; Giraudon, Louvre, Paris *Alexander the Great,* portrait head (3rd century BC) Greek (marble) 32tr; House of Masks, Delos *Mosaic of Dionysus Riding a Leopard* (c.AD 180) 35t; Guildhall Art Library *Clytemnestra,* John Collier 179c; Louvre, Paris *Double Bust of Aristophanes and Sophocles* (15th century) 56t; National Archaeological Museum, Athens *Bronze Statue of Poseidon* (c.460–450 BC) photo Bernard Cox 52ca; Private Collection *Two-tiered Icon of the Virgin and Child and Two Saints, Cretan School* (15th century) 38cl; © THE BRITISH MUSEUM: 26clb, 27cb, 28t, 30cb, 31clb, 53tr(d), 53br, 55c(d), 60tl, 61tl, 61tr, 100br, 173cla(d), 185bl.

CAMERA PRESS, London: ANAG 43tl, 43bl(d); Wim Swaan 62–3, 243t; BRUCE COLEMAN LTD: Udo Hirsch 236b; Dr Eckart Pott 257c; Hans Reinhard 22t, 23cla, 206b. COURTESY OF THE CITY OF ATHENS DEVELOPMENT AND DESTINATION AGENCY: 304br; C M DIXON PHOTO RESOURCES: 27ca; Staatliche Antiken-sammlung und Glyptotek, München 32tr; CORBIS: John Heseltine 280cl; Kevin Schafer 10cl; Zefa/Rainer Hackenberg 11tl.

DIVANI APOLLON PALACE & SPA: 261tl; DK IMAGES: ©The Trustees of the British Museum/ Nick Nicholls 10tc; DREAMSTIME.COM: Dudau 310bl; Kalousp 304cla; MARC DUBIN: 19t, 168b, 206t, 208cr, 253t, 253br; L DUPRÉ: Bibliotheque des Artes Decoratifs 24(d). ECOLE NATIONALE SUPERIEURE DES BEAUX ARTS, Paris: *Delphes*

Restauration du Sanctuaire Envoi Tourn-aire (1894) 30–1; EKDOTIKI ATHINON: 21br, 26crb; ELIA: 186c; ET ARCHIVE: British Museum 185c; National Archaeology Museum, Naples 32ca; EUROPEAN COMMISSION: 305; MARY EVANS PICTURE LIBRARY: 241b.

FERENS ART GALLERY: Hull City Museums and Art Galleries and Archives *Electra at the Tomb of Agamennon* (1869), Lord Frederick Leighton 55b; FOLK ART MUSEUM, Athens: 110t, 110b.

G7AHN ON FLICKER: 319c; GIRAUDON, Paris: Laruros Versailles Chateau *Le Batille de Navarin,* Louis Ambroise Garneray 200t; Louvre, Paris 60c, *Scene de Massacres de Scio,* Delacroix 40ca(d); Musee Nationale Gustave Moreau *Hesiode et Les Muses* Gustave Moreau 56ca; Musee d'Art Catalan, Barcelona 95bra; National Portrait Gallery, London *Portrait of George Gordon Byron,* Thomas Phillips (1813) 149tr(d); GRANDE BRETAGNE HOTEL: 261br; GREEK NATIONAL TOURIST ORGANIZATION: 304tc; NICHOLAS P GOULANDRIS FOUNDATION MUSEUM OF CYCLADIC AND ANCIENT GREEK ART: 65tr, 74–5 all.

ROBERT HARDING PICTURE LIBRARY: David Beatty 44br; N A Callow 263t; Tony Gervis 44cla, 44bl; Adam Woolfitt 46c; HELIO PHOTO: 254b; HELLENIC POST SERVICE: 43cla, 313tl; MICHAEL HOLFORD: British Museum 32cb, 52t; HOTEL KRITSA: 277br; HULTON GETTY COLLECTION: 41cb(d); Central Press Photo 42clb(d); HUTCHISON LIBRARY: Hilly Janes 98t.

IDEAL PHOTO SA: N. Adams 116cl; T Dassios 45br, 175t, 232, 252t, 252bl, 252br, 253cl, 262b; C. Vergas 48b,178b; IMAGES COLOUR LIBRARY: 99b; IMPACT PHOTOS: Caroline Penn 45bl.

KARAVOSTASI BEACH HOTEL: 263cl; KOSTOS KONTOS: 26cr, 42cra, 42cla, 45crb, 119b, 120b, 140, 152tr, 153tl, 153ca, 153b, 170t, 175c, 178c, 184t, 189tr; KTEL BUS: 322cla; ILIAS LALAOUNIS: 297cla.

LAMPROPOULOS:114c. MAGNUM PHOTOS LTD: Constantine Manos 44t; MANSELL COLLECTION: 52–3; MUNICIPAL ART GALLERY OF ATHENS: *Despinis TK* Mitarakis Yannis 88t.

NATIONAL GALLERY OF VICTORIA, Melbourne: Felton Bequest (1956) *Greek by the Inscriptions Painter Challidian* 54b; NATIONAL HISTORICAL MUSEUM, Athens: 38t, 40t, 40–1(d), 41t, 42b, 173clb, 188c(d), 194c; NATURAL IMAGE: Bob Gibbons 23rb; Peter Wilson 237cr; NATURE PHOTOGRAPHERS: S C Bisserot 236c; Brinsley Burbridge 23clb, 23br; N A Callow 22b; Andrew Cleave 23bc, 237b; Peter Craig Cooper 237cl; Paul Sterry 23t, 23cra, 225cr; NEW ACROPOLIS MUSEUM: 100cl; ANTONIS NICOLOPOULOS: 299t.

Octopus Sea Trips: Peter Nicolaides 300tr; Olympic Airways: 317tl; Oronoz Archivo Fotografico: 211b; Biblioteca National Madrid *Invasions Bulgares Historia Matriksiscronica FIIIV* 36cb(d); Charlottenberg, Berlin 54tr; El Escorial, Madrid *Battle Lepanto Cambiaso Luca* 38cr(d); Museo Julia 53c(d); Musee Louvre 60b; Museo Vaticano 61bl, 221tr.

Romylos Parisis: 14t, 104b, 136–7, 218b; City of Athens Museum 40cb; Pictures: 12, 14b, 44crb, 298c; Popperfoto: 42crb, 43cra, 43br, 98b, 180t, 262t; Michalis Pornalis: 218c, 219cb, 219b; Private Collections: 5t, 216t, 217t, 217b.

Ride World Wide: 299tl; Rex Features: 17c; Argyropoulos/Sipa 48t; Sipa/C.Brown 43tr.

Scala, Florence: Gallerie degli Uffizi 28b; Museo Archeologico, Firenze 29t; Museo Mandralisca Cefalu 30ca; Museo Nationale Tarquinia 61br; Museo de Villa Giulia 28–9, 60tr; Spathario Shadow Theatre Museum: 151c; Spectrum Colour Library: 244b; STASY/Attiko Metro Operation Company S.A. (AMEL): 325cr; Maria Stefossi: 118b; Theodoros-Patroklos Stellakis: 154b; Carmel Stewart: 279c; Tony Stone Images: Aperion 152tl(d); Sunvil: 300bl; Swan Hellenic: 300cr.

Tap Service Archaeological Receipts Fund Hellenic Republic Ministry of Culture: A Epharat of Antiquities 5b, 43cb, 58b, 94bl, 94br, 95t, 95c, 96b, 97c, 97tl, 98c, 99cr; Acropolis Museum 96t, 100tl; Ancient Corinth Archaeological Museum 166c; B Epharat of Antiquities 82, 141b, 144 all, 146c, 146bl, 146br, 147tl, 147c, 148c, 148b; Byzantine Museum, Athens 67t, 76 all; D Epharat of Antiquities 139c, 139bl, 162–3 all, 164–5, 167bl, 177b, 178t, 179t, 179b, 180c, 181c; Delphi Archaeological Museum 50–1, 228t, 230tl, 231t, 231b; E Epharat of Antiquities 174cb; Elefis Archaeological Museum 156b; 11th Epharat of Byzantine Antiquities 237tr;

5th Epharat of Byzantine Antiquities 21tl, 21cl, 37c, 190–1, 192t, 192b; 1st Epharat of Byzantine Antiquities 139cra, 152c, 153cb, 222–3 all; I Epharat of Antiquities 138ca, 205t, 226–7, 228b, 229c, 230tr, 230b; IB Epharat of Antiquities 211t, 212c; IO Epharat of Antiquities 256c; IST Epharat of Antiquities 241c; Keramikos Archaeological Museum 89t, 89cr, 89br, 91t, 91car; Marathon Archaeological Museum 145c; National Archeological Museum, Athens 3c, 26t, 28tr, 65tl, 68t, 68c, 68b, 69t, 69c, 69b, 70–1 all, 99t, 155t, 157cr; 9th Epharat of Byzantine Antiquities 248c, 248b; Pireaus Archaeological Museum 21tr; 6th Epharat of Byzantine Antiquities 13t, 21cr; 7th Epharat of Byzantine Antiquities 21bl, 218tl, 219ca; Thebes Archaeological Museum 221t; Thessaloníki Archaeological Museum 31t, 139t, 233t, 242b(d), 244t, 246t, 246ca, 246b, 247 all; I Epharat of Antiquities 88c, 88b, 89cl, 89bl, 90t, 90b, 91t, 91cla, 91cb, 91b, 156t, 156c, 157cl, 157bl, 157bc; Z Epharat of Antiquities 138cb, 170c, 170b, 171t, 171b, 172 all, 201c, 201b, 298c; Trekking Hellas: 298tc; Trip Photographic Library: Marc Dubin 250–1; Yannis Tsarouhis Foundation: Private Collection *Barber Shop in Marousi* (1947) 42tr.

Wadsworth Atheneum, Hartford Connecticut: T Pierpont Morgan Collection 189b; Werner Forman Archive: 36t; Alan Williams: 49t; Peter Wilson: 59bl, 92–3, 94t, 97br, 106–7, 214–5, 216c; Woodfin Camp & Associates: John Marmaras 254t; Adam Woolfitt 45clb.

Front Endpaper: all special photography except Rt Ideal Photo SA: T Dassios and Rbl Kostos Kontos (d).

Jacket
Front – AWL Images: Jon Arnold. Back – Alamy Images: Chris Batson cla; Images&Stories clb; Dorling Kindersley: Joe Cornish tl; Peter Wilson clb. Spine – AWL Images: Jon Arnold t.

All other images © Dorling Kindersley. For further information see: www.dkimages.com

SPECIAL EDITIONS OF DK TRAVEL GUIDES

Phrase Book

There is no universally accepted system for representing the modern Greek language in the Roman alphabet. The system of transliteration adopted in this guide is the one used by the Greek Government. Though not yet fully applied throughout Greece, most of the street and place names have been transliterated according to this system. For Classical names this guide uses the k, os, on and f spelling, in keeping with the modern system of transliteration. In a few cases, such as Socrates, the more familiar Latin form has been used. Classical names do not have accents. Where a well-known English form of a name exists, such as Athens or Corfu, this has been used. Variations in transliteration are given in the index.

GUIDELINES FOR PRONUNCIATION

The accent over Greek and transliterated words indicates the stressed syllable. In this guide the accent is not written over capital letters nor over monosyllables, except for question words and the conjunction ή (meaning "or"). In the right-hand "Pronunciation" column below, the syllable to stress is given in bold type.

On the following pages, the English is given in the left-hand column with the Greek and its transliteration in the middle column. The right-hand column provides a literal system of pronunciation and indicates the stressed syllable in bold.

THE GREEK ALPHABET

Α α	A a	**ar**m
Β β	V v	**v**ote
Γ γ	G g	**y**ear (when followed by e and i sounds) **n**o (when followed by ξ or γ)
Δ δ	D d	**th**at
Ε ε	E e	**e**gg
Ζ ζ	Z z	**z**oo
Η η	I i	bel**ie**ve
Θ θ	Th th	**th**ink
Ι ι	I i	bel**ie**ve
Κ κ	K k	**k**id
Λ λ	L l	**l**and
Μ μ	M m	**m**an
Ν ν	N n	**n**o
Ξ ξ	X x	ta**xi**
Ο ο	O o	**f**ox
Π π	P p	**p**ort
Ρ ρ	R r	**r**oom
Σ σ	S s	**s**orry (zero when followed by μ)
ς	s	(used at end of word)
Τ τ	T t	**t**ea
Υ υ	Y y	bel**ie**ve
Φ φ	F f	**f**ish
Χ χ	Ch ch	lo**ch** in most cases, but **h**e when followed by a, e or i sounds
Ψ ψ	Ps ps	ma**ps**
Ω ω	O o	f**o**x

COMBINATIONS OF LETTERS

In Greek there are two-letter vowels that are pronounced as one sound:

Αι αι	Ai ai	**e**gg
Ει ει	Ei ei	bel**ie**ve
Οι οι	Oi oi	bel**ie**ve
Ου ου	Ou ou	l**u**te

There are also some two-letter consonants that are pronounced as one sound:

Μπ μπ	Mp mp	**b**ut, sometimes nu**mb**er in the middle of a word
Ντ ντ	Nt nt	**d**esk, sometimes un**d**er in the middle of a word
Γκ γκ	Gk gk	**g**o, sometimes bi**ng**o in the middle of a word
Γξ γξ	Nx	a**nx**iety
Τζ τζ	Tz tz	ha**nds**
Τσ τσ	Ts ts	i**t's**
Γγ γγ	Gg gg	bi**ng**o

In an Emergency

Help!	Βοήθεια! Voítheia	vo-ee-theea
Stop!	Σταματήστε! Stamatíste	sta-ma-tee-steh
Call a doctor!	Φωνάξτε ένα γιατρό Fonáxte éna giatró	fo-nak-steh e-na ya-tro
Call an ambulance/ the police/the fire brigade!	Καλέστε το ασθενοφόρο/την αστυνομία/την πυροσβεστική Kaléste to asthenofóro/tin astynomía/tin pyrosvestikí	ka-le-steh to as-the-no-fo-ro/teen a-sti-no-mia/teen pee-ro-zve-stee-kee
Where is the nearest telephone/hospital/ pharmacy?	Πού είναι το πλησιέστερο τήλεφωνο/νοσοκο-μείο/φαρμακείο; Poú eínai to plisiés-tero tiléfono/nosoko-meío/farmakeío?	poo ee-ne to plee-see-e-ste-ro tee-le-pho-no/no-so-ko-mee-o/far-ma-kee-o?

Communication Essentials

Yes	Ναι Nai	neh
No	Όχι Ochi	o-chee
Please	Παρακαλώ Parakaló	pa-ra-ka-lo
Thank you	Ευχαριστώ Efcharistó	ef-cha-ree-sto
You are welcome	Παρακαλώ Parakaló	pa-ra-ka-lo
OK/alright	Εντάξει Entáxei	en-dak-zee
Excuse me	Με συγχωρείτε Me synchoreíte	me seen-cho-ree-teh
Hello	Γειά σας Geiá sas	yeea sas
Goodbye	Αντίο Antío	an-dee-o
Good morning	Καλημέρα Kaliméra	ka-lee-me-ra
Good night	Καληνύχτα Kalinýchta	ka-lee-neech-ta
Morning	Πρωί Proí	pro-ee
Afternoon	Απόγευμα Apógevma	a-po-yev-ma
Evening	Βράδυ Vrádi	vrath-i
This morning	Σήμερα το πρωί Símera to proí	see-me-ra to pro-ee
Yesterday	Χθές Chthés	chthes
Today	Σήμερα Símera	see-me-ra
Tomorrow	Αύριο Avrio	av-ree-o
Here	Εδώ Edó	ed-o
There	Εκεί Ekeí	c-kee
What?	Τι; Τi?	tee?
Why?	Γιατί; Giatí?	ya-tee?
Where?	Πού; Poú?	poo?
How?	Πώς; Pós?	pos?
Wait!	Περίμενε! Perímene!	pe-ree-me-neh

Useful Phrases

How are you?	Τί κάνεις;	tee ka-nees
	Ti kάáneis?	
Very well, thank you	Πολύ καλά, ευχαριστώ	po-lee ka-la, ef-cha-ree-sto
	Poly kalá, efcharistó	
How do you do?	Πώς είστε;	pos ees-te?
	Pós eíste?	
Pleased to meet you	Χαίρω πολύ	che-ro po-lee
	Chaíro polý	
What is your name?	Πώς λέγεστε;	pos le-ye-ste?
	Pós légeste?	
Where is/are...?	Πού είναι;	poo ee-ne?
	Poú eínai?	
How far is it to...?	Πόσο απέχει...;	po-so a-pe-chee?
	Póso apéchei...?	
How do I get to?	Πώς μπορώ να πάω....;	pos bo-ro-na pa-o?
	Pós moró na páo...?	
Do you speak English?	Μιλάτε Αγγλικά;	mee-la-te an-glee-ka?
	Miláte Angliká?	
I understand	Καταλαβαίνω	ka-ta-la-ve-no
	Katalavaíno	
I don't understand	Δεν καταλαβαίνω	then ka-ta-la-ve-no
	Den katalavaíno	
Could you speak slowly?	Μιλάτε λίγο πιο αργά παρακαλώ;	mee-la-te lee-go pyo ar-ga pa-ra-ka-lo?
	Miláte lígo pio argá parakaló?	
I'm sorry	Με συγχωρείτε	me seen-cho-ree teh
	Me synchoreíte	
Does anyone have a key?	Εχει κανένας κλειδί;	e-chee ka-ne-nas klee-dee?
	Echei kanénas kleidí?	

Useful Words

big	Μεγάλο	me-ga-lo
	Megálo	
small	Μικρό	mi-kro
	Mikró	
hot	Ζεστό	zes-to
	Zestó	
cold	Κρύο	kree-o
	Krýo	
good	Καλό	ka-lo
	Kaló	
bad	Κακό	ka-ko
	Kakó	
enough	Αρκετά	ar-ke-ta
	Arketá	
well	Καλά	ka-la
	Kalá	
open	Ανοιχτά	a-neech-ta
	Anoichtá	
closed	Κλειστά	klee-sta
	Kleistá	
left	Αριστερά	a-ree-ste-ra
	Aristerá	
right	Δεξιά	dek-see-a
	Dexiá	
straight on	Ευθεία	ef-thee-a
	Eftheía	
between	Ανάμεσα / Μεταξύ	a-na-me-sa/me-tak-see
	Anámesa / Metaxý	
on the corner of....	Στη γωνία του...	stee go-nee-a too
	Sti gonía tou...	
near	Κοντά	kon-da
	Kontá	
far	Μακριά	ma-kree-a
	Makriá	
up	Επάνω	e-pa-no
	Epáno	
down	Κάτω	ka-to
	Káto	
early	Νωρίς	no-rees
	Norís	
late	Αργά	ar-ga
	Argá	
entrance	Η είσοδος	ee ee-so-thos
	I eísodos	
exit	Η έξοδος	eee-kso-dos
	I éxodos	
toilet	Οι τουαλέτες /WC	ee-too-a-le-tes
	Oi toualétes / WC	
occupied/engaged	Κατειλημμένη	ka-tee-lee-me-nee
	Kateiliméni	

unoccupied/vacant	Ελεύθερη	e-lef-the-ree
	Eléftheri	
free/no charge	Δωρεάν	tho-re-an
	Doreán	
in/out	Μέσα /Έξω	me-sa/ek-so
	Mésa/ Exo	

Making a Telephone Call

Where is the nearest public telephone ?	Πού βρίσκεται ο πλησιέστερος τηλεφωνικός θάλαμος;	poo vrees-ke-teh o plee-see-e-ste-ros tee-le-fo-ni-kos tha-la-mos?
	Poú vrísketai o plisiésteros tilefonikòs thálamos?	
I would like to place a long-distance call	Θα ήθελα να κάνω ένα υπεραστικό τηλεφώνημα	tha ee-the-la na ka-no e-na ee-pe-ra-sti-ko tee-le-fo-nee-ma
	Tha íthela na kάno éna yperastikó tilefónima	
I would like to reverse the charges	Θα ήθελα να χρεώσω το τηλεφώνημα στον παραλήπτη	tha ee-the-la na chre-o-so to tee-le-fo-nee-ma ston pa-ra-lep-tee
	Tha íthela na chreóso to tilefónima ston paralípti	
I will try again later	Θα ξανατηλεφωνήσω αργότερα	tha ksa-na-tee-le-fo-ni so ar-go-te-ra
	Tha xanatilefoníso argótera	
Can I leave a message?	Μπορείτε να του αφήσετε ένα μήνυμα;	bo-ree-te na too a-fee-se-teh e-na mee-nee-ma?
	Mporeíte na tou afísete éna mínyma?	
Could you speak up a little please?	Μιλάτε δυνατότερα, παρακαλώ;	mee-la-teh dee-na-to-te-ra, pa-ra-ka-lo
	Miláte dynatótera, parakaló	
Local call	Τοπικό τηλεφώνημα	to-pi-ko tee-le-fo-nee-ma
	Topikó tilefónima	
Hold on	Περιμένετε	pe-ri-me-ne-teh
	Periménete	
OTE telephone office	Ο OTE / Το τηλεφωνείο	o O-TE/To tee-le-fo-nee-o
	O OTE / To tilefoneío	
Phone box/kiosk	Ο τηλεφωνικός θάλαμος	o tee-le fo ni kos tha la-mos
	O tilefonikós thálamos	
Phone card	Η τηλεκάρτα	ee tee-le-kar-ta
	I tilekárta	

Shopping

How much does this cost?	Πόσο κάνει;	po-so ka-nee?
	Póso kάnei?	
I would like....	Θα ήθελα...	tha ee-the-la...
	Tha íthela...	
Do you have....?	Εχετε...;	e-che-teh
	Echete...?	
I am just looking	Απλώς κοιτάω	a-plos kee-ta-o
	Aplós koitáo	
Do you take credit cards/travellers' cheques?	Δέχεστε πιστωτικές κάρτες / travellers' cheques;	the-ches-teh pee-sto-tee-kes kar-tes/ travellers' cheques?
	Déchente pistotikés kártes / travellers' cheques?	
What time do you open/close?	Ποτέ ανοίγετε/ κλείνετε;	po-teh a-nee-ye-teh/ klee-ne-teh?
	Póte anoígete/ kleínete?	
Can you ship this overseas?	Μπορείτε να το στείλετε στο εξωτερικό;	bo-ree-teh na to stee-le-teh sto e-xo-te-ree ko?
	Mporeíte na to steílete sto exoterikó?	
This one	Αυτό εδώ	af-to e-do
	Aftó edó	
That one	Εκείνο	e-kee-no
	Ekeíno	

expensive	Ακριβό / Akrivó	a-kree-vo
cheap	Φθηνό / Fthinó	fthee-no
size	Το μέγεθος / To mégethos	to me-ge-thos
white	Λευκό / Lefkó	lef-ko
black	Μαύρο / Mávro	mav-ro
red	Κόκκινο / Kókkino	ko-kee-no
yellow	Κίτρινο / Kítrino	kee-tree-no
green	Πράσινο / Prásino	pra-see-no
blue	Μπλε / Mple	bleh

Types of Shop

antique shop	Μαγαζί με αντίκες / Magazí me antíkes	ma-ga-zee me an-dee-kes
bakery	Ο φούρνος / O foúrnos	o foor-nos
bank	Η τράπεζα / I trápeza	ee tra-pe-za
bazaar	Το παζάρι / To pazári	to pa-za-ree
bookshop	Το βιβλιοπωλείο / To vivliopoleío	to vee-vlee-o-po-lee-o
butcher	Το κρεοπωλείο / To kreopoleío	to kre-o-po-lee-o
cake shop	Το ζαχαροπλαστείο / To zacharoplasteío	to za-cha-ro-pla-stee-o
cheese shop	Μαγαζί με αλλαντικά / Magazí me allantiká	ma-ga-zee me a-lan-dee-ka
department store	Πολυκάταστημα / Polykatástima	Po-lee-ka-ta-stee-ma
fishmarket	Το ιχθυοπωλείο/ ψαράδικο / To ichthyopoleío/ psarádiko	to eech-thee-o-po-lee-o/psa-rá-dee-ko
greengrocer	Το μανάβικο / To manáviko	to ma-na-vee-ko
hairdresser	Το κομμωτήριο / To kommotírio	to ko-mo-tee-ree-o
kiosk	Το περίπτερο / To períptero	to pe-reep-te-ro
leather shop	Μαγαζί με δερμάτινα είδη / Magazí me dermátina eídi	ma-ga-zee me ther-ma-tee-na ee-thee
street market	Η λαϊκή αγορά / I laïkí agorá	ee la-ee-kee a-go-ra
newsagent	Ο εφημεριδοπώλης / O efimeridopólis	O e-fee-me-ree-tho-po-lees
pharmacy	Το φαρμακείο / To farmakeío	to far-ma-kee-o
post office	Το ταχυδρομείο / To tachydromeío	to ta-chee-thro-mee-o
shoe shop	Κατάστημα υποδημάτων / Katástima ypodimáton	ka-ta-stee-ma ee-po-dee-ma-ton
souvenir shop	Μαγαζί με "souvenir" / Magazí me "souvenir"	ma-ga-zee meh "souvenir"
supermarket	Σουπερμάρκετ/ Υπεραγορά / "Supermarket"/ Yperagorá	"Supermarket"/ee-per-a-go-ra
tobacconist	Είδη καπνιστού / Eídi kapnistoú	Ee-thee kap-nees
travel agent	Το ταξειδιωτικό γραφείο / To taxeidiotikó grafeío	to tak-see-thy-o-tee-ko gra-fee-o

Sightseeing

tourist information	Ο ΕΟΤ / O EOT	o E-OT
tourist police	Η τουριστική αστυνομία / I touristikí astynomía	ee too-rees-tee-kee a-stee-no-mee-a
archaeological	αρχαιολογικός / archaiologikós	ar-che-o-lo-yee-kos

art gallery	Η γκαλερί / I gkalerí	ee ga-le-ree
beach	Η παραλία / I paralía	ee pa-ra-lee-a
Byzantine	βυζαντινός / vyzantinós	vee-zan-dee-nos
castle	Το κάστρο / To kástro	to ka-stro
cathedral	Η μητρόπολη / I mitrópoli	ee mee-tro-po-lee
cave	Το σπήλαιο / To spílaio	to spee-le-o
church	Η εκκλησία / I ekklisía	ee e-klee-see-a
folk art	λαϊκή τέχνη / laïkí téchni	la-ee-kee tech-nee
fountain	Το συντριβάνι / To syntriváni	to seen-dree-va-nee
garden	Ο κήπος / O kípos	o kee-pos
gorge	Το φαράγγι / To farángi	to fa-ran-gee
grave of....	Ο τάφος του...	o ta-fos too
hill	Ο λόφος / O lófos	o lo-fos
historical	ιστορικός / istorikós	ee-sto-ree-kos
island	Το νησί / To nisí	to nee-see
lake	Η λίμνη / I límni	ee leem-nee
library	Η βιβλιοθήκη / I vivliothíki	ee veev-lee-o-thee-kee
mansion	Η έπαυλις / I épavlis	eee-pav-lees
monastery	Μονή / moní	mo-ni
mountain	Το βουνό / To vounó	to voo-no
municipal	δημοτικός / dimotikós	thee-mo-tee-kos
museum	Το μουσείο / To mouseío	to moo-see-o
national	εθνικός / ethnikós	eth-nee-kos
park	Το πάρκο / To párko	to par-ko
river	Το ποτάμι / To potámi	to po-ta-mee
road	Ο δρόμος / O drómos	o thro-mos
saint	άγιος/άγιου/αγία /αγίες / ágios/ágioi/agía/agíes	a-yee-os/a-yee-ee/a-yee-es
spring	Η πηγή / I pigí	ee pee-yee
square	Η πλατεία / I plateía	ee pla-tee-a
stadium	Το στάδιο / To stádio	to sta-thee-o
statue	Το άγαλμα / To ágalma	to a-gal-ma
theatre	Το θέατρο / To théatro	to the-a-tro
town hall	Το δημαρχείο / To dimarcheío	To thee-mar-chee-o
closed on public holidays	κλειστό τις αργίες / kleistó tis argíes	klee-sto tees aryee-es

Transport

When does the .... leave?	Πότε φεύγει το ....; / Póte févgei to...?	po-teh fev-yee to...?
Where is the bus stop?	Πού είναι η στάση του λεωφορείου; Ποú eínai i stási tou leoforeíou?	poo ee-neh ee sta-see too le-o-fo-ree-oo?
Is there a bus to...?	Υπάρχει λεωφορείο για...; Ypárchei leoforeío gia...?	ee-par-chee le-o-fo-ree-o yia...?
ticket office	Εκδοτήρια εισιτηρίων / Ekdotíria eisitiríon	Ek-tho-tee-reea ee-see-tee-ree-on
return ticket	Εισιτήριο με επιστροφή / Eisitírio me epistrofí	ee-see-tee-ree-o meh e-pee-stro-fee
single journey	Απλό εισιτήριο / Apló eisitírio	a-plo ee-see-tee-reeo

bus station	Ο σταθμός λεωφορείων / Ο stathmós leoforeíon	o stath-mos leo-fo-ree-on
bus ticket	Εισιτήριο λεωφορείου / Eisitírio leoforeíou	ee-see-tee-ree-o leo-fo-ree-oo
trolley bus	Το τρόλλεϋ / Το trólley	to tro-le-ee
port	Το λιμάνι / Το limáni	to lee-ma-nee
train/metro	Το τρένο / Το tréno	to tre-no
railway station	σιδηροδρομικός σταθμός / sidirodromikós stathmós	see-thee-ro-thro-mee-kos stath-mos
moped	Το μοτοποδήλατο / το μηχανάκι / Το motopodílato / Το michanáki	to mo-to-po-thee-la-to/to mee-cha-na-kee

bicycle	Το ποδήλατο / Το podílato	to po-thee-la-to
taxi	Το ταξί / Το taxi	to tak-see
airport	Το αεροδρόμιο / Το aerodrómio	to a-e-ro-thro-mee-o
ferry	Το φερυμπότ / Το "ferry-boat"	to fe-ree-bot
hydrofoil	Το δελφίνι / Το υδροπτέρυγο / Το delfíni / Το ydroptérygo	to del-fee-nee/To ee-throp-te-ree-go
catamaran	Το καταμαράν / Το katamarán	to catamaran
for hire	Ενοικιάζονται / Enoikiázontai	e-nee-kya-zon-deh

Staying in a Hotel

Do you have a vacant room?	Εχετε δωμάτια; / Echete domátia?	e-che-teh tho-ma-tee-a?
double room with double bed	Δίκλινο με διπλό κρεβάτι / Díklino me dipló kreváti	thee-klee-no meh thee-plo kre-va-tee
twin room	Δίκλινο με μονά κρεβάτια / Díklino me moná krevátia	thee-klee-no meh mo-na kre-vat-ya
single room	Μονόκλινο / Monóklino	mo-no-klee-no
room with a bath	Δωμάτιο με μπανιο / Domátio me mpánio	tho-ma-tee-o meh ban-yo
shower	Το ντουζ / Το douz	To dooz
porter	Ο πορτιέρης / Ο portiéris	o por-tye-rees
key	Το κλειδί / Το kleidí	to klee-dee
I have a reservation	Εχω κάνει κράτηση / Echo káni krátisi	e-cho ka-nee kra-tee-see
room with a sea view/balcony	Δωμάτιο με θέα στη θάλασσα/μπαλκόνι / Domátio me théa sti thálassa / mpalkóni	tho-ma-tee-o meh the-a stee tha-la-sa/bal- ko-nee
Does the price include breakfast?	Το πρωινό συμπεριλαμβάνεται στην τιμή; / Το proïnó symperilamvánetai stin timí?	to pro-ee-no seem-be-ree-lam-va-ne-teh steen tee-mee?

Eating Out

Have you got a table?	Εχετε τραπέζι; / Echete trapézi?	e-che-te tra-pe-zee?
I want to reserve a table	Θέλω να κρατήσω ένα τραπέζι / Thélo na kratíso éna trapézi	the-lo na kra-tee-so e-na tra-pe-zee
The bill, please	Τον λογαριασμό, παρακαλώ / Ton logariazmó parakaló	ton lo-gar-yas-mo pa-ra-ka-lo
I am a vegetarian	Είμαι χορτοφάγος / Eímai chortofágos	ee-meh chor-to-fa-gos
What is fresh today?	Τί φρέσκο έχετε σήμερα; / Tí frésko échete símera?	tee fres-ko e-che-teh see-me-ra?

waiter/waitress	Κύριε / Γκαρσόν / Κυρία (female) / Kýrie/Garson/Kyría	Kee-ree-eh/Garson/Kee-ree-a
menu	Ο κατάλογος / Ο katálogos	o ka-ta-lo-gos
cover charge	Το κουβέρ / Το "couvert"	to koo-ver
wine list	Ο κατάλογος με τα οινοπνευματώδη / Ο katálogos me ta oinopnevmatódi	o ka-ta-lo-gos meh ta ee-no-pnev-ma-to-thee
glass	Το ποτήρι / Το potíri	to po-tee-ree
bottle	Το μπουκάλι / Το mpoukáli	to bou-ka-lee
knife	Το μαχαίρι / Το machaíri	to ma-che-ree
fork	Το πηρούνι / Το piroúni	to pee-roo-nee
spoon	Το κουτάλι / Το koutáli	to koo-ta-lee
breakfast	Το πρωινό / Το proïnó	to pro-ee-no
lunch	Το μεσημεριανό / Το mesimerianó	to me-see-mer-ya-no
dinner	Το δείπνο / Το deípno	to theep-no
main course	Το κυρίως γεύμα / Το kyríos gévma	to kee-ree-os yev-ma
starter/first course	Τα ορεκτικά / Τα orektiká	ta o-rek-tee-ka
dessert	Το γλυκό / Το glykó	to ylee-ko
dish of the day	Το πιάτο της ημέρας / Το piáto tis iméras	to pya-to tees ee-me-ras
bar	Το μπαρ / Το "bar"	To bar
taverna	Η ταβέρνα / I tavérna	ee ta-ver-na
café	Το καφενείο / Το kafeneío	to ka-fe-nee-o
fish taverna	Η ψαροταβέρνα / I psarotavérna	ee psa-ro-ta-ver-na
grill house	Η ψησταριά / I psistariá	ee psee-sta-rya
wine shop	Το οινοπωλείο / Το oinopoleío	to ee-no-po-lee-o
dairy shop	Το γαλακτοπωλείο / Το galaktopoleío	to ga-lak-to-po-lee-o
restaurant	Το εστιατόριο / Το estiatório	to e-stee-a-to-ree-o
ouzeri	Το ουζερί / Το ouzeri	to oo-ze-ree
meze shop	Το μεζεδοπωλείο / Το mezedopoleío	To me-ze-do-po-lee-o
take away kebabs	Το σουβλατζίδικο / Το souvlatzídiko	To soo-vlat-zee-dee-ko
rare	Ελάχιστα ψημένο / Eláchista psiméno	e-lach-ees-ta psee-me-no
medium	Μέτρια ψημένο / Métria psiméno	met-ree-a psee-me-no
well done	Καλοψημένο / Kalopsiméno	ka-lo-psee-me-no

Basic Food and Drink

coffee	Ο καφές / Ο Kafés	o ka-fes
with milk	με γάλα / me gála	me ga-la
black coffee	σκέτος / skétos	ske-tos
without sugar	χωρίς ζάχαρη / chorís záchari	cho-rees za-cha-ree
medium sweet	μέτριος / métrios	me-tree-os
very sweet	γλυκύς / glykýs	glee-kees
tea	τσάι / tsái	tsa-ee
hot chocolate	ζεστή σοκολάτα / zestí sokoláta	ze-stee so-ko-la-ta
wine	κρασί / krasí	kra-see
red	κόκκινο / kókkino	ko-kee-no
white	λευκό / lefkó	lef-ko
rosé	ροζέ / rozé	ro-ze

raki	Το ρακί	to ra-kee
	Το rakí	
ouzo	Το ούζο	to oo-zo
	Το oúzo	
retsina	Η ρετσίνα	ee ret-see-na
	I retsína	
water	Το νερό	to ne-ro
	Το neró	
octopus	Το χταπόδι	to chta-po-dee
	Το chtapódi	
fish	Το ψάρι	to psa-ree
	Το psári	
cheese	Το τυρί	to tee-ree
	Το tyrí	
halloumi	Το χαλούμι	to cha-loo-mee
	Το chaloúmi	
feta	Η φέτα	ee fe-ta
	I féta	
bread	Το ψωμί	to pso-mee
	Το psomí	
bean soup	Η φασολάδα	ee fa-so-la-da
	I fasoláda	
houmous	Το χούμους	to choo-moos
	Το houmous	
halva	Ο χαλβάς	o chal-vas
	O chalvás	
meat kebabs	Ο γύρος	o yee-ros
	O gýros	
Turkish delight	Το λουκούμι	to loo-koo-mee
	Το loukoúmi	
baklava	Ο μπακλαβάς	o bak-la-vas
	O mpaklavás	
klephtiko	Το κλέφτικο	to klef-tee-ko
	Το kléftiko	

Numbers

1	ένα	e-na
	éna	
2	δύο	thee-o
	dýo	
3	τρία	tree-a
	tría	
4	τέσσερα	te-se-ra
	téssera	
5	πέντε	pen-deh
	pénte	
6	έξι	ek-si
	éxi	
7	επτά	ep-ta
	eptá	
8	οχτώ	och-to
	ochtó	
9	εννέα	e-ne-a
	ennéa	
10	δέκα	the-ka
	déka	
11	έντεκα	en-de-ka
	énteka	
12	δώδεκα	tho-the-ka
	dódeka	
13	δεκατρία	de-ka-tree-a
	dekatría	
14	δεκατέσσερα	the-ka-tes-se-ra
	dekatéssera	
15	δεκαπέντε	the-ka-pen-de
	dekapénte	
16	δεκαέξι	the-ka-ek-si
	dekaéxi	
17	δεκαεπτά	the-ka-ep-ta
	dekaeptá	
18	δεκαοχτώ	the-ka-och-to
	dekaochtó	
19	δεκαεννέα	the-ka-e-ne-a
	dekaennéa	
20	είκοσι	ee-ko-see
	eíkosi	
21	εικοσιένα	ee-ko-see-e-na
	eikosiéna	
30	τριάντα	tree-an-da
	triánta	
40	σαράντα	sa-ran-da
	saránta	
50	πενήντα	pe-neen-da
	penínta	
60	εξήντα	ek-seen-da
	exínta	
70	εβδομήντα	ev-tho-meen-da
	evdomínta	

80	ογδόντα	og-thon-da
	ogdónta	
90	ενενήντα	e-ne-neen-da
	enenínta	
100	εκατό	e-ka-to
	ekató	
200	διακόσια	thya-kos-ya
	diakósia	
1,000	χίλια	cheel-ya
	chília	
2,000	δύο χιλιάδες	thee-o cheel-ya-thes
	dýo chiliádes	
1,000,000	ένα εκατομμύριο	e-na e-ka-to-mee-ree-o
	éna ekatommýrio	

Time, Days and Dates

one minute	ένα λεπτό	e-na lep-to
	éna leptó	
one hour	μία ώρα	mee-a o-ra
	mía óra	
half an hour	μισή ώρα	mee-see o-ra
	misí óra	
quarter of an hour	ένα τέταρτο	e-na te-tar-to
	éna tétarto	
half past one	μία και μισή	mee-a keh mee-see
	mía kai misí	
quarter past one	μία και τέταρτο	mee-a keh te-tar-to
	mía kai tétarto	
ten past one	μία και δέκα	mee-a keh the-ka
	mía kai déka	
quarter to two	δύο παρά τέταρτο	thee-o pa-ra te-tar-to
	dýo pará tétarto	
ten to two	δύο παρά δέκα	thee-o pa-ra the-ka
	dýo pará déka	
a day	μία μέρα	mee-a me-ra
	mía méra	
a week	μία εβδομάδα	mee-a ev-tho-ma-tha
	mía evdomáda	
a month	ένας μήνας	e-nas mee-nas
	énas mínas	
a year	ένας χρόνος	e-nas chro-nos
	énas chrónos	
Monday	Δευτέρα	thef-te-ra
	Deftéra	
Tuesday	Τρίτη	tree-tee
	Tríti	
Wednesday	Τετάρτη	te-tar-tee
	Tetárti	
Thursday	Πέμπτη	pemp-tee
	Pémpti	
Friday	Παρασκευή	pa-ras-ke-vee
	Paraskeví	
Saturday	Σάββατο	sa-va-to
	Sávvato	
Sunday	Κυριακή	keer-ee-a-kee
	Kyriakí	
January	Ιανουάριος	ee-a-noo-a-ree-os
	Ianouários	
February	Φεβρουάριος	fev-roo-a-ree-os
	Fevrouários	
March	Μάρτιος	mar-tee-os
	Mártios	
April	Απρίλιος	a-pree-lee-os
	Aprílios	
May	Μάιος	ma-ee-os
	Máios	
June	Ιούνιος	ee-oo-nee-os
	Ioúnios	
July	Ιούλιος	ee-oo-lee-os
	Ioúlios	
August	Αύγουστος	av-goo-stos
	Avgoustos	
September	Σεπτέμβριος	sep-tem-vree-os
	Septémvrios	
October	Οκτώβριος	ok-to-vree-os
	Októvrios	
November	Νοέμβριος	no-em-vree-os
	Noémvrios	
December	Δεκέμβριος	the-kem-vree-os
	Dekémvrios	